Sacred Sexuality

Listening to Our Bodies

Leslie Blackburn

First Edition: 2024

ISBN 979-8-9918710-3-7 (paperback)

Published by Purple Platypus Press, Ann Arbor, Michigan USA

This book is published on the traditional lands of the Anishinaabe people of the Three Fires Confederacy — the Ojibwe, Ottawa and Potawatomi — and the Wyandot. We acknowledge the history of colonization and the continued presence of Indigenous peoples in this region.

CONTENTS

"Be really whole and all things will come to you."

~ Lao Tzu

PREFACE

Hello, Sweet Reader!

Sacred Sexuality: Listening to Our Bodies is the first of a series of books in which I share my personal journey to serve as a vehicle for others to awaken into richer, more fulfilling lives and ultimately co-create a more vibrant and meaningful future. As you read this book, my hope is that you will see parts of your own story and find inspiration to deepen in the process of your unfolding and self-discovery.

Here we explore a journey with elements common to many. It's a journey from being stuck to waking up, unfurling, seeing the light, beginning the process of remembering who we are, including unwinding old stories and healing old traumas carried in the body.

I also describe my journey of feeling that I never quite fit into white, academic, corporate, heteronormative structures, yet walked blindly in those structures until I finally realized they were just structures and did not define me.

It's the story of learning to see those structures for what they are, waking up, and starting to recognize my place as a unique being on this planet among many more unique beings. It's the story of how I shifted my identification away from inherited structures as I moved toward self-discovery and self-definition.

It is a journey *outward* — into new lands, ideas, cultures and subcultures, new practices, new kinds of work, new arts and skills. It's also a journey *inward* — toward realization, growth, discovery and overcoming limitations.

This is a journey many of us are called to.

Central along the way has been a new approach to sex and sexuality, with an emerging recognition that how we approach sexuality tends to show up everywhere in our lives. Because of this, healing sexual wounds and shame can have a transformative impact, and not just on what our culture has compartmentalized to call our "love life." It also affects how we radiate from the core of our being and how we connect with all other beings, finding new depths from which we are able to participate in all areas of life.

This is the essence of tantra: wholeness.

Honestly, at the beginning of the story, I didn't even know I was on a journey, let alone one of my own unfolding. I bumped into walls I didn't know were there, and I felt barriers inside myself that often outlined areas of trauma and limiting beliefs. Feeling my way forward, patterns began to emerge, and in the process I realized that the living body carries the wisdom needed for our continued growth. For this reason, as the journey progressed, I began to gather resources and ideas, practices and modalities, guides and mentors to further my own process and help me to share what I was learning with others as part of my life's work. All of this I offer with gratitude in the hope that it may be helpful to you wherever you are on your path of self-discovery and fulfillment.

What I've Learned Since I Finished This Book

I am writing this preface in a new home and temple space located at the confluence of three streams merging into one on their way to join the River Raisin and then on to Lake Erie. I started this book over a decade ago. It should go without saying — but I feel it needs to be said anyhow — that I've learned a lot since then. My personal growth journey has spiraled out to encompass both larger cultural understandings and deeper personal ones. For a while, I felt frustrated that my writing couldn't keep pace with my own learning. The conflicts I felt about this slowed down my completion of this book, but eventually I came to understand that I don't need to go back and reframe all my experiences within my current understandings. Much as I can love the small streams near my home before they merge to form a larger river, I can honor all stages of my own growth. At the same time, right here at the outset, it is important to me to acknowledge these new and broader flows, even though they are not fully reflected in the pages that follow.

My journey out of the dominant cultural paradigm led me to cultures both outside the one I grew up in and to subcultures within it. Staring me in the face the whole time, though I didn't see it until much more recently, was the fact that having the ability and the resources to reject the dominant culture was a privilege conferred by being an accepted part of that culture. As a successful white engineer in a managerial role in a large corporation, I enjoyed privileges. What I now know to be true, informing my current work and extending well beyond the timeframe of this book, is that the racial and social justice issues I was able to temporarily bypass in my own spiritual journey are in fact central to the conditions that motivated me to embark upon it.

In other words, having made my way through one turn on the spiral of personal transformation, I'm now circling back with greater vision to embrace the need for social change in tandem with personal transformation.

I used to think racism was a construct that existed within "mean people," not me, so I wasn't a part of the injustice. I thought that because I am not part of the KKK, do not believe that white people are better than black people, and because I don't physically, violently harm anyone, that I am not part of the problem. I would cringe when people in my family or network used racial slurs or made mean remarks, but I didn't take a clear stand against it, nor did I take any action to create or advocate for change.

This book is a chronicle of many awakenings. Early in 2019, I had another awakening in which I began to see the impact of embodied racial dominance in our culture. I began to recognize the way our bodies carry racial trauma — not only from our own lifetimes, but from our lineages. Actions that arise from trauma often create injustices, inflicted sometimes without realizing it. I began to see the ongoing, daily impact of racial injustices rooted in past traumas, including even experiences that occurred hundreds and even thousands of years ago.

I've moved through many layers of shame around not seeing this more clearly before, and yet I am being gentle on myself to walk the path of no longer hiding from the conversation or pretending this doesn't exist. I am meeting these questions in my body. I am slowing down to listen. I am acknowledging my "whiteness," and learning more about my ancestral lineage. I am acknowledging the way white culture permeates all of our mainstream functions and continues to mean folx in black and brown bodies are disproportionately impacted by oppression. I am taking action to make change, no longer ignoring the need for it. Most of all, I know there is more to learn, and more to do on this path.

I spent a lot of my adult life rejecting my own lineage and trying to find other ways to trust and come into relationship with myself that would soothe me and support me to grow. I tended to lean on teachers and other traditions to come into better relationship with myself. Through those, I did find ways of connection and spiritual support, and I am very grateful. As you read on, you will see these connections and support, and how important they are. I also now know that the work of reclaiming my bloodline lineage, repairing relationships with my ancestors and offering healing there are a huge part of the next steps of my personal path.

The second influence informing my current work that I had only begun to explore as I wrote this book is a widening gender identity as well as sexual preferences. I woke up to my queerness many years ago, but in more recent years I have understood this more fully in my case as being not only a reference to sexual preference but also to gender and self-expression. Only in the past few years did I come out publicly, and even more recently with my mother and father. I felt a misalignment between my emerging authentic identity and the prevailing binary norms of our culture. To me, being queer is a celebration of my authentic self expression. Previously, I was afraid to truly claim my queerness and rested in the fact that I can pass as straight/heteronormative even as I noticed the way my ability to "pass" flavored my sexuality, my journey on this path, and the stories in this book. I'm now clearer about my queerness and gender nonconformance, the way I don't feel aligned only with the sex I was assigned at birth as defining my gender.

I also know that as much as I see now, there is more I don't know or see yet. I notice that my identity and awareness have changed numerous times in my life. I notice that it feels important to be seen in my current identity, and yet, there are so many older identities reflected in this book. I acknowledge that I will likely continue to change even after I write this. So it's a slippery concept to try to be seen in that fluidity yet get words captured on the solidity of printed paper. It's even a struggle with the English language. We are verbs, not nouns — ever changing.

So, my solution to these problems is that I'm owning all of this. The book you're about to read recounts my journey — from being socialized and passing as a white heterosexual girl/woman living in dominant mainstream US culture, fighting to be recognized as credible and competent in a predominantly male field, and then through a major spiritual awakening. You will see how these identities shift as we go. Waking up to being human in our human family is ongoing.

I am certain there are others who will find resonance in this story, and feel support on their own paths. But I am not intending this book only be seen or read by cisgender, white, heterosexual women and men whose journeys may parallel my own.

I acknowledge and welcome the gender spectrum. I offer this book as an LGBTQIA2S+ friendly exploration of being in a human body and expressing and being in our sexual energy. And amidst all that breadth and multiplicity, there is my journey walking my own specific path. Each of you is walking your own, and all are welcome: non-binary, gender non-conforming, trans woman, trans man, lesbian, gay, asexual, cis woman, cis man, beings of all gender and sexual expressions.

My evolving understandings about racism and gender have become an important part of my life and will continue to inform my work. I am continually changing as a being. I am not the same person I was when I started to write this book. I am not the same person I was when I was halfway through writing this book. I am not the same person I was yesterday. I will be different tomorrow. And I will be different years down the road.

And so will you, dear reader. We are all changing. My hope is that these changes move in the direction of honoring each of our unique identities while building our connection as fellow humans. Just as the land where I now write this contains multiple distinct yet merging streams, so do we, both within us and among us. Let us recognize both our uniqueness and our connection as we co-create a culture of love and respect for our bodies and ourselves, for one another, Spirit, nature and the planet.

INTRODUCTION

I remember a time not so long ago when I would hear stories about 'energetic orgasm' or 'psychic awareness' or other seemingly impossible occurrences, and my first reaction was to assume that something in me was inherently flawed. I couldn't fathom the possibility of experiencing an orgasm without touching my body (heck, I could barely reach one when I *did* touch my body!), or communication without words, or trusting that I could know something without backing it up with research and scientific proof. Surely, I thought, I must be incapable of these things, or that they must not be real. From there, I would either spiral into the depths of self-pity, or climb the tower of self-righteousness, closing my heart to any potential growth or possibility that could be opened by hearing stories about these kinds of experiences.

This is common. Recently a client excitedly expressed her elation upon learning that there was a point in my life that I didn't "get" this stuff either, when I felt stuck and not in my own body. She realized that if I could transcend those challenges and become an explorer of my own inner depths, she could do it too, and so can anyone. Yes.

For the early part of my life, though, 'energy healing,' 'shamanism' and 'sacred sexuality' were so far from my conscious experience that even the phrases and the vocabulary were foreign to me. I felt frustrated without knowing where to start. I had a deep sense that there must be more to life and sexuality than I had experienced in my many years on Earth thus far, but no clue how to find it.

Until something happened: that something I now call my "Spiritual Awakening." This experience required me to move toward a new vocabulary, and if these words don't currently resonate with anything in your experience, I ask you to be patient and open-minded as you read this, because at one time if I encountered them in a book I would have been in exactly the same position. But then something changed.

To start, what do I even mean by Spirit?

What is Spirit?

For me and many others who choose to walk the path of sacred sexuality, spirituality involves tapping into an expansive realm where energy flows and shapes infinite possibilities.

Spirit exists all the time, everywhere, within us and around us. It's how we are all connected. All we have to do is be open to listening to the messages around us and pay attention. Spiritual messages can take many forms, from traditional prayers to "coincidences" that awaken us. For example: picking up the phone to make a call and the person you were about to dial is already on the line. Or thinking about someone then getting a text from them in the next minute. Or tapping into "the zone" in athletics where you don't even need to think about what your body is doing, you just do it. These are not just coincidences or random occurrences. This is what I mean by connecting with Spirit.

Spirit is known by many names: Great Creator, God, Goddess, Source, Universe, Divine, Higher Power, the Tao. Any or all of these can be shorthand for your experience of this flow space, this "spiritual electricity," to borrow the words of artist and best-selling author Julia Cameron, whose work has enabled millions to realize their creative dreams.[1] Naming it is not important to the potential of connecting with that flow. As Cameron notes, "You do not need to understand electricity to use it."[2]

This book is the story of my spiritual journey as well as a guidebook for personal transformation where I share practices, exploring the Body as a primary modality for reclaiming our inner authentic wisdom, power and our own Sacred Sexuality. Sacred Sexuality is an invitation to experience the spiritual/sacred/intentional as embodied, physical, and sexual. Sacred Sexuality is a way of being that encompasses much more than sex as people commonly think of it. It's a

---

[1] *The Artist's Way* by Julia Cameron.

[2] Cameron, pg xxii.

powerful potential for healing our bodies, connecting deeply with others, manifesting our hearts' desires, and illuminating a path of connection with Spirit, the Universe, the Divine. As we embark on this spiritual journey, I acknowledge there are as many spiritual paths as there are beings on this planet. When you see me use the words Spirit, Universe, Source or Divine, feel free to substitute whatever name or words feel good for you, and don't force yourself to believe in something that you do not believe in. Tapping into this flow, this electricity, doesn't require having a specific path or belief system. As you read these pages, invite an open mind. Allow your connection with your truth to be your guide.

As a part of this spiritual path, the shamanic way also became very important to me and started weaving into the story. For me, the shamanic path begins with honoring the ancient ways and rhythms of nature and the Earth, opening to the realm of Spirit as well as the physical world, opening to the dreamtime. Shamanism is a tangible, embodied path, one that is not accessed through reading or talking about it, but through living and breathing it. It's about remembering who we are by allowing ourselves to reconnect with the Earth and all the beings here, opening to the nature-based wisdom through that connection. When we open to the possibility, we can learn much through our relating with animals, plants, other humans and more, as well as to the spiritual realm and messages from our dreams. More recently, I have come to know and also identify with this as 'animism.' According to Wikipedia, "Although each culture has its own different mythologies and rituals, 'animism' is said to describe the most common, foundational thread of indigenous peoples' 'spiritual' or 'supernatural' perspectives."[3] You will see me refer to this foundational thread as shamanism throughout the book.

These topics may be familiar to some readers and new to others, as they once were to me. Like the people I knew from school, work, social environment and family, I would have turned my nose up at any idea that wasn't rational or scientifically provable. Yet now, nature-based wisdom, Spirit, and Sacred Sexuality are at the foundation of my life, not because somebody told me they should be, but because I felt into what my body knows and then aligned with my own truth. As you read on, if nature-based wisdom, Spirit, Sacred Sexuality or

---

[3] https://en.wikipedia.org/wiki/Animism

other concepts or stories trigger resistance in your body, as they once did for me, I invite you to open your eyes and your heart wide in wonder and childlike curiosity. Let these pages be what they are for you, which will be different than what they are for other readers. Feel into what is your truth, and what isn't. You can create the life you choose to experience, one step at a time. You are good enough. It is possible. Go slow, and be gentle with yourself.

Bringing the Story to Light

In 2012, my self-realization studies brought me once again to vision quest on sacred land in upstate New York. I went there to seek wisdom from within and through connection with Nature and Spirit. Afterwards, I had this dream:

I am a powerful mama figure, centered in myself and connected with the wisdom of the Earth. My head is wrapped in a cloth, and I'm carrying a little baby in a sling, who is nursing happily. I'm round, curvy, wearing sumptuous, flowing clothes that are simple, comfortable, and pleasing to wear. Four or five women are walking with me; I'm surrounded and supported by community. I'm talking on a cell phone, excited to share about my new baby. Joyful, happy, blissful. Comfortable. At ease.

Returning from the three-day fast on the land during the vision quest, I experienced this dream as I came back into three-dimensional (3D) reality. This dream felt pivotal to highlighting the combination of strengths and gifts I bring to these teachings. In it, the technology of today (the cell phone) blends with indigenous, Earth-honoring tradition (the setting, my clothing) and with the need for me, as an empowered mother, to speak my voice and share my story (the baby). This book is my "baby," and by reading it you are helping to midwife a new consciousness.

This book is about the journey of my unfolding, as well as the inspiration and possibilities that have opened up in that. My intention to share about my journey is not to suggest that it is the only way, but instead to illuminate options and possibilities and to offer tools. I offer these tools to help you find the gems, and to discern between the wounded self/ego-driven voices in your mind and the authentic wisdom and exquisite messages of your body as you align with your internal compass and authentic path.[4]

Stepping Into Vulnerability

There's a vulnerability in sharing one's story. I feel vulnerable in sharing mine. Dr. Brené Brown, a research professor at the University of Houston, has spent many years studying vulnerability, courage, worthiness, and shame. In her bestselling book *Daring Greatly*, she shares a prayer offering about the courage to be vulnerable:

"Give me the courage to show up and let myself be seen."[5]

The journey of getting this book onto the page has been one of tremendous self-inquiry and growth. Part of me just wanted to sweep all the shit under the rug, smile and share all the glamorous, sexy, ecstatic parts, and say, "Hey reader, look at all this amazing stuff!"

And yet Spirit got very clear with me fast: "Oh no, you don't get the easy way out! This is not just about offering the juicy bits. You need to bare your soul."

Gulp. Really? More?

I had already shared parts of my story in speaking engagements and videos, on my radio shows, in my classes, through my performance art and in sessions with clients. Each time, there has been a new layer of exposure that felt spiritually guided. People would come up to me after classes and speaking engagements or performance art pieces so grateful, often in tears, sharing how some aspect of my story struck a chord with them, that their life felt changed by the experience, that they felt a new introduction to themselves. It wasn't the didactic bits that were tugging at their hearts, it was the personal story. Their feedback validated the growing confidence within my body that yes, I was meant

---

[4] I was inspired by many teachers and authors in my own journey of connecting with my authentic purpose. To name a few that influenced these early years for me: Martha Beck encourages *Finding Your North Star*. Jean Houston invites us to align with our entelechy (our soul's purpose, for example an acorn's entelechy is to become an oak tree). Julia Cameron has us connect with intuition and creativity through *The Artist's Way*. See Resource List for these and more.

[5] Brené Brown, *Daring Greatly: How the Courage to Be Vulnerable Transforms the Way We Live, Love, Parent, and Lead*, pg 42.

to share these stories. Yet each time, I felt another layer of exposed self, tender and raw, and afterward I'd be hit with a huge vulnerability hangover.[6]

Couldn't I just sort all of this down to the teaching nuggets, share those and let it be at that? That felt easier, yet not as rich, and not as authentic. Spirit kept nudging me, saying, "Yes! More! Share your story. Trust." I kept creating ways to meet the edgy bits in my body to let the tenderness find healing so that I had a new layer of safety from which to share a new layer of vulnerability. And it continued. As I healed the old wounds within me, my body said yes to more exposure. It was like a spiral… an old story rising up, me meeting it and listening to the wisdom through my body and finding a new layer of healing, celebrating the new place of feeling good. Then my body would rebuild, becoming a new foundation to allow the next layer to be revealed. Deeply listening to my body turned out to be integral to both the content of this book and *the process of its creation*. Yes, yes!

"Give me the courage to show up and let myself be seen."

As I type this, part of me is still engaged in that old tantrum, kicking and screaming. "I only want the parts of me that are pretty and likable to be seen," this part pouts and whines. "These dark bits, I am not so sure about. Can't we just ignore those?"

Um, no. No, we can't.

This journey includes the raw gritty experiences of human life, the grist for the mill which came from my own path and human homework. This is not just happy fluffy rainbows and unicorns![7] We all have this stuff of experience. Our experiences, unedited and unadorned, are the essential raw material for remembering who we are. You are not alone when you feel the darkness, the smallness or the "not-good-enough-ness." You are not alone when you feel like wanting to crawl out of your skin, or into a hole, or when you can't feel much at all. You are not alone when you feel like you aren't worthy of love. I have felt all these, too. I've related with thousands more who have, as well.

---

[6] Gratitude to Brené Brown for coining this phrase that self describes exactly that sensation; *Daring Greatly*, pg 42.

[7] Although, don't get me wrong, rainbows and unicorns are also awesome!

Yes, there is a way through. The work I share in this book is an embodied spiritual practice, a Sacred Sexual practice that can help you:

- Create the life you choose.
- Rejuvenate your body.
- Reclaim your sexual sovereignty.
- Witness and learn from places in your body.
- Release old patterns and limiting beliefs.
- Build the foundation to explore your unique ecstatic, orgasmic repertoire.
- Reclaim your power and your choice.
- Feel really good about feeling good.

What I share on these pages has been guided to move through me and be offered. It's not always pretty. It IS always authentic. I trust that it is what it's meant to be.

ACKNOWLEDGEMENTS

The seeds of this book were planted long ago. I am grateful for all the pieces that come together now as the weavings begin, and for all the people in my life who have been part of my journey, no matter how difficult or easy the interface. We all learn from and teach each other, and I'm thankful for each of you teachers in my life who've been a part of my growth and unfurling. You've taken the form of mother, father, grandmothers, grandfathers, girlfriends, boyfriends, fellow athletes, colleagues, bosses, partners, lovers, daughter and more. Some of you have taken on the formal roles of teachers, mentors, therapists and guides. I hold the gifts all of you have shared with me in great gratitude. Whether consciously or unconsciously, you have been mirrors and catalysts for seeding changes in myself. I believe all the major players in our lives incarnate and come together by choice. At an energetic being or soul level, I chose the parents I stepped into this lifetime with, I chose the interactions with friends, lovers and even enemies.

While some of what I am going to share may cast a dark light, I intend no harm nor blame. On a human level, yes, portions of this journey sucked. Yet these painful experiences also carried within them a gift, a redemption, a reclamation of joy and light. As the pain dies away, the joy issues forth.

Brad, you taught me that I MUST let go of the anger I had been holding inside for so long, or I would not survive. Re-creating our lives so that we could be apart yet continue to both raise our daughter to be the powerful, confident person she is says much for what can happen when the healing happens — and I know it hasn't always been easy. Thank you for being in my life; I am proud of us and our daughter.

Mom, wow — we had no idea how much fragmentation existed behind the curtain pulled over your mom's past, right?! I see now how this rupture had an impact on your journey as a young mother and then on me as your child. This was really hard for me in ways I couldn't articulate, and I can't imagine all the ways that must have felt for you. New layers of forgiveness bloom from my body and heart. Through ways I didn't expect, I've learned how to gently let my own eyes open and meet the world with new curiosity, and allow people in to help me. Thank you.

Dad, I can only imagine how hard things must have felt as you grew up fighting to make your way. You've taught me: "Never give up, baby — never give up." And in ways I didn't expect, I've learned how to find my own balance of drive and action with compassion and love. Thank you.

Deb, you helped me open my eyes and start to peel my white-knuckle grip off of the steering wheel! Quite literally, you compassionately and directly introduced me to myself. You helped me see vast new possibilities and to realize I could create my own reality. For this and for your love, support and encouragement for me to be me, I am eternally grateful.

Beautiful sweet Paul, I thank you. You helped me transition into my authentic beauty and power, and encouraged me to contribute to the world in these ways. I am eternally grateful for what we shared, how you helped me slow down and see that life was so much richer and juicier than the hectic, dry experience I had been living.

In the fullest biggest heart gratitude I say thank you, my Love, Dixon, for all you've done to support me in my path and in this book. I have opened in love like I never knew was possible, emotionally connecting in ways that I didn't know existed. Thank you for holding my heart safely. I love sharing life with you!

And my daughter, Hannah — it is to you I dedicate this expansion of possibility. You woke me up, sweet one! Thank you. I am so glad you were born, and I am forever grateful to be your mom and to share this life together. I've witnessed you grow into adulthood and move through important initiations to land here and share your light. I love watching you connect with *your* authentic gift to contribute to the world... full, vibrant, and alive.

Cliff, where do I begin? Our journey with editing became a deep, rich, phenomenal relationship of intimacy and connection. I feel I learned so much more about myself through your lens, and the guidance you've given me has deepened my capacity with my own voice. I literally couldn't have done this without you.

There are so many more beings that have been invaluable in my journey, too numerous to name here, including friends and Patreon supporters. Here I offer my gratitude to those of you who supported me with claiming my voice, clarifying my message and/or editing this book: Sky, Barry Callen, Emily Canosa, Stefanie Cohen, Zahava Griss, KT, Michele DeVoe Lussky, Genie Nordskog, Emily Otto, Jim Parker, Leela Sinha, KJ Song, Rebecca Staffend, Janine Taylor, Michelle Tupko, Sara Vos. Thank you.

HOW TO USE THIS BOOK

There are so many ways a book can flow. Novels tend to share a story, have one consistent flow, a narrative, sometimes with poetic prose. Technical writing tends to have different topics delineated and include a lot of footnotes and information. Self-help books often offer practices and exercises to explore for your own integration and transformation.

This book is a unique blend of story, teachings, embodied practices and exercises, self-reflection prompts and more.

This is intended to be a full, multidimensional experience. Even though the words are lined up in neat little rows on the page, it's really about stepping into the nonlinear. You may notice times when you feel triggered or uncomfortable. You may notice times when you feel turned-on or filled with pleasure... and then maybe even feel the internal tension of "I don't know if I should be feeling turned on by this." You may stiffen up at the thought of touch. You may notice judgment or resentment. You may feel gratitude in recognizing you're not alone in this journey. You may feel like celebrating.

Feeling our feelings is important. To consciously notice our feelings is to connect with information emerging from the body in real time. Our emotional response opens the way. This is the nature of the sacred sexual tantric path and this book: meeting what is alive and present and now. This is the nature of becoming more accessible to yourself.

That said, take it slow. Don't expect to read this book in one sitting. Give yourself time and space. Move with this material at the pace you feel called to do. Setting the book down is an opportunity to integrate and to go deeper in your journey of self. Yes, do that when you feel called. Take time for self care. And be sure to come back to the book to continue. There is an intentional cycle of exploration here, so commit to yourself to hold space for that completion.

Check in with your body as you read. Notice your breath, notice your heart rate, the sensations in your gut. There may be times when you notice yourself having a hard time staying present or feeling unsettled — take pauses and support your body to settle. This is important, not to ignore the discomfort arising and put our heads in the sand, but instead to settle the nervous system so that the possibility of change, of building resilience, can happen. Some ways to do this are:

- Turn your head and look to your left. Notice what you see. Name the colors, textures and shapes that you notice.
- Turn your head and look to your right. Notice what you see. Name the colors, textures and shapes that you notice.
- Take a deep belly breath.
- Stand up and stretch.
- Step outside and get your feet or other parts of your body in direct contact with the Earth. You may do this standing, or sitting down, lying on your back, or lying on your belly, just to name a few positions.
- Pause and begin to hum deeply for a few breaths — really let the hum vibrate through your body.[8]
- Slowly stroke your own face with self-love.
- Take a warm bath to surround and soak your body in water.
- Snuggle with a pet or fellow human.
- Share eye contact and smile with someone you care about.

As we move with this book, we will explore practices to support our path of Listening to Our Bodies. To support this exploration, many of the **footnotes** offer a path to cool ideas and resources — use those.

If you come across a word or phrase you are unfamiliar with, refer to the **Glossary** at the end where I summarize the terms that may be the most unusual.

And if you would like to follow even more threads to new ideas, see the **Additional Resources to Explore** for a list of books and other materials that supported me on this journey. I offer them to support you as you explore experiences and concepts through this book.

---

[8] Resmaa Menakem shares some wonderful body settling practices, including humming, in his book *My Grandmother's Hands*.

There are as many ways of reading this book as there are readers. Here's my suggested approach. Of course, feel free to modify, adapt and innovate what works best for you:

Read it through once at the pace and rhythm that feels right for you to read and absorb. When you see a **Recipe** introduced, flip to the Recipe section and read it. Read, and breathe. Do the practices that feel right for now.

As you read through this book, you'll start to notice places in your body that are wanting to communicate with you. Harvest that, become aware, journal about it. Keep reading. If something catches you or triggers you or feels hard to get through, skip it for now. Take your pause, do one or more of the practices above, and come back. If it still feels hard to get through, then scan ahead, grab the next thing and keep rolling.

Once you've completed the book, then come back and explore the Recipes more deeply. I incorporated the practices at the core of the book into my life over the span of 12 years. Each one has the potential for producing life-changing shifts.

Give yourself the time and space to read this at a pace that is right for you. If you notice a place where you feel stuck, this is important. The stuck places are often where you will find your gifts. If you are wondering what to do, keep reading. See how the pieces come together. Trust that they will.

Overall, being aware of your intentions is helpful, and finding a level of commitment will support you in this process. What attracted you to this book? What are you seeking? The practices provided along the way will also help. Try them. Embodied practice means trying new things. It's exciting! Trying something new can be daunting at times, and it can feel silly as easily as it can feel exalted and illuminating... sometimes at the same time. This is the space of growth.

And finally, you may need or desire additional support on your path in the form of a healer, therapist, teacher or guide. Seek out someone who is trauma-informed and works with embodiment practices. I sought many people within the timeframe this book encompasses. We're not in this alone.

One more thing: I want to acknowledge the "hard." What's hard for each person is different. This is not about comparing trauma levels. The hard things this work brought up in me might feel like no big deal for someone else, or they may feel really overwhelming for another. Many people have experienced traumatic events much more intense than the ones I describe here. What you've experienced may seem much harder than some of the things that I've experienced, and I honor that. Whatever you experience as "hard" is what's true for you.[9] Let your journey meet you and your body with care. Notice if you brush off your own journey as silly or unimportant. Or if you do that as you witness someone else's. Or if you feel overwhelmed in the hard places.

Be kind and gentle with yourself and the process. Take good care, and follow through with your commitment to you.

May this book be of service on your path.

---

[9] Ash Beckham shares about how hard is not relative, it's not about comparing with others' versions of hard. Hard is just hard. TED talk "Coming Out of Your Closet," https://youtu.be/kSR4xuU07sc?si=MILNDAcStnW5ISAz

IT'S JUST THE BEGINNING

"Our bodies merged in new ways. The raging, fiery passion filled with deep rumbling roars and tear-filled screams opened ways into joyous delight, laughter and blissful cries. Tender, slow, deep silent moments settled into releasing heaving trembles, or peaceful sinking sleep. Sweaty and hot, we pressed into each other to the point of not feeling where our individual selves ended and the other began. We moved gracefully from sweetly snuggling together to powerfully merging with raw intensity."

"...I invite the energy of the tree to penetrate me, feel the energy enter me, pulse through me, build... build... bump against an edge, release some ejaculate. More building. I let go with sound, feeling a little restricted but nothing like in the past, even in my bedroom... and now here I am in the wide open park! It's okay to feel nervous; I let myself feel it. Press palms of hands with thumbs. Take off shoes, press into arches with my thumbs... oh yes! Builds more, pulses of an orgasm... spreads... then builds again and my legs tense, the energy shifts and it's okay, straight tight legs, pelvic tilt, thrust ungh yes mmmm... intense... and finally it lets go! Orgasm pulsing, ejaculating, pouring through me. Mmmm wide, I remind myself and send my intention to the Universe that only beings of Light are welcome here! Oh yes, you are safe! I hear a bird..."

"...Sharing love with all beings: with trees, with nature, with partners male, female or any gender identity, or multiple partners. That it wasn't about gender, it *was about opening in love, AS love. Embodying the STATE of love! I was beginning to see the expansiveness of possibilities."*

These are excerpts from stories I wrote describing my personal experiences with body opening and sexual awakening, Female Ejaculation and Energetic Orgasms (fully clothed, in nature, without touching my genitals) that blew my body and mind. My capacity to feel good about myself and experience ecstatic pleasure and bliss states began to open. YES! I have GOT to stand on top of a mountain and shout to the world how EVERY PERSON DESERVES TO KNOW ABOUT THIS! It feels like no one talks about this stuff, and it's time: I'm going to!

I felt so deeply called that it literally changed my life on every level and in deeply personal ways, so much so that I felt called to seek out teachers and guides so that I could also bring this work to others. As I wove teachings from many teachers and ancient traditions along with direct experience and Spiritual guidance, I gestated and created even my very profession.[10] I moved from Engineer to Sacred Sexual Healer and Transformational Guide. When I began writing this book, I was a Sex Educator and a Spiritual Coach. Now having worked with thousands of people to support them on their paths, and as I continue on my own path of self-awareness and sacred sexuality, I know it is time for more to be revealed.

To set the stage for that, I would like to share with you my story. Like any good, deep heart story, this deserves presence. Let's sink in together — share a cup of tea, light a candle and settle in. We're going into deep territory and that deserves a safe space to be held.

---

[10] I acknowledge many great colleagues in the field of sacred sexuality. What I mean by "creating my own profession" is that we all bring our unique medicine to this work, and there is no standard way that sacred sexuality is taught. I didn't use a script, a protocol nor a standard methodology. Yet I did bring a balance of education, training, experience and tangible practices with spiritual and intuitive guidance while honoring the intention of the being(s) I worked with. I offered meeting and listening to the authentic wisdom in the body.

PART ONE

NORMAL-VILLE

CHAPTER ONE

Dragonflies and Armor

The sun was warm and bright the day I met Dragonfly.

I was at a corporate company picnic at a local park, complete with plasticware and foil catering trays brimming with hot dogs, burgers and macaroni salad. The picnic tables sat aligned in grid-like military fashion on the cement under the pavilion, as if mocking our attempt to get out in nature.

Walking the company line, like most everyone else, I was dressed in traditional corporate casual: khakis and polo shirt.

Yet this day would be different: Something was about to change.

Conversations stay safe and familiar — lamenting about recent layoffs and organizational changes (aka "reorg"), comments about the weather and the food. I sit across the table from a fellow engineering manager named Lisa. Lisa with the perfect makeup and hair, Ann Taylor slacks and fitted shirt, her fork poised delicately beneath her perfectly manicured nails, painted a subtle beige that makes me wonder why she bothers painting them at all. Between us on the plastic-covered table sits my unsuspecting bottle of water.

At some point between the woes of reorg and "please pass the salt," a dragonfly lands on the cap of the water bottle. It looks at me.

I pause in awe, looking back.

Lisa shrieks in disgust, waving it away, brushing it off like a freaky ugly nuisance of a creature. "Ew! A bug!"

I grimace at the difference in our perception, giggle a little, and dismiss it without much of a thought.

A moment later it returns and lands on my sleeve. I notice: Wow, it is so beautiful, intricate, delicate yet strong… precise movements of its head and eyes. Lisa notices and freaks out again. I say, "Hey, it's really cool! Nothing to be afraid of!" It flies off.

Finally, a third time, it lands directly on my skin… right on my hand, which is propped up near my face. It looks at me as if to beckon: "Are you listening now?" I feel tingles, and my heart is racing.

I am.

Wow, the people at our table are kind of surprised that it keeps coming over. They make a comment or two and then the subject shifts back to speculation on who's getting canned and who's heading up the new department.

Meanwhile, it hits me: This is really important. I need to pay attention. I look at the dragonfly: What are you saying to me? What message are you bringing me?

Six months earlier I had "a hit" (an intuitive knowing) of clarity. After walking the company line and being really successful at doing what I did for 15 years, I finally realized I was not a "lifer" after all. I had assumed, like so many in the culture of our industry in the decades prior, that I was going to be employed there for 30+ years until I retired: a lifetime of paychecks and benefits, the safety of the known. However, a shift in the Universe made it clear to me that I was meant to do other work in this world. My time here was coming to a close. It had served me well, yet now my calling guided me elsewhere.

Only 10 days prior I had set the wheels in motion, reconnecting with my inner panther/cougar. As a child I had a longstanding fascination with panthers but had only recently started to take my relationship with them seriously as an adult. With panther nudging me forward in encouragement, I asked to be considered for a severance package to leave the company. That opportunity indeed became available. Now the day drew near when I needed to make the final decision.

So here, now, in the park under the pavilion, it becomes clear… Dragonfly. She sees through the illusion, she tells me to free myself, she beckons: "Fly with me, see things a different way, through many more facets and dimensions. Move in ways new and different!"

Yes, thank you! I committed that day to do my best to honor that guidance. Four days later I had a conversation with my management and they set the wheels in motion. It was sealed. I was to leave the corporate world less than two months later.

These images are directly from my journal the day this happened in 2008.

But wait… How did I get here? What led me to this place, and how the heck did I, the uber-logical brainy science geek who became a successful corporate engineer and business leader, start believing animals were talking to me? And how did I begin trusting to *listen* to them? How did I begin to notice and trust that there is an infinite realm, a world beyond the 3D reality that my conventional sight and senses could grasp? How did I connect with this realm of the infinite that opened up amazing new vistas of possibility?

The Landing

In recent years on my birthday, I have been asking my mother for stories of my birth. I wanted to hear how her pregnancy with me and the birth process went. What I've learned has informed my compassion for her and myself with new perspectives on how I stored things in my body. She shared with me that the night before, she had been on hands and knees scrubbing the kitchen floor of the old farmhouse in rural Ohio where they lived. My dad came home and chided her for doing this work so late in her pregnancy. That night she went into labor and they made the 25-mile journey to the nearest hospital.

Born in that small-town hospital to young conservative parents, like so many other babies in the 60s and 70s, I was whisked away to an isolated bassinet across the hall, only to be brought to mom for bottle feedings at prescribed times. My mother later told me that she felt lucky that the nursery was a short distance away from her room so she only had to "waddle across the hall" to get a view of me through the glass window. She noted that I looked older than I was. To her, I "didn't even look like a newborn."

This isolated existence the first five days of my life was common among people of that time and place. Still, it would have been considered cruel and insane by those cultures that remember interconnection. This experience probably contributed to my sense of separateness and not really fitting in. It's as if I landed, alien, on this new planet... [blink blink] looking out into the world with sort of stunned recognition that I really didn't belong here. Who are these people, anyway?

As a little child I was shy, timid, reserved and introverted. I was also ready to grow up fast — no longer wanting to be in this child body.

I am five years old, walking along on the sidewalk in the sunlight to visit my friend down the street. I am chanting "half an hour" over and over in my head, because that is how much time my mom has given me to go play, and I need to remember to be back on time. My awareness suddenly pops out, it feels like it goes wide, as if I am no longer only inside this tiny body but am also suddenly inhabiting the space around me. I feel as if I am stationary at the center of the movement, and the earth is actually rolling underneath my feet below me as I walk. Wow, this feels really neat!

It wasn't a feeling of being the center of the universe — that would've been far too bold — so much as a sense that I was participating in an illusion of a story unfolding around me, one that didn't exist until it came into my view.

During my childhood, I often tried to be seen as older than I really was, this grasping at social acceptance in part due to being younger than the others in my class. It was as if my Soul Being was not happy with having to do human birth and the childhood thing again — can't we just skip to the adult part? I hated being looked down on for my age, and I constantly felt the need to prove myself.

This alien feeling of not quite belonging here was exacerbated by the teasing of my family that I was adopted or somehow not a part of their natural family. My fair blond locks and hazel eyes stood in stark contrast to the dark hair and eyes of my sister, mother and father. While part of me may have wondered if this was true, it was also quite clear that as much as I felt strange and different, I was very much biologically a part of this family. Whether I liked it or not.

The Armor (Building the Walls)

Thus began a childhood of never quite feeling like I fit in or knowing who I was. My parents did their best to raise my sister and me, and we had what I would've called a good and fairly "normal"[11] childhood: family vacations, board games at the kitchen table, public school for my sister and me, work for my father who was hardly ever at home, and childrearing and household chores for my mother. It wasn't until much later that I started to notice how deeply my childhood experiences affected me.

Childhood is when our ideas of what is normal are established. We're building the lens through which we view the world, and then we don't see it anymore because it's a lens. Because of that we can easily normalize things that are not okay, including things that were profoundly traumatizing. It's very easy to carry that into adulthood and not really see the impact of these traumas until much later, if at all. For me, layers continue to reveal themselves, which in turn reveal more options for continued healing and liberation. I believe this is an important part of our "human homework."

Connecting with other kids was always really difficult. My closest connections were usually adult friends of the family. My father moved us around a lot, and while there were some upsides, like exploring new places and learning new things, it was super hard on me. In the beginning I believe it was to get us a fresh start from the rural, farming and small-town lifestyle that he and my mom had experienced growing up. Perhaps he wanted to give us a new perspective on the world? Perhaps he wanted to escape a world that had been incredibly hard on

---

[11] "Normal" for me then meant through the lens of white dominant, middle class, US culture of the 1970s and 80s.

him? Whatever his reasons, he kept driving himself into new and "better" jobs and careers that required us to be in different places across the country. While my mother went along with it, I am not sure how much she loved it either. My father's pursuit of his entrepreneurial spirit resulted in my going to five different schools in three states by the time I was in sixth grade. I believe this nurtured the seeds of my own entrepreneurial and adventurous spirit within me from an early age. I certainly loved experiencing new things that would not have been possible in rural farm country:

I am seven years old, arms wrapped around my dad's neck as he carries me across the deep water to the shallow part and sets me down. Here, my little sister and I get to have nets and walk beside the small boat my dad is now in and steering to navigate through the clear water of this ocean bay. I feel the sunlight on my skin, tanned a golden brown, my long blond hair pulled back into a low ponytail. I breathe in the salty ocean breeze. We start looking… there's one!! We squeal and scoop our nets at the small, shelled creatures darting through the seagrasses. Scallops! We are catching them and gazing at the little blue eyes all along the edge between the shells. Intrigued, I count the little eyes, 42… wow! And as we collect them in our repurposed mesh orange bags, the little creatures open and close their two shells like a bellows and squirt water out at us. Giggles of delight! At the time this tickled me — I was not really thinking about how they were in fact gasping for the last bit of oxygen, now deprived of their salty waters of life, in their dying moments.

The sadness of the dying was lost on me… we'd come home, my dad would clean them and sauté them up in garlic and butter. Oh, how we relished the succulent fresh taste of seafood we had caught on our own.

There were times like this where I had fun and enjoyed life — catching blue crab, digging for clams, collecting sand dollars and shells on the beach. These were intriguing, new experiences and I felt proud to be learning new things.

However, as much as I enjoyed the new experiences, my family's last move devastated me.

I am 11 years old, in sixth grade. I finally made a friend this year, and we've become close. It's a first, and I am so excited! However, Dad recently announced we're moving… AGAIN, and I just hate it. I feel so awkward, puberty is starting and I have this mouthful of braces on my huge teeth paired with my very narrow face and fast-growing body — I've grown five inches in height this year alone! I feel barely able to keep up with my own very skinny and rapidly growing body, and I feel so uncomfortable in my own skin.

So now I am here, a shy, skinny kid with long blond hair, staring sullenly out of the window of our green van stuffed with bodies, boxes and belongings. Tears stream down my face as I gaze down the street toward the house of a friend that I will never see again. We drive away from our life here to start over, yet again.

In my awkwardness, I felt ashamed and embarrassed. I would often get teased by other kids — it made me feel awful, unimportant, not good enough, small. But the worst part was that it mostly came from my own father. I don't think he ever consciously was trying to hurt me. I really believe he just thought it was "all in good fun." To make matters worse, when I did respond in a way that showed how much it hurt, I got laughed at even more. Teased about being too sensitive, I was trained early on that my emotions were not valuable; they were a burden. He would say things like, "Aw, c'mon... I'm just kidding. It's no big deal." I felt that now my reaction to the teasing was another bad thing about me to be ashamed of: I shouldn't cry, I shouldn't express the hurt or the anger, and I felt like I couldn't do anything right. Although my mom was physically present, I didn't feel her as emotionally available for support.

I am 10 years old, in fifth grade. My body is beginning to change, and I am developing breasts. While this alone makes me nervous, I feel even more awkward as I notice my friends have started wearing bras and I haven't. I want one too, and timidly and nervously I shop for one with my mother, a "training bra." As if that terminology isn't embarrassing enough (thank Spirit they don't label them that way anymore!), my father laughs when he sees me and asks, "So what are you training those things to do?!" He is referring to my newly sprouting breasts that I am tenuously proud of having. I feel this as a punch in the stomach, totally deflating what is left of my confidence, and literally feel my body round into a hunch to hide my breasts from view. My height is already daunting for me to step into, and now I feel like I need to be even smaller. This adds another brick weighing onto my already hunching posture.

I could not express my emotions without being shamed. So I hid them, stuffed as much away as I could, held on, tightened up. I remember gnawing on a small blue rubber figurine of Mickey Mouse. I would grind my teeth and bite into the ears of that toy in a way that seemed to release some of the anger. Tears welling up, intense clenching in my jaw. I couldn't scream or speak any of it without being yelled at, so at least this way perhaps I could let some of it seep out. Yet mostly, I bottled it inside.

And then there were the "knowings," times when I had knowledge about someone or something that really I had no way of knowing overtly through conventional, "3D reality" means. These would also get shut down. Or these experiences would fill me with fear, then I couldn't separate the sensations of others from my own. In fact, I had no idea that there was any difference. So it registered as a threat or that I was doing something wrong. I subconsciously started to put up shields to keep it out since I didn't know how to handle it. This "it" being an awareness of realms other than the 3D reality/physical world I had been socialized to believe was the only truth. It felt like every time I started to shine my light, I would get squashed. So in addition to putting up the shields, I learned to dim myself down. I learned that my own body and intuition were not to be trusted. I also learned that to ask questions or to look at people was intrusive and that I should never do it. All of these influences were adding more layers of weight, dimming my light and making me smaller.

I felt safe when I could hide away in my closet: it was dark, warm, cozy. With a flashlight and a pad of paper in my lap, I could draw in there. Drawing was one of my favorite things to do. I would create: draw cartoons and flow visual stories onto the page. That felt nourishing, safe and helpful. I felt alone, and that drawing space inside the closet provided the closest I could come to feeling held.

My shame, embarrassment and shyness grew, coupled with my overachiever desire to accomplish more and more and do better and better so that I would feel good about myself so that maybe *they* would see me, maybe *they* would stop laughing at me, and maybe *they* would be proud of me. Who were "they"? My parents, my peers, even the world, perhaps. This began to be the theme of my life: "Don't let anyone in, and don't feel."

Don't Let Anyone In, and Don't Feel

How did this happen? How did I shut myself away from the world while still interacting in it and pushing myself harder and harder to achieve? How did I numb out my emotions, creating a persona of success while crumbling inside?

One part of me went on overachiever autopilot and excelled in school, skipping third grade and continuing to excel in ongoing honors programs, dean's lists, and student leadership. I received straight As and excelled as a swimmer, winning ribbons and medals by the armload. Another part of me went into numbness and closure. Then two traumatic events happened in my life.

Parents' Divorce

My parents announced their divorce when I was 11 years old. It was rather matter-of-fact. I had sensed a tension and a lot of "stuffing away" between my parents leading up to it. But then again, that was really nothing new. Showing emotions was not encouraged in our household, and my parents were very secretive about their personal affairs, especially my father. I remember feeling a little stunned and a bit awkward at the irony of having to go to the courthouse to state my desire to live with my mother when all I had ever really known was life with my mother. My father's work and life seemed to keep him away from our home for most of my younger years, so him moving away now just seemed aligned with my normal realm of experience. In fact, I remember feeling very awkward once when I was home with him alone (it was a weekend where my mother was away). I felt this deep in the pit of my stomach — a longing, as if I were homesick. I thought that this was really odd, given that I was in my own home with my own father.

Therefore, my father moving out really didn't seem to directly affect me much at the time. What did hit me really hard was how it affected my mother.

I am 11, I hear crying and come in to see that my mother is trying to install a towel rod in the bathroom. She's using wood screws in the drywall, and it isn't installing properly — rod and wall are crumbling away into her hands. I feel her feeling overwhelmed, I sense that to her this means she is failing yet again. Such a simple project that she would've relied on my father to do in the past now leaves her struggling on her own. I feel despair in her tears. I vow in this moment that I will never rely solely on another person anymore — especially not a man. I will always just do it myself. I will never let anyone in. I will be strong and independent, able to take care of myself and do anything I need to do.

And I did. The impact of the divorce landed in my body, and I unknowingly carried this as trauma. I built walls to keep people out and strove to control everything myself. While there's value in the skills of independence, it can be taken too far, something that I would learn very viscerally in my journey yet to come.

Heartbreak

The second traumatic event was the breakup of my first love. I felt first love at age 14: I a freshman, he a sophomore.

It is the summer of '85. My geeky, awkward, shy and terrorizing middle school years are finally behind me. I am feeling pretty good about myself: My braces are off, my body has filled out and I consciously made the choice heading into my freshman year of high school last summer to smile more, to meet new people and to stand a little taller. In the process, I connect with a guy I know from swim team, and he becomes my first love. We have been dating for most of the year, I have visions of romantic "forever"-ness. Maybe we'll get married someday, have kids.

As our relationship grows deeper, the question of sex keeps coming up. Neither of us had ever had sex before. I was curious; he was persistent. Despite my visions of a romantic connection — warm, soft bed and candlelight, surely that would be perfect for our first time — we know our parents wouldn't approve. Instead, we have to be secretive. We make plans for it to be tonight, sneak out of our respective houses and make what has become a fairly regular midnight trek across our neighborhoods. We meet at our community swim club where, as a lifeguard manager, he has the benefit of a key to the office.

Now here we are together, in the dark, on the floor of the pool office, with a bottle of Seagram's 7. It's a warm summer night outside, but in here with naked butts on a cold linoleum floor, there's stale air and a secretive darkness that weighs as heavy as the large metal desk pressing into the tiny room. After having drunk alcohol to "loosen up," we pull out the condoms. Fueled by my own motivation to constantly try to prove myself socially and to grasp at the love I didn't realize I was missing, we consummate our relationship. It is awkward, painful even, and I feel isolated. Yet part of me is glad we did it. I am no longer a virgin. I feel pride: I can explore sex with my boyfriend now, so surely I've entered the cool kid ranks. I also feel defensive — I want to claim that I can like sex too, that it's not just a guy thing.

There is an older group of girls on the swim team, and I desperately want to be seen by them. I have overheard them talking about sex before, something I haven't known much about. I want to be cool, so I assume that by having sex I can be "one of them," too. So now that I have, I feel really eager to share with them about it.

I proudly walk up to the coolest of the cool girls, planning to share my story about having sex with my boyfriend the past weekend. I am so sure that this will be the key to having them accept me, I eagerly await her smile and open arms and being greeted by "Welcome to the cool girls club!" — perhaps even an engraved invitation!

Only that's not at all how it landed.

As I eagerly share my story, she looks down her nose at me with disgust. She's appalled that I would do such a thing, and then worse, tell about it.

I suddenly feel incredibly small. I feel nauseated. A shroud of shame descends upon me, I hunch over, deflated. Oh no, what have I done?! I feel defensive. I want to say, "I am not a slut or a whore! This is my boyfriend and I love him, so that makes it okay!" I begin to "pattern into" my body/brain that the only way it's okay to want to have sex is in a long-term relationship, and therefore I had better stay in this one.

This first love, I recognized much later, was at least in part an attempt to grasp at the love I wasn't feeling at home. I grasped for and attached to the object of my affection in unhealthy ways, perhaps smothering him, in an attempt to find and connect with the emotional support I was missing from my parents. Now that we had sex together, there was a bond that, while I didn't consciously understand it, I believe was also a part of what fueled how hard what happened next landed for me. When he ended it a year later, I went into a severe depression.

I am 15, a sophomore, sitting at my desk in the 200-wing of our high school wearing jeans, a dumpy gray sweatshirt and too much black eye makeup. The undersized leather shoes I am wearing are closing in far too tight around my feet, some of the stitches are broken, a hole starting to form at the toe. I poke at it. I feel much too awkward and ashamed about being too big to dare wear a larger size that might offer a little relief to my suffocated feet. I pull further away. I close my eyes. As a wave of feelings and tears closes in around me, I realize that if I just numb out it doesn't hurt so much. I find relief in that.

From then on I made the choice to numb out to avoid feeling the pain. And so emerged the second piece of armor: I made the decision not to feel.

"Don't let anyone in, and don't feel." Thus the bricks began: the mortar, the walls, the barriers — body armor, shields I constructed around myself to not let anyone in and not feel. This armor also served to block any fledgling awareness of realms other than the normative, mainstream, three-dimensional view of the world I had been trained to see.

And in the meantime, my overachiever self just kicked into hyperdrive.

Overachiever

As my body began to numb out, my head was happy to take over. All of my focus was centered on achievement. At the age of 17, I graduated with honors in the top of my high school class. My world was designed to excel academically in preparation for college, and it felt like I practically lived at my high school and YMCA. Whether it was waking up early to dive into a cold pool in preparation for the next swim meet, or staying late at school to organize events and publish a newspaper, always there was a list of things to do that would bring me closer to my goals. I excelled in all the college prep courses, especially math and science, which I loved. I could buzz through complicated equations with ease. At the same time I was also an art geek, and having been selected to be a part of an honors art course, I found myself regularly driving to a nearby university for a nude figure drawing class. Art had been a part of my life since a very young age in addition to my abilities in math and science, and my desire to blend these together framed my choice of a major to be between graphic design/arts and engineering.

Actually, engineering had been a foreign concept to me. I knew nothing about engineering until one day in my high school physics class, my teacher — a woman — invited in a female engineering student from the state university to talk about engineering. I saw her walk through the door, hair pulled back in a neat ponytail, proudly wearing her college sweatshirt and beaming with confidence. As she shared about her experiences, she sounded so together. I heard her describe the field of engineering, and I fell in love with it! I liked the idea that I could combine my love of art and creativity with my math and science skills through problem solving. I also liked the idea of entering a predominantly male field with the challenge of proving myself capable there. At the time I still viewed gender as a "binary" and limited to our "sex" (male/female or man/

woman). I felt like I had to do a lot of fighting to prove myself as a "woman," but I did not yet see how limiting that was.

I also chose engineering because that was how I could "make the most money." I felt no real pressure for that goal outside myself. It was just my logic brain kicking in, reporting that was what I should do. All of this resonated with me, and my decision was made. My parents really didn't have much to say about it, and once it clicked for me, it stuck. I later entered college knowing my choice of major.

While my overachiever self was setting and meeting goals, I was also attracting the attention of guys once again.

I am 16, with permed and feathered hair and tight jeans pegged at the ankles: totally '80s. Standing on the brown linoleum floor, I lean against the mustard-colored refrigerator, light filtering in from the window in the back door. Feeling better about myself and back in the dating scene after the breakup, I'm starting to enjoy the attention of multiple guys and feel my social life starting to gain some momentum. I read through the phone messages scrawled in pencil on the scrap of paper on the kitchen counter of our tiny cube of a house. I return the calls, excited about some more than others. I'm not surprised to see several from the same boy, a friend of some friends from my summer swim club.

It started with him persistently contacting me; I wasn't all that interested. Dressed in a leather jacket and jeans, he rode up on his motorcycle, a dark blue Honda Nighthawk, to see me at a local root beer stand where I worked as a carhop. His persistence and charm prevailed and I finally agreed to go out with him when he said, "C'mon, let's just go have dinner. What's the harm in dinner?" I agreed to dinner, yet what we got was a 12-pack of beer, and we snuck cans into the theater to see a movie. Despite the awkward foreshadowing lost on me in the shift in plans, I began to enjoy my time with him, finding that I was loving him for loving me so much. His attention and adoration of me won me over, and I just figured the rest of what I needed would catch up. Seven years later I would marry this man.

Meanwhile, home life was tense and awkward at best. My sister and mother were both struggling with issues of their own. I did not realize that I was creating distractions in order to avoid being at home. Little did I know that this 17-year-old summer was the last time I would live with a parent.

CHAPTER TWO

Purses and Fear

I am 19, in college. It is dark and smoky in the bar, and it's loud… too loud. With the music and lights blaring at the dance floor and the screaming near an ear to be heard in conversation — all of it feels like too much. There are so many people around. My head hurts. My body cringes, resistant to inhale the cigarette smoke, fake fog and stale alcohol in the air, yet the instinctual survival need to breathe wins out and keeps me going. I am in college, and have caved to peer pressure: I'm out at a dance club.

I drink. Heavily. Cheap draft beer from a bucket — quantity over quality is my motto, and it is about all my starving student budget can afford. I really don't like going to dance bars. I don't dance. I don't feel comfortable in my skin, afraid of how I will look and that people will laugh at me. So I sit. I drink. I am the reliable "girl who sits at the bar with the purses." Since there's no risk of me getting up to dance, I am the safe zone. My friends stash all their valuables at the table with me: purses, jackets pile up. The safe place with no fear of them being stolen or vandalized, common occurrences in the college bar scene in our town. My friends rely on me and then head out to the freedom of the dance floor to get their groove on. The persistent over-achiever in me does not have a checklist for the bar scene. This social setting has no rules or things to accomplish. I feel lost. I sit, buried in sensory overload and hanging on… not only to the pile of stuff at the table, but to the baggage I've begun accumulating the last few years. Carrying the weight of it all, I continue to numb out and not feel.

While my body continued to numb out and avoid emotions, my head and intellect were fueled with things to do. College suited me well and I voraciously soaked it all in. Classes, labs, papers, projects — I did them all with self-imposed high standards of perfection. I also loved the freedom to step into owning my life. I continued to excel at school, my mind and intellect riding high on top of it, all the while disconnecting from my body in more and more ways. I continued with the heavy binge drinking that began in high school, along with the weight gain and emotional numbness that comes with such behavior.

I remember being really organized with my drinking, planning it out in such a way as to not to interfere with school, my work at my several jobs or any other responsibilities or commitments. I would complete assignments and work ahead of time, so I could carve away time to "get wasted" without worry. I was so thorough that I would plan shoes and outfits that wouldn't get ruined in the sludge ever-present on the floors of the college bars, and earrings with backs so they wouldn't get lost in a drunken, out-of-control moment. Often these nights would end in blackouts and pass-outs.

The next day I would startle awake, grimacing, head pounding, eyes wincing at the light, feeling tremendous guilt and shame as I turned over and over in my head what I might have done or said the night before. Every now and again I would wonder why I was doing this to myself, opening little windows into my body that was screaming for help. Yet mostly I just tried to avoid listening to those inner messages, continuing to numb out and stuff them away.

I stuffed away so much. I kept forcing any glimpse of inner knowing down and away. I stuffed away all the pain and dirtiness, the shadows. I had to keep my outer facade clear, pretty, likable...

...just as I had learned to do so many years before.

Holding On and Holding In

I'm seven years old, lying in bed at night in our house in Florida. My room is the one at the end of the hall, with the dark olive shag carpet. It's late — I'm supposed to be sleeping. I look to my left and see the hall light peek in around the crack in the door. It soothes my fears a little. I don't feel well. I'm coughing. And coughing. And coughing. The coughs are getting stronger and stronger. I am uncomfortable, not able to sleep. But I don't know what to do. I am hoping for comfort in some way but I don't know how to ask for it. My mother is in her room down the hall and I assume she can hear me, but she isn't coming to help. The coughing keeps getting stronger, and I don't expect what happens next.

The force of the cough brings up the contents of my stomach and I vomit all over myself, the bed and down over the side onto some of my toys and games. Ewwww! I am so scared! What did my body just do?! What is this? It smells awful and hot. I am scared and begin crying for help... I don't know what to do. The hot, rancid wetness soaks my skin through my thin pajamas.

My mother finally comes into my room — I don't hear her words, I just feel the energy: I woke her up, I am inconveniencing her. I feel I am dirty, gross, and disgusting. I am messy and a bad girl for making her have to clean up after me. What happened is all my fault and I am a bad girl, unworthy of love or nurturing. I feel cold and alone, I feel awful and needy, yet I suck it up so that I won't be even more of a bother. I want to make her feel better. I draw in the fear and the pain and I hold it inside. Maybe if I do that more, swallow up the fear and the pain, me and the space around me will be prettier and she'll feel okay to be near me. Maybe she'll even hold me.

What I learned that day created a pattern in how I related to the world: I learned that life could feel terrifying, but those problems were mine to fix. Nobody could be counted on to support me. I felt alone, disgusting, unworthy, needy. So I began figuring out how to just do it all myself and not let anyone in to help.

I also learned ways to take it in and hold it there, not let any of this vile stuff out. Keep it hidden away, take it on from the world around me so I could be a good girl and be worthy of love. My hope was that then the people around me would like me better and be willing to hold me. I didn't realize the danger of holding on to it then.

My body carried this experience so strongly that later what arose was this visceral fear in my gut when I was near anyone, including myself, who may be on the verge of vomiting. I couldn't watch it in movies, just the gag reflex itself would send terror through me. Clenching in my body, I would flush with sweat and heat and feel nauseated and near vomiting myself, which I would then violently oppose. I would force myself to hold back from that feeling, to the point of making myself quite sick. It came up often in my drinking years. My binge drinking with friends became a mirror to reflect back on similar behaviors. Noticing an acquaintance had recently vomited down the side of a car door as I arrived at a high school party scene, I stepped in to clean it up. I was cleaning up their messes while living out my own mess. Was this a mirror? Was I trying to fill my own need for nurturing? Was I trying to hide the vileness to present the pretty, likable facade?

Feeling like life was going well, at least from my head's perspective, I continued to enjoy school and the success I was achieving. My boyfriend Brad was still living in our hometown, and the frequent trips to come visit me at school over one hundred miles away were wearing on us. After my first year of college we decided to move in together. I had been offered and accepted a prestigious engineering internship at a major corporation that summer, which required relocating to New York. The plan was that Brad would join me there, and then we'd move into an apartment near campus at the university in Ohio when school started back up in the fall.

For some reason, I felt compelled to tell my father that Brad and I were making this new step. I had hardly seen my father since my parents' divorce when I was 11. We only had one or two weeks a year to visit in one of the many states he lived, a weekend here and there, and maybe the occasional holiday.

My father really had no control over what I could do by this point, but I had a deep-seated need for his approval that I wouldn't have been able to articulate at the time. Was I subconsciously reaching out for his support, his blessing? Was I really excited to share about my new engineering internship (an honor to receive, having completed only one year of university) and our planned journey across the country for this new adventure? I was hoping for an "I'm proud of you" or maybe just an encouraging word.

What I got was something very different, something that changed the course of my life.

The Rift

I am 18, the late spring sunshine in the courtyard shines through the window of my college dorm room as I near completion of my first year of engineering studies. I am sitting in a ball on the gray linoleum of my dorm room floor by the mini-refrigerator. The long, coiled, manila phone cord drapes at least 10 feet across the room like a looming snake awaiting a time to strike. I hear my father's voice on the line, the little girl in me magnetized toward him, craving his approval, sharing my news.

His voice becomes sharp, harsh, booming. I feel his unprecedented anger and rage directed right at me. I'm scared. I sense I have evoked a monster and I must deserve the acid being spewed through the line and raining down across my body. The only actual words I can now hear booming and slamming around in my head like the echo of cannon fire are him screaming at me: "*IF ALL YOU WANT TO DO IS FUCK! ... IF ALL YOU WANT TO DO IS FUCK ... IF ALL YOU WANT TO DO IS FUCK ...*"

As I leave my body, I don't even consciously hear what comes next, something about how I shouldn't make this move. He's yelling something that makes me believe that he thinks I am ruining my life to make this choice.

I am sobbing, hitching, my breath catching short in my throat, crying. I take it all in, absorbing, carrying, stuffing away all this rage. My body is in a tight ball, I'm rocking, hiding my face, choking on my tears and high-pitched whimpers and cries. My belly feels tightly contracted, I feel nauseous. Surely I'm about to vomit, and this scares me even more. My breath is shallow, my body barely receiving its life-giving force. I am pulling away... I see my body there... I'm disconnecting even further from my body. These words and his energy, like a dagger, stab me deeply in my core and I feel my tender belly entrails ripped open, dripping, exposed...

Did he know that my perception of his words and how I thought he felt about me would later lock me (by my own choice) into marrying this man? A part of me felt I needed to prove that I was worthy of my father's approval by eventually getting married to the man I wanted "to fuck." This was a respectable outcome. Otherwise, I was clearly some kind of prostitute or whore, unworthy of love, a bad girl, not good enough. This is the story that locked into my body that day.

CHAPTER THREE

Pearls and Triathlon

The divide between my body and my soul was deepening. The hyper-achiever in me was again succeeding in spades. I had chosen to stay on and complete my master's degree in mechanical engineering when I was offered the opportunity to do an honors combined program that included an undergraduate thesis as a part of my bachelor's degree as well as a graduate thesis with my master's degree, completing both in five years total. I graduated in 1992 and again in 1993, Summa Cum Laude, with honors, full robes, sashes and regalia each time. In my master of science in mechanical engineering program, I specialized in quantum physics, my thesis on "Vibrational Excitation of Carbon Monoxide (CO) Molecules Using an Argon Fluoride (ArF) Excimer Laser" involved practical lab experience, literally building and manipulating lasers. Now, at age 22, I was launching my new engineering career at a huge prestigious corporation in the automotive industry, relocating myself and my soon-to-be husband to the very hub of the global automobile industry in Southeast Michigan.

I'm in my early 20s, dressed in a navy blue skirt suit and heels, blond hair pulled back and clipped in a tidy, low ponytail. Wearing pearl earrings and necklace, with a respectable amount of makeup — not too much and not too little — I sit at a boardroom table in one of the many high-rise office buildings of the major corporation to which I now give much of my waking life. The table is long, the fluorescent lights above us adding to the daunting sterility of the space. My place at the side of the table denotes my rank, as many of us gaze the length of the table to await the arrival of those expected to sit at its head. My leather planner and various reports are opened in front of me, displaying my sense of eager preparedness. I am here to present our team's progress on a project to senior management.

The meeting commences and we proceed to address the various items on that day's agenda. As my item comes to the forefront, I begin to speak. As soon as I begin my recommendation on how to proceed with "I feel that we...," I am harshly interrupted with a booming voice and a slammed hand on the table: "I don't CARE how you feel, show me the data!!"

I suddenly feel small, a welling up in my throat, a hot burning in my face and eyes. Doing my best to hold back tears, I take it in as I had so many times before, assuming I was the one in the wrong, that my ways of processing had to be adjusted to fit corporate norms. I do have the data, I share it, I am able to back up what I have to say, and it is received. Yet I vow to myself that I will do better in the future. I watch my language more carefully. I continue to "man up" and walk that line.

As I walked this heavily patriarchal world of corporate America as a woman, I found myself doing my best to fit in by changing who I was. Not listening to my body, stuffing away emotions, I found myself having to numb out even more to take on the heavy loads of analyzing and doing.

I am sitting at my desk under the fluorescent lights, the gray walls of my cubicle and stacks of papers closing in around me. Another email, another phone call. Someone does or says something that triggers it. As so many times before, I feel the anger well up inside, the stress, the anxiety building... I do my best to shove it down. I pull away, I don't even notice my body other than my hand compulsively going to my eyes once again. I'm not really here, I see myself as if from afar and yet I can't stop it. My fingers grasping at my eyelashes, I pull at them. Obsessing... I have to pull at my lashes, pull the mascara off of them, feel the sensation of the tug at the lid, as if scratching a deep itch.

I look in my fingers: they're shaking, I see the mascara clumps and smears, rub them off of my fingers onto paper. Go back for more... I pull, look again at my fingertips, I see eyelashes. At first one or two. "Likely," I tell myself to make it okay, "they were ready to come out anyway." Then more. I keep pulling. I feel repulsed at seeing them come out in my fingers: four, five... more. They come out in small clumps, stuck together with mascara. Part of me begs this other part of me to stop. But I can't stop myself from pulling more. My jaw is clenching, pulsing, over and over, my face swells hot, holding back tears. I'm grasping at my eyelids, it hurts, I pull. More come out, I even see blood at the root. I pull out a small cosmetic mirror, I look... there's blood on the rim of my eyelid where the eyelashes had been, and gaps in the line of lashes. I'm shaking. I fear someone will see me and yell at me. I feel deep shame. I'm a bad person for this. I stick the eyelashes to the adhesive on a sticky-note and shove it into my desk drawer.

Why do I do this? Why do I hurt myself? Why do I save the little lashes instead of letting them fall away? Why can't I let go of this compulsive action? What's wrong with me? I shove these questions, along with what I've just done, deeper away. I have to be strong. I get back to work. I vow to myself to tell no one about this for fear of what they would think of me.

My body was screaming for support, for some way to ease the load I was placing upon it. However, I couldn't hear it. I couldn't ask for help to offset the load. I had to carry it myself. I just kept shoving more, deeper inside. This is one example of the odd behaviors and impact that all the shoving things away and holding on was having on my body.

Another way those loads manifested was as a tremendous amount of physical weight that I gained, starting with the "freshman 15." People teased that gaining weight was a "normal" part of the college life transition, but this was nothing compared to what had crept up on me over time. Sure, I had noticed an extra pound or two every so often, but I had been trying to ignore how they were adding up. I was ashamed to admit it was more like 50 by then than 15, but it had started at the university.

I am lying in bed in our small apartment in college. Overweight and hungover, I squint my eyes to the light coming in the bedroom door. I hear the shower running, I feel gripping in my belly, a fear. I am feeling horny. I want to have sex, yet my attempts this morning at initiating with Brad have failed. He's not interested. He's gotten up and gone into the bathroom, and now as the shower only thinly veils the movements of his stroking and the muffled sounds I can feel that he's masturbating. I receive this as a knife in my belly, a rejection of me. I am not good enough: I am too fat, not sexy. He'd rather touch himself than touch ugly me. This is not the first time; it's becoming a pattern, and I am feeling unwanted.

This time I decide to touch myself instead. I rub my clitoris with my fingers, it feels swollen and tender from the rough, dry sex I can barely remember we had the night before, but I push it anyway. I rub out a fast, tight and clenched orgasm. It feels temporarily good, a relief from the tension. However, I quickly move to feeling dejected and ashamed. Tears stream down my face. I roll over and try to ignore the feelings.

Ignoring feelings and drinking were both ways I was distancing myself from the world around me and building up more armor. Drinking took its toll in my years in college, and by the time I was establishing myself as a young adult in corporate America, I was starting to really feel the effects of it. Drinking and time at bars became less enjoyable. I really only went to bars anymore because Brad wanted to.

I had an "Aha Moment" at a health expo at work, a time of seeing something I hadn't seen before, or getting it in a deeper way. A coworker friend and I casually strolled through the event during lunch break and filled out the survey out of curiosity. As the woman working the expo reviewed my survey results, she compassionately brought awareness to the quantity of alcohol I had shared I consumed on weekends (six to 12 beers at a sitting) as being "excessive." Really? It wasn't just what everyone did?

I began to see that no, it wasn't. It really didn't have to be this way anymore. The amount of drinking I had been doing was unhealthy, and I was finally feeling called to change it for myself, despite my fiancé's continued need for it.

My body felt awful, and the extra weight was impacting how I felt about myself. Clothes were uncomfortable. I got on the scale one day and the persistent fog that had been obstructing my view of myself finally lifted: I saw a number that scared me. I was way heavier than I had been in high school, terrifyingly close to a number I couldn't fathom would ever describe my weight. I couldn't keep living like this. It was time. I felt called to swimming again, having been away from it since I was young.

There's a knock at the door.

We are newly moved into our house in South Carolina — was this move three or four? I am nine years old and feeling really shy. I don't have any friends in the area. I tag along with my mom as she goes to answer.

A man is there. He's from the community pool down the street. There's a swim team, and he's welcoming us into the neighborhood and recruiting kids to join. When he asks if anyone in the household would be interested in joining the team, my mom answers, "No, we're not interested."

I pipe up! "Wait! I want to be on the swim team!" I declare to my mom and to the man. My mom is shocked. I am shocked. Where did that come from? I rarely speak up much, especially not to counter something one of my parents says, and especially not in front of somebody else.

I had only learned HOW to swim two years before, when we lived in Florida. I used to be afraid of the water. Why now am I so clear that I want to be a part of this?

I found out many years later that my mom, growing up in the background of the intergenerational trauma of WWII, had a really traumatic experience at her local community pool when she was a little girl. She was pushed and held underwater by some boys and it really affected her. She had been unable to swim since then. When we lived in Florida prior to this experience with the swim team recruiter, my dad had insisted that my sister and I learn to swim. I had more fear than my sister did, yet we both made it through the Red Cross lesson sequence to learn the basics.

With my mom's past experiences and fear, I imagine how hard it may have been for her to let me embark on this, yet she allowed me to sign up. And perhaps little me had an unconscious desire, the way children often do, to overcome our parents' fears and traumas as a way to heal our lineages.

Now we're at the pool for the first practice. Reality sets in fast and hard. Yeah, I had learned how to swim, but to swim laps in a pool is completely different than "learning how to swim."

I swim a grand total of two lengths of the pool, 50 yards, and I am in tears. It is so hard! I get out of the water and run to my mom, who is sitting in one of the deck chairs with the other moms watching the practice.

I am crying, and say, "It's too hard, I can't do this." My mom, so young and inexperienced with anything water-related, not to mention fearful herself, is ready to let me drop out then and there.

Then something happens. An olive-skinned, buxom woman with dark hair, bold red lipstick and a bright floral dress speaks up: "Excuse me." She looks me in the eyes and says to me, "Honey, you got this!! No no no, you don't have to give this up. Yeah, it's a little hard. That's okay. You just keeping going… you can do it, don't you stop." I feel this coming from a genuine place of love and encouragement. She sees me. My tears slow, and then stop. I feel empowered. Maybe she's right. Yes, I can do it. I turn around and dive back in.

This marks the first day of training and competitive swimming that lasts my entire childhood. It's interesting to me to reflect now on the nature of water. Water is a medium that is not solid ground, yet it is supportive. Like our spiritual experiences, supportive but not solid. Water puts us in touch with our depths. If it had not been for this woman that day, I would not have stayed with swimming, yet with her encouragement to help me believe in myself, I dove back in. Over time, as I grew in my confidence, strength and skills, I ended up feeling quite comfortable in the water. My grandparents later came to call my sister and me "little fish."

Swimming and being in the water became a resource — something I knew was for me and I could be good at.

So here it was years later — I'm an adult and haven't done much swimming since high school. But I knew it was time to get back in the water and swim. I knew it could help me lose the weight.

Meanwhile, Brad and I were planning to marry. Of course I went into hyper-planner mode with binders and charts and calendars, and proceeded to plan all of the details of our wedding.

I began to swim with a club at work, changed my eating habits, cut way back on drinking. The weight started to drop. The seamstress fitting me for my wedding dress, taking it in smaller and smaller as I dropped six sizes over two years of engagement, lightheartedly complained that if I kept going she'd have no material left to stitch! I felt my body reshaping, physically transforming through better ways of eating, much less drinking, and more moving in exercise.

Losing 50 pounds felt wonderful! Yet my control freak self stayed in worry mode: Would I suddenly gain it all back? Could I keep it off? I was still so disconnected from the wisdom in my body that I thought I had to analyze it to death. I weighed myself obsessively, daily, sometimes even multiple times a day.

And I kept adding layers of control, my hyper-achiever self stepping in to help out often, with all of the associated worry, stress and anxiety that comes along with it. The details of the wedding needed to be perfect, succeeding in my career was a priority, as was working long hours and proving I was worthy of the next promotion. The rewards of raises, bonuses, promotions and praise helped fill my ever-constant need for approval. Part of me felt really good!

I proceeded to accomplish and acquire. We had the classic large wedding, with 13 attendants, flower girl, ring boy, awkward family dynamics and party at the reception. Me in a long dress with a train and intricate bead work and veil, he in the standard tuxedo. We married in a church that we picked because we thought we had to, and alcohol abounded at the reception with over 120 guests.

Self-imposed needs for proving my success began to stack up in the list of "get it done": marriage, car, house, career, student loans paid off, weight loss, training. I was finally making enough income to basically buy anything we needed. It felt so good to not have the pressure of supporting myself through school, I could finally reap the rewards of a lot of hard work. I felt good about my accomplishments, and I was feeling a bit better about my body. But still, something was missing.

My interests were shifting, and they didn't line up with my husband's very well. He was still interested in hanging out at bars, watching sports and drinking as a primary pastime. At the time, it was no big deal. We led our parallel lives, and my overachiever self found a new passion.

It's a cool morning, dark and still, the air is filled with the electric tension of 1,800 athletes and their support crews gathering in readiness. I had slept fairly well at the hotel, considering my nervousness. I walk down to the race area. The grounds roped off, as an athlete I am able to step beyond them. I double-check that all my preparations the night before are still in place… my bike and gear are awaiting me, my transition bags all in place. Okanagan Lake lies in waiting: still, vast, cool, deep, mysterious. All that's left now is me. I feel as ready as I can be. My father is here, a rare occurrence, this being perhaps the first time in most of my life he's come to a competition of mine. He gives me a hug and whispers in my ear: "Don't give up, Baby. Don't ever give up." I cry. I feel his way of supporting me. I crave it. In fact, is this drive I have to run my body being fueled by the scarce gift of his presence and attention? If I keep driving myself, will it make up for how I disappointed him? Regardless, as his words seep into my being, I think "just one step at a time." I have 2.4 miles of swimming, 112 miles of biking and 26.2 miles of running ahead of me, to be completed before midnight. My first Ironman Triathlon. Can I do it?

Swimming again felt good, reconnecting with muscles and body movement that had long been a part of my life growing up. It supported me in losing weight, and of course my competitive achiever self wanted the next goal to meet. I had connected with a swim and triathlon club at work, which was how I found access to a pool. So as I swam with this new community, my hyper-achiever self found excitement in both reconnecting with competition via masters swimming (it was like the old days, only for adults: swim meets and medals and races, oh my!), as well as by moving into uncharted new territory: triathlon.

At first I resisted. Traditional triathlon consists of swimming, biking and running varying distances ranging from long to excruciatingly long! The first two I could handle, but the running? I didn't think so. A unique, locally hosted event called "Alternative Triathlon" came to my attention: swimming, mountain biking, roller blading... aha! Now that I can handle! I began my self-enforced strict training regimen immediately. I met new friends, and loved every minute of it!

But that was only one event. If I wanted to continue exploring this bright new vista that was feeling so vibrant and fun, supporting my body to come alive and opening up my social life, I had to face the facts: Running was around me, everywhere.

Overcoming a perceived distaste for running left over from a bad middle school track experience, I said to myself, "Really, Leslie? You think you don't like running because of something that happened so long before?" I gave myself permission to try again. Inspired by a new friend I swam with who was also a triathlete, I stepped out for my first run in the fall of 1996.

And like everything else I set my mind to, I got it done! By the next autumn I had completed my first marathon, completed many shorter triathlons and signed up for my first Ironman Triathlon (2.4 mile swim, 112 mile bike, 26.2 mile run) to be completed in the summer of 1998. Not only did I sign up to participate, I organized over 25 other club members to take the journey across the continent to British Columbia and race in what was at the time the only Ironman competition in mainland North America.

Over the next years, I dove into the club with all my zeal and energy, held several officer positions including president and race director, organizing and leading events, racing in as many as I could fit in. Training, racing and my leadership role in the club, as well as nurturing my blossoming new social life (yay running buddies!), became my new obsession. I finished two Ironman Triathlons and nine marathons in addition to over 100 running, biking and swimming races.

Meanwhile, I was being rewarded and promoted at work, working long hours, pouring my energy into the company. I was getting rave reviews. I did my best to fit in with the party line, and the only criticism I would receive was, "You're too emotional." I did my best to stuff away tears, to "man up," to get tough. The overachiever me was in hyperdrive. The sensitive little girl in me that I had begun to ignore so long ago got shoved even deeper away. Little did I know how loud she was beginning to scream.

I experienced injuries and bizarre overuse intensity in my body, which was now in hard-pack mode: muscles tight and intense, limited flexibility, my weight dropped to an all-time low. I was pushing myself too hard and my body was trying to tell me, but I was ignoring her. Emergency room visits started adding up: my neck froze with such sharp pain during a practice that I could barely make it out of the pool, I lost vision in one eye during a swim meet and later learned that I had burst a blood vessel from the high internal pressure building in my body. Runs started including regular ice downs of the outside of my knee due to the iliotibial band (ITB) syndrome I had developed. When I was supposedly down-and-out with bronchitis, did I stop and rest to recover? No, I just puffed on the prescribed inhaler as I hung on to the wall of the pool between sets of laps. I was not alone in this approach: I observed the mentality of "being weak if you let anything like that stop you" in my friends as well. One of the powerful women I really looked up to broke her wrist before a major race she had been planning and training for. She ended up finishing her tenth Ironman with that broken wrist.

I hit the alarm as it goes off at 4:15 a.m. I am exhausted, so tired, but I have to keep going. I drag myself out of bed, put on running clothes, grab a protein bar, bottle of water, my gym bag and work clothes. My brain is not awake yet: Do I need gloves? Which jacket? Shorts or long pants? What's the temperature this morning? I find myself running late as I grab what I can and throw it in my truck.

Fearing wrath for my lateness, I speedily pull into the parking lot where my friends and I meet to run before work. The rule is "ready to run by 5 a.m.," not 5:01 and certainly not 5:05. Ready to run at 5 a.m. means that as I pull in the lot at 4:59 they are already out of their cars and about to move. I tear out of my truck, grab my water bottle carrier and start to clip it on as I run to catch up to them, already in motion down the street. I realize too late that I am still wearing my wedding ring. I usually take it off when I run. Oh well, not for today. I turn it around so the diamonds are on the inside of my cupped hand, as if somehow protecting the stones. We are embarking on a 10-mile run across the city, a common occurrence in my world right now, one of three or more runs each week.

I find myself straggling a bit. Still exhausted, my body is dragging. One friend and I fall back from the group. There is a strange meditative quality in these runs that I enjoy: The early morning darkness is calm, the roads are quiet in the neighborhoods. The shadows shift as we pass under streetlights, as if the ground itself is moving. I'm doing my best to pull myself together, to catch back up, but I am barely able to pick up my feet. Suddenly a crack in the road rises up, my foot strikes the uneven pavement and I launch myself into the air.

Launch...

...airborne...

...crash to the ground.

The fingers of my left hand, subconsciously because of the ring, create a protective tent and, as I hit pavement, they strike the ground "tippy-toe" style instead of flat palms. The pain in my fingers is immediate and excruciating. I don't even notice the large bright red patch where the pavement has removed the skin from my shoulder. My friends turn around; they had heard the scuff and the airborne silence before the crash. We are now about five miles into a 10-mile loop — no option but to keep running to get back to the cars. Luckily, we remember the little coffee shop whose owner comes early to open. We reroute our path to run by, and sure enough the store owner gifts me with a bag of ice. My friends and I and my bag of ice finish the run and I drive straight to the emergency room at my medical center. I have broken three fingers, the hyperextension essentially snapped them backwards, tearing a part of the bone from the third knuckle of all three of them. The ring, a symbol of my marriage, made it through fine.

Was protecting it at the expense of my body worth it?

The stress was immense, but I couldn't see it. I remember a doctor asking me, during one of my many visits, whether I had stress in my job. I shrugged it off: "Eh, not any more than 'normal,' right?" It wasn't until much later that I could reflect and see the vast understatement in that. At the time, it *was* my "normal." I didn't see any other way. I didn't know any other possibility. For all I knew, I just wasn't doing it well enough, and that was why I was sick or hurt. I needed to get tougher, be better. Surely, that would make me be good enough. So I added more workouts, more cross-training, more time in the gym to toughen up. I got faster, tougher, leaner.

During this time it became increasingly clear that my interests were shifting drastically from those of my husband. We had met and connected around a mutual interest in partying and drinking. As we grew, he kept that interest, expanding from high school and college parties to a lot of social time at bars. I started to pull away from drinking, and my social experience shifted to become centered around workouts and races. He finished college and began his analyst and project management career, yet remained with a foot in the door at the bars. At the time, it didn't seem to matter much. He did his thing and I did mine. We had a very 50/50 partnership kind of existence, sharing a household and splitting up chores, yet each having our own friends and doing our own thing outside of the house. We had a sex life that I believe we each would've said was pretty good, yet lacked emotional intimacy and deep passion. At the time I didn't realize I needed that. This was my normal.

At the time, in the mental checklist of life, I felt I had accomplished quite a lot: marriage, career, school, cars, house, getting in shape, awards, promotions, salary, bonuses. Yet there was something still missing: I could feel my biological clock ticking.

CHAPTER FOUR

Plane Crashes and Pregnancy Tests

It is late summer of 2001. I am inside our huge office complex, rows of cubicles bathed in stale, lifeless fluorescent lighting. I leave a meeting and briskly walk back to my office with folders of papers under my arm. A woman who works for me rushes up and shares the news that a plane had just crashed into the World Trade Center. Spiraling disbelief is swirling through the office and all work has come to a halt as people gather around monitors and screens, absorbing bits of information about what's happening in New York. After a short time, an unprecedented release of all employees from our product development center sends us home for the afternoon.

I step outside in shock. I have been working here eight years, we NEVER get sent home. This is big.

Although it was lost on me in the windowless building, I now notice the day is gorgeous: a clear, bright blue sky with full sun shining down upon me. It feels eerie, ironic. I make my way home in a stupor. The next thing I know, I am sitting in my living room with the sun shining in the window at my left. From where I sit perched on the big tan sofa, the TV appears large, heavy and ominous in the home entertainment center across the room. News of the unfolding tragedy is pouring through the screen as I sit with tears pouring down my face. Why am I feeling like this?

Only five days before, I had joyously discovered I was pregnant! Is this new emotion connected with the pregnancy? Why can't I control the tears? I'm not used to this. I feel out of control. What's happening?

Much later I realized that this moment on that day was a time where the armor I had built around my body started to split open, just a bit, and I began to feel the expansion of feelings again.

I was glad to be pregnant. I had known I wanted a child, well… ever since I was one. I always just knew I would be a mom someday, and yet until this time it had just not entered my mind. Something inside me clicked, and it became quite clear it was time: I wanted to have a baby. And my husband was ready, too. So we made the decision that I would go off of the birth control pills that had regulated my cycle since I was 16 years old.

As with everything else in my life, my hyper-control self stepped in to get this done! My logic brain tackled it like anything: If I do A, B and C, I'll get D, just like all the goal-setting, planning and organizing I had done to accomplish so many things in my life. Just one more thing to put on the list, right?!

Boy, was I in for a surprise!

We excitedly began the fun of having sex as often as we could to up the chances of one of those little sperms reaching my egg. The first few months went by with no luck, and I began to get discouraged. We kept trying, having now settled into task-like, mechanical actions in bed. I began charting my basal body temperature in Excel spreadsheets. These measurements, taken diligently every morning could help determine time of ovulation. This process was exhausting. Sex became rigid and routine. Tension was building between us, and yet we kept on trying. However, I had very little patience, so we also reached out for medical support.

With that came the appointments with fertility specialists, tests, monitoring and a decision for me to go on an oral fertility drug called clomiphene to enhance the possibility of my egg coming out to play. The drug had intense side effects for me, hot flashes among them. I had never understood before why perimenopausal women that experienced hot flashes had complained of them. I mean, really, what could be so hard about feeling warm? I learned very quickly: These were miserable, out of control, intensely hot, icky feelings that took over at random moments and sent me reeling. Yet if it meant I had a better chance of getting pregnant, I was all for it.

A few months later, as I was still racing through life at top speed, we were thrilled to find out that the fertility medications worked! We were pregnant! I was nervous, unsure, and yet excited to begin planning for our new baby. We found out very early in the pregnancy. Yet, it was so near the holidays that despite our gut feeling and advice from doctors to wait before announcing to anyone, we elected to share the exciting news with our families at Christmas. Soon-to-be grandparents were thrilled! News spread quickly.

Since I was being monitored so closely, I had an appointment for another ultrasound shortly after the holidays. I had an oddly uncomfortable feeling that the pregnancy wasn't thriving, yet brushed it off as just being nervous since we had tried so hard for so long. When the ultrasound showed that there was no longer a heartbeat, I was crushed. Yet a part of me already knew: I'd had a miscarriage.

We took very little time to mourn. I swept grief away rather quickly (or so I thought) as the drive to try again took over. I really did feel like the first pregnancy just wasn't meant to be. Yet my logic brain still took over and I took the approach that since clomiphene had worked the first time we should just do it again. Certainly that would be the answer?

Not exactly.

The doctor supported us in the choice of another round of clomiphene. Yet, despite working the first time, this time it did not. There were only so many months in a row he would let me be on the drug before giving my body a break. This series ended without a pregnancy. By then I was maxing out: the side effects of the fertility medication were overwhelming, adding to the stresses of work, training and controlling everything I could, and I just couldn't take it anymore.

I broke down.

It's 5 a.m. I am at the running track, in the dark. My two closest friends and running partners are there. Dressed in shorts, running bra, singlet and running shoes, with my hair pulled back in a ponytail, I run. Arms and legs pumping, fast and hard... running away from feeling, running away from listening to my body. Finally at the curve by the pine trees, sweaty and tired it all catches up to me. I collapse in a pile, crying, screaming with sweat, snot and tears pouring over me. I give up; I can't do it anymore. My body needs a break. I have to stop trying to force my life into waiting to see if I would be pregnant. I make the decision to stop trying.

I viscerally,
for the first time ever...
...LET GO!

Not just in my head as a cognitive decision, but at a body level, I let go of grasping at trying to DO something. It was a big deal, HUGE. My husband and I released the attempts at pregnancy. We made love to make love, not because it was on the to-do list. I let myself continue with life.

For the piece of me that needed to plan everything out, this was hard to do. So I created a plan, signed up for the next big thing, booked flights to California, made plans to climb Mt. Whitney again, as I had the year before, with my dad — something that I would not have been able to do if I were pregnant due to the significant altitude changes. I moved on. Viscerally, at a body level, I let go of the need to keep trying to get pregnant.

I stopped charting...
I stopped taking temperatures...
I stopped tracking...
I stopped controlling.

I allowed my life to continue. I focused on new ventures. I felt my life take on a life of its own.

It's 5 a.m., I'm up as usual, getting ready for the day. The house is dark. I flip the light on in the bathroom and shuffle in. Sleepily, I begin to brush my teeth. My mind wanders to the day's events, recapping to-do lists, and suddenly something hits me. Wait a minute, how long has it been? I had let go of the tracking and counting. I don't even know when my last period was. Nah, it can't be. Today is the day we have the final appointment with the fertility specialist. We left it on the books, just to wrap up and close out our journey with him. To tell him we were done trying. I must just be subconsciously thinking about that.

Yet something deeper tells me to check. It's easy enough. I mean, I have a drawer full of home pregnancy tests. I open the drawer and pull one out. Perfect timing for first morning pee! Yep, right in the stream... Okay, here we go. I set it aside.

Three minutes later my life is changed.

I'm PREGNANT!!!

Literally the month we stopped trying, when I let go, viscerally, of the need to control the process, was the month our beautiful baby girl began her journey of growing inside my body to eventually join us in this world!

This cracked me open... it was an epic experience in my awakening. For the first time in my entire life, something big that I wanted happened not because I had planned every step, tracked it and put it on a goal sheet. For the first time in my life something happened because I LET GO. I surrendered. It didn't happen gracefully or elegantly, but it happened: I stopped forcing, gripping, trying and DOING. This was a glimpse into divine order, the sense of something greater, a flow, a divine current that, ever present, was going to simply BE, whether or not I was at the controls. My eyes started to open, ever so slowly, into the awareness of the realm of the infinite, the nature of the world and my own being that is real and yet beyond the scope of my scientific, rational brain and traditional senses. This immense cracking open catalyzed the tiny baby step, a drop of water in the huge pool of possibility, that began my Spiritual Awakening. I couldn't fully articulate it back then, but by the time I sat crying in front of the television after being sent home from work on 9/11, I was already swimming in this pool and things were already well underway.

CHAPTER FIVE

Placenta and Holding On

As my eyes opened to this new way of being, I started to see, a little bit at a time. I was so thrilled to be pregnant. Happily rearranging plans, I canceled my mountain climbing trip and the flights, and soon I began mommy and baby planning! As with everything else in my life, I poured all my energy into this new focus: preparing the nursery and house, and organizing work to prepare for my maternity leave. I ate as well as I knew how, continued working out and swimming. I even kept running until about seven and a half months, when it felt as if a bowling ball was bouncing up and down on my pelvic floor and I finally decided to take a break.

The final week before my daughter's birth was an oddity to me. I was home from work on leave, and her due date had passed. All the planning and organizing was done. I had everything bundled up and planned out so neatly that I was down to rolling the loose coins in the house for something to do! I could sleep as much as I needed to, at any time. All I had to do was wait. Sounds simple? Relaxing, even? Oh no! How hard that was for me! Just being and allowing, instead of doing. My first real experience with it. I remember coming up with ways to fill the time, certainly I must "do" something, right? Only much later did I see the lesson in the value of slowing down that this was bringing me.

"Push, Leslie! Push!"

What?! Wait I've just given birth. I'm basking in sweaty exhaustion in the hospital room. My beautiful, healthy little one is nearby, being measured and cared for, and I'm on the phone with my mother, sharing the news. She's here! We're so excited and proud. However, I hear faintly, as if from across a long distance, Ann, the certified nurse midwife who supported me and my daughter in this journey so beautifully, calling to me. Ann's voice gets closer, louder.

"Leslie, it's really important... you need to push."

Suddenly I am brought back in. I rush to get off the phone as it's whisked away, I reluctantly shift my focus. I thought I was done with the pushing. I'm tired, I'm sore, I just want to hold my baby and rest together. Why are you asking more from me?

"It's the placenta — it hasn't delivered yet. This is dangerous. You need to push!"

The urgency grew. Apparently there was a risk of hemorrhage that could be quite dangerous if the placenta didn't let go soon. My body was still holding on. Such an analogy for so much in my life.

Only moments before, or was it hours... the timelessness is striking, I had been pushing and pushing, thinking I was bearing down in a way that would invite my daughter into the world with ease. But it was so hard! All the Kegel exercises I had done, the birthing classes and yogic breathing, the running, the swimming, all the workouts were supposed to prepare me. I thought I was strong and ready. I can do this, I don't want drugs, I am a strong, independent woman: I got this! All my pushing was focused in the one way I knew. As hours went by I got scared: Is this ever going to work? Is she ever going to come out? What if I just stop? I'm tired — what if I just rest now? As I sensed into that, it hit me:

If you don't push her out, they will cut you open.

The fear of an emergency C-section kicked my hyper-achiever self into top mode and I pushed more, despite the pain. What I didn't know then was that there is another way. A way I learned much later.[12]

So I push, push in the only way I know. I feel defeated; it isn't working. I am done, I have nothing left. "Leslie, the placenta is still not delivering. I've got to call in an emergency physician."

---

[12] Pushing with the contractions, or so I thought, began. It hurt and I found myself resisting. Much later I realized all the pushing I was doing was actually pulling up in my pelvic floor, retaining her rather than encouraging her down and out. The body awareness that came much, much later actually opened up an amazing door of orgasmic empowerment and confidence in life. This was a huge part of the sacred sexual path I was following, unbeknownst to me at the time.

"What does that mean?" I wonder.

In an instant, a strange man walks through the door, a man I had never met or even seen before. He introduces himself and says maybe five words before plunging his arm elbow-deep inside my vagina and into my uterus, grabs, tears away from the uterine wall and pulls out the placenta that was refusing to budge.

"HUH" [Sharp breath in!] I leave my body. "AAAAAUUUNNNGH!!!" [Blood curdling scream!] I hear from my body. This sharp, intense, terrorizing pain makes the hours of birth process so far seem like a gentle float on a river.

He leaves as quickly as he came in. I am left in tears and pain and shock. My beautiful baby has grown in my womb, my cervix has opened to allow her to come out, and this doctor reaches in and pulls where no man, no human other than my newborn, has ever touched me before. I feel violated. This harsh shift from the connected support and holistic care of my midwife that had been cultivated over years to the heartless "get-it-done" energy of the Western medical system felt so shocking. What just happened to me? Am I really here?

My body in its holding on was underscoring the need for new layers of letting go. And I was only beginning to notice.

After the shock of the experience was over and Ann was reassuring me that everything was okay, I finally was able to relax a tiny notch, as the new anxiety of being a mother set in.

My little baby girl I love so deeply — Hannah! I snuggled her into my chest, she began to nurse, and we settled into the new, fragile learning process of becoming mommy and daughter… together.

New Motherhood

Not surprisingly given my history, I was in high anxiety mode after Hannah's birth. I felt this overwhelming obsession with trying to keep track of everything. I took photos of her every day, I wrote down in a log when and how long I was nursing her. I wanted to make sure everything was perfect, that she was getting the best care from me I knew how to give.

I was desperately sleep deprived, yet during any moment that was available for sleep I would be so overwhelmed with the anxiety of needing sleep that I couldn't! It went something like this:

Okay, I just finished nursing her, she's finally asleep. She eats approximately every three hours, and it takes 45 minutes to nurse her. So now that she's done, I need to use the bathroom, grab a snack or take care of my own needs as briefly as possible so that I have a shot of sleep for perhaps an hour and a half before she'll be awake again wanting more. So okay, an hour and a half, here we go: Let's hurry up and fall asleep. Lie here, mind spinning, can't slow down, OMG another 15 minutes have passed and I am missing sleep, OMG hurry up and fall asleep! Lie there, mind spinning, can't slow down... repeat, until baby cries to be fed again.

Ugh. I was exhausted.

But I couldn't stop holding on, trying to control everything. As Hannah grew, I started learning, letting go, little by little. As I would slow down to feed her, or bathe her, or simply hold her and love her, I would finally start feeling my heart open up. Nursing her was one of the most amazing experiences of my life. I absolutely loved it! It was hard the first couple of weeks, my tender nipples were not used to this much attention and my body struggled. Once we got into the flow, it was blissful. It was slowdown time for me in a big way. Not only when we were together, but when I went back to work I chose to pump breast milk to support her during the day. I had never experienced slowing down for breaks at work before in my life. However, now it was a must: two times each workday, every day, not just when I felt like I had time.

Breastfeeding forced me to slow down, to see that it is important to nurture my daughter, and in doing so, I realized later, I was nurturing me, too. The little girl inside me who had been screaming for attention for so long — I started to hear her.

And it scared me.

I am rocking gently in the yellow glider chair and ottoman. Hannah is snuggled in, nursing at my breast, lying in my arms with the blue nursing pillow that has little bees printed all over it. The warm summer sun is shining in through her window, casting an exquisite yellow glow all over and around us. Feeling the amazing nurturing love pouring between us, my heart smiles, yet I am overwhelmed with tears. I cry as I hold her, feeling guilt and shame. I so desperately want her in my life, and I feel totally and completely sure that she is meant to be with us here in the world. Yet...

...I realize I don't want to be married to her daddy anymore.

As Brad and I had moved through pregnancy and the birth, there were struggles, disconnects. But we had always managed to sweep them under the rug. Ignore them and they will go away, right? Well, no, and that became glaringly obvious when Hannah came into our lives and suddenly we could no longer function on separate schedules. We needed to care for our daughter together, and our lives just didn't line up for it. The growing apart that had been happening silently, unnoticed for so long, became strikingly obvious now. I was no longer interested in drinking and hanging out at bars, and this was a crucial piece of life to Brad. This is the way we handled it before Hannah: He would "go out with the boys" on Fridays, get drunk, come home and pass out, while I would stay in, get up early on Saturday mornings and leave to go swim, hang out with my friends and shop or run errands most of the day. By the time I got home, he would be up and about and we would move on with our weekend.

However, now I couldn't leave in the morning if he wasn't able to awaken and care for our infant daughter. His mornings of being so passed out he wasn't responsive could no longer be ignored. And my escaping to run and swim it all away couldn't either. So it began: a cycle of weekly tears and anger, arguments and frustrations, his apologies and saying, "I'll try to be better," his frustrations with me for not being around, with it starting all over again the next week.

Another night, another morning. The sun of early afternoon pours through the window. Hannah is safely sleeping in another room. I'm back home from half a day's activity: workouts, shopping, breakfast with friends. The pattern is wearing on me. Brad was out late again, drinking, heavily. Back home he passes out in bed beside me... I awaken, smell him, revolted. I roll away from the cigarette smoke, stale beer and bar stench, stewing in hatred. My body is tense and guarded. I tolerate fits of sleep through the night as he cycles near death: breath stopping, starting, stopping again. A sleep apnea undiagnosed until years later. Unbeknownst to me, my body grips and holds all night, on alert. I feel this as terror. Beneath cognitive reasoning, my body senses a fear that in any one of these moments I am losing him to death's grip. I lurch awake, as if I alone am responsible for making sure he survives, shaking him under the guise of getting him to stop snoring... an inhale, thank god... then a stew of resentment for him doing this to me. Finally, I doze back off. The cycle repeats. All night.

I try to hold it in and just make my way through another weekend, as I had been doing for so long. This day I can't. I snap. He is now sitting there on the bed in a dull, hungover haze. He looks at me with eyes glazed over. I am screaming at him, SCREAMING some version of the same thing, about his drinking, about the snoring, about the things he hasn't done, yet the topic itself is only the trigger for all the things I've held inside all my life, and he himself the unwitting target. "YOU BLAH BLAH BLAH BLAH!!" I vomit this anger all over him. I feel rage pouring through me, tears hot on my face. My jaw tight, fists clenched in balls at my side, tense angry body.

He simply slouches and looks at me, dull eyes, straight face. He says, unemotionally: "You have an anger management problem."

I FLIP! This statement and the dull, emotionless tone in which he says it infuriate me even more.

I scream...
"I DO NOT FUCKING HAVE AN ANGER MANAGEMENT PROBLEM! YOU..." and I proceed to yell all sorts of things about this being all his fault and all about him. I rattle off some sequence of things I think he should change about himself, and worse, I carry the responsibility of thinking I need to change him. I take no ownership for myself. I've gotten really good at proving how right I am. Surely anyone could see this.

Yet the seed of awareness was planted. He even went on to say, "I cannot make you happy, only you can make you happy." This was a nugget of wisdom, guidance for human homework that didn't sink in until we chatted about this years later. As for this and my anger management problem, he was absolutely right. Yet my ego hated being called out on it. Later I realized I did have a problem. And this was a light to shine in on myself. I was carrying too much, trying to control too much, and I needed to let go. I needed to nurture myself, release the anger, and begin to heal. I needed to look at the layers underneath the anger: What gift was this mirroring for me to see inside myself? What old wounds were being triggered that felt so raw? How could I safely shift the anger I was carrying so that I didn't take it out on others? And most vulnerably: How could I heal so that I don't pass this pattern on to my daughter?

Yes, there were things happening that did not feel good for me, yet I wasn't owning my power of choice. I was bottling it up and holding on, trying to blame everyone around me for my misery.

That moment stuck and came back later. My eyes continued to open. I continued seeing how life was not what I had assumed for so long. I began by taking responsibility for me, not blaming others, yet knowing when, if necessary, to make a shift and hold space for myself to be who I am. I could no longer squash myself away or be small to avoid making others feel uncomfortable. It continued slowly. New keys unlocking new levels of my awareness began to come into view. It began with Deb.

PART TWO

WE'RE NOT IN KANSAS ANYMORE

CHAPTER SIX
Opening Eyes

I am sitting in Deb's office on a soft yet supportive chair that is richly colored and textured. Now familiar, stunning objects of delight sparkle around me: colorful crystals, figurines, art. This space holds a warmth, a potency and a vibrancy that stands in stark contrast to the drab gray cubicles of my corporate life where I've learned to keep my defense mechanisms on guard. Here I begin to let down the shields, in this space I've come to know as a safe sanctuary during the months of our journey together. Sitting across from me, Deb gazes softly and compassionately my way, her eyes so clear and penetrating. She waits patiently for my response. Her inquiry has landed on me like a white elephant and I don't know what to do with it:

"What does your body have to say?"

My what?! I don't speak from my body, I speak from what goes on inside my head, and it comes out through my mouth — my decisions come from thought processes. I basically operate the controls from the neck up. The idea of listening to my body throws me for a loop. I feel my face flush with embarrassment that I don't know what she means. Even a bit of anger... why would she ask such a question? My rational brain is in a huff and totally censoring this. Asking my body seems ridiculous, and part of me wants to resist, as if being told that pigs fly and I should climb aboard.

Yet the time in my journey is now. Something happens. I can feel it. I trust her, I slow down, notice my censor and set it aside for a moment. I drop in, down, and I listen. What does my body have to say? Now, finally, months into my visits with Deb, I listen...

Who is Deb? She is Deborah Austin, M.A. Transpersonal Psychology, an intuitive healer and lifelong student of a broad spectrum of spiritual philosophies. Deb with the sparkling smile, witty humor and colorful hair and clothes. She came into my life in another one of those spiritually guided ways, long before I would have called it spiritually guided! It was like the Universe was conspiring to get her into my life, whispering to me, "Go! Go! She will be the resource you need for this next big cycle, Little One! Go see her!"

Only it came through like this:

We're running at "oh-dark-thirty" in the a.m., as always. Running with Theo and Clair has become my lifeline. They are my two closest friends, both also in the corporate world: Theo a fellow engineering manager, Clair a financial executive. We met through running and our triathlon club, and our times together have become my emotional support and social life, workout and energy release, all tied up in one.

We're chatting about the latest life stuff. Clair, a headstrong, get-shit-done type of person who just completed a divorce, had in recent weeks been encouraging Theo to see through a new lens. She'd found support therapy in a nontraditional modality, and had convinced Theo to go. Theo in his logical, scientific self, with a snarky sense of humor, recaps his first experience in Deb's office:

"So I walked into her office and said, 'You're a psychic, eh? So where's your crystal ball?'

"And she goes: 'Oh, I don't need one.' And then she smiled, looking directly at me! I followed her into her office, wondering what I'd gotten myself into."

The session proceeds to be life-changing for Theo. He shares vulnerably how surprised and humbled he was that Deb was really able to offer deep wisdom and guidance that resonated for him.

So now both he and Clair have spoken highly of their experiences with Deb. Despite my own scientific, logical and conservative background, I hear myself saying: "Oh yes, I believe that someone can be psychic."

I feel a moment of shock as these words come out of my own mouth, and yet I know it to be true.

I have been feeling the weight of the world, so much anger and unhappiness in my life despite the joy of new motherhood. Something has to change, I just don't know what or how. This therapy just may be the answer. My choice to reach out to Deb is sealed by the experience of my fellow engineer friend. His opinion weighs strongly with my analytical side, which carries a lot of skepticism. If he can go and open to the possibility of this type of therapy, I can, too.

My first appointment to see Deb was while I was still married and Hannah was an infant. She helped me open my eyes to the awareness that I couldn't keep gripping the steering wheel of life. I had to let go of control and trust in the flow. I needed to get into my body and be present. Oh my, was it hard to see these things at first! She was helping me to "repattern" the very web of existence I had known all my life. With her help I was rewriting my framework for what life is all about, and not only how to exist in it, but to connect with and nurture my authentic self and allow my gifts to emerge to share with the world.

Deb, whom I came to know as an amazing spiritual mentor, therapist, and intuitive healer, helped me see myself in a new way. In my time with her, I would absorb like a sponge, take volumes of notes, and carry away suggestions and assignments to incorporate into my life. I devoured books[13] and voraciously poured my energy and focus into self-awareness, growth and transformation.

One of the first big book inspirations that resonated with me was *The Artist's Way* by Julia Cameron.[14] Reconnecting with my juiciness, my Divine Feminine, had become the theme for me, and a huge part of that was reconnecting with my creative self. This book really helped me take steps to do so. I embodied the work, lived and breathed it. I experienced a supportive blend of allowing the deep shadowy bits within that I didn't want to see to come to the surface, along with ways to rewrite the story and open to new possibilities. I began journaling, writing Morning Pages to clear out the mess in my head. In Morning Pages, the author encourages a stream-of-consciousness writing style that helped me clear a bunch of junk. **I had not realized how constant the voices in my head were until I started listening.**

Very first Morning Page – Day 1: Morning Pages — so what do I write? Just have to fill the page (three pages?!) — how about one page. I need to find myself, find my true Artist... the Artist's Way. Morning Pages, Artist Date. Will I be able to do this? Brain dumps on paper... I have a stressful day at work ahead — presentations. But first, track work and a swim. Clair probably wonders why I am still in my truck! Theo is with his buddies up north — I'd like to call but best not to bug him while he's hanging out. I need to find a plan for Sunday... Bike? Run? Muncie [a half-Ironman Triathlon race I am

---

[13] See Additional Resources to Explore.

[14] *The Artist's Way* by Julia Cameron.

planning to compete in] is approaching fast — need to finish it, and feel strong on the run. No need for a PR [personal record], but I want to feel good afterwards.

What more do I write, need to unblock. How about my Dad... haven't chatted in awhile — I should call him. Maybe tonight. I'm sure Brad is going out as usual — even though he went out late last night and came home plowed at 2:30 a.m. Why is that so important to him? Can't he enjoy other ways of relief? When he got laid off — needed the bar. Then he gets the good news of a new job — needed the bar. Does he ever need me?

A month later, I journal my answers to the Virtue Trap quiz[15] from *The Artist's Way*:

1. *Biggest lack in my life: emotional intimacy with my husband*
2. *Greatest joy: my daughter*
3. *Largest time commitment: work*
4. *As I play more, I work: less*
5. *I feel guilty that I am: considering divorce*
6. *I worry that: I'll mess up Hannah*
7. *If my dreams come true my family will: Affirmation – benefit; Blurt – suffer*
8. *I sabotage myself so people will: like me, not be mad*
9. *If I let myself feel it, I am angry that: I went so long without opening my eyes to how I really feel in my marriage*
10. *One reason I get sad sometimes is: I'm lonely*

Seeing the dark stuff gently come out was so hard and yet so helpful. I wrote those pages assuming no one would ever read them, and that I would never look at them again. In fact, I thought that I might burn them. That helped me let stuff out to be seen that I typically censored out of my awareness.

To support the shifting, I created play dates with myself, dancing with abandon in the living room, buying sparkly stickers for my journal and colorful new art supplies. I started painting and drawing again, deep loves from my childhood that I had squashed away over time as I entered the realm of analytical engineering-land. I looked at old patterns, limiting beliefs, rewrote the old stories, and stopped mentally beating myself up so much. I snuggled with Hannah and delighted in seeing her grow.

---

[15] Cameron, pg 101.

My beautiful baby girl! It's a glorious sunny day and the sunlight is streaming in the living room window. Hannah is wearing the little yellow outfit with the bees and smiling and giggling as she moves her hands at the dangling toys. I am filled with love for her. Somehow deep inside I know everything is going to be okay.

The spiritual synchronicity of the 12 weeks suggested in *The Artist's Way* process ended up aligning with the time it took for Brad and me to hone in on the decision to divorce. We had separated, sorting through the logistics of living apart and raising a child. Hannah was our number one priority, and our biggest challenge was sorting through how to create two happy homes for her instead of one miserable one. Yet, the way slowly presented itself clearly and with relative ease. One might call this… luck? I began to recognize it as "synchronicity," being in the flow with Spirit, following my authentic path. I was learning that when I make choices that align with the deep authentic purpose within me, the Universe aligns to make available the support and resources to make it happen.

Questioning Spirit

I had begun recognizing and noticing "coincidences" in my life, starting to pay attention to how they weren't coincidences at all but were the Universe's way of supporting me, sending me messages and guidance. I was so skeptical in so many ways, yet also so hopeful. I began to trust and notice things I just couldn't brush away as random any longer. I started asking for help and guidance from the Universe, from Spirit. This included first questioning my relationship with Spirit.

I came from a loosely Christian background. Baptized Methodist, I went to Sunday school until about age five, then any regular practice just faded away and my only connection with church came at funerals and weddings.

Going to church always felt very mechanical and filled with guilt and shame. It never resonated in my heart, and frankly I didn't really know what it meant for something to resonate in my heart, so I just took it in at face value. I sort of thought I had to believe in God and then follow the rules someone else put in place, but it just never felt right and I couldn't articulate that or see any way to change it at the time. So as I branched out on my own, I had come to a sort of flat agreement that God must exist, but I just didn't buy into the rigidity of religion. I thought I had to deal with it to get married, for example, so we just made a choice on a church we liked aesthetically and went for it without much thought. For awhile I even thought there just must not be a god, but there was still a part of me that knew that didn't feel right, either.

It wasn't until later, with Deb's support, with my friends, and in my yoga practice, that I really started to feel my connection with the Universe, with Spirit, with the infinite potential and energy that we are. A few windows started to open. For example, as I was sitting with whether or not to divorce, I kept asking Spirit for help.

Two months into Morning Pages excerpt:

Why am I doing this to myself? Why am I splitting up a family... we've spent so many years building it up — a home, a life, career, a baby girl. Why, when it's not all bad? A lot of it is okay, a little happy. Is that emotional piece that's missing so important? Shouldn't I just stay in the relationship for the other pieces we do have? Am I asking for too much? How do I know?!

Please PLEASE send me a sign. I can't bear it.

Help me see. I need to know if I've screwed up —
Maybe I should go see Deb again, she may be able to provide some insight.

Last night was our last night — Brad moves out today [to begin a trial separation period, and he has Hannah for the first night while I travel]. I miss Hannah already. I don't want to travel tomorrow. The thought of work sucks right now. But I need it — the routine to help me get through. But why? Why am I doing this? Is this really what I want? It hurts, badly.

I don't know what I want.

In that process, one of those "coincidences" happened — a synchronicity.

I am in my Explorer under the huge oak tree, getting ready to pull out of my driveway to head to work. Out of habit I put a CD in the stereo, not thinking much of that action. Meanwhile I ask for a sign, asking Spirit, "Please help: Should I proceed with this divorce? Please show me in a way that it is clear and I know it's from you!"

I put the CD in and randomly pick a track. In the song that comes on the stereo, I hear these words from REM:

"It's the end of the world as we know it, and I feel fine!"

YES! I feel it! This is the message! I had no idea that the message would come through in this way. I feel tingles in my body! It isn't a coincidence, or random or something to be ignored and not trusted. It is real!

I was learning to trust resonance in my body as a spiritual compass.

My jaw dropped, tears poured and joy, fear and the reality that things were no longer going to be the same became clear. In a vision, Deb had seen Brad and me on inner tubes in a lake, floating away from each other. That's exactly what it felt like. It didn't need to be a struggle or a fight, it was simply time to end this phase of my life, shedding the old skins of marriage, and enter my rebirth into myself. Not long after, I found myself in the parking lot of my lawyer's office, the decision made, the paperwork complete. I sat in my parked car with tears pouring down my face as it poured rain around me. Cleansing, releasing, it felt good to let go.

What unfurled was perhaps one of the simplest, calmest divorces I had ever heard of. Sure there was emotion, tears, frustrations, even anger, yet I learned new ways of working with intention, choice and energy that totally changed the way Brad and I communicated. I really felt Spirit support me: As I was stepping along this authentic path of what I needed to do, Spirit was encouraging and guiding me, releasing obstacles, opening doors and helping me compassionately close old ones. Brad and I reached agreements together and quickly had a plan that we settled in court with a single lawyer and a request for a waiver of the waiting period. Our divorce was amicable and final before Hannah turned two. I actually felt I had created a better relationship with him than ever before, and now we were creating two happy homes for Hannah, with 50/50 shared custody.

As I started to see patterns, I would notice that I had the power to change them. I was learning that I didn't have to live with the anger, frustration, and superficial relating with the world that I was experiencing.

Releasing Distractions

An example of this superficial relating that was a huge distraction in my life was my relationship with TV. Over our years building a home together, Brad and

I had developed a weekday rhythm. For me that started as: go to work, come home, eat dinner, then "unwind" in front of the TV for several hours before bed. Over time, as I began workouts to support my triathlon fix before work, plus longer work hours, the amount of my TV time began to get squeezed. I had let go of watching the news years before, and now I had to choose which of my shows were my favorites and carve away time for them. I reluctantly told myself: "Maybe I will be okay with only two of the half-hour primetime shows?!"

Then I began to notice that even that small amount was really not satisfying. The superficial "addiction" to needing to see what happened next in my shows gnawed at me, yet I was finally able to see that other things in my life felt more important and to begin unplugging from the bottomless pit of photons bombarding my eyes and body.

In my home life with Brad, it had been really common that the TV would be on during the day on weekends, even when neither of us were watching it! I started turning it off more and more.

After Hannah was born, and in the process of separating from Brad and beginning to shape my home life in the way I chose to create it, the day came when I turned it off for good.

I notice the TV is on again: Why am I doing this? This is totally an unconscious thing, an old habit. Do I really need it on right now?

No.

Click.

Silence in the house.

Wow. What do I do? It's so quiet. I am not sure how to be with this. I notice these thoughts spinning in my head: work, training, ending my marriage with Brad, being a momma, loving my daughter, opening to these new facets of self. All of this means letting go of my old me. Old ways of being, noticing when I am doing something authentically versus when it is like a broken record... stuck in a groove I have built over so many years. Sometimes it is so hard to just realize I can make it go another way.

Wow this is uncomfortable... am I ready to lean into that discomfort? Yes I am. It's okay to change!

I remember how hard it was! Those first few times turning the TV off and leaving it off... AACK! I felt overwhelmed with the voices in my head. What do I do in this silence as I can now hear my own voices?! Suddenly I could pay more attention to myself and, in a way, I didn't really want to, and it was scary. Yet I also knew I needed to stop indulging in the habitual distractions I had been using to numb out. A new life was knocking on my door. To receive it, I had to clear the clutter.

What is Clutter?

Clutter can express as the piles of physical stuff sitting in our homes or at our desks that are taking up space but not adding value to our lives. Clutter also has an energy and time aspect. Things we do to distract ourselves, kill time or waste time also clutter our energy field.

Let's explore two main types of clutter: Time and Space.

Time Clutter

Time clutter happens during watching TV, "killing time" or "wasting time." It's doing random things that don't really serve a purpose or feel that good other than to distract us from ourselves and what's really going on with us and our experience.

Notice in the story above how I finally recognized my relationship with TV was a major time clutter, and how I finally let it go. Later, people in my life shared similar stories about how releasing time clutter helped open their path to new and more satisfying careers and lifestyles.

There are many kinds of time clutter. Clearing it opens space for personal growth and stepping into one's power. It also leads to better sex, better connections with others, more intimacy, and better connections within.

Space Clutter

Space clutter is the physical stuff in our lives that we hang on to beyond its useful time. This can include boxes of old papers and files, clothing, dishware, trinkets, and more.

I notice that some people have more proclivity for hanging on to things than others. Some of this may be passed on intergenerationally: I have felt threads of this tendency in myself coming from my grandparents living through the Depression era. When my grandmother died in 2004, we found food dating from the 1950s in her deep freeze. For many people in the Great Depression, survival was dependent on saving things.

Both clutter and decluttering tend to involve emotion. Real urgency motivated my grandparents to save everything they could. The tension was passed on through their descendants to me. Until we recognize this, we don't even know why we need to save something and yet, we're saving it. The feeling that we need to do so is often rooted in the past.

Another way I noticed my own unhealthy pack-rat qualities showing up was with a sense of: "If I destroy these documents or get rid of this box of stuff from college, then somehow that part of me, that phase of life, disappears. If I do this systematically, I am going to erase myself!" Over more than a decade, as I did serious phases of clearing physical clutter from my home, I noticed a lot of emotional overwhelm. I know I am not alone in this.

Because of this dynamic, going through the decluttering process involved body-level fear. Although I was rationally aware that I would survive discarding some stuff, it felt like I wouldn't. It didn't feel safe to my system. When that happens, it's common to override the body and ignore its messages. When the body talks we need to listen. So I listened. This brought up a real question: "What does my body need to feel safe as I clear this?"

As I discovered ways to support myself emotionally through my clearing process, releasing clutter from my life became much easier. I also collected some tips to support our decluttering journeys and I share a practice later in this chapter.

Deb encouraged this clutter clearing as well, and in session one day, as I was sharing about doing this and that and this and that, she stopped me: "Leslie you need to cull the herd!" Thin out and create some space. Thin out the time commitments.

I was deep into being an endurance athlete, living an intense, highly successful corporate career, taking on extra leadership roles and adding more to my life. Deb nudged and gently helped me see, "Uh, this is crazy! I am going to burn up and fry if I keep adding things to my plate!"

While her invitation to "cull the herd" at the time was a frustrating one, it was also really welcome. I was like: "What do you mean? What am I going to give up? I can't give up any of these things! I enjoy doing them!" But I was also avoiding looking at me. Looking within. And looking at what I really needed to see at that point in my life. I was doing a good job escaping and avoiding it by putting all these things in its place.

I invite you as well: Slow down and start to cull the herd, thin out time commitments, give up the distractions.

I am not saying it was easy. Sometimes it's really hard to change old habits, feeling the tender rawness that gets created as we open to new ways. It's like the well worn grooves of our brain/body wiring get ripped open and the baby skin underneath needs some time to strengthen. That's why those distractions are there... they are padding something. There's a comfort zone to them. And yet I encourage us to notice the role such distractions play in our lives. As we let go of these things, previously unthinkable possibilities emerge.

Letting go of the TV habit — and it was but one of many — supported my journey of recognizing I could create my own reality by waking up, being conscious about my choices and taking ownership of my life and the world around me. That included learning how to discern when I was trying to control something that was not mine to get involved with, slowly letting go of the need to make everything "perfect."

Rescripting Life

The divorce supported an even deeper change within me. I now had the freedom to re-create my life and truly carve out space for me, as well as deeply focus on raising my daughter. I was able to release boxes that I had been assuming I must fit into for decades. I really began to explore my own deep path of self-realization. Who am I when I am no longer someone's wife? What fills my heart with joy when it's not about compromising with another person's choices? Can I connect with my own personal well of life-giving energy? What's it like to connect with what feels juicy and alive? How can I be even more present with my growing daughter as I create space to be more present to the little girl within me? Slowly I felt myself let go.

A memory comes in...

"You're going to make yourself sick!"

I am a little girl. My mother is in the front seat of the car and I am crying in the seat behind her, unhappy, miserable. She's not paying any attention to me. I cry harder. As her frustration builds, she finally bursts out, yelling at me with disdain in her voice: "Stop it! You're going to make yourself sick!"

While it wasn't nice in the moment, I eventually came to realize something: She was right. I could make myself sick.

…And if that were true, could I also make myself well?

That second part took longer to realize, but the truth is, YES! We can make ourselves sick, we can make ourselves well, we can support ourselves through that whole spectrum.

As we've now seen, for many years I hated my body or parts of it. I worried about weight. I was tense and analytical, and I gained weight, lost and gained it back again. I criticized how different parts of me looked and felt. I tried to control it, and the harder I tried to control it the worse the relationship became.

And finally, finally, I started to shift this pattern.

One of the catalysts for my shift came from an unlikely place — a movie! A new film had come out in independent theaters, and Deb brought it to my attention. It was a big deal, a human homework assignment not to be taken lightly. The movie invites opening up to viewing consciousness and our power to create our reality in a whole new way. Deb strongly encourages Theo, Clair and me to go see it: *What the Bleep Do We Know!?*[16] We go. We see.

In the film, the lead character, a woman, is feeling really unhappy with her body. After fighting with it for some time, she finally decides to change it. She sits in the tub and draws beautiful purple spirals on her body and loves herself, really loves herself.

That had a huge impact on me — it really struck me. Shortly after seeing that movie when it came out in 2004, I did that ritual with myself. I decided:

---

[16] *What the Bleep Do We Know!?* is a 2004 film that combines documentary-style interviews, computer-animated graphics, and a narrative that posits a spiritual connection between quantum physics and consciousness. Wikipedia, accessed 2016.

"I want to shift how I see my body and how my body sees me. I want my body to know that I love it."

I got a sweet purple eye pencil and sat in the tub and drew hearts and spirals and soft, lush waves all over my body; I wrote *"I love you"* and other loving messages all over myself. I shifted how I interacted with my body at that moment.

"I've been hating you in many ways, or trying to force you to be something you're not. What's it like to invite you to be who you are, and to really let yourself be you?"

I gave myself space and permission and ritual to love my body, just as it was — all the stresses and imperfections still right there, and me in the middle, part of it all.

With that, along with all the pieces of my self practice and new spiritual awareness, my life that used to revolve around running my body instead of listening to it, control, weight loss, fear and insecurity started to shift to, *"I don't need to control that so hard. Let's let my body be what it is."*

As I started to sink into that — not by force — I released the worrying about my weight and my shape. I took on new practices. For example, I began body brushing, which feels so supportive and connecting. It was an opportunity to love my body, to relate to my body in a sweet and loving way.

It's been a huge emergence, and my body responds: As I love my body, it loves me, and we have a co-existence instead of fighting against each other.

The Recipes

Now, here in Part 2, is where we begin to explore together. I will be offering practices and talking with you more directly as we go. We're on a journey of listening to our bodies, and our bodies need nourishment. Our attention, care and love are the main ingredients in this nourishment. This takes the form of exercises and practices that support our bodies and allow our wisdom to pour forth so that we:

- remember who we are,
- trust our power, and
- claim our sexual sovereignty.

From here on, as we meet various places throughout the book, you will find these practices referenced in the text and gathered in the Recipe section at the end of the book.

They are for you to explore as a supplement to the story and teachings I offer here. I share them in a Recipe format to support you with clarity on what ingredients you'll need to gather, how much time to allow and what steps to take. Each Recipe includes:

- Title of Exercise
- Time to Allow: minimum needed to fullest extended
- Description & Benefits: short, easily accessible description and outline of main benefits, short-term and long-term
- Ingredients: space, settings, materials
- How-to: the steps to take
- Stories and other resources

The main thing that needs to be added to these recipes is you. As you explore your personal chef style, you may find following the structure helps it land in your body, then your body will guide you to modifications that support you at different times and spaces. The practices, while set up with structure, become art and flow. Yet that transition needs some time.

Giving Your Brain a Chance

Chances are, whatever pattern you are currently meeting in your body has been around for awhile — often rooted in years and even decades. So your brain has established a groove, a pattern, that has a lot of momentum behind it. Give your brain a chance. If you are feeling the call to make a shift and want to make a change for yourself, give the change a chance to take root. By inviting a structured practice, and creating the fertile ground for new practices and concepts to take root, we support ourselves into the best chances possible for transforming our lives.

Allow the time and space of at least 21 days with a new pattern. Explore new practices for at least that length of time before making a decision about them.

In my own practice, I've found this sort of structure balances well with body awareness, intuition and fluidity. I invite you to allow a structure to support you.

Intention

Let's take a moment with the concept of setting intention. The dictionary shares that "intention" is what one has in mind as a purpose or goal, or a determination to act a certain way. Energy moves where our intention and attention guide it. It can be very powerful to make choices with intention, and later in this book we'll explore how intention can impact what we manifest in our lives and be an important practice in our human homework. As we work with building resilience in our body, using the practices described in this book, we increase our capacity as a conduit for energy moving through our bodies. That, combined with grounded presence and intention, can be a powerful way to work with that energy to transform our lives, our consciousness, and together, our collective human family.

That said, while intention-setting is indeed powerful, it can be easy to get in our own way with what we "think" should be. We can also allow Spirit to do what needs to be done without interfering with our own ideas of what should be done or what questions we think should be asked. There is a place for both types of energies: intention (masculine/animus/yang) and allowing (feminine/anima/yin). As a spiritually aware friend once put it, "I believe that my cells are smarter than me!"

I have found that being as clear as I can about my intentions can be very helpful when healing old body-deep wounds. Have you ever felt unworthy to receive love? Do you ever feel hatred for your body or wish it were different than it is?

Are you ready to transmute your own Self-Loathing to Self-Love? Explore the following recipes for rituals and daily practices of body love and care. Also included are the practices to complement the stories shared earlier in this chapter about journaling and clearing clutter.

RECIPE 1: Self-Love & Acceptance Practice, pg 298

RECIPE 2: Body Brushing, pg 301

RECIPE 3: Journaling & Free Writing, pg 303

RECIPE 4: Clearing Clutter, pg 306

Even though I began to feel good about my body, I still continued to wear drab, oversized items that I found myself hiding behind. Ready for a change, I went shopping for some new clothes.

Standing in front of a set of mirrors with glaring lights washing down, I see myself in clothing I've selected in sizes I habitually choose. I'm stuck. They're not right, but I'm not sure why, or what to change or what to do about it. Here at this women's clothing store, filled with fun, trendy, modern and professional options, I feel a little shy. I know I want something new and this place feels right, yet I am a little unsure how to go about it. I am holding the intention that the Universe will show me the way. I open a bit. I trust.

Sure enough, a woman who works at the store comes over and offers to help. I feel tingles! What a synchronicity! I would not have sought out or asked for help, yet this is exactly what I need. Yes, I accept! She sees me swallowed up in sizes that are far too large for my frame and, with one hand on her hip she waves toward me exuberantly with the other, proclaiming: "Oh, honey, we are gonna make you POP!"

The salesperson begins gathering clothing that invites my curves to show instead of the clothing I had been hiding behind. Inviting my breasts, that had been shamed into hiding so many years before, to be present and seen. I had patterned in my head that I am a "large." Sure, I acknowledge, I weigh less than I had in the days of being seriously overweight, yet I still think that I have a large frame and I don't even consider trying on a size "small" and especially not an "extra small"! These are exactly what she brings me, in styles and colors I would not have even considered before. I find they fit beautifully and feel great!

I can see curves and color in my body and my clothes that I never would have considered in the past. Fitted shirts instead of baggy sweats... I try them on. I can see my shape underneath. I start paying attention to how clothing hangs on me, how it actually fits, rather than what size is on the label. I begin to see myself in the mirror differently. The salesperson helps me learn how to change the way I see my body and clothing. I carry this with me — it becomes a lasting change! I feel such gratitude!

It was happening: I was opening to the flow and support of Spirit and the Universe. It was exactly the help I needed at the time, for which I didn't know how to consciously ask. I let it in. Today, as my style and body continue to change, I stay open to meeting myself where I am and feeling how things fit from the inside. I am finding new balance, and ways to flow and change with that.

My theme as I went through these changes became one of reconnecting with my Divine Feminine energy and feeling love move through me again. I had gotten so dry and crispy that my body was begging for juiciness, for the fullness and richness of life that I had squashed away for so long.

I reconnected with my art and began drawing and painting again. It felt good to express myself, and also scary. The blank page could feel so daunting: How should I fill it? What if I mess up? The process of meeting those inquiries, of letting myself mess up, of doing more of what felt hard, all this became part of the journey as well. I found an ad in a local spiritual journal for an Intuitive Painting class. Yes! My body said yes to that, even though I really didn't have a clue as to what to expect and I had already missed the class time that was published. The spiritual guidance was so strong that I reached out to the teacher and she happily agreed to create a private class for me and a friend of mine. Yay! We were making it happen!

"Think back to your earliest childhood memory — feel it. What are the colors? The textures? Who is there? What do they mean to you? What's happening? Now paint that, bring it to the paper."

My "Intuitive Painting" teacher is asking these questions. I sit facing a large piece of white watercolor paper with a paintbrush in hand. I'm not quite sure what to do with them. I have a memory that comes in, but is it really my earliest? I may have had earlier ones. I mentally search. My rational brain tries to censor it away, as if it's not meeting the letter of the instructions. I ask about it and she compassionately affirms: "Trust your body. That one coming in — that's the one!"

So I paint, the dark colors of the background, the memory:

> *I'm four years old. It's evening, my mother has to leave quickly, and an adult friend of the family takes her place, sitting behind me on the sofa, putting my freshly washed hair up in rollers — the soft, pink spongy ones I can sleep on. My father, I can't see him. He's outside, hurt. I'm scared. My mother rushes out of the house, they leave. They leave so fast, they don't even say good bye. Are they leaving me forever?*

I paint: my little girl hair, my closed eyes, distant door. The little circles with faces inside and rays emanating outwards, what I call "sunshines" from the drawing when I was three years old that my mother kept for me. The sunshine faces look blank, emotionless, almost sad or angry; it's hard to tell. I draw them. I stop. I feel stuck.

My teacher comes to me as I am frozen with the painting. She asks, "What's emerging for you?"

I answer, "I don't like it. I'm stuck. I don't know what to do."

"What don't you like?"

I point to these little stick figures and the bland sunshines.

"Then do more of them," she invites.

More of them?! But I don't like them, I want to erase them and I can't.

So I give it a go. I trust. I do more of them. More and more and more... yes!! Something breaks free, yes YES! I paint. More of them, and the colors pour forth and it works and something moves in me and I let go of a layer. I let go of anger for them leaving me, for them not showing up. I let go of grief, for me carrying all the anger and the sadness and hiding it and taking it on inside so the outside will still look pretty and acceptable. I let go of carrying it. Another layer I don't have to keep hauling around with me. A layer I can let go... I let it go. Ahhhh...

CHAPTER SEVEN

Omnisexuality and G-Spot Healing

As I reconnected with my art, drawing and painting, my body continued to open and my creativity began to flow. I also began to acknowledge facets of my sexuality that I had not looked at before. I felt a newness in the freedom to explore what I authentically wanted instead of what society was scripting for me. I started to realize I was interested in exploring sexually with women. I began to open that discussion with two close friends of mine: a man with whom I already had a sexual connection and a female friend of ours. We discovered that all three of us were eager to explore this newness together in a safe space. We talked about it ahead of time, exploring what the concept could possibly bring about. So the time came where we chose to get together to explore, with no expectations, and just see where it took us.

I feel 16 again, however I'm at least twice that age. We're in my living room, the three of us: he, she and I, lights dimmed, dirty martinis poured, just one or two to "loosen up." We're watching a movie, an incredibly erotic movie. We've come together with the possibility of sharing a sexual connection. The next thing I know, tops are off and I am sharing my first kiss with a woman! I feel the tingling of excitement, the newness. The texture of her lips and skin are so different, softer, than the men I've kissed. Her energy different. She says this is her first time too, but she seems so much more comfortable than I, so much more experienced as she slides down to bring her mouth to my vulva. I wonder briefly if I don't have the whole story and realize that it doesn't matter. We explore more through the night. It is so interesting to explore her body and to feel the softness and smoothness so different than when I would kiss or touch or be touched by a man. I am so turned on! It's exciting, it's new!

That night I felt what I later refer to as my giggly and immature masculine energy: that of my inner 16-year-old boy. It felt like "Oooo! I get to touch a booby!" And while it was an important facet of opening in my sexuality, it was also very much filled with nervousness, uncertainty and newness. I had a hard time really being conscious and present. The alcohol we consumed I now equate with numbing out, and no longer feels good. Yet that evening was an important turning point for me.

Omnisexuality

This experience brought some of my internal questions about my sexuality to the forefront of my awareness.

First, I woke up the next day with the old familiar script of self-shaming. Questions circled as I reflected on the evening's events: Did I hurt anyone? Did I do something wrong? Am I bad for what I did? Did I just put my friendships at risk? It may be easy to look at now and say, "Of course not! You are so allowed to make conscious choices with other adults to share and connect as you wish." Yet the layers of social and family programming are deep in our bodies, and sometimes we do put relationships at risk when we try new things or step into new versions of ourselves.

The questions continued. What did this mean? I pondered. Was I a lesbian who just didn't get it right for 16 years? No, I was still really interested in men. So then did that mean I am bisexual? Hmmm... No, even that still seemed too limiting, the "bi-" prefix implying only two options. It was Deb who helped me realize that I didn't need to put a label on it, and yet a label that might be closer suited was 'omnisexual'! Yes indeed, 'omnisexual' felt better. It had the energy of "yes AND!"[17] Sharing love with all beings: with trees, with nature, with partners

---

[17] In the technicalities of the English language, I remember way back in school learning the use of "but" as a way to set up a counterpoint. For example: "She's really pretty but she has a scar on her face." Much later the use of language and the way it can land energetically came into my awareness. I have noticed that the "but" can feel awful. In the example given, it's as if she cannot be pretty because of the scar. I call bullshit! I invite us to change this. Both are possible. "She's really pretty AND she has a scar on her face." Or "Yes I feel better than I ever have in my life AND I am excited about the continued possibilities of opening." Or "Yes I can feel good about my sex life AND explore new layers of pleasure and ecstasy." It's not that the new stuff means you aren't powerful and

of any gender identity, or multiple partners. The word suggests that it isn't about gender, it's about opening in love, AS love. Embodying the state of love. I was beginning to see the expansiveness of possibilities.

And I did explore: with men and women, and with multiple partners. It was fun and it was exciting; it was a learning experience and an important part of my growth. The growth included meeting the raw vulnerability and noticing shame. It has been a journey of unpacking layers of old stories from the body.

In my experience, this takes time. My journey with vulnerability and shame continues. As my body continues letting go, I need to process the layers of shame that emerge. Each time, feeling a bit softer, I let go a bit more, creating a bit more space for self-acceptance and care for myself and for my partners. This building of resilience is so much different than the building of walls and armor. And although my early explorations were important, it wasn't until later that I began to really be present with my sexual energy in a conscious way with my lovers of any gender.

I learned a lot in this era of my life about new love, about myself, about my sexuality. I shared connections with new friends. And it was only the beginning!

As I started dating, I felt like I was fumbling around like a teenager. I realized it really was the first time that I had dated since very early on in high school. So I felt really out of practice, unsure of myself, and awkward. It was like those old times of childhood flooding back to the surface. I learned a lot about really checking in with what I wanted, and for the first time, I really began to hold space for what I needed.

A friend at work sets me up on a lunch date with this guy she knows. We meet and decide to go out on a dinner date. It happens to be on New Year's Eve, and I dress up in some stunning new clothing — casual yet evening-appropriate and sexy. Ahead of time he asks where I'd like to go, and I say, "I don't know." So he picks his favorite restaurant: one with red and white checkered tablecloths and rolls of paper towel to sop up the grease from the fried finger foods being served. While this is not my first pick and feels awkward given the outfit choices I'd made, I realize I had not given him any information to go on about my preferences, so I suck it up and deal with it, not letting on that I don't like it. We eat and move on.

———————————

wonderful just as you are, it's "YES you are powerful and wonderful AND there may be even more to explore."

Our next stop is possible dancing, but the cover charge at a nearby club scares us off and we end up at a familiar sports bar, a bar that is in my comfort zone from my old days, but not nearly the elegance or excitement I had hoped for in my new life and with a new person. I begin to realize we've spent the whole night hearing about him and his life plans since his divorce. In his view he has all the perfect pieces: two careers that he loves, two kids (a boy "junior" and a girl), and all he needs now is a wife to make it complete. I feel like I am in the running to be a trophy for him to sit on a shelf. Somehow we manage to share a kiss at midnight to bring in the New Year. It feels awkward kissing someone new who I am really not attracted to. He's a lovely person, and we end the date pleasantly, yet I know in my heart and feel clearly that this is not a match.

A few days later he calls. As I am on the phone with him, I hear him sharing how he enjoyed our time together and would like to see me again. I pull away. Suddenly from above and to my left, I look down to see myself holding the receiver of the phone and cringing. I realize that I am about to agree to go out on a date with him again! Not because I want to, but because I don't want to hurt his feelings… and I don't know how to say "no."

Luckily I am able to reconnect with myself, barely in time. I scream to myself inside my head: "Oh no, you are NOT going out with this person again!"

I manage an awkward decline, not at all graceful. It's really bumbling and yet I do it. I say "no" because that's what my body was clearly wanting even though it feels really awkward and hard and I worry about how it will land. That day I begin to access a new layer of how to hold space for what I need.

So it began — I started getting clearer about what I want and need. As I did, I met a man who became an important part of the next opening of my life and the more tangible beginnings of my sacred sexual healing: unwinding old information from my body and reclaiming my power. I found myself bumping against my biggest body block (energetic stuck spot) and awakening to what is stored there.

Connecting with Music and the Arts and Meeting My Biggest Body Block

The social dating scene felt awkward, so I turned to the only thing I thought I had available: online dating. I began the process of filling out profiles and identifying answers to questions so that I could potentially find "a match." I proceeded to meet a few of the people I found online, and the first few awkward meetings were interesting. I was grateful that shortly into the process I met a man I felt very attracted to. We began a relationship that proceeded to unfold for a couple of years. Jay adored me, and he helped me connect with new cultural and artistic experiences. Music and the arts: We enjoyed art shows together, visited galleries and attended concerts. It was an exciting time in my life, and a new chance to deepen with someone, something I hadn't done, basically, in my whole life. I had been with one man all of my adult life until my divorce and omnisexual awakening, so this new relationship was a new opening. We enjoyed doing some of the same things together: I was a triathlete and he was a runner. One of the strengths we found was truly enjoying spending time together.

Our sexual relationship grew quickly from awkward early beginnings. I remember calling my friend before heading out on an early date with this man, wondering whether should I bring condoms or not! Realizing that this question had not crossed my mind in years, I quickly moved through some repatterning around allowing myself to enjoy connecting in a sexual relationship. I realized it was okay, that I was an adult and I had my choices to make and it really was completely up to me.

As Jay and I began our sexual relationship, I started to experience new things. I was experiencing new levels of orgasm and my orgasms became slightly more accessible. I had only known orgasm literally by my own hand, externally clitorally stimulated, in all my years, and for the first time I began to feel what it was a like to allow a partner to bring me to orgasm: the early beginnings of my sexual, orgasmic letting go!

I began to find that after orgasm, behind closed eyes, I would see waves of indigo and purple swirling lights that I later came to know as the opening of my intuition and my vision of energy. With some guidance from Deb later, I felt and connected with that as my third eye opening.[18]

Jay and I also began to explore what I later came to understand as sacred spot healing in my body. At the time all I knew is that I was acknowledging new

---

[18] A reference to one of our chakras, or energy centers, as commonly referred to in the yogic tradition.

sensations in my vagina. Specifically we began to really explore my G-spot,[19] which I had not done since early explorations with my boyfriend at age 16.

Jay and I are in his bed sharing a sexual connection. I am lying on my back and he has two fingers inside my vagina and is pressing against my G-spot, stroking and pushing. I feel only a little sensation, and urge him to press harder, faster. He proceeds to increase the intensity of his contact over and over at my request... "Harder, more!" I feel tense and tight, the pressure evokes only small sparks of sensation, and I keep grasping for more. As I do, I feel pleasure turn into pain. We shift positions, he continues with the pressure. I am grasping toward sensation and pleasure, yet it's elusive; it feels so out of reach. Thoughts that seem random keep coming in, and I keep pushing them aside, "Go away!" as I try to focus on feeling pleasure.

He finally stops me, "I don't want to push any harder — I'm afraid I am going to hurt you!" He pulls his fingers out of my vagina and presses them against my thigh to demonstrate the amount of pressure he is giving inside. I am shocked! I had no idea this was how hard he was pressing, I can hardly feel anything in comparison.

Later I get up to pee. I am shocked once again: I see blood in my urine.

What I found was I carried so much numbness that it took a ton of pressure to feel any sort of sensation at all, and by the time the sensation would unfurl, it quickly moved into pain. I was carrying that much shielding in my body. I started experiencing what I thought were random thoughts, random memories that would come up during our sexual encounters — specifically when we explored vaginal penetration and G-spot stimulation.

Finally, with the assistance of Deb, I started to explore these seemingly random memories that were coming up in my intense sexual experiences. It would be years before I would come to call these "Fruit Flies" and document the process of releasing them. We will explore Fruit Flies and the process of listening to them in much more detail in Part 3.

---

[19] The G-spot is actually a misnomer that has gathered enough traction in popular culture that I leave it here for simplicity. Counter to the idea that it is a "spot on the wall" of the vagina, it is actually a whole three-dimensional body of erectile tissue that includes the glands that support ejaculation. The full exploration of anatomy is out of scope for this book. *A New View of a Woman's Body: A Fully Illustrated Guide by the Federation of Feminist Women's Health Centers* by Suzann Gage and Sylvia Morales is an excellent and empowering resource for female body anatomy.

For now, all I knew was that disturbing memories kept popping up, and I kept swatting at them trying to make them go away, often at the most intense moments just before orgasm. I would often feel frustrated or want to cry as I was making love with my partner and these feelings created waves of guilt and shame, like, "Wait, I should be enjoying making love with my partner and feeling happy and blissful, not feeling these sensations of frustration or anger or sadness." So I beat myself up and tried to ignore them, hoping they would go away.

I talked to Deb about these experiences, and what I found in that exploration and learned more deeply over time is that it is okay to allow these memories to present themselves. Connecting with these memories as they emerged and when they emerged, prompted by body wisdom and when I was resourced to meet them, was essential to my healing, opening my path to being in my body and being alive.

The memory attached to this part of my body came up during certain contact or certain energetic explorations, and it was very specific. It involved having my genitals touched by a babysitter when I was about 10 years old. Our bodies carry trauma and stuck energy, and our very sacred center deep in the pelvis holds our entire sexual history. This was why this memory kept popping up for me during intimate moments with my new partner as an adult. While I wasn't able to articulate how to work with these memories at the time, noticing them was crucial to the journey ahead of me.

The thing is, when the babysitter memory popped in during sex, I didn't acknowledge it as being inappropriate touch. I just saw it as this male babysitter, probably 18 or more years old, who would touch my genitals under a pillow I held against my front body. I hadn't repressed the memory; I knew it was there. I just kept shoving it away, not REALLY looking at it: "I mean surely it wasn't important, right? It wasn't 'abuse' or anything — he didn't rape me, after all." These were some of the thoughts going through my head. I thought these were helping me deal with it by rationalizing and trying to make it go away. Instead, these thoughts were limiting my ability to release it.

Finally, I let myself unfurl in it. Deb guided me into going into the FEELING of the experience. I felt myself clutching a pillow against my body, me on my back, slid down into the couch, him beside me, his hand sliding under the pillow to find my genitals. It felt sneaky, like I was a bad girl, yet there was my body response of curiosity and arousal that made me want to know more. Part of me liked it; I eagerly awaited his next visit and lay on the couch with the pillow, as if non-verbally asking to be touched again. Yet I felt tremendous guilt and shame — clearly, it had patterned in my mind that I was a bad girl for feeling pleasure. Yet I was desperate for attention, and perhaps this was the way I could receive love. I had felt it absent in my life, with my parents divorcing, my dad moving away, my mother physically present yet not emotionally available. This very pattern of "I am a bad girl for feeling pleasure" got unconsciously rooted into the wiring in my brain and body. It became deeply, deeply rooted.

Now as an adult, crying, feeling the deep shame that had rooted in my body from that time, curled in a ball clutching a pillow, I was able to begin the re-patterning. Deb, along with a book she recommended (one I not-so-affectionately at first nicknamed "the big fucking book!"),[20] helped me acknowledge and feel in my body the powerful pieces that helped unlock the keys: It was NOT my fault. It WAS trauma because I was still carrying around the pain associated with the experience in my body, no matter how "no big deal" my intellect tried to label it. That my body responded with arousal and sexy feelings is simply because our genitals are wired that way. As Ellen Bass and Laura Davis write in their book *The Courage to Heal: A Guide for Women Survivors of Child Sexual Abuse*:

> It is important to recognize that it is natural to have had sexual feelings, and that even if you had sexual responses to the abuse and those responses felt good, it still doesn't mean that you were responsible in any way.

> Our bodies are created to respond to stimulation. When we are touched sexually our whole physiology is designed to give us pleasure. These are natural bodily responses over which we do not always have control. When we eat a sandwich, our stomachs digest the sandwich. We can't stop our stomachs from digesting the sandwich. In a similar way, when we're stimulated sexually, we can't always stop our bodies from responding.[21]

And importantly: It was not a betrayal by my body. It is okay to feel pleasure, despite the contrary pattern that sunk in that day. In the process of healing, I learned to make peace with my body and rewrite the script that had been patterned in.

---

[20] *The Courage to Heal: A Guide for Women Survivors of Child Sexual Abuse* by Ellen Bass and Laura Davis.

[21] Bass and Davis, pg 117.

I found that what I was really seeking in my desire to be touched was love: the love and acceptance I didn't realize at the time I was desperate for from my parents, particularly from my father. While that love may have been in him somewhere, my need to feel it was not being met.

What happened was that my feelings of guilt and shame in response to the fear of being a "bad girl" patterned in with the sensation in my body. So, when I felt similar sensations in the future, the memory was triggered to resurface. That energy gets stuck in the body, and the body is the key to unlocking it.

ℭ ✣ ☙

While my relationship with Jay bloomed open in many ways, an emotional undercurrent was also looming inside me.

Jay and I plan to meet at a park for a bike ride with my friends, a triathlon training ride. I pull in and see a brand new road bike leaning against his truck. I get out and read the note attached to it: "Because you love to bike."

He's bought himself a brand new bike because of his perception that I like to bike?! Argh! I actually don't even like biking that much. Of the three events in triathlon it is by far my least favorite, and I train for it just to support my triathlon fix. I've always felt kind of awkward on a bike, chalking it up to not really riding one much as a kid, so I just don't have that same embodied familiarity with biking that so many of my friends seem to have.

Now I see this note on his bike and it makes my skin crawl. Why would he put the responsibility of a brand new purchase on me? I cringe. Yet as he comes out to greet me, I smile weakly and say nothing. Once again, letting him believe that I feel good about it. I've done this too many times already. The resentment continues piling up.

By not saying anything then, I was taking on a responsibility that I didn't want. Jay was trying to hand me his power and I was taking it. He couldn't really put that on me unless I let him. Unfortunately, I let him, and I didn't see at the time how not to.

After a lot of self growth, I have learned more ways to hold my energetic boundaries. What I would say now with clarity and compassion is, "Yay, you got yourself a bike! I hope you enjoy it. To be clear, your bike is for you and I celebrate that for you, not for me. I am not taking the responsibility of your bike purchase."

This pattern continued, with gifts that felt like too much, with what he called "random acts of kindness," that often really did seem to come from a genuine place of wanting to share kindness. Yet these unwanted gifts also landed on me as attempts at grabbing at me, seeking attention, trying to draw me in. These acts left me feeling guilty and confused. He's just trying to do something nice, right? I should appreciate it and feel good about it, right? But I didn't, and I couldn't understand why. It wasn't until much later that I started to recognize that the shadow side of this type of "giving" without consent manifests as being a martyr, a "do-gooder" and "rescuer."[22] Yet I was allowing it instead of holding space for what I needed.

I was starting to recognize my time with Jay was coming to a close, but I really didn't want to admit it to myself. As I continued with my journey of self-awareness, I began to feel Spirit calling me to travel.

---

[22] Dr. Betty Martin, The Wheel of Consent, https://bettymartin.org

CHAPTER EIGHT

Peru, Heart Opening and Intuition

"Spirit calling me to travel." What does that even mean, you may wonder? I didn't know how to name it then. I found words later to go back and name these experiences. I was having experiences that I didn't have vocabulary for. I wasn't able to describe it in words. I just knew.

Sitting in Deb's office, I would watch her go into a kind of meditative state, gazing off beyond my shoulder or closing her eyes. After a short time, her face would light up with clarity, her eyes would meet mine, and she'd share something with me. In her words, she would "listen to Spirit." My exploration with and trust of such words came later. At the time, it appeared to me simply as Deb checking in with me: "Have you seen this?" "Have you heard of that?" She would suggest a book or person or teachings to look up. Such gifts were like little human homework assignments that I loved receiving. Often I would feel a sense of "You gotta be kidding me?!" in terms of how much each new offering she would share would resonate for me. Things I had never heard of before would light me up. I felt tingles down my neck and I just knew I needed to follow it. So I would grab these things Deb offered and go home with them to integrate. I would take 11 pages of notes in her office, and then come home, reflect back on what she said and voraciously look up the things, find and read the books, absorb it in, feel a resonance and get blown away, then follow the next thing.

It was changing me. It was helping me remember who I am and why I'm here. It was like she was offering these keys that kept unlocking doors and leading to the next thing and the next thing.

Frankly, it wasn't until later that I could trust the vocabulary Deb was using. Deb was the one saying 'Spirit.' She was the one pausing and saying "let me tune in" or "check in" as she would come to stillness, close her eyes or gaze out wide, as if listening intently to something I could not hear.

At first I was like, "I don't even know what's going on!" Over time, as I shared earlier, my trust in her opened, as did my trust in similar processes in my own awareness. I could pause and allow more space, too, and this seemed to support the flow of gifts that kept flooding through her to me. I sensed something above or around us and I felt like, "What was that?" Then it would come through her to me.

I began to see that Deb was a vessel for receiving these nuggets of offering who then shaped English spoken words to describe these experiences. I would go follow a suggestion and feel how it would impact me, try new things, and parts of it would become a part of my truth. Others would fall away. As this continued, I would talk about it with close friends who were also opening to this new vocabulary, and that reinforced the learning. As I started to learn this new vocabulary, I could take it and apply it back to the things I was exploring.

At first though, I was really not clear: I had no idea how it was working! Just like in my engineering days, it took many years of training to learn new vocabulary and formulas and structures that described shared experiences. Faced with new experiences, I created new mental frameworks on which to hang the new information. I began to realize that everything we do has a language associated with it, and it takes time to become fluent in it.

What became clear much later, and what I offer now, is that I was undergoing another language acquisition. It can feel crunchy and awkward and uncomfortable. It's new! Like when we are toddlers learning new words and phrasing. Yet it's necessary, and it weaves inextricably into the rest of the book. And here, dear readers for whom the vocabulary we are dipping into in the following chapters and later parts of the book is new and potentially uncomfortable, I invite you also into this additional language acquisition. Like me, you very possibly had your primary language acquisition very early on in life with your primary caregivers. They pointed at an apple, let you touch, taste, feel and smell the apple, experience it. Ultimately the apple is a mysterious object, but you name it an "apple." It's still mysterious, but we now have a name for it so that we can have a shared way to refer to it. "Spirit" (or any other of these new terms) isn't all that much different than "apple." Yes, the thing "Spirit" refers to is harder to point to, but the experience of it can be shared.

Essentially what is happening at this point in my story is a rebirth that required another period of language acquisition, similar to primary language acquisition in my family, and later learning a new kind of language in engineering school. New people (in my case Deb, Theo, Clair and others), along with new books, films and teachings appeared in my life along with a new set of experiences and understandings. Along the way, I gained a new vocabulary to help me navigate this new space.

As you move further into the material in this book, my hope is that you will find the models (as Deb was for me) and the kinds of experiences that give this new vocabulary real meaning. Your vocabulary will then add additional bandwidth to your current use of language, and it will be both uniquely your own and shared with others.

New terminology can also be a point of departure for your own explorations as you look up words and read or interact with others who use them. To support your exploration, flip to the end of the book for the Glossary, where I summarize the terms that may be the most unusual, and Additional Resources to Explore for a list of books and other materials.

As we now continue with the story, I began to feel Spirit calling me to travel…

I am noticing pieces coming together. The journey I'd begun exploring unknown parts of myself is calling me to unknown parts of my world. Big cat energy has long surrounded me. Panthers have been my favorite animal since as long as I can remember: stuffed animals when I was small, pictures on my wall in high school. I even drew a self-portrait in college with half of my face a panther. In second grade I made a papier-mâché Sphinx for a school project, and my more recent calling into Sacred Geometry and Drunvalo Melchizedek's work has me steeped in its ancient mysteries. The theme woven through them all is Egypt. Egypt is calling me.

As I reflect on all this sitting in Deb's office, she smiles with those knowing eyes and excuses herself for a moment. Upon returning, she plunks down an exquisite statue of a powerful female figure with a male lion head in front of me, and introduces me to Sekhmet, the lion-headed goddess of ancient Egypt. I feel tingles of knowing all through my body. Yes, yes, I have a connection with her! Yet I sense, and she suggests, to take this one step at a time; this powerful connection is not to be taken lightly.

That day Deb also connected me to Sarah, the leader of a tour group heading to Egypt a few weeks away. It was too near the departure time for me to join, yet as I connected with her and her work, I found a resonance open up with Peru. I felt the shift happen. I was meant to align with Peru for now. Perhaps my call to Egypt was just to guide me to Sarah and her Peru trip, planned for June of the following year? As I deepened with that, really let this idea of traveling to Peru seep in, feel it, and explore all the facets of what that meant to me, Sarah indicated people often journeyed with her to both places. I brushed that off, thinking, "How could I possibly afford both such extensive and expensive journeys in this lifetime?" I knew Peru was right for now, so I released Egypt and sank into preparations for the journey to South America. Spirit was calling me.

Peru is a powerfully deep, sacred feminine center on this planet, located in the juicy jungles and mountains of South America. Egypt is a powerful masculine center located in the deserts of the African continent. Tibet is the sacred child of the divine feminine and masculine union. As I read about this through Drunvalo's[23] work, it felt more like a remembering from deep within my being than new information. I realized that of course I needed to connect with Peru to open my heart, to deepen with my theme of connecting with my Divine Feminine.

So I made my plans, read books in preparation,[24] did my human homework — the practices and paying attention that supported me to continue to learn and grow — and set off alone to join the tour at an airport in the southern US. We all flew in from various areas of the world, and met there to fly into Lima, Peru, together for what would be the most powerfully heart-opening 10 days of my life to that point.

On the way there I connected with three amazing new friends: Kirsten, Ed and Teresa. Kirsten is a tall, beautiful woman of German heritage with long flowing blond hair and a beaming smile. We connected deeply and quickly. Ed, a former technical career guy turned spiritual author and mystic, had a way of sensing energetics and articulating about them that was totally new to me, sparking a lot

---

[23] Drunvalo Melchizedek speaks of this in his book *The Ancient Secret of the Flower of Life, Volume 1*, pg 118.

[24] To name two: *Initiation: A Woman's Spiritual Adventure in the Heart of the Andes* by Elizabeth B. Jenkins and *The Celestine Prophecy* by James Redfield.

of skepticism, and yet I couldn't deny that I felt the things he would invite me to see. It was so simple and authentic, yet so foreign and against the typical views of the world I had been raised to believe. Teresa is a woman of Chinese heritage, soft spoken and kind. The four of us came together as Lightworkers — beings with a desire to be on a path of self-realization, remember who they are, and support others to remember and align with their soul path as well. Still new to this kind of experience, I shared in our growing sense that we had been brought together by the Universe. We meditated together, chanted together, and offered healing to the planet during our short 10 days together. The synchronicities were astounding in the way we kept finding ourselves in situations enabling this group healing. At the time I didn't see it quite like that. I simply thought things were happening in a "normal" sort of way. The significance of it wasn't as clear until later.

We are now four days into our journey. After the train ride from Ollantaytambo to Aguas Calientes, we check into our hotel then take a bus to our next sacred site. Looking out of the bus window, I feel a stirring in my pelvis as I gaze at the feminine mountains, lush and green, their vulva-like valleys moist with life. We arrive and continue by foot. I stop on the hike up.

I breathe in the cool moistness of the earthen wall… stretch my hands and fingers into the tiny green plants, feel the cool moisture and breathe in the vibrant fecundity that fills the air.

As we approach the top, we pause, close our eyes, link hands, and our guide leads us the final few steps to the top. Trust, surrender, walk on. At the top we unclasp our hands and open our eyes to see majestic Machu Picchu and the surrounding peaks, with the river Urubamba deep below. We offer coca leaves and our intention as we ask Spirit for support, and surrender to be received into the land. My companions Kirsten, Ed, Teresa and I feel as if we had been called back here — we've been here before in another life, another dimension.

As we meditate at the cardinal points of a specific ceremonial area of the ruins, I can feel a sludgy, heavy energy. Afterwards, Ed conveys that he sees that we were called back here to do important work: to help clear the path and the energy at this spot, a portal of connection with other realms. This makes sense to me based on what I felt as we meditated, and it resonates as true for me.

I am honored that my new friends can help me see these deeper callings. I feel so new to the awareness of having a deep soul purpose, being so used to life in 3D reality where the main purpose is often purported to be getting up to go to work at a "job" in the morning. This felt so much more real, more profound. A deeper layer of my newly emerging Truth.

As we moved to another area of the ruins, I experienced memories of myself as a young one playing and dancing through the stone structures as if living there as a child, giggling, alive! Or perhaps it was simply my consciousness tapping into the field of awareness of that ancient time? The specifics didn't matter. The feeling of aliveness — of waking up and remembering who I am — was what was important, and it was real and present for me.

Peru, June 2006 – Today we journey to the floating reed islands on Lake Titicaca. We're encouraged to bring gifts for the families that live on the islands. I buy some fruit and some colored pencils for the children. As we arrive in our small boats, we are literally greeted with open arms by the indigenous people. The men are elsewhere, fishing and working with the reeds. The older children are in school, the schoolhouse being a simple reed structure on one of the other floating islands nearby. The women in their colorful wool skirts and small hats are holding the babies and have their crafts and wares laid out on cloths with hopes of selling them to us, we Western tourists.

I feel a little awkward and anxious. So many questions fill my head. When am I supposed to share the gifts? With whom? As I browse through the various items for sale, I wonder how much am I supposed to bargain? Or do I pay full asking price? The process feels stressful. My analytical brain just wants it all clearly laid out, to get rid of the guesswork. I don't know what to "do." I struggle a bit. I choose a few things. A beautiful cloth textile, woven and sewn by hand, catches my eye. The Uros woman selling them smiles, and her eyes beam from her brown cherubic face. She barely speaks anything other than her native Quechuan language, and I struggle with some basic Spanish, a tenuous language bridge helping us to connect (that I later acknowledge came from colonization generations ago). Yet somehow, we communicate. Her name is Julia. I offer Julia the money for her work and she gratefully receives it. She neatly wraps and hands me my purchase and smiles as she hands me a small, hand-painted pendant on a cord.

I am confused and shake my head for a moment... no, I didn't buy a pendant, there must be some mistake. She smiles and insists in broken English... a "gift" for me. I am in awe: A gift? For me? Wow, what a special moment, and an honor to receive a special piece of art, when it appears to me that the money exchanged for her work must be so important to support her family. I share deep gratitude, I thank her and then turn to walk away. I still feel a bit awestruck, and something begins to shift in me.

When I get back to the boat, I see our trip leader Sarah, and I excitedly begin to recap the story, planning to share how sweet and surprising it was to receive a gift in this way. I take the cloth textile that I just purchased out of its wrap and begin unfolding it to show her what I had selected. As I do, an item tumbles from the folds to the reed island bed we are standing on. It's another pendant! Julia had slipped yet another gift inside the cloth without my noticing! She clearly did it with no expectation of anything in return. I uncontrollably drop to my knees in tears… I cry and cry.

I cry and grieve the times I've kept love out.

I cry and feel the joy of letting love in.

And I cry as I feel love and unconditional bliss. I feel my heart bursting open.

It was yet another big letting go. The dam around my heart that had been touched with a tiny, hairline fracture some years ago, finally cracked and crumbled away as the waters that had been slowly seeping through burst forth in a rush of emotion. I had no idea it was possible to be met with such unconditional, supporting love. This act of kindness, something so simple, so human, touched me deeply, and in a way I had never known before. It was the day my heart burst open.

Shamanic Initiations

In addition to supporting me in opening my heart, the journey to Peru marked many other initiations on my spiritual journey as well.

I look up at the sky. I feel a deep mysterious wonder… I've never seen so many stars. They are different here in the Southern Hemisphere. I feel a little disoriented… I don't see the constellations I am familiar with. There are billions and billions of stars, so thickly blanketing the sky they nearly cover it completely! I sink in, reflecting on this powerful time, nearing the end of my journey in Peru.

Mmmm… singing through my body are the colors and sounds of my recent experiences: The bittersweet native flute tones, floating through the winds from the *mountainsides as we hiked and sat with the land and the sacred energies there. The reds, blacks and multi-rainbow palette of the exquisitely woven fabrics that make up the clothing and ceremonial wraps of the native people here. The Q'ero elders, dark, weathered skin taut on their solemn faces evoking a familiar chord in me, a recognition... as if they could be my biological grandparents. While they are not, I still know and feel we are connected.*

I sit in reverence. We are holding ceremony, the creation of the despacho — a dispatch to Spirit of an offering, a prayer, sharing love, a request for support and guidance. Watching the elders in this facet of their shamanic practice — slow intentional placement of each piece, breathing intention and prayer into each of the coca leaves, flower petals, herbs and sweets, which they then arrange into exquisitely colorful mandalas of offering. Wines and other sacred elixirs are added, along with prayers and intention for healing, and they are folded and tied into bundles. They listen deeply. The bundles are placed against our bodies, offering a healing and initiation. I receive this initiation with honor and respect. We send our prayers to Spirit. We sing.

The threads of these teachings wove into fabric that is now a part of me in many ways. One is my mesa: my medicine bag or spiritual bundle that I carry and hold sacred. The woven cloth, with traditional patterns in reds and blacks, formed the foundation for the meeting of ordinary and non-ordinary worlds: the physical realm and the spiritual realm. Along my journey, crystals found me, as well as other sacred objects that came to be a part of my initiation into these teachings: a rose quartz sphere that fits heavy in the palm of my hand and represents the deep heart opening I received on this trip, a quartz crystal pyramid honoring the constant visions and experiences of pyramids I had as we sunk in at the sacred, ancient Incan sites, a remembering of my roots. Small sculptures of Puma, Condor, Serpent (representing the Middle, Upper and Lower worlds respectively) and Pachamama/Pachapapa also graced my newly created bundle, representing divine feminine and divine masculine and my quest of integrating and finding a balance of these energies in my body. Ways to connect and make offerings to Spirit... to the Apus (Mountain Beings), Inti (Sun Being), Pachamama (Earth Being) with intention and purpose emerged, and have also changed as I continued my journey. Relating to Beings — whether plant, animal, crystal, human, Earth, Sun and more — is how we learn and grow as Energetic Beings ourselves.

Remembering who we are, remembering our roots, cultivating our connection with the Earth, Spirit and all that is. This is the nature of the earth-based spirituality that opened before me from deep within my Being.

As the darkness of the night enveloped us and I felt in awe with the stars, I also felt a fear. Nighttimes of my past weighed heavy — they used to signify numb, drunken experiences, often with anger and usually resulting in sick sensations. Unconsciously throwing myself into altered states, I would feel tremendous guilt and shame as I would emerge on the other side, hungover, cringing in pain and wondering what I had done.

That night we headed into a deep ceremony, one that offered the possibility of meeting Huachuma, also known as San Pedro cactus. This powerful plant medicine is known as "Grandfather," a masculine energy that supports spiritual healing and teaching.

I am feeling nervousness and, in fact, fear. My longtime fear of vomiting is one of the worries that comes up — not only for myself, but the fear that someone else in circle may vomit and I will have to be near it. The old body fears rise up. I meet them.

Yet as I check in with my guidance, I know I am meant to explore this journey. The differences between this and the many nights of intoxication I had experienced are vast: This is an intentional journey, honoring the spirit of the plant, opening to it, asking for its guidance. We are held in safe space, a conscious container with our community of seekers and shamans. I feel ready, and I acknowledge my nervousness. I pray. I ask Spirit for support.

What follows is a gentle yet powerful experience. Perfectly matched for me is this gentle, conscious new introduction to the power of plant medicine when held in sacred container. The old scripts start to drop away. I feel a gentle opening, my body relaxes a layer. I experience some visuals that are light and easy — a deepening into the wisdom of many of the visual experiences I had already been having in meditations that involved no alterants. My rose quartz sphere glows with me, holds me safely. Familiar, soothing… as I gaze into the candlelight I feel Grandfather gently remind me, "Everything is going to be okay."

At one point in the ceremony I feel a strong pressure at my forehead. As I relax into the pressure, I get a strong sense of Sarah, with whom I had begun to really feel a motherly sense of support. She is not here in sacred circle with us — in fact, she's in another building, but I feel her say to me, "Just relax; all is well."

The next day, I spoke with Sarah and thanked her. I told her about the pressure and the message I felt I heard from her. She replied, "Oh yes! I was holding space and sending Reiki energy to all of you to relax."

WOW! I got it! This was my first conscious and acknowledged experience of telepathic communication and energy exchange. The gates into my innate knowing were opening.

This connection with support from Sarah I received as a sweet mother energy, one aspect of the divine feminine. In addition, I connected with another feminine aspect in sisterhood through Kirsten, perhaps in part because of our similar stature, and even similar smiles. She and I met as we arrived in the airport together for this trip, yet we bonded so quickly and deeply that within a day or so, others in our tour group thought we were actual sisters!

We are all sitting and watching a native dance demonstration. Our donations to the community are supporting these artists, and we are being honored with dance. Kirsten and I are next to each other, and as we sit on the earth, an insect flies onto Kirsten's shirt. I see it and instinctively flick it off. She notices, and I make a comment about seeing a bug and getting rid of it for her — as if this is a good thing friends do for each other. Somehow I immediately feel a message from her, unspoken — she is so kind as to not shame me or make me feel bad with words. I sense it somehow, though: The insect was welcome, there was no need to flick it away. The pattern in me is old and I am gently invited to look at it a new way. Something changes in me. I receive this gift, another way that another layer of relating with the world reveals itself to me.

This is only one example of many ways in which I seemed to absorb Kirsten's compassionate, unspoken guidance for clean living, sustainable approaches, love and aliveness. I welcomed seeing through the new lens, with refreshing and empowering new views on life. It was wonderful to connect so deeply with a new female friend — to open to new awareness and learn new ways of relating in sisterhood.

One of the ways she met me was with her wisdom on relationships. As I was lamenting about my relationship with Jay, wondering if I should end it yet fearful of another awkward journey into dating, saying, "I don't even like bars anymore! Why would I want to go there to meet people?" and so on, she gave me the most inspiring advice. "Oh no, sweet sister. You don't have to go out looking. Simply follow your authentic path, focus on healing and your own life journey. Then feel what you want to connect with in a person. Hold space for that energy to enter your life, and that person will walk through your front door!"

This was my first real lesson in 'manifesting,' consciously creating the life I choose.

Nine Spiritual Objectives

Nearing the end of our journey, I am running out of soles, the local currency. An opportunity to receive a special spiritual reading arises, a Coca Leaf reading from a native shaman, and I assume I won't be able to participate since I don't have the cash to offer in exchange. Spirit steps in, and a special gift emerges: A friend from our tour group gifts me with the reading! Wow, I feel so grateful!

The shaman sits beside me, hunched over his medicine bag and altar. With dark hair and skin, a wool hat pulled down over his ears, he prays and shares an offering to Spirit. He opens the sacred space. His hands are curled and worn, taut skin covers the knuckles. He gazes at the leaves that have presented themselves. He has an interpreter with him, and through that exchange I hear him say:

> *It is rare that I see this. You are here for a special purpose. You are important. You are successful and are here on the planet to be successful. But you are deciding not to make some choices on the path. You need to set some spiritual objectives. The issues you are having with your second and fourth chakras (sexual and heart centers) are because you are not taking actions on your path; your emotions are unstable. Take these nine leaves. Decide on a spiritual objective for each one. As you reach each objective, eat the leaf. When you reach them all, you will have no leaves left. Also you need to do a Flowering Ceremony.*

He hands me nine coca leaves, which I receive with honor, and I commit to proceed with this quest: I intend to set and meet nine Spiritual Objectives on my journey. I commit to ask for help and receive more guidance on what he means by a "Flowering Ceremony" since I have no clue what that means in the moment. I feel the initiation. It feels very big. I can feel that something big will shift as I enter and bring this cycle into culmination. I share deep gratitude to him, to Spirit, and later to my friend who gifted me the reading. I am deeply humbled and honored.

My time in Peru drew to a close. I deepened in my human homework, connected deeply with Pachamama (earth being) and Inti (sun being), and with the infinite realm of the stars. I continued along the path of remembering who I am.

Painting by author: Opening – acrylic on canvas 12''x12'', 2007

When I returned to the US and began to integrate all of these experiences, I felt excited yet a little overwhelmed with this idea of nine objectives. What are they? How will I know? My meditations, spiritual practices and support from Deb helped guide me to recognizing that these objectives would come in waves of three. The first three became clear within the first month. I journaled about them, planned for them, completed them and honored their completion with a coca leaf ceremony over the course of the next several months:

1. Transformational Breath – a powerful embodied practice of breathing that opens pathways in the body (7/27/06)

2. Painting – Intuitive Painting workshop, finding my guidance on drawing and painting what I see in meditation, and exploring what I am authentically moving through my body to paint (8/12/06)

3. "Flowering Ceremony" – Flower of Life workshop, exploring Drunvalo Melchizedek's teachings through local teacher Lorna Brown (11/24/06)

During this time, I actively engaged in my path of self-realization. My journals are filled with "aha moments" and guidance from meditations, visits with Deb, dream guidance, "Angel Card"[25] readings to myself, and spiritual revelations. Outwardly, I still walked in corporate shoes, drove through rush hour, wore button-down shirts and tailored pants. I still went into a bland, air-conditioned office each day, managed people, ran projects and moaned when timing was not met or costs were exceeded.

Yet, this other part of me began to flourish. I explored the inward path, meditated regularly, practiced yoga. I sought out alternative, creative ways to meet my body and the world. I took my nine Spiritual Objectives seriously, did my human homework, and as I did, more of the path was revealed…

November 24, 2006 – I celebrated in my journal this day with colorful stickers of flowers, an orange butterfly and words stating "Nurture Your Soul" as well as spiraling doodles and smiles:

In meditation this morning I asked, "How will I meet my love?" And I got the message that I need to eat my coca leaf for completing my "Flowering Ceremony," then set my next three objectives… So I do! I use my pendulum, a divination tool that can be used to gain spiritual insight,[26] to select which leaf. I thank my guides and my higher self. I blow my gratitude and intent into the leaf. I eat the leaf.

Objective #3 is complete!

And the next three are revealed:

4. *Jean Houston workshop*

5. *Alex Grey's art gallery – "Chapel of Sacred Mirrors" (CoSM)*

6. *Paint spirals? Labyrinth?*

---

[25] *Healing with the Angels: Oracle Cards* by Doreen Virtue.

[26] For more about the spiritual use of pendulums, search for dowsing or using pendulums for divination.

I do an Angel Card reading for myself: "What do I need to know right now?"

The first card leaps out, the others follow:

(1) STUDY – I am engaged in learning and study right now – take time to read, listen and grow! Don't rush to apply these teachings, enjoy the process of learning! :-)

(2) MIRACLES – are occurring – notice and experience even more of them. Expect a miracle on the item I can't see a solution to right now

(3) MUSIC – immerse myself in beautiful music, lifts my spirits and elevates thoughts to Divine love! Play soft background music while I dress, work, play

(4) SOULMATE – my prayer is answered – follow guidance. Great passion & spiritual companionship with the same person? YES! Trust and follow, the guidance will give me clear steps

I trusted, I continued to explore my path, I made plans to go to New York, the location of CoSM and Jean Houston's Mystery School workshop.

ഔ ❀ ൟ

Additionally, as I returned from Peru, I had to meet the growing fear in myself about my relationship with Jay. I had been fearing it might be time to bring it to a close. Finally, I got up the courage and had a tough conversation with him, saying that I needed the relationship to shift, but I was having a hard time really ending it. After the conversation, we left it open to continue as friends. This felt good, for awhile. But the unwanted gifting continued, and while I tried to convey that I wanted him to stop, I kept holding in how much it really bothered me. Until something happened.

My five-year-old daughter is so excited to bring home some newly sprouted flower seedlings from day care. "Mommy, look!" As she hands me the little paper cup half-filled with moist soil, bursting with tender new life.

"Yay!" I celebrate with her. "Let's find a spot to plant them in the backyard!" We find a little corner of the back garden bed, roughly delineate a little patch with some sticks to mark the new home of the little plants. We clear out some weeds, dig some holes and place the flowers-to-be in the ground. Yay again! Mommy-daughter gardening feels good to share together.

A few days later, I come home from work and as I am gazing out into the backyard my stomach drops. The whole back garden bed has been cleared out and a set of store-bought

*annuals has been planted. I feel an intake of breath, a shock, nausea, a sense of violation…
and of denial. This can't be! Am I really seeing flowers planted in my backyard that I did
not put there? The sensations in my body are similar to times I've noticed my belongings
have been stolen, or that a burglar has been in the house: a void in my stomach, hard to
breathe.*

*It becomes clear within seconds: It was Jay. He came during the day while I was at
work and cleared out the back garden bed, presuming all the small plants to be weeds. He
unknowingly ripped out the new plantings in his unwelcome attempt at sharing a gift of
flowers.*

*I am furious! It's the last straw! It feels like I am being stalked; it feels intrusive and
disrespectful. Now I fear that if I tell him that he ripped out Hannah's baby plants, he
will feel guilty and try to do more or create some other gift in an attempt to make up for
it. I can't handle that thought, and I do the only thing I know how: I email him to tell him
to stop the gifts, stop the emails, and never contact me again. He says he will honor my
wishes, and then proceeds to keep sending emails. I feel like the only way to stop this is to
stop engaging. I begin to ignore all of his attempts at contact.*

As I look back on this time, only the clarity of 20/20 hindsight reveals how
much I was NOT clear in setting and holding the boundaries[27] I needed, nor was
I bringing compassionate communication to the situation. Yes, the actions he
took were not okay, yet in my lack of speaking what I needed, I allowed
something to build to the point of feeling very icky and then having to take more
extreme measures. I had thought I was being clear, but really I was relying on old
tools of defensiveness and passive aggression that I had learned in childhood
from my parents. Jay provided a mirror for me to see this, and it was
uncomfortable for me — probably for both of us. Yet now through my journey I
continue to find healing and new ways to relate. As I have cleared much of this
old wounding around passive-aggressive behavior (both receiving it and giving
it), I now work with these kinds of situations in more direct and energetically
clear ways.

So as my relationship with Jay ended, I felt sadness and grief… as well as the
space of freedom. I really stepped into my journey, the next piece of my spiritual
path, and focused cleanly on myself. Kirsten's manifestation advice was in the

---

[27] We'll explore the nature of Boundaries more in the chapters on Container and
Foundation.

forefront of my awareness: the suggestion to not "do" and simply "be." She had invited me to let go of trying to force meeting someone and just be who I am. With the invitation to create the space for what I was seeking, I stopped stressing out about meeting someone. I journaled about what I was seeking in a partner, at an energetic quality level, not a physical one. I even left gender open. I held space, and simply followed my path. I released "trying to find someone" and continued on my journey of self-awareness. My yoga and meditation practices really began to open up, and with them, my power of intuition.

Opening My Power of Intuition: Visionary Art Begins

Back in my endurance athlete days, as a way to try to manage all the bizarre injuries I was struggling with, I began a yoga practice. I came to it in a very physical way, seeking a way to gain some additional flexibility and strengthen the little balancing muscles in my body. As I continued my practice, what had started as me striving for which poses (asanas) I could accomplish shifted into opening my awareness of what the poses offered me. The spiritual side of yoga emerged, the yoga that invites self-awareness and connection with the realm of the subtle. I began to value not only the outer body "workout" aspect, but the deep space of inner self-exploration.[28] As my journey with meditation deepened, I sought out a meditation retreat to learn even more about it. I came back with a newfound awareness of the benefits and the how-tos of seated meditation in conjunction with hatha yoga. As I explored it, I felt a sense of clarity and peace. It helped me find my center, ease stress, decompress from my day, and get clarity on my spiritual guidance. In so doing, meditation and yoga became a part of my regular practice.

By then, I had started meditating regularly, and my yoga practice was deepening. My eyes opened to see there is much more than my traditional senses claim to know. I kept feeling the "flow space" that opens as I align to this guidance. Yet my rational brain was still having a hard time trusting my body, trusting these "knowings." My inner skeptic still wanted more proof: Is there really such a thing as this realm of Spirit that I can trust? That will be there to

---

[28] See the Additional Resources to Explore for more on this.

guide me? And support me to connect with someone if that is meant to be, as well?

My connection with Sacred Geometry became a huge part of my path, a way in for me. Sacred Geometry was a language bridge: linking spirituality (which was so new for me) with science, math and geometry (which were very familiar). I read a ton about it, felt the resonance. Yet I also found that resonance as I *experienced* Sacred Geometry by drawing the symbols, feeling the connections, building physical models, recreating the pathways. This opened up new pathways of knowing in my body that created space for so much of this new knowledge, like hanging things in new slots in my brain.

Drunvalo Melchizedek's work had been resonating deeply in my body. In his books *The Ancient Secret of the Flower of Life: Volumes 1 & 2*, I found a suggestion, what he calls "Testing the Reality of Your Connection with Your Higher Self,"[29] and I sat down in meditation to explore it:

2006 – I am in my meditation space at night. A single white candle illuminates the otherwise dark space my daughter affectionately calls the "color room." I've painted the walls a deep coral orange, with gem-like reds and purples on the fabrics surrounding me. I am seated on my purple satin zafu (meditation cushion), and I have just written my intention in my journal. It's time; I need to know. Spirit, please prove to me your existence, and my connection to you. This is what I have written:

"What can I do as a physical act in this dimension to prove to me my connection to You, and help me in my spiritual growth? And please show me in such a way that I will know it is You."

I set it aside and go into meditation, sinking in deeply. About 30 minutes or more into the meditation I know it is time, and I ask my Higher Self to enter.

I ask the question. I wait.

I see some images that have been familiar to me in meditation since the unlocking in Peru: the eye in the pyramid and a few others. I see them and think, "Yeah, yeah — I see these all the time now. So what is that saying?" I wonder, what do I do with these? What is the "physical act in this dimension"? Then I get a hit... just ASK! So I do.

I ask: "Okay, I see these images, what am I supposed to do with them?"

---

[29] Melchizedek, *The Ancient Secret of the Flower of Life*, Volume 2, pg 407.

Instantly the visuals change from the general dark, vague imagery of my mind's eye in meditation to a crisp, bright, photographic quality. I see my hands at my white art table with the black work light shining upon them. They are holding colored pencils, and drawing on dark paper the very image I had just seen. The color choices are clear, the lines, the smudging. I feel tingles of knowing up my spine: YES! This is an assignment! I am supposed to draw these images, paint them! THAT is the action. I thank Spirit for this guidance and I promise to honor the message, I promise to do the drawing. I am giddy and excited, yet I hold space for the continuation of other pieces of the message and find closure with the meditation.

I had been tired heading into this evening meditation. I thought I was going to bed right afterwards. As I came out of it, though, I immediately wrote about it in my journal, a crucial step to get the transmission captured before ego-mind takes over and judges it or rewrites it. After I did, I relaxed a bit and I briefly thought I would come back to the drawing part tomorrow, after I slept. However, the zing of the new knowing and the power of Spirit drew me to my art table immediately. I couldn't avoid this deep call, and the time is NOW! I drew the image with colored pencils on black paper. It flowed out fast, clear, purposeful. It felt wonderful to be in the moment. I knew this was meant to be.

Shortly afterwards, I painted it. This calling to create my Higher Self painting launched a whole new phase of my spiritual journey as my art bloomed out into the world.

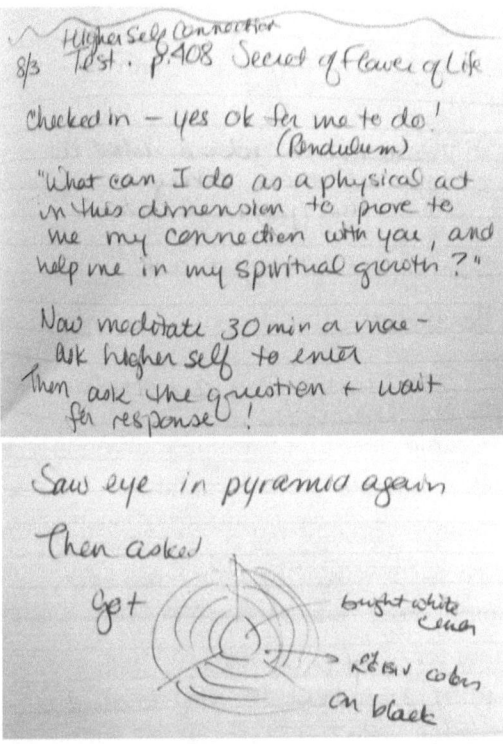

My journal entry as I head into Higher Self meditation, followed by the journal notes about what I saw. August 3, 2006

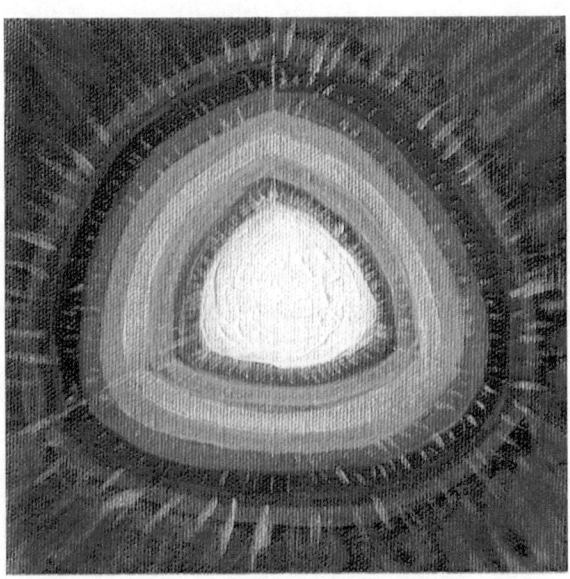

Painting by author: Higher Self – acrylic on canvas 6"x6", 2006

As I continued to focus on following my path of self-realization,[30] and in support of my Spiritual Objectives, my journey took me to New York to work with Jean Houston, PhD, a scholar, philosopher and researcher in human capacities.[31] I had been introduced to Jean's work by Deb, and her upcoming workshop planned for December 2006 caught my eye. Yet my calling to it came in the way that I was coming to know as Spiritual guidance and a body resonance that didn't necessarily line up with rational thought. In fact, despite reading the description of the workshop over and over, it just couldn't quite sink in! As I was debating about whether or not to go, the synchronicities started pointing the way. It became clear that I was to journey into Manhattan, see Alex Grey's Chapel of Sacred Mirrors (CoSM) gallery and do some drawing there, then head upstate to Jean's weekend workshop. I didn't even know what it was about, yet I had a strong sense that I needed to be there. When the woman I called to inquire about it boldly stated in her New York accent that I was to come, and opened up the door for how to pay for it, my plans were sealed.

So off I went, and sure enough, it was only the beginning!

Tucked away in the woods in upstate New York, I drive in after dark. After a morning flight, two taxi rides for my journey to see CoSM in Manhattan, and then a rental car and a several-hour drive away from the city, I finally arrive at the retreat center camp where the workshop with Jean is to be held. I am new to this and know no one here. Sleeping in a cabin shared with many other people, I find myself nervously excited to embark on this weekend experience. My typical self steeped in old patterns always prefers solo rooms over group bunkhouses, and in fact I had even paid extra to create that on my trip earlier this year to Peru. However, this time a private room was not an option: We will all sleep in a communal space. I meet my anxiety and allow myself to be present. Despite this nervousness, I am definitely feeling the call to be here, a sense of "Just let go and trust. It will be fine."

The weekend's programming opened the next morning. We embarked on a journey exploring "the Mystery of Inner Fire" through Jean's signature four levels: the physical/sensory realm, the psychological/historic realm, the mythic/

---

[30] A journey of awakening and remembering who we are. See also Glossary.

[31] www.jeanhouston.com

symbolic realm, and the integral/unitive realm. At one point we were invited to dance through the world's music. For me, this was brand new territory! Only in the past few years had I begun to move my body in new ways, yet mostly those scripts were athletic ones. My body knew how to run, to bike and to swim, plus some new yoga positions… but dance? The invitation to dance bumped a bit against my old "girl at the bar with the purses" era, yet I was ready to break free of it. I danced!

14th century Renaissance music …I danced!

Balinese music …I danced!

Country folk songs …I danced!

Native American songs …I danced!

I let my body move to the new rhythms in whatever way I felt called. I noticed when I would worry about how I looked, or wonder whether I was doing it "right," and I let it go and danced! Then the African music came on, and as I moved to the deep driving beat and explored the multistep pattern being offered to us, I felt my body connect with the rhythm and open up: I saw my grandmother! My father's mother who had passed away two years prior: I saw her! I *saw* her, smiling on me, connecting with me. I cried. I felt her begin the call to me, to remember who I am and to co-create in something very special many years later. This was my first conscious connection with an ancestor, and later the bridge to my consciously doing ancestral healing work.[32]

That weekend, in addition to this new relationship that began to emerge with my grandmother, I spoke my intention of working with sacred sexuality to the audience of fellow participants, as if sharing with the ambassadors of the world. It felt like yet another initiation, one of me speaking my truth and claiming my intention for my life's work. In the process, I met one of the most amazing men I've been honored to connect with in my life — Paul. After I spoke my introduction and intention to the group, he walked up to me and handed me a CD of his brilliant, ethereal guitar music. He solemnly and profoundly said, "You need to paint to my music."

I looked up at him, smiling and accepting. I somehow knew that yes, yes I did.

---

[32] For more about the need for and how to support ancestral healing and lineage repair see the book *Ancestral Medicine* by Daniel Foor.

In fact, later in meditation it became clear: *This* is the sixth Spiritual Objective that had been fuzzy when I first felt it! The experience of painting to his CD ends up becoming the sixth of my Spiritual Objectives and sets the stage for creating art together in person, yet to come.

Thus began the deepest, most powerful relationship I had ever experienced in my life.

CHAPTER NINE

Slowing Down and Letting Go

Despite all my rational logic, after meeting Paul for only a brief lunch during the weekend workshop in New York, we made plans for him to come visit me in Michigan a few weeks later. Again, Spirit was guiding this. I could feel it. Part of me was freaking out that I was inviting a man I had hardly met into my home for a several-day stay. All my logic and hyper-preparation style upbringing was screaming at me. I even, only partially joking,[33] set up a "code word" system with my friends should I need to call for help. It was simple, really: We decided on "get the fuck over here!" as a phrase I would use if I needed some support.

Yet a deeper place in me trusted that yes, indeed, having this man in my home would be not only safe, but deeply and powerfully important in my process of slowing down and learning to let go. We had opened a remote relationship, spent a ton of time in email and on the phone and just adored the process of getting to know each other. Paul lived in Oregon, and we had met in New York, while I was living in Michigan! Wheee! Little did we know how well we would grow and maintain a relationship from afar. I already knew I needed a tremendous amount of personal space, so it seemed to be a great fit.

We had connected right away from the moment we met, and during that first visit we bonded physically and sexually at levels of depth I had never experienced before. It was over Christmas of that year, and though we hadn't discussed sharing gifts ahead of time, we both found that the gifts we were meant to share with one another had been guided to us before we even met!

---

[33] The lighthearted way in which this flowed was important to me at the time, and yet is not meant to undermine the very real and important need for safe words and clear communication regarding body needs as we journey with sexuality and intimacy. See Creating Container in Part 3.

It is the fall of 2006. I'm at a popular book and music store and a display of CDs catches my eye. I glance over but don't feel particularly called to what I see. I walk on. A few moments later it grabs me again, so I walk over, pick up a CD and read about it. Hmmm, I don't really feel particularly called to the style of music. I put it down and walk away. A third time the display beckons me, I find it strangely odd that I feel literally almost as if something is pulling at me to turn around and buy it. I realize this CD will NOT let me leave the store without buying it! Okay, I'm curious. It must be music that I will love and it will be a surprise — I'm game! So I pick it up and add it to my purchases and check out.

Excited, I decide to unwrap it and pop it in my car stereo on the drive home. I do and I listen to the pieces... track 1, track 2, I skip through, listen to parts, don't feel it and decide to eject it and put it away. Wow, I wonder why I felt so strongly that I had to buy this CD? The style of music is really not resonating with me. I set it aside.

Time went by. I met Paul and my plans with him began emerging. Aha! I get a very strong hit as we were planning the visit that the CD was meant for Paul. I shared the gift and found out that he not only loved it, it was a collection he had not explored yet and was a perfect fit for him. I was blown away. Had I tried to think about purchasing a gift for him, I would not have come close to this choice. Synchronicity yet again!

For his part, Paul had been making jewelry with an artist friend some time ago, and he bought one of her pieces. He didn't know why at the time, it had just called to him in that same strange way. When he gave it to me and shared the story, we were both filled with delight and gratitude. I beheld a necklace of unparalleled beauty... garnet sparkle and feminine fire, coupled with oxidized, industrial edginess. Mmmm! It was perfect, gorgeous: five stones dropping down to my chest at my heart. A flowing style, dripping with rich red garnets, which are a favorite color of mine as well as my birthstone. I wore this deeply sensual piece with honor and loved how it helped me connect with my feminine juiciness. It remains one of my favorites to this day.

December 29, 2006 – From my journal the last day of Paul's first visit:
    Where do I begin?! Three days of bliss :-) My new lover, my new friend.

    Connection beyond my wildest imagination.

Sacred Sexuality: Listening to Our Bodies

We've known each other before, we fit... interlock, soak in each other. We made passionate love for five hours on the first night, after savoring the flavors and textures of sushi (his first). We walked, we talked... we discovered our bubble. I felt this energy field around us, containing us, merged as yin/yang inside. Awareness of the world outside our bubble would diminish as we were absorbed in each other, exploring, learning, touching, growing. It happened before on the phone, then first time in person at the sushi restaurant — then again so many times later. As we made love — the energy connections — like when we were on the phone, were phenomenal. I was safe, trusted him fully, immensely. I opened to him and he to me and he entered me fully, each of us absorbing each other.

I painted, he played guitar, we created, merged, shared more than we ever could have imagined. We went further in three days than either of us had in a lifetime with others...

And it was clean, comfortable, safe. Open communication — more than ever before, no expectations.

I love what he does to me, his magical hands, his energy, his touch, his words, his music, sharing his space, love of chocolate, fire, passion.

He is my lover.

I love our day-to-day comforts, no drama over our food choices or tousled bed clothes, we share styles — neither of us require newspapers or TV, etc.

We live in similar ways.

He helps me slow down and enjoy and savor.

We slept, deeply, comfortably, together... no anxiety, it was phenomenal, beautiful, perfect.

He left me a small note...

It really says it all, so simply, so cleanly.

We've done our human homework to be here.

We knew we'd meet each other — neither knew when or how...

We have been and we are together once again — we will learn our past lives experience again some day.

Paul... my lover.

We manifested each other — we could feel it. This was my first relationship that was so conscious. Our awareness of self, each as individuals, as well as the desire to deepen in a partnership together, was powerful. I felt an attraction I later would be able to articulate as my masculine being attracted to his feminine. And, his feminine was attracted to my masculine. We began to support each other in growth, love and sexual awakening.

Female Ejaculation

Simply put, Paul helped me to slowwwww wayyyyy downnnnn. He helped me soften, connecting more with my body during our sexual explorations. I started to really allow myself to relax, and as I did, I realized how much tension I was carrying, all day, every day, day after day. I still worked in corporate engineering at the time, and during my time with Paul, I would soon recognize the need to leave that career to follow my bliss full time.

Also, we began to explore G-spot healing with more conscious awareness. And with that came learning about something I had never heard of before: Female Ejaculation.[34]

Female Ejaculation — what is that? As we begin a bit of research into this expression of fluid during sexual arousal in female bodies, my first reaction is: "What? No way! That is just a porn star trick!" Then we dig deeper. I see a homemade video showing a woman's slow gentle gushing, I hear her soft breath and sighs, I see the gentle flow of her ejaculate and I feel drawn in, I drop into my body. Whoa, this feels legitimate. I absorb information, do research, read more about it. "Wow, okay, this is for real... but clearly it must be that only some women are capable — and I am not one of them," I assume. But

---

[34] Acknowledging I am using words that may not align for all bodies with vaginas. "Female Ejaculation" is intended to acknowledge the distinction from ejaculation more commonly known from bodies with penises. And G-spot is a name created by a man for a part of a body with a vagina that is actually much more extensive than known at his time.

wait, no, that doesn't feel right either. "Maybe I can learn this? Really?! Yes!" I feel called. I must explore this for myself!

During the times between our visits, we shared in our connection from afar. Paul bought some videos, a book and a toy to support our learning! He packaged them up and sent them my way. It was so wonderful to get the book in the mail after he had read it and circled important parts and drawn smiley faces, hearts and notes all over the place, encouraging me from afar in my self practice.

I'm lying on the hardwood floor of my second-floor bedroom at the foot of the bed with a folded towel under my butt. It feels so good to be in my space, with art that I love and have collected on the walls: some nude photography, a print of one of Alex Grey's paintings, a framed drawing of my own. I have the book "Female Ejaculation and the G-Spot"[35] in one hand and the deluxe crystal wand in the other. Enjoying self-pleasure, I am in a curious place of exploration. My own journey of self-awareness and sacred sexuality has brought me to this place of exploring my body and my yoni[36] with newfound knowledge and curiosity! The tips and suggestions in the book inspire me, and I've found that in order to create a safe space for my body to let go… I need to listen to her!

As I listen, I notice a deeply embedded fear of "wetting the bed" or peeing, rooted from childhood — all the training since age two to not let anything out of that place in my body unless I was sitting on a potty. Later a deep shame was rooted in: a time in second grade when the rule in class was that if you asked to go to the bathroom outside of the designated time, you would lose recess privileges. I had to go so badly, but was ashamed to ask for fear of being on the "bad kid" list. As I tried to hold it, I simply couldn't anymore and I peed in my pants on my chair. We were finally excused to go as a class, and I ran out of the classroom, mortified. I was deeply embarrassed, felt tremendous shame, and locked this energy into my urethra and pelvis in a way that stayed with me for decades. This was now holding me back during my new exploration. My body was clamping down to avoid being a "bad girl."

To acknowledge these fears, I decided to simply prepare for "So what if I do?!" by moving from the bed to the hardwood floor and adding the towel. My body drops into

---

[35] *Female Ejaculation and the G-spot* by Deborah Sundahl.

[36] Meaning "sacred space" in Sanskrit, Yoni is a term I used to honor the womb, vagina, vulva during this era. See Glossary.

another notch of relaxation because it will be super easy to clean up from here, no matter what happens. I let go of the worries of making a mess.

The wand reaches a delightful place inside my yoni... what I come to learn to be a "hot spot" of pleasure about two knuckles deep, on the anterior wall of my vagina. A place that I later come to recognize as only a small portion of the three-dimensional body of tissue that I come to delightfully know as my prostate. No, it's not only a "dime-sized spot on the wall" that I had been searching for decades ago. It's a whole body of tissue that responds as I listen to her, slowly, over time, beginning to release the layers of armor she has been hiding behind.

Lying on the floor as my G-spot continues to wake up, I feel myself building in arousal. The sexual energy I am cultivating is growing, and I find myself exploring the "bearing down" action encouraged in Sundahl's book that I had never known before — even through childbirth. This bearing down action finally awakens in me as I am learning to relax. The opposite of clenching and lifting upward that I am so used to in my orgasms, "bearing down" is about relaxing enough to have access to the muscles, then pushing when I feel the intensity of pleasure rising, and the sensation of "needing to pee."

I build and build, then relax and push. The energy shifts, it feels so good! I cycle through again and again. Building to near orgasm, I intentionally keep my fingers off of the exterior portion of my clitoris, which is hard for me! Touching my clit is my former "go-to" style of self-pleasure, and what I formerly exclusively relied on to reach orgasm. I feel that if I cascade over into a clitorally stimulated orgasm I may miss the opportunity to bloom open into an ejaculation. So I stroke internally with the wand, and I build and delight in the pleasure! And sure enough, after many prior "practice" sessions, today it happens...

...I build and push and AHHHH!! I ejaculate! Only a tiny few drops — which makes me giggle. All the worry about ruining the mattress, my first experience can be absorbed with a mere tissue! And yet the sensation is wildly pleasurable! WOW! I had no idea something like this was possible! I am filled with delight. I build more and more... and climax in a delightful orgasm that does not include another ejaculation (the ability to ejaculate through my orgasm doesn't happen until much later for me). I smile so big at the newfound opening in my body. Gratitude!

As I integrate and reflect on this experience by phone with Paul, who is on the West Coast, and later with a friend as we are out for a run... I realize how big this is. This is so big, feels so profound for me on this journey. And it is just the beginning! I feel at the *cusp of even more possibility! I've cracked open a glimmer into a realm of opening and feeling in my body, something I had to consciously make a choice to learn about. I had never heard of anything like this before and I feel as if no one ever talks about this stuff. No one in my world at the time, that is! I feel called to share... to stand on top of the mountain and shout "EVERY WOMAN AND THE PEOPLE WHO LOVE THEM DESERVE TO KNOW ABOUT THIS!"[37]*

Thus began my own personal journey of female ejaculation as well as stepping into my power and what soon became my life's work as a sex educator, transformational guide and healer.

Shibari – More Letting Go!

As if beginning my female ejaculation journey wasn't blowing my mind enough, Paul and I began to explore a new art form, one that I never would have expected would become a welcomed part of my life. In it, my journey of letting go bloomed open even more.

Paul and I are in my bedroom, a safe comfortable space with lavender walls, carefully chosen art, sacred objects from my travels and a deep soft comforter on my bed. It has been several hours since we began. Paul has the space heater on, and blankets and pillows surround me on the bed, creating the most nourishing pod of safe space. The white rope slides gently across my skin as Paul guides it into position along my inner thigh. He has planned knots and ties along my torso in such a way that I feel a supportive bind and gentle resistance to my breath, which I invite in full and deep, delighting in the pressure. Mmmmm... the compression delights me, and I drop into my body.

He honors my request not to remove the use of my arms and legs... I am not ready for that in these early explorations. I feel like this is a deep, dark, vast pool of mysterious possibility, and right now just dipping my toes in feels perfect. Instead, we focus on presencing into the moment. We explore the slow, exquisite art of the knots and ropes against the softness and curves of my body. He stays so present with me, focused, aware, checking in with my breath, my body, and my words as he works the rope with exquisite detail. I feel my skin open and my pores expand.

---

[37] I also acknowledge the gender spectrum — not all people with yonis identify as women. I acknowledge us all with love, and honor this journey as unique for all Beings.

We begin to explore the nature of my body opening, his touch, his mouth, his fingers playing the exquisite lute strings of my yoni lips, cultivating me open, coaxing me to come to him. With his fingers inside my yoni and the encouragement of his tongue and lips, my ejaculations begin, and become more and more voluminous. I am gushing and opening in pleasure. Mmmm! I feel myself letting go, Letting Go!

I find myself in a deep tingling space, trance-like, submissive, which is so powerfully new to me as a recovering control freak. I murmur in a deep soft voice, sensually, erotically: "I had no idea, I had no idea!" Together we feel the pleasure of what holding space for the divine feminine to move through our bodies can offer.

Afterwards I feel deeply present, plugged into my womb and my pelvis, in addition to being deeply relaxed. I feel empowered, strong and confident. The co-creation of this space is the embodiment of co-creating a "container," the safe space to feel supported to open, a concept we will be exploring in much more detail in Part 3.

We have opened into the ancient art of *shibari*, a Japanese rope art commonly associated with bondage and domination. This was definitely something that at first glance I wasn't so sure I wanted to do. When looking up *shibari*, I saw photos of bodies that seemed to be contorted and in pain, and pain was NOT what I was looking for.

Yet I felt safe with Paul, and I knew we could go slow, so when he asked me to consider exploring it with him, my adventurous self figured what the heck, "It can't hurt to try it once!" He was excited to get a chance to experience actively roping me.

I ended up deeply in an altered state of consciousness and a state of relaxed, submissive bliss. My body relaxed more then ever, my skin opened up, I experienced feeling very cold, even in a very warm room, and Paul would take care of putting on heaters and blankets to make me feel comfortable.

This external binding, in ways that felt safe and within my current body resources — also to be explored in Part 3 — can support a loosening and unwinding of internal body binding, places where we feel stuck. In my case, the internal bondage resulted in large measure from my emotional response to untrustworthy caregivers. I also lovingly refer to these internal binds or stuck spots as skills learned to protect myself. Those skills are not "bad" per se — they got me through a lot of things. Yet as I build new resources I can learn new skills of trusting myself and my body and learn new ways of letting go. Here, having the bondage in place with a trusted partner addresses both the physical knots within and their emotional precursors. This is powerful practice for healing all the impacted layers of our being: emotional, mental, spiritual, physical — not just one layer. Addressing and shifting our whole selves, not just one facet, is what creates lasting and cumulative change.

In the sacred sessions with *shibari* that continued, we explored states of letting go that my body had never experienced before, and my ejaculations became more and more accessible and abundant. We had opened a new door in my sexuality, and there was no turning back.

Art, Music, Sound Healing

Paul and I co-created in other ways. We had been called since the moment we first met to explore me painting as he played music. We spent many hours like this, me moving paint across the canvas as he played improvisational guitar. He had many guitars, each a different lover, and he danced with them and me. I felt him move through me in song and vibration. Each of us muse for the other.

My art bloomed open. I created more and more pieces as he and I deepened together. With his support, I felt myself taking more emotional risks in my painting. I also began to notice the types and styles of music that I felt called to listen to changed, and healing happened as I resonated with new layers of vibration. His playing also grew and changed as he met my energies of support and validation, allowing him to be even more fully himself.

જી ❁ ୠ

Meanwhile, my study with Jean Houston's Mystery School had been ongoing since that first workshop. Jean and her associate Peggy Rubin, who brought in her work with Sacred Studies of the Divine Feminine and Sacred Theatre,[38] were the core leaders in Mystery School. Jean and Peggy also encouraged co-creation of the Teaching/Learning Community with all of us as students and teachers contributing. This marked the completion of my fourth Spiritual Objective and opened the door to Paul and I connecting as well as the gates to my final three objectives:

---

[38] https://peggyrubin.com/

7. Live creating, painting with Paul playing improv guitar in person together

8. Jean's Mystery School workshop series (completed the series in 2007, and continued for two more years)

9. And finally… full circle, completion, the very thing that started it all comes back….

But first, through those years with Jean and Peggy and our Mystery School community, I had been learning how to connect with my 'entelechy' — my authentic soul purpose, and my gift to share with the world. My vision of supporting people to find and connect with their true paths had become clear: "illuminating the path of self-realization." I knew that yoga, meditation, art, sound/music, sacred geometry and sacred sexuality were all a part of it. Yet, the specifics were vague. Honing in on those details was the next piece. My intellectual, control-freak self wanted to see the whole picture clear ahead of me, yet my spiritual self knew that trusting in each step of unfolding had been working and would continue to support me in that knowing. Trust: Take the leap and the net appears… or you grow wings to soar! Yes, indeed!

Painting by author, from a vision in meditation: Entelechy — acrylic on canvas 16''x20'', 2007

So in May 2007, I started my company, One Space, LLC: "Illuminating the Path of Self-Realization through Art, Yoga, Meditation, Sacred Geometry, Sacred Sexuality and more." The pieces started clicking into place.

First, I designed and built my website by myself, incorporating my art and sacred geometry into the design. Building the website was like the first bridge between these worlds under my feet as I made this leap — a way to take my science and art background and apply it to my new work in the world. Learning the new software tools to do this was accessible, something that I could wrap my brain around in my rapidly changing world. It felt safe, and I felt some accomplishment toward my new path.

Second, I prepared web images of my artwork to create an online gallery and created and sold prints of the paintings in addition to the originals. I began submitting to art shows, and was honored to have several pieces at Alex Grey's CoSM Gallery in New York for a show in the summer of 2007.

Also, as I mentioned earlier, Sacred Geometry had become a large influence in my journey, serving as a way to connect spirituality and science. I came to know Sacred Geometry as a language of creation. As I began developing and teaching sacred geometry classes, I also learned how to shape my teaching so that I could better share this way to bridge the physical and the metaphysical with others. This helped me illuminate a path to offer esoteric wisdom to folx who were more familiar with the science of 3D reality.

This was a new growth edge for me: how to teach from a place that was not simply reading from a book or using a presentation. It was much more tender for me than learning to build a website, or creating prints of my art. As a student in public schools in the Midwest in the 70s and 80s, I primarily learned through books and being "talked to." I am now recognizing the importance in my life and career shift of shaping and teaching those early Sacred Geometry classes. I had to begin to trust that the knowledge was in the experience, not just in the words I offered. I shaped the classes to offer words and background about metaphysical world history that may not look like what people expected it to be. Plus, I offered quite directly: "Don't just take the words I am saying at face value — go in and draw the circles." The experience of putting pencil to paper and actually shaping and recreating these forms invites the deeper learning. The drawing tools and physical experience through the body of using them teaches us.

I recall at the time totally doubting myself in that. I had never consciously experienced receiving teachings in this way, although I am sure it happened. I had always associated learning with lectures and books, so to offer an experience of inviting my students into their own visceral experience of creating something and having that wisdom arise from physical experience was hard for me as a teacher. I recall being really shy about it, thinking things like: "Oh my god, are people going to think that this is silly?" Or: "How can I fill this experience with more words so it can be more credible?" Plus other stories arising from doubt.

Developing my own teaching style in this way was a perfect way to begin other kinds of both teaching and learning. The pieces were beginning to fall into place, and my Ninth Spiritual Objective was drawing near: a spiritual journey to Egypt.

CHAPTER TEN
Egypt and Healthy Masculine

Manifesting Egypt

Fall 2006 — I feel Egypt calling me again. It's now several months after returning from Peru. I feel drawn to make a spiritual pilgrimage to Egypt, to bring a balance of the energies. Peru was such a divinely feminine opening, and I felt Egypt calling me in to support a healing of my masculine. Yet despite the spiritual call, my rational self can't see how it will happen. These are both major trips, taking a large amount of time and money that my rational self can't compute in the logistical realm. These are the thoughts in my rational brain: Clearly since I did one major trip, I must be done for now. How can I do another one? How can I afford it?

Yet I feel the call. It's strong. Finally I declare, "Okay, Spirit, I hear you telling me I am to go to Egypt. Please help. This is the budget I need to go. Please show me how, and bring me the abundance I need to make the trip."

At work, we are at a time of serious downturn in the industry and economy, and the company I work for has already announced there will be no raises or bonuses this year. I find myself in a position of needing to release to the Universe the means of obtaining the extra money. I logically see no way that I will get it. Yet I am convinced in my heart that if I am meant to travel to Egypt, the Universe will show me the way. So I put out the call to Spirit, I journal about it, I continue to do my human homework, and I release it.

It is now a week or two later. I am called into the office by my director for a private discussion. He shares with me that while the company is navigating a serious downturn, they acknowledge that there are key individuals whose services they value to keep the company moving through hard times. I am one of those people, and they are offering me a one-time bonus. He slides a piece of paper across the table to me and I look to see that, after taxes, it is exactly the amount I had asked for from the Universe!

Wow, it happened. My request for support from the Universe has been answered. I smile and say to my boss, as well as to Spirit, "I am so grateful! Thank you so much. I know exactly what this money is for."[39]

This was the final piece clearing the way for me to complete the ninth and final Spiritual Objective: I am going to Egypt. Preparations begin for this journey to take place the following year:

Spiritual Objective #9: Egypt, November 2007

Egypt

Paul and I are in a hotel room in Giza, Egypt. Making love, we feel a soft energy, and relax into it. In the end I have a soft ejaculatory orgasm after he ejaculates inside me. Although sometimes we will choose to retain his semen and recirculate the energy, it is also a gift to receive him in this way, allowing our fluids to blend alchemically... ah... sweet, soft sounds emanate from our bodies.

Then something amazing happens: the "seeing thing." Like many times before as I move sexual energy, I am starting to see visuals, typically with my eyes closed. However this time is different, more powerful. This time my eyes are open in the darkened room. I see swirls of energy, spirals that then move to light the way, as if illuminating an ancient Egyptian wall covered in markings, inscriptions of some sort. The energy moves and lights up different parts. Then I see what I call "the grids," these geometries and lines connecting, eyes abundant, in a lattice-like field... and then: Orbs!!

Thousands of them, just like in the digital photographs we've been taking here. In the digital photographs, often we would capture not only what our regular vision saw but also little round dots of transparent light. People in our group, and many others, have theorized that they are energetic beings surrounding us, perhaps spirit guides or ancestors, their presence less obvious to the naked eye. Yet they were able to be captured in the photographic images. This was a new concept to me; I felt a little unsure about it. So to see them now with my naked eye feels even more unique, and yet very affirming of the theory. I can see the orbs and I play with watching them for a long time, moving in

---

[39] I acknowledge that privilege is a huge player in my capacity to manifest in this example and often overlooked in white spiritual circles, and I was not aware of it in this era.

and out of focus, shifting my awareness. I see energies, like wisps of light on my fingers, then on Paul's fingers and like an aura line around us.

In my preparations through the year for Egypt, I set intention, absorbed information about initiations and the ancient sacred sites through a DVD[40] and several books, and meditated for support and guidance. I continued my spiritual journey, completing Objectives Seven and Eight and honoring their completion with a leaf eating ritual. The visionary paintings I was creating at the time were inspired by the visuals during meditations. Early in the year, we realized Paul was meant to go as well, and he and I together prepared our bodies through our sacred sexual connections as well.

As a masculine center on the planet, Egypt was dryer, hotter and more fiery than Peru. I knew this would be a different experience, the polar opposite in fact, and a very necessary balance to my earlier journey. I anticipated a deepening with my divine feminine through healing my masculine, holding space. My beautiful partner Paul and I set off once again to meet our tour leader Sarah and the others in our group, this time in Cairo, Egypt.

It is a hot, sunny day with reds and oranges, like fire in the sky. We arrive at Dahshur by bus and step out into the desert, dry, hot. Inside the Red Pyramid, we go down through a tunnel into the cool inner chambers. My body appreciates the shift in temperature. We are in the vibration chambers, and my rose quartz sphere sings along with a tuning fork struck by one of our trip guides. I see more orbs, in the ceilings. I feel. We move on. I collect stones near the Bent Pyramid before we move to the Step Pyramid and the healing temples at Sakkara, the ancient hospital, this center for sound and vibrational healing.

We take turns moving into a chamber with three niches in the walls... one to the left, one to the right and one in the center. I place my head inside the left niche and make sounds with my voice and my body (I "tone") and feel. I notice a feminine, soft quality. In the niche to my right, as I place my head inside and tone, I notice a more linear, direct energy, more masculine. Then I move to the center niche. I place my head inside and tone and, as I do, I see a column of white and blue energy with a billowing top and experience a sense of coming together, of integration of the masculine and feminine. I feel a gratitude

---

[40] *Nine Initiations on the Nile* by Barbara Hand Clow.

for this initiation, and a sense of new balance. As we exit this temple, our guides ask what we notice, as I share about my experience I receive an affirmation: I am not the only one who sensed this feminine/masculine integration. It is only then that they reveal that is also what they knew to be true about this space, and why they invited us to explore it.

Later, I paint what I saw in the center and it becomes the Integration at Sakkara, 2007, acrylic on canvas, 12''x12''.

This journey was another piece of my Spiritual quest for deepening my connection with the sacred masculine and feminine energies and integrating them together with balance. It was about remembering, in fact reactivating, the cellular memory of who I am. I feel a knowing of having been a sacred sexual priestess in Egypt in prior lifetimes, and this visit supported pieces of me to reawaken to my authentic path. Recall how my initial draw in my calling to Egypt started with the big cat energy with which I had felt a kinship all my life, from deep within and as a part of me. I met this deep energy once again. This time, I met her face to face.

Sekhmet Initiation

We arrive at the Temple of Karnak. Ram sphinxes line our way into the vast main complex with towering pillars, filled with hieroglyphs. After we spend time in the main structure, we are guided into a special hidden temple space where we have the honor of meeting Sekhmet in her chapel! We slowly make our way through the antechambers, honoring each of the keepers of the space. We finally step deep into the holy of holies, the dark chamber of Sekhmet herself. We hold ceremony. I open to receiving her energies. At her statue, our tour guides tell us it is made of a dark green basalt, so dark it appears black, and that it is ancient, of the era of 4000 BCE.

With deep reverence and respect, I feel the essence of her there. I breathe in the energy of her fierce compassion. Warrior Goddess, Goddess of Love, Opener of Ways, I call to Sekhmet for sexual healing, and find my body offering a heart-opening backbend as I meet her. I am filled with deep gratitude as I begin my journey of walking with her in this lifetime.

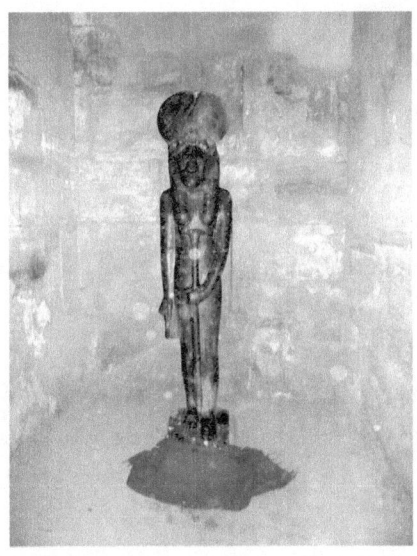

Sekhmet in her temple at Karnak, 2007

My initiation with Sekhmet in the temple, 2007

As I have done at each of the temples, I also held space for my mesa bundle of sacred items to be charged with the vibration of the space, in particular here the rose quartz sphere and the quartz pyramid ask to be seen, as well as the garnet necklace, the sweet gift from Paul.

While still at Karnak, we also explored the large statue of a scarab, seen to be a representation of renewal and immortality, and a symbol of good luck. It was said that if one walks seven times in a circle around the scarab and shares a wish, it would come true. I walked the seven circles, and I offered the intention I had been working with in my life at the time:

> *"I have clarity in my gift to share with the world and I step into this new space with grace and confidence. I have the abundance to leave my corporate career with safety and peace."*

Indeed, the intention I set that day was realized. Less than a year later, I left my corporate career and began my deep authentic work in the world. Was it the seven circles around a scarab statue in Egypt? Perhaps it helped. Yet within my being, I know that I am empowered in the creation and re-creation of my life. My transition away from career world wasn't only a leap into the unknown. I had been preparing for it for years. The power of the changes we can create in our lives is in our own hands. Doing my human homework, finding my connection with Spirit, opening to the support of my partners and allies, and walking the path of listening deeply to my body supported me in making these changes.

Egypt was also about connecting with my joys, not even knowing all the reasons why at the time, just knowing I had to make certain connections. For example, I had hoped to find and see the ancient inscription of the Flower of Life in person, its deep mysteries a rich and important part of my journey on the path of Sacred Geometry, and of Drunvalo's work. From his books, I knew I would be able to find it here.

As we explore the temples at Abydos, the Sacred Geometry geek in me is filled with joy. We learn about the story of Isis and Osiris, and do a ceremony to clear the old and move through death to rebirth. Additionally, I am thrilled to witness the balance of feminine and masculine once again as I am introduced to Seshat, the lesser known neter (the word for the Egyptian deity, god/goddess, or archetype) of Sacred Geometry. Having first learned about Thoth as the neter of Sacred Geometry, it resonated deeply to see that there were really two, in balance, both as scribes: the feminine and masculine neters of language and sacred geometry. I see them opposite each other on the walls here, often in support of each other.

Seshat – the neter (Egyptian goddess) of Sacred Geometry

Thoth – the neter (Egyptian god) of Sacred Geometry

After we explore inside the large, columned structure at Abydos, we walk outside of the dark inner temples and into the bright sunlight. I know that I will be able to see, in person, the ancient symbol of the Flower of Life inscribed on the ancient stone walls. Sure enough, here it is! At the Osireon, there are large stone columns rising out of a pool of water at their base, with openings between them. On the shadowy wall inside one of the openings, I finally see it: the familiar interlocking circles. I feel in awe and wonder to gaze upon this mystery. I feel tingles and receive the vibration of being in the presence of this ancient Flower of Life inscription. The Flower of Life represents the knowledge and wisdom of creation using the language of geometry, and it offers the keys to unlock wisdom of the creation cycle.[41]

---

[41] For more exploration, see *The Ancient Secret of the Flower of Life: Volumes 1 & 2* by Drunvalo Melchizedek.

Flower of Life. CAD drawing by author, 2008

As I continued to explore, I felt the strength and power in the vulnerability of my opening at the temple of Sekhmet. The beauty of music being created and shared as Paul played guitar at the temple at Edfu even inspired the birds to come to join us. I collected scarves, essential oils, galabeyas (a traditional type of clothing worn in the Nile Valley) and sacred objects for my mesa. The trip was filled with initiations, temples, sound healing, sacred sexuality. My moon time (menstrual cycle) ended with the New Moon, and happened to be on the day we spent at Kom Ombo, the temple associated with the second chakra or sexual center. This connection of my moon time, womb and the sexual center's relationship with the temple was not lost on me. I felt a moon rebirthing as I cleansed and moved into my own rebirth.

Throughout the trip I learned more about sacred sexuality and how to raise the life force energy (sekhem, kundalini) up the spine (djed), symbolized in the divine union of Isis and Osiris. I met deep inquiry in my body, gazing upon the tools of resurrection inscribed on the walls, used in these ancient times. This connection of sacred sexuality and consciousness, divine connection and transcendence — there are keys here that unlock these pieces. I felt curiosity and wonder as my experiences generated questions rather than answers, opening the gates to learning even more upon my return. And in a similar way, I introduce these topics for you to explore if you wish. You may find a sense of familiarity, a remembering, intrigue, mystery and excitement in this study, as I did.

As our guides and speakers shared with us, these ancient sites and their energies have been in existence since a time before and during the age of Aten, when awareness and understanding transcended the need for written communication. We are now leaving the Age of Amen, the darkness, heading toward a major shift, awakening to the light and to a new dawn.

Take a breath with me, exhale. Notice your body. What a beautiful time to be alive, to be a part of this amazing transformation, and to teach and learn from others along the way. The deep mystery — the more I open to knowing, the more I know I don't know.

During and around this trip, my dreams were rich and many. I saw themes of getting guidance about corporate life: A little more time is needed, and I will know when it's time. Many of the dreams had the number nine, and even the preparatory information I was reviewing had nines in the titles. Nine to me represents a closing, the ending of a cycle, the last single digit before beginning a new cycle with the number 10. The message that my time in corporate life was coming to a close was clarifying, but when and how were still quite foggy.

The journey also brought us back full circle, serving as a completion of the invitation from the shaman in Peru 18 months prior to set and meet my Nine Spiritual Objectives. And it also happened to be exactly one year after Paul and I met. Back at home, I held ceremony to complete the final ritual, lighting a red candle and a white candle to honor the integration of feminine and masculine energies respectively, and I ate the final coca leaf, bringing closure to this set of Spiritual Objectives:

1. Transformational Breath – a powerful embodied practice of breathing that opens pathways in the body (7/27/06)
2. Painting – Intuitive Painting workshop, finding my guidance on drawing and painting what I see in meditation, and exploring my content (8/12/06)
3. "Flowering Ceremony" – Flower of Life workshop, exploring Drunvalo Melchizedek's teachings through a local teacher Lorna Brown (11/24/06)
4. Jean Houston workshop (12/5/06)
5. Alex Grey's art gallery – "Chapel of Sacred Mirrors" (CoSM) (12/5/06)
6. Paint to Paul's music (remotely via CD) (12/21/06)
7. Live creating, painting with Paul playing improv guitar in person together (1/14/07)
8. Jean's Mystery School workshop series (completed the series in 2007, and continued for two more years)
9. Egypt, November 2007

I acknowledged it was just the beginning as the spiral continued into the next cycle. With this completion, going into 2008 I held intention to receive clarity on my gift to share with the world and my move into teaching, supporting others on their path with grace and confidence. Open and loving with purpose and direction: Love in Action!

ଚ ❀ ଚ

The big change drew closer.

The auto industry continued its serious downturn. Since I was in the top-performance tier of my position, I felt very secure that I would not be a target of the layoffs. However, in my management role, I was frequently in the position of delivering notices of job terminations to other people on my team. It was a hard time. When the company first started offering severance packages and asking for voluntary terminations, I didn't even pause to consider them. I still very much had it in my head that I would be there until retirement.

Until something happened.

The downturn started hitting so hard that the company was making cuts everywhere. One day an announcement came that the company-subsidized childcare centers that had been an enormous value to me and many other parents were being closed down. I was flabbergasted. The decision was unilateral and final. A huge call from parent employees went out within the company. One plea was to consider allowing the parents the choice of paying more for the childcare and keeping the centers open, relieving the company of the cost yet keeping the much-needed value to the parents. The response to our offer was paltry and appalling: We had been brushed off. The centers were closing with no further consideration.

I had much gratitude that the closing had coincided with an opportunity for summer care at another center, followed by Hannah's beginning kindergarten that autumn. Because of this, we as a family were able to recover easily. Not so much for other parents.

This was the key that clicked open the door of awareness for me. Was it because it hit such a core place in my being: taking away the support of my little girl? Yes. It directly impacted my young daughter. But it was it also a mirror, helping me see and connect with the little girl within myself. I saw how she was asking for support from *me*, and that I couldn't just expect it from organizations outside of myself. It was time. I felt myself ready to stand up for her… for me. I felt myself owning a new level of my healthy masculine, holding space for the support of that little one inside me.

Seeing how my daughter could be impacted, the inner messages and dreams now precipitated into action. It became clear that this was the long-awaited time. After 15 years in corporate engineering, my time there, while it had been important for me and served me well, had come to an end. I went to my director to ask about the severance package offer.

Leaving Corporate Life

The process of leaving was a pivotal shift in my life, trusting animal wisdom, spirit guidance, vision quest intention. Spirit guided me to leave, but I couldn't see more than a step or two in front of me, and I was making one of the biggest changes of my life. Part of me was really scared. A deeper, more authentic part knew and trusted completely. As I shared in Part 1, Dragonfly showed me the way. And, as my playful side started getting some breathing room, my stuffy, conservative self started recognizing the need for change.

I am working from home, a common occurrence in my last year or so with the company. I find I can be more productive in an environment that allows me to be comfortable, rather than having to dress in constrictive formal business clothing and steep in stale windowless buildings and stuffy cubicles. I am effective working remotely, and because of this I am given the opportunity. It also allows me to be flexible with my work schedule.

As I now have one foot in corporate America and the other in my sacred sexual path, the combination begins to paint new pictures of productivity. It also fills me with joy and makes me giggle!

Paul and I are in the living room. He has tied me up, which has my erotic juices flowing, my yoni dripping with ecstasy as he takes photos and slides his cock inside me. Mmmm, yes. More please!

We explore and delight in each other.

Then... Bing!

Clock time calls, and I respond to the call of duty: It's time for my weekly meeting. I get up, naked except for the ropes still bound across my torso, grab a blanket to wrap up in and walk to my home office in our back room. I set up the conference call, and dial in to run the weekly meeting. Sitting at my desk with my headset on, typing at my laptop, and speaking with my corporate tone of voice — all of this as I sit wrapped in nothing but a blanket and ropes. Eeeee! Yes! This is what I call work-life balance!

I giggle as I replay this image in my head! It was happening: My body knew it was time to move on. The transition time brought a lot of planning and reorganizing. Everything in my life had been woven in and through the company. Choosing to leave meant I had to turn in my company car and buy a new one on my own. New insurance, shifts in bank accounts and retirement savings, changing ways I had been doing things for years. I needed to figure out how to streamline my life to live without a paycheck for the first time since I was 15 years old. And at the same time, the universe supported me each step of the way. Doors opened that I hadn't even known existed, let alone could have asked for. Finally, the day came.

I am wearing a vibrantly colored silk wrap skirt with my favorite oranges and reds richly flowing around me. I love this skirt and until today have not worn it to work for fear of it not being "conservative" enough. Today is my last day in the corporate world. I walk in, my boxes already packed, my desk cleared. The only thing left is the formal meeting with my manager. He delivers the speech and the papers, I thank him and I leave.

It's an odd feeling... walking out of the huge building and complex for the last time, and so early in the "workday."

I drive home. Paul is waiting as we had planned, and I feel so grateful. He receives me, holds me in his arms as I pour open in a pool of tears... grief and sadness, joy and overwhelm... all of these emotions flowing and just pouring through me.

I feel a strange space, the place where the heaviness of the stress and responsibilities of the corporate career are no longer here. Yet knowing they are there, left behind, I just no longer choose to carry them. I release them. I feel lighter, brighter more colorful! Wheeeeee! It is time!

And it was just the beginning.

The life changes felt natural to me. I took the opportunity to create much more time with my daughter and shape my new career as a self-employed person around my schedule with her.

Since I no longer had a paycheck, it seemed logical to start to spend less. Yet while things like spending way less money might have seemed hard to do, they weren't. They didn't feel forced, and I didn't feel lacking. I chose to release the need for "stuff." It no longer felt good to buy unnecessary things. I let go of wearing business clothing that no longer suited me, which also meant releasing dry cleaning bills and hassle. I was teaching my daughter by example: At only six years old she was noticing how many toys were over-packaged in materials that just ended up in a landfill, and she started to see the value of choosing options that helped support the Earth.

Here's an example of how simplifying my life worked for both my own new financial situation and the planet. For years I had been paying money to turn on lawn sprinklers in the spring, pay for extra water to run them during the summer, pay for lawn care service to spray chemicals on my grass, pay for a service to cut the growth, then pay for the sprinklers to be turned off again in the fall. I released this cycle of destructive consumption, and began to manage my own lawn organically, with no extra water and a non-motorized mower. Not only did I save money, I was helping the environment, and in fact spending less time on it because the need for mowing lessened as it grew less! Breaking this pattern freed up energy and resources for other uses — recall the Clearing Clutter discussion in Chapter 6 and Recipe R4. What a win-win situation! Things like this started happening like crazy. Spirit was showing me the way, affirming each step I took toward my authentic life.

As I did, my next spiritual steps became clear. Spirit had been calling me to a new level. The outward journeys had served well in preparation, and now I felt the call was guiding me deep within. Spirit kept nudging me: The words "Vision Quest" kept coming my way. I wasn't even sure what that was at first. I began to learn that a Vision Quest is about stripping away the exterior world and journeying into nature for connection to spirit guidance and deep self-inquiry and awareness. This resonated strongly, and I felt much gratitude when a friend from Mystery School pointed the way so that I found myself connected to Rose Khalsa, a powerful woman with long mahogany hair and a huge heart. Rose integrates Native American (Ojibway), Celtic and Tibetan Buddhist practices into her life and work, and shares these as part of her Medicine and nature-based shamanic teachings.[42]

---

[42] Rose Khalsa, http://polaritycenter.org/

CHAPTER ELEVEN

Vision Quest and Throat Opening

2008 — I am hot, scared. I feel crowded-in, suffocated. Sweat pours off my face, down my neck. I feel repulsion as I stick to myself, and my sarong clings heavy against my skin. Sitting on the bare Earth, I pull myself in, I feel I should be smaller, take up less space. So many of us have crowded into this small, handmade structure of wood and canvas, sitting in a tight circle: 11… maybe 12? Yet I know I feel called to this. I trust.

The smoldering hot stones — grandfathers — rest in a sacred pile in the center of the circle in the earthen floor. Every so often another is very intentionally put in place. Water and herbs are added to the hot stones, creating steam, and the healing medicines fill the air in the tiny space. They open a portal. My teacher sits next to the opening of the tiny structure we are inside, and I realize that because of the order we filed in, I have landed in the spot directly opposite the opening to the sweat lodge and the fire outside. A place of honor, I find out later. At the moment, it doesn't feel that way. It feels awful, as if I have the worst possible escape route. There's no way past all the people between me and the door, in either direction. I am doing my best to be with the process and not freak out.

My teacher begins to sing, inviting us to join.

Sing? I don't sing. I don't have a good voice. This is the story I told myself long ago. Fifth grade chorus. My parents, maybe? Someone told me I wasn't good enough. I learned I should keep my mouth shut. Don't ask questions. This is what I know. I don't sing, so what do I do? This feels so hard. I hold it in. I feel worse.

I hear a cricket… gently calling. Right behind me, he must be on the wall of the sweat lodge. He's calling to me. The sound carries directly to my ear, as if meant just for me. Cricket sings his sweet song, so close…

"Don't be afraid to use your voice."

I find a strange reassurance in it.

Yes, I must sing. I let go into it. I sing. The vibrations, the sound, the songs. I begin slowly, quietly. Nervous, someone might hear me and tell me to stop. I worry about being a bother to someone. Yet the sounds move through me — I let go into them, I rely on them, they carry me. They carry me through the tough spots, I ride above the pain and intensity. They free me of my old story. I see the colors, indigos, purples, swirling, even in the darkness with my eyes open. The amazing, powerful voice vibrations create a resonance in my body and give me the strength to move through the four rounds of the sweat lodge. I SING! I TONE! I VIBRATE with sound, I AM sound, I AM rhythm, I feel the healing of trusting into this flow. I let go!

I was filled with gratitude: for Spirit, for Cricket, for trusting and letting go. This experience in sweat lodge was a part of our journey inward in preparation for a three-day Vision Quest that followed. It marked an important step in my journey to find my voice, to speak my truth. My throat began to awaken that day, initiating the long journey of finding and using my voice.

My first Vision Quest, a deep initiation into spirit guidance and awareness of self, was guided by Spirit to happen synchronistically just three weeks after I left the corporate world in 2008. I couldn't have planned it better if I had tried. Luckily, I was getting used to these 'flow spaces,' the ways the Universe aligns and supports ease when I am following my authentic path without me needing to control it, and my analytical brain wasn't nearly as jealous. It was an initiatory experience, as if inviting me to cross the threshold into my authentic life and calling. There I released my old life into the fire and created space for new beginnings. This late-summer journey, taken on sacred land in upstate New York, was where I remembered my name.

I am tired and cold. There's no sun yet in my sacred space, the area of land I have claimed as Vision Quest camp. This space I have delineated with spiritual intention and prayer flags, I am not to leave unless to walk to the sacred fire. I am nearly 48 hours into the 72-hour fast and solo time on the land that is part of this intentional spiritual journey. My body is feeling the exhaustion, lack of food and lack of warmth. I decide to walk to the fire, to feel the heat, to move, and dare I say… to pray.

To pray?

I have a hard time with this word... it carries a lot of baggage for me. It rings of dogmatic religion and a history that does not resonate for me. Yet now I've come to know that by "pray," I mean to connect with Spirit with intention, to ask, to receive, to offer, to love. Yes please, that resonates: I walk to the fire to pray.

Head shrouded in my sarong to keep my intention of deepening in inward awareness, I slowly, one foot in front of the other, make the trek down the hillside from my tree-lined camp, through the switchbacks into the meadow and to the sacred fire at its center. I pray. I call to the seven directions for support and guidance and protection. I feel the call. It's time to ask. Spirit, please help me remember: What is my Spirit name? I wait.

My body is a clear channel now, I feel myself connected to the rhythms of the sun and Earth. I know time not by a clock or watch but by the sun's position, by the feel of the shadows, the sensations in my body. It feels so good to be present with these sensations, and the movements and rhythms.

I wait. I listen. I pray.

This question has been part of my intention for this journey. To remember deeply who I am. I am nervous to ask — what if I don't get an answer? What if I don't like the answer?

I brush that off... no, I am ready. I am a channel for the answer.

What is my Spirit name?

"Light Bearer"

It comes through simply. Cleanly, concisely. Like, "Of course this is the answer, haven't you known all along?" It hits strongly. It feels BIG. Too big? Is this really it? Can I live up to this?

"YES you can."

Is this my calling?

"Yes it is."

I breathe, I cry, I share deep gratitude. I rest. Gently, I allow myself to receive this. I feel the "yes" in my body, the tingles, the knowing. Yet, for good measure I decide to sit with it for the day.

I walk back to my sacred space and ask: "Is this my name? Is Light Bearer really the one?" Just then, a shiny black salamander with an electric blue tail reveals itself, and looks so out of place. Wow! I haven't seen you before. Other creatures — slugs and insects, even deer — have been here, but not once have I seen anything so brightly colored and seemingly out of place in this forest.

"I'm not like everybody else," she says.

Indeed. Thank you for encouraging me to remember my calling. Yes, being unique is wonderful, and we ALL are beautifully unique in our authenticity. I am the only one who can be me. You are the only one who can be you. I commit to being me in the fullest.

Days later, after returning from solo time on the land, integrating with the group and preparing to return home, my teacher and I share a beautiful goodbye. She gazes deeply into my eyes and says, "You too are from the Star Nation, but I think you already knew that. We're Light Beings. Share that light, Light Bearer." It felt good, validating, clean.

We are all unique beings. You are the only one in the Universe who can be you so well. What's calling to you? How do you wish to express yourself? What are you feeling called to do? Who do you feel called to learn from? To be around?

Re-Entry

Wow! During the months after leaving the corporate world, and in the integration time post Vision Quest, I felt as if I had just landed on another planet. The strange sensation of having all of this space and time available felt liberating, yet part of me worried that because I wasn't at a job with a paycheck, that somehow it wouldn't work.

Through my connection with Paul, I was grateful to see other templates, other possibilities of making a living. His work as a musician and sound engineer, creating sound for and recording workshops led by prominent authors and teachers, took him across the country for stretches: a weekend workshop here, week-long intensive there, then a week or two of post-processing time back in his home office. All of this peppered with downtime that could last a couple of weeks. Often, this is when he would visit. I could see, through this model, ways that were much more fluid, much more creative in time and space. Ways that didn't include life in a colorless cubicle, inside buildings with no windows, 7 a.m. to 6 p.m. Monday through Friday, and daily commutes in rush-hour traffic. I could begin to create my own days and hours, shape how and when I spent my energy and time.

I was also grateful to have a nest egg of financial support from my leaving the company that would give me the space to sink in to learning, deepening and undergoing the process of creating, gestating and giving birth to the authentic path: my gift to share with the world. Yet that nest egg had a fixed size, and my logical self worried that it wouldn't last long enough. Thankfully, the authentic self in me was trusting more and more. I knew the way would present itself; I was trusting in the flow, taking steps to follow the guidance, and opening to receive more.

This time was a slow process of sinking in with myself and body sensation, and like layers of an onion, I'd pull each layer back and go: "Wow, I wonder if there's more?!" It was no longer just the self-directed will that had driven me from old times, it was the light from within me illuminating the way. I felt my higher self beckoning: "Come to me, come to me, I want to show you who you are. I want you to know who you are!"

Even now, so many years later, as I reflect with Paul, he shares his memory of me during that time:

> You were driving and doing the to-do list, but your inner self was saying: "Just Be." Like my Great Aunt Marty used to say: "Don't push. Let."

> It was a hard thing for you to do.

> The higher self in all of us, it wants to be seen, wants to be heard. It wants us to know, it beckons us. Higher self says, "Don't be so distracted! That takes you away from being who you are. Stop for a moment."

> HARD! This was so hard for you... as you were so much in a driven corporate world.

> You have made the journey, you have heard that call! You have felt that spark inside you and to feel and to go, "Oh, hey — what's over there? How can I explore this? What's over there?" And you had the guts, and courage. You left a really big thing!

> I am so proud — I was at the time and I am now — so proud of you for doing that. What greater thing is there to see than someone you love and care for grow? It's like seeing a miracle.

> The way you touch people makes a difference in their lives. When we smile, when we spread love, that's our work. Now more than ever.

I realized fairly early on that this was bigger than just "doing" something different — it also meant I must "be" and process differently. I felt that if I tried to do the new things with my old way of processing, I was going to be in the same pattern of burning up and frying in no time.

I began viscerally shifting the way I approached life. Slowing down and noticing became a big part of how I processed. Certainly many of the business skills I had acquired during the corporate career helped me in what I was doing now. I was grateful for that.

Yet I realized this was about finding balance — the balance of the masculine analytical business processing skills that I had honed so sharply, with the feminine: slowing down, opening to intuitive and spiritual guidance and wisdom, and feeling and sensing messages of the body. This was new to me and the very balance of it was crucial.

Sometimes finding this balance felt really klutzy and uncomfortable. It wasn't as graceful as I had hoped. Sometimes it meant scheduling the time to slow down. Or forgetting to, and then noticing much later that I was still zooming around and hadn't noticed much at all. When it went well, I intentionally planned when I would take a few breaths outside, or reminded myself to sit for a minute. It may seem counterintuitive, but "the slow down and listen" had to be consciously planned into my day at first. Over time, it became more fluid and arose more spontaneously. And still it's true that creating the spaces and times for this letting go process actually helps it. It's not a bad thing to analyze and plan, it just needs to be balanced with space, breath, creative flow. This creates a Container that gives space for the change to happen. By planning it and practicing, it gave my brain a chance to rewire with the new patterns. Those new brain patterns then become a more natural flow. Recall our exploration of "Giving Your Brain a Chance" in Chapter 6.

My teacher Rose encourages me to spend more time in nature. More time in nature?! How the heck am I going to do that? I live in corporate suburbia: a grid of houses, sidewalks, neighborhood streets and power lines. Sure I can get in my car and drive to a local park or nature area, yet that isn't practical for day to day.

One step at a time. Time goes by, and I dip into my backyard for a breath here and there. It is nice to get outside, and yet still rare. I spend most of my time indoors. It feels weird to be outside in my backyard. I have no real privacy from my neighbors. I worry they will see me and wonder why I am just sitting here. Then I get a hit: The Earth is everywhere. While it can be nice to disappear in nature and be away from buildings and traffic, the reality is nature is also right here in my backyard. The spot of lawn by the cherry tree is just as much in connection with Earth as other places, and it is time to claim it in my being.

As I become more familiar with earth practices, I am able to do a ritual to clear the land and offer healing there. As I do, I feel a welcoming and a new safety. I can be in my backyard differently than before. It feels safer to simply rest here. Sure my neighbors are still in homes right near me, yet my own safety of roots in my space deepens. I can trust myself more, and simply be with the processes that are showing up. This spot becomes a resource, and I give myself more and more permission to spend time here.

Eventually, acknowledging my need to get my body connected, I began getting my bare feet on the ground back there. Over time, I began to lie down there. This is the spot where I later set up the teepee to create additional privacy and allowed my moon blood to flow in ritual connection with the earth. I danced there, moved, drummed, sang.

I listened to my body when it resonated and acted on something that I felt I needed to do, even when my logic brain questioned why. One such hit was the opportunity to do a yoga teacher training. I felt the call.

Yoga Teacher Training – Wisdom for Sharing My Medicine

At first I couldn't conceive of how it would be possible. I questioned my intuition: "Why are you doing this training? Teaching yoga isn't what you are planning to do for your new career. How does this fit?" Yet I felt the call from Spirit and I knew I must do the training. Rationally I figured this much: Maybe I would teach yoga for a bit as a transition, as it is a worthy skill all on its own. I knew the training was coming to me for many more reasons, although at that point I didn't know what they were. At the same time, I also realized I didn't need to plan it out, I simply needed to open up the possibilities and allow. Organizing how to handle the care of my daughter quickly opened up the door of opportunity for what the weekly training on Saturdays would look like, despite my initial logical resistance. With extreme gratitude to the Universe for showing me the way, I stepped into what would be yet another life-changing journey.

I am sitting with a circle of fellow students and our teacher. The large studio space is simple and quiet, with wooden floors, plain walls and a soft, low light. Shelves in the front of the room hold cotton blankets, bolsters, and other props for supporting asanas (yoga postures). We are seated on the floor, chanting, opening our sacred space, embarking on a 25-week journey, a 250-hour yoga teacher training.

Through the course of our first day, I diligently take notes in my journal, capturing various thoughts and bits from what our teacher is sharing with us, including:

- *Teacher will teach based on students capability to seek*
- *Don't try to change a student, you cannot – only they can*
- *Just suggest, recommend and get out of the way*
- *You are a channel for them to see their own truth*
- *Humility – recognize areas in ourselves we haven't opened up yet*
- *If you know you made a mistake, admit it*
- *Empower your students*
- *If ever in doubt, don't do it – err on the side of safety*
- *Be adaptive, come with a plan, but be prepared to throw it away*
- *Learn techniques – then intuitively weave the class together*
- *Process is more important than the destination*

We continue with more teachings, receive a binder with handouts and logs to be completed, lists of required texts. As we complete our closing chanting and meditation, I feel the potency.

We close and I step out into the bright August sunlight outside the studio and leave this first day of class feeling bright, tall, enthusiastic! It feels inspiring on so many levels. I love that I get to go buy books and supplies. It hearkens back to the excitement I used to feel getting ready for the first day of school — gathering supplies, organizing them. The geek in me loves this.

I also feel gratitude that Spirit aligned me with this teacher. He is from India, and is sharing such deep teachings from his culture and beliefs. This training is far more than how to do which pose, it is the deep essence of the philosophy of yoga as a way of life — preparation of the body, mind and spirit, ethics for the inner and outer realms. He's also including the richness of teaching us the exquisite, vibrational language of Sanskrit that carries profound meaning beyond the characters written on a page. This resonates deeply with me. I so look forward to soaking it in, absorbing and integrating. I am motivated to continue my meditation and journaling practices, both of which he has also assigned as homework. He also invites us to be mindful with food, and keep track of what we eat, and in our journals, how we feel. Yes, I take it all on: I am in for this journey.

As my yoga teacher training continued, I sank in with the many hours of observations, practice teachings, self practice. I wrote a paper, completed the final exam and finally was honored with receiving the certificate of completion for the 250-hour class that exceeded the Yoga Alliance (RYT-200) training requirements. This training became a foundation for teaching and sharing in ways that I hadn't expected in the beginning when I felt the call to sign up. Those nuggets of wisdom I captured, even on Day 1, became a foundation not only for teaching yoga, but for all of my teachings that continued to emerge.

Aerial Arts

As yoga teacher training and my own yoga practice progressed, I met another synchronistic opening: One of my yoga teachers began to teach aerial arts. The aerial fabrics and apparatus I had previously only seen used in Cirque du Soleil beckoned me; this style of performance was new to our area and I felt called to go learn more. I immediately fell in love with it. Once again my logical brain came in and said, "Why are you going to pursue this? You don't have time for this, you don't have money for this. What is it going to do for you?" These were old familiar ways my "censor" would come in and try to stop me from following a piece of my path.

Yet my heart and my body were ringing with such aliveness that I knew it would be an important piece of my journey. This was a part of my processing shift, my new approach to life. I HAD to do things differently. I had come so far with this spiritual journey, I wasn't about to stop now. So I followed my heart and stepped into this new phase of aliveness in my body as I began to learn aerial arts.

As I moved into this practice, the horizontal, forward-moving awareness of my swim, bike, run days was to get blown open into a whole new dimension: vertical. The vertical gave the space for new pieces of healing to happen, opening up levels of body awareness in an entirely different dimension. Old stories rose to the surface to be met.

I am seven years old. A warm, sunny day at the park, there are trees all around that are new to me, cypress, with that curious, curly, silvery moss. It looks different here; we had just moved. My hands are on the monkey bars, and I am swinging to bring my feet up to the bars, wheee!!

Only....
My hands slip, my feet don't reach the bar, and I see the sky.
THUMP!
I land on my back and upper shoulders and neck, on the earth.
I feel rocketed forward, up, out of my body. My breath is gone, I can't feel it. It's dark.
Hehhh! <sharp intake of breath> I open my eyes, light returns. Where am I? Who are these people? Where are my mom and dad?
I cry. I'm scared. What just happened?!

Thank God/dess it was sandy soil and not concrete! And gratitude that people were there to help me, but they were strangers to me. Eventually my parents were found, but it was shocking for me to have this intense experience and not feel safe to reintegrate. This was a traumatic event for little me. I realized later how the force of the impact knocked me up and forward out of my body. As a result, my capacity to fully inhabit the back of my body and the space surrounding it was rifted. Such energetic dislocations are actually quite common in car accidents, falls and other major impact events, and depending on how the body is resourced in the moment, are one way physical trauma can manifest in the body. We will touch on this more in Part 3.

While I didn't recognize in advance that this healing was needed, it came up as I was introduced to a new drop in aerial. It was an intellectually "simple" move on the static trapeze called "Bird's Nest." The performer is seated, hands on the bar, then leans back with legs wide. As long as you keep holding on to the bar and your legs go wide, they easily catch on the ropes and you are now in an upside down position in a new equilibrium.

However, there is a moment that you have to let go of control and allow your body to drop backwards. You are suspended in a moment of chaos. I felt a huge fear, and later realized the fear was tied to this time as a child when my body fell back like that and I got hurt. I feared losing the connection of my hands with the bar and my feet not landing where I wanted them to. My body remembered this event, even if I didn't cognitively remember right away.

Yet the drop is relatively simple, and really can be done easily for many people. My daughter, Hannah, who was only six at the time, was doing aerial with me. She was like, "Wheee! Look Mom, no problem! You can do it too!" as she easily learned the new move. Seeing her joy and ease helped spark my own courage. I thought: "Yes. I can do this, too." With Hannah and my teachers and fellow students cheering me on, I was able to perform the move and allow this exciting drop for the first time. Working through this rewrote the script I had written all those years ago that I couldn't be safe in this part of my body. I felt myself meet this space behind my heart and back with a new foundation. Over time, with practice, it became a space I could be in safely.

It was huge. This example was one of many ways in which aerial and other movement arts helped me to reintegrate and love my own inner child, support and care for my daughter in new ways, unwind old stories in my body and open to new possibilities. It helped with my overall reclaiming of my whole self and my ability to fully inhabit my space.

Our cultural focus is very narrow. We tend to inhabit the front side of our bodies, moving forward throughout the day, getting things done. Yet the omni-directional awareness of self — noticing the space behind the body, to the sides, below, above as well as in front — is important on the journey of wholeness and can come in many ways. How do you notice the space around your body? Within your body?

RECIPE 5: Widening Awareness of Self, pg 310

RECIPE 6: Center Ground Orient, pg 312

RECIPE 7: Exhale with Sound, pg 314

I soaked up the learning and healing and expanded my skills. I practiced regularly and built strength, callouses on my hands, and more confidence in trusting my body. Over time, I began to perform for others and eventually teach aerial arts.

By this time I had completely abandoned my fear of dancing in public. I now embrace my body and express myself through my body in front of audiences. Yet that doesn't mean it was easy.

I am dressed in a white unitard, with a Butoh-inspired, white painted face and hair pulled up in tight, random spirals on my head. The lights are low — an eery blue haze illuminates the darkened warehouse gallery space, and the mood is somber. The music, haunting and deep, guides my slow, intentional movements as I climb the white aerial fabric, hand-over-hand, foot wrapping and un-wrapping...

...one

...step

...at

...a

...time.

I feel my body strong, powerful, graceful. I am present, here, connected with my body, and together with my troupe partners we are offering an experience to the audience. They gaze, enraptured with wonder and curiosity, as if asking themselves: "What's going to happen next? How is what they are doing possible?"

I am now in a solo performance. I twist, turn, climb and create shapes with my body. Finally, I make my way to the top of the fabric, where I invert and begin to wrap my body in a way that will support a big flourishing drop.

Suddenly I freeze, my breath locked high in my chest. My grip on the fabric tightens. I am hanging upside down on an aerial fabric, with a bare, unforgiving concrete floor looming 25 feet below me. I feel myself at the brink of panic. What if I fall head first to the ground? There would be no second chance. I might not survive it. The audience is agape, waiting... My troupe members are holding space, not noticing what's emerging for me.

I breathe. Oh my god, they're waiting. I have to do something...

I remind myself... slow down... "Leslie, you've done this move hundreds of times with ease. You've got this!" I realize all the months of practice, all the many prior performances, all of these were at a height of about 15 feet. This is the first performance space that enables such a high rig point for the fabric. It means we have more room to climb. When I was upright climbing, my rational brain was like, "Hey let's go! Higher is no different, let's do this drop!" Yet now, hanging upside down, my body feels the difference.

I take another breath. Only moments have passed and yet it feels like lifetimes. I release the brain math on the height and I allow myself to be present with my body to trust myself... close my eyes, feel inside, I KNOW this move inside my body, I KNOW I have wrapped safely, it IS okay to let go...

It is okay to let go

...yes, to let go

...I

...LET

...GO

... and I move gracefully and powerfully through the drop sequence, rolling, dropping, flying and engaging once again to my final position about half way down the fabric, where my body offers the wide flourish of completion... and Ahhhh! The audience breathes again. They clap! It feels amazing. It's well received! No one even realizes how much I had been freaking out.

I breathe, I smile, I continue my routine to completion with grace and power and come down to take my place in our circle as the next member of our troupe begins.

I did it: I let go! Yes it was scary, AND it was freeing, exhilarating.

I realize everything is going to be okay.

This deep lesson was one of many that came from within my body during this time. My work with the aerial arts helped me face fears, learn ways to let go, trust, to find my foundation safely and learn to really let go into expansive freedom: the very nature of the work of my journey of sacred sexuality. Moving into the practice, the reasons I was called to do this became more clear, and the therapeutic value of my aerial work became crucial to my personal unfolding. I also built confidence in my body and movement as I stepped into performing with this new group. My teacher, a small-business owner herself, also helped me see new ways of relating with clients and a more fluid, organic business model for a small business, a refreshing alternative to the stoic, lifeless versions of business structure that I had grown accustomed to in my corporate years.

And frankly, I began to learn the value of play!

During a yoga class I took around that time, my teacher asked us to reflect back on the earliest memories of being a child just spinning around in circles in the yard until falling over in exhaustion and laughter. She encouraged us to bring that element of playful freedom into our practice that morning. I realized I didn't have those blissful childhood memories. As a young girl I was always so shy and hard on myself that I never really allowed myself to let go into that carefree bliss. But I did have more recent experiences, so I enjoyed playing in that freedom during my practice:

Now, a few days later after my yoga teacher's illuminating suggestion, unseasonably warm weather inspires my nine-year-old daughter and me to spend some time at the park. We are playing on the play structure in a very open space near the ball fields. I have a blast hanging upside down on the monkey bars — thanks to my recent love of the aerial arts totally healing my traumatic experience of falling from them as a child.

But now she asks me to play hide-and-seek. My initial analytical reaction is to decline with "Oh no, there's really no place to hide around here, and I don't like playing hide-and-seek, and..." Immediately the inspiration from yoga floods back in through my body... "YES! I WILL play hide-and-seek, because, well why not?!"

So we do! "3, 2, 1... ready or not, here I come!!"

The wide open space we are in makes "logical" hiding spots limited. I quickly realize I don't always need logic... and I encourage myself to just PLAY!

It's my turn to hide first. I curl up in a ball on the grass underneath the picnic blanket we brought. Surely she won't see me. She'll see it as just a crumple on the ground.

I wait.

I giggle... no, I stop myself.

I giggle again.

As I wait for the countdown my ribs heave with the laughter I am trying to suppress... which makes me laugh even harder at the thought! Of course she quickly comes up behind me. Then she announces, "I can see your shoes!" We both explode in laughter as she pounces on top of me, blanket and all!!

My next turn I "hide" in plain view on top of the play structure in a ball. She walks about two steps before being directly in my line of sight and of course she sees me clearly.

"WAIT!" I declare, stopping her from calling out. She waits and looks at me.

I place a pebble on my head.

"I am hiding under a rock and you can't see me!!"

BWWAHHH HA HA! We roared again and again!!!...

I can't recall the last time I laughed so hard and let go in play so deeply! It feels sooooo good! My connection with my daughter deepens, and I feel so alive and vibrant! Truly a healing, blissful experience. :)

How did it feel when you read this story? Did it feel worth your while? Did it feel familiar? Invite yourself to play: What do you notice? Do any "should" or "should not" statements arise from within? Can you set them aside and explore play? Notice what emerges as you do. Can you experience laughter? How does it feel in your body?

This path of unwinding and reclaiming my creative playful self integrated into how I approached building my business. I recognized that the two were not separate at all. In fact, the deep inner journey of self revealed what I was meant to offer in my work. Soon I came to feel these two aspects of my growth slam together in the most important lesson of my personal and professional journey to this point.

CHAPTER TWELVE
Relearning About Power

Through travels, personal exploration and shifting relationships, I delighted in learning more about who I am and connecting with new templates for existence in the world. At the same time, some more tough lessons appeared on my path. Tough lessons that actually softened me.

In my aerial training, I unpacked a lot of old trauma from my body, reclaimed portions of my playful self and learned new movement skills as well as fire performance skills beyond the aerial arts. I felt excited and wanted to share them. I also wanted to find balance of how I would share what I'd learned with others and also honor one of my many teachers. I made a suggestion on how to offer the work, but the teacher was not interested in hearing it. While this hurt, what felt even worse was that I sensed her feeling threatened as I grew in my own presence and abilities with these arts. I had no intention to step on toes or create hurt; I didn't even want to do something that wouldn't feel good for her. However, in making my suggestion and attempting to take a more active role in the community, apparently I pushed too far.

In fact, let's be honest, what I know about myself from that era is that my ideas of leadership came from the way I was raised and my corporate work history, still quite recent then. As a result of these experiences, my ideas of leadership had become embedded with competitive scripts. Looking back, it seems likely my actions were steeped in those scripts in ways I couldn't even see at the time. However, after things started to go badly, I did try to open the doors for communication with my teacher, with the intention of finding a balance that would bring ease to both of us. Despite this, I began to be shunned from the troupe and the school. I felt myself getting pushed away, as if this person's sword came out and I was on the receiving end.

At first I felt awful. I wanted to make it better.

I am in a parking lot in my car talking on my cell phone, and the heat of the asphalt baking in the sun is suffocating. I am crying huge tears, with my body heaving in that "hitchy" sort of way I last remember in my college dorm room on the phone with my father. Only this time, it's not my father on the other end of the line, it's my teacher, who has also really become a friend. I don't understand why I feel this way, I intended no harm and I am happy to make shifts. Can we talk about this? Can we find a balance together? It feels like she's not hearing me. And I hear her words that I don't understand. I feel myself pulling away from my body again, and this time it feels like a sword in the gut. I feel like I must be a really bad person, like that time in college. We hang up. My tears flow even more.

Afterwards, as I reflected and shared with my new partner (whom I will introduce later in this book), I could hold myself in a different light than I had that day in the dorm on the phone with my father many years before.

The conversation with my father had been particularly devastating because he was an authority figure, and not just any outside authority figure: I wanted him to be my caregiver, my parent, someone whose thoughtful advice and encouragement would help me feel safe as I navigated this major life transition. The response I got from my father would have been abusive in any situation, but it landed particularly hard because I was so open with him. This broke my trust. It's a recipe for huge trauma when our trust in our caregivers is broken, and this event reinforced my belief that I couldn't count on others to help me as I made life decisions. It was all up to me, so I had to take charge.

In the situation with my teacher, I was feeling a similar power dynamic. As a teacher of mine, this friend was also an authority figure. As with my father, I felt vulnerable because of many of the ways I learned and grew under her guidance, unwinding old traumas from my body. Because of this, her words landed all the more harshly, and especially coming from a woman. I had such a hard time having female friends all my life, so there was something even deeper about the way I would cower and withdraw from my own power around women that wouldn't happen in the same way with men.

At the same time, I was bumping into my hyper-achiever drive. In some ways, this drive is a natural expression of who I am and in that way it is a beautiful thing. But when it gets compulsive, it pulls me off center. That's when it doesn't feel good for me and definitely not for those around me.

I thought about this interaction for years, still feeling the hurt around it. In retrospect, years later I began to sense that my drive towards hyper-achieving was happening without my even knowing, and it triggered her into defense mode.

I had learned the patriarchal ways of domination and power over another as a way to "success," and my sense was, like most of us, my teacher had, too. And because it was a woman this time, I was being invited into healing in the way we treat each other as women and femme-identified folx, healing that sisterhood by releasing old competitive scripts.

Even at the time, I could feel myself open to a new level of self-awareness around these events. The experience might in some ways echo past events, but it wasn't going to be a total repeat. I had acquired new self-resourcing skills and had at the time recently found a partner in life who could really have my back. Both my own inner resources and the external resource of my new partnership became key to my capacity to transform and grow in new layers this time around. We will explore more about what I mean by Resources and how to tap into them in Part 3.

A big part of my growth at the time came from realizing that I was also not holding myself with the same loving compassion that I was extending to my teacher as I grew through these issues. As this became clear, it became equally clear that the level of cowering and subordination that would be required of me to stay in relationship with that community no longer felt good for my body. I shouldn't have to revert back to my old ways of making myself small and insignificant to be accepted.

That said, despite the frustration that had built up in me, I also didn't need to fight, put my teacher down, or prove myself "right" to feel better. Instead, I gently let it go. I stepped away. I beamed loving kindness to my teacher and let myself focus on my own path, which I felt turning gently in a different direction. I grieved, and I moved on.

This was hard for me! I was so used to proving worthiness through competition and winning. I had always felt the need to "come out on top." However, contrary to what I learned in the corporate world, stepping into one's power is not about pushing one's own forward, or "being better than." It's gentler than that, and even more profound. As we allow it to emerge, it's a soft power.

Also, it was about claiming that my feelings matter, too. And, being aware that if I was on the receiving end of the "come out on top" energy, I didn't have to crumple. It does not need to feel like being hit by a cannonball in the gut, like the day on the phone with my dad in college. I didn't need to cower, feeling like I did something wrong, like the day of the slammed fist in the corporate boardroom.

So overall, I met this experience differently. I was reclaiming my authenticity as power. This was another layer of "coming out" — meaning, being honest with myself and others about who I really am. That is the very nature of this book. Sexuality without authenticity is a pretty thin soup. To meet and be with our power, our sexual sovereignty, means to really look deeply within and claim and be who we authentically are. This is not easy. However, living a repressed version of ourselves, especially in the deep areas of our root and sexual centers, can be particularly damaging. This is why healing in this area of our lives, Sacred Sexual healing, can be so liberating and empowering. The rewards of feeling vibrantly alive make the tough spots all the more worth it.

This reclaiming of power in a soft way was very much about letting go. It's about letting go of control mechanisms, thought patterns and body habits that have become part of a shell of a false identity. Yes, it can be painful as that false identity drops away — or gets ripped away, chewed off and swallowed in the chaos as we meet change. Even if we find it painful at times, it's important that we remember that this whole process is empowered by our larger identity.

Everybody has them: dysfunctional patterns that often we really can't see in ourselves. These patterns are not only our own, they often also come from the collective, social constructs and the shared or inherited traumas that so often drive them. Such patterns can be so deeply embedded in our society that we "can't see the forest for the trees." Born of colonizer energy embedded in the dominant culture are things like chemical agriculture, atomic weapons and even the non-stop urge to do more and work harder to prove our worth, which is fueled by the violence of linear clock time — another construct.

I am only now really starting to see these larger, cultural contexts that I couldn't see for so long. At the time, it was all I knew. And I know I am not alone in that. But I am now starting to see the damage they create, and the violence inherent in these patterns. The urgency that comes with this energy can be felt, and it can be damaging and violent to our own nervous systems without even realizing there is another way.

Part of the answer is found in creating relational space. We can create a relational space with any being: person, animal, plant, stones, water, fire, Earth and other elemental energies and celestial bodies. It's through the relational space with other beings that we can be offered the gift of seeing things about ourselves. Slowing down, listening to our bodies, being present with ourselves and each other, witnessing another person and hearing their hopes, dreams and fears opens a new space of possibility. As we see these patterns, we can begin to let them go. To unwind.

Unwinding the Patterns

As I gaze back over the time covered in this book, I can now see many of the patterns that were hard to recognize when I was in them. For example, I moved from a thinking orientation, which was all I knew, to more of a feeling orientation — which I had previously derided or dismissed as weak. This took courage. As I began to bring in the balance of both, I began being more open for things like spontaneity to spark the joy of play, even amidst my daily schedule.

That pattern can also be seen from the lens of moving from a "head" focus where my thoughts and mind ran and controlled my body in ways I thought it "should be," like swimming, biking and running to extreme limits — to a "body" focus where slowing down and listening to body messages now guides the actions and choices I am making. For example, choosing to take rest when my body asks for it even if it doesn't fit the workout "plan," or slowing down and touching my yoni in a way that opened my first ejaculation.

In the journey, I witnessed my dismissive, skeptical attitude toward spirituality soften and widen to include and embrace this unseen dimension of experience as powerful additional information that can be trusted. Noticing when dragonflies (or deer, bats, owls, chipmunks, slugs, plants) beckon my attention, taking a moment to honor the connection, and noticing what changes next, are now a daily part of my life. I now feel much more comfortable calling upon unseen support for guidance, and feeling the answers resonate in my body, often through tingles or goose bumps that flush over me. Many times the answer comes in a new and different way, one I don't expect.

I see now how this movement was also from an outside-in approach, "operating on" life — times when I would take on more projects and leadership roles as a way to gain acceptance, or "rub out a quick orgasm" simply to get it done — to an inside-out approach to living. Here, my subjectivity and inner connections form my compass. For example: "Let's try this Japanese rope tying thing and see how it feels," or allowing myself space to feel and see the way new clothing fits on my body rather than prescribing my shirt or pant size with a mental pattern.

Through all this, I moved from a prescribed, inherited, culturally mandated/approved life and career path as an engineer to a self-directed and idiosyncratically sculpted one as a sacred sexual healer.

All of these patterns point to the same primary theme of slowing down, paying attention and Listening to the Body as a path of Letting Go. A powerful journey of life and sacred sexual healing that is just the beginning.

These early experiences with the teaching dynamic opened the start of the lesson of meeting soft power that continued to unfurl for years. Along the way, I had also already begun the next phase of my training, to support my becoming a sacred sexual practitioner.

ဆ ✿ ⚋

As I had left the corporate world a few years before, in parallel with the yoga and aerial path that had called me, I had also been deepening into my own path of sacred sexuality as well as my vision of sharing it with the world. My body guided me to seek teachers who would help me with the practical aspects: the structure, tools, and how to tangibly share the power of this amazing path with others. I had been looking for several years, considering many options of intensives and workshops around the country in places like Hawaii, California or New York, hosted by various schools and teachers. Finally, the right one for me at the time presented itself. I read the book *Sacred Sexual Healing: The SHAMAN Method of Sex Magic* by Baba Dez Nichols and Kamala Devi, and felt the call. I found my way to the International School of Temple Arts (ISTA). Paul, my lover and tantric consort at the time, was also very interested in the work, and he and I chose to travel there together for an intensive training program.

The training changed my life. In a very short amount of 3D linear clock time, yet a lifetime or more in the Spirit realm, I learned powerful lessons and began to make tangible, physical body changes in my own healing path. For example, I noticed how much I clenched my buttocks, yoni and anus on a daily basis. Even as I stood or walked, the clench and tightness were strong. Related, I also noticed how my breathing was held high in my body for fear of letting my belly "hang out." The conscious choice to relax to allow my breath into my lower belly, anus, vaginal muscles and buttocks became regular practices. I began to notice how I was standing to brush my teeth, crooked with my hip cocked to one side, and consciously began to get curious about aligning to allow the energy flow through my pelvis and legs.

These starbursts of awareness, often but not always fueled by a sparkling sensation of energy flow, I came to call Body Awakenings. Additionally, the training and experiences introduced many tools and processes that helped me understand how to share this path with others.[43] These I combined with practices from many traditions, teachers, and other influences as I moved forward to creatively design my own approach to this work.

In Part 3, we will introduce foundational concepts and practices that will help you open up to and explore your own Body Awakenings. The training also gave me a practical awareness of how to structure such a business, and led to questions I needed to explore for myself that were important as I launched my work in the world. With the tangible support of the training, in conjunction with my spiritual and body guidance, I felt clear and empowered to step out into the world as the Sacred Sexual Healer and Transformational Guide that I had felt and nurtured in myself. The final pieces of what had been years of my life's work brewing and gestating slotted into place, and I launched a mystery school, the sacred sexuality aspect of One Space, shortly thereafter.

---

[43] While I appreciated many things I learned from ISTA, the school was not without its issues. I encourage you to do your own research should you wish to explore these topics in a school environment. Know your truth, and listen to your body as you make choices that are right for you.

Teaching About Sexuality and Spirituality

When I started the One Space journey, it began with: Illuminating the path of self-realization through art, yoga, meditation and sacred geometry. Sacred sexuality, always part of the vision, had now become a reality.

I feel so honored and grateful to have had this powerful work move through me. I am in service, honored to be sharing from the most authentic source place inside. That all of this was emerging in a time of vast acceleration of conscious shifts on the planet felt so aligned. My work with clients unfolded for 14 years, and I continuously learned and grew with each one. I loved witnessing how Spirit brought me unique situations and people as we went. As I learned and grew in my own practice, my capacity to support deep healing in others grew, also. As a healer, I am a vessel for supporting each person into their own journey of healing themselves. It's about finding your truth, acknowledging it, and stepping into it. As Franklyn Sills, author of *Foundations in Craniosacral Biodynamics* and pioneer in Biodynamic Craniosacral Therapy, says: "It is not we (the practitioners) who do the healing; it is the unerring forces from within."[44]

Sacred Sexuality

I am at a Thai yoga massage weekend immersion retreat. Now a few years into my sacred sexual healing practice, training in this intentional touch modality becomes another of the diverse modalities that weave into my work. Kneeling on the thick, sage green cotton mat resting on the hardwood floor, my hands are in gentle contact with another person, and I am moving from my center. I enjoy the lush experience of a meditative, centering, deep inquiry into my own essence while being supported by others. The feeling of deep familiarity, ancient memory rekindled... present, aware touch, slower breath, and conscious movement from the core of my very being. Inspiration flows as I connect the dots: This foundational physical reality of breath, sound, movement, touch and visualization is a Divine web, illuminating a path of self-realization.

Sacred Sexuality is an energetic healing path of authenticity which seeks to unwind old stories and held patterns and uncover the wisdom encoded in our own bodies. These teachings turned out to be an authentic gift and passion of

---

[44] *Foundations in Craniosacral Biodynamics (Volumes 1 & 2)* by Franklyn Sills.

mine to share with the world. The essence of working with energy in the body is about balance, finding healing in the spectrum of feminine and masculine aspects of ourselves. Integrating these aspects together creates wholeness in our body, which projects outwardly into our lives. This method of healing and self-knowledge carries a powerful potential for releasing held emotions, improving our health, creating richer and more meaningful relationships with others, manifesting our heart's desires, and for walking a path of connection with pleasure, the process of enlightenment and the Divine. Sacred Sexuality is a lifestyle and calling, going way beyond sex as we commonly think of it.

A big part of this, as we've seen in my own story, is that despite all the hanging-on and control mechanisms, we actually can let go to step into new patterns. We've all been trained in various ways to ignore feelings, to stuff away, and hold on too long. Many of us, myself included, hold on too long to past relationships, old ways of thinking, and clutter in our homes. Quite literally this manifests as holding in our bodies and pelvises, including even our bladder and bowels. When we suppress our grief and pain, we suppress our joy and laughter as well. We suppress our love. This is what we're overcoming through the Sacred Sexual healing path.

Because all life is connected and sexuality is deeply connected with wellsprings of life, our embedded habit patterns surrounding power and control, along with layers of trauma and other patterning that we hold in our bodies, are going to show up in our sexuality and be liberated through our sexual empowerment.

Part of the reason sexual healing is needed is that, as a culture, we do have sexual traumas, rife with power and control dynamics, places where sexual abuse has run amok. Sexual abuse perpetrated by priests in the Catholic Church, human trafficking, child sex rings involving and perpetrated by people in major corporate and government leadership roles, and abuses reported by survivors in the #MeToo movement are only some of many such examples. Whether we are directly impacted by such crimes, more subtly affected by institutional or familial guilt and shame, or simply trying to live in a society where these and other sexual traumas are more the rule than the exception, everyone is impacted. So where does the healing start?

The answer is: We can undo the control paradigm in ourselves and unwind trauma from our bodies. We can notice, unpack, and let go of the inhibitions that show up in ourselves (thoughts, body, etc.). To do this, we must listen to the body. For example, I can breathe and notice restrictions in my breath, or places in my body. I can notice when I hold back joy or self-expression. If I listen to my body, I can understand where the control patterns that I've instituted reside. I may even recall how and when these patterns got established. With greater awareness, I can then start to navigate toward a true self, a wholeness that is always available.

This is the bigger picture, the deeper purpose for this work. Sacred Sexuality is not only about having a better experience with a lover, although it supports that as well. Sacred Sexuality is about having a greater experience of the whole, of all of life. Encountering one another and co-creating.

The tantric path is about meeting what is now, the present moment. That is what is. The now guides us and informs us. We meet what emerges in the now because it is ready to be seen and worked with. The container we have created and the resourcing we currently have make it possible to be in the now. We meet it, see it, hold space, listen. In tantra, this is the way of the whole of life, not only sex in the bedroom.

Listening to our own body enables us to deeply listen to another person and their body as well. Such listening yields actionable information. As we listen to our body, we can actually begin to trust the letting go process. We learn ways that are not only about "doing," we honor the "being." If we are "trying to let go" we aren't letting go. It's such a sweetly discombobulating paradox.

And as we do this with our own selves and our own bodies, it empowers us to be able to co-create in that space with other humans. Other beings and bodies. The relational space becomes really important. Since our traumas typically are rooted in relationship, we often have to return to relational space to heal them — though not often with the same person. This is why powerful healing can happen when we let ourselves reach out for the support of other people. Healing happens in the stillness that can emerge as the relational space settles. Healing happens when what is ready to rise up to be met, is met and held with care and love. We literally love these parts of ourself and others back into wholeness.

This was the nature of my evolving work with clients for 14 years, and the foundation of Sacred Sexual healing: Together we co-create a container. We slow way down, bringing love and respect to support each person to feel safe, seen, heard and cared for. As the settled relational field emerges, information that the body is holding can be revealed, and the results of cultural and individual trauma can be loved back into wholeness.

Often, for example, cisgender men came to me with the desire to learn how to touch a woman, or be a better lover or "make my girlfriend _____." Maybe it's "orgasm" or "ejaculate" or something else they perceive as important. The approach I took began with honoring their desire, and also offering a new way to see. This includes a shift in vocabulary, because the energy of our words is so important, as well as teaching self-awareness that offers a new way to be with this desire. It also requires learning boundary and communication tools, tools to navigate consensual touch and contact. The result is a practice that builds confidence, bringing new patterns into the body so these new patterns become a part of how we can interact with lovers and partners on our own.

In working with people who bring a "results oriented" mindset, I clarified that it was not about "making anyone" do anything. It's not about some technique or which button to push when. Instead, it is about LISTENING to your partner's body, which starts with grounding and listening to your own body first. I then taught ways to deeply come into your own experience of your own body as a guide, and then gently meet the relational space with another human.

In our culture, it is common for the eyes, hands and fingers to be trained to be active "do-ers." This can feel abrasive, sharp, and even painful to a partner, yet often neither person even realizes why. Reality is, our culture tends to encourage habits that don't work for lovemaking, and that's not even counting the individual traumas both partners bring to their lovemaking, including things we don't even think of as traumas. These take the form of body constrictions and emotional blocks. But if most people we meet seem to be constricted in their bodies and emotionally blocked, this can seem "normal."

However, people showed up in my practice because they were aware that something wasn't working, and they wanted some aspect of their life to change. They came with good intentions. Maybe they wanted to "be good at sex" or to do well with a new partner they care about: "I want my lover to feel good." But until we learn to listen to our own bodies, we can't successfully feel our way forward with our partners. In the example of the cisgendered male "doer," it can be incredibly confusing for his partner to know that he has every good intention, but... it just doesn't feel right. The partner may feel, but not even know how to articulate: "Would you please back up, create some more space, and slow down?"

For couples caught in this pattern, it may seem like a problem without a solution. But healing this is possible. I saw it all the time. As I taught one-on-one with people or guided couples, I often paused and invited my clients to close their eyes. I would ask: "Where's your attention right now? What are you noticing? Where's your awareness?"

Much of the time, especially if they were new to Body Listening, at first they may not have known how to assess where their attention was placed. If they were able to articulate, the response to my question almost always began with descriptions of the other person. For example, they would say "I feel the softness of her skin" instead of what they themselves were noticing in their own body. In these cases, I offered "Yes AND" and invited them into the noticing of their own body in that moment, guiding them into a present awareness of their physical self. For example: "Can you feel where your leg or buttocks are in contact with the cushions or floor? Do you notice your breath? Where do you feel it in your body?"

As we went, I often inquired deeper: "Are you noticing your own pelvis? Where is your ground line? Where's a part of you that's connected with the earth? Do you notice that? Can you feel your foot right now?"

In the relational space we had created, such questions could be received as they were intended: as curious inquiries, instead of a threat. There aren't right or wrong answers, there aren't tests or quizzes to be mastered. This is about learning self-awareness. A client may then have had a huge "aha moment" and realized: "Oh my god, my feet disappeared like eons ago and I am all in this forward center of my brain, and my eyeballs and fingertips are like pointy little daggers! Wow! No wonder this is hard for my partner. I had no idea!"

So in this process of working together, people learn how to soften the body, especially eyes, hands and fingers and other body parts, so that they can better receive information from their partners through these channels. They learn to listen and share what's being received, then make choices and take right action using this information with love, care and respect for their own bodies and their partners'. This is often not easily grasped through language or just by reading the pages of a book. However, the experience of being guided and supported in a loving space can be life-changing.

Love and care for our fellow humans: to remember who we are and feel good about being our authentic selves together. This is the core of what I hold space for in my work.

Everything starts with being in your own body, finding your own ground and your own caring presence for yourself. This is essential if we want to open the space in ourselves that supports listening and responding in real time to others in our intimate relating. These are capacities and practices I introduced to my clients and will share the foundations of in Part 3. They will help support you as you learn new ways to touch and listen. After you begin working with these practices, many of the ideas I've shared in these pages, and even the personal stories I have shared in this book, will take on greater meaning. For example, the cultural conditioning around power and control that we were exploring at the beginning of this chapter can be transformed.

These concepts and practices in the pages that follow will help us open into our body of awareness as we continue our journey into this powerful path of self-realization, of learning to let go, of listening deeply to the body and supporting energetic and orgasmic awakenings from within... this path of Sacred Sexuality.

Part Three

New Structure for Life

Welcome to Part 3.

Here we are. How has the journey been, so far?

What part have you found compelling? What parts could you relate to? What parts did you find inspiring? Were there any parts where you felt uncomfortable, or felt judgments come up as you were reading? Anything you really wanted to skip? I encourage you to slow down for a moment and to notice all of these things. Reflect.

I'm also curious: Why did you pick up this book? What were you hoping to get from it? Did you start out with a desire? Did you find any new ones along the way? And now that we've come this far, what are you still hoping to find?

What do you WANT?

Asking these kinds of questions and being really honest about your answers could make the rest of this book much more meaningful and impactful.

You may have noticed that in Part 2 I started addressing you, the reader. In Part 3 that will continue at a higher level.

And yes, in Part 3, my personal journey continues. I step more and more into the role of guide and teacher. Of course, as part of this transition, there will be more discoveries and deeper understandings of the dynamics of a full, exciting, and spiritually informed life.

Yes, this includes sacred sexuality.

But since tantra is a journey of weaving levels of integration and wholeness, the healing we're embarking upon will involve yet more inner and outer adventures, new kinds of risk-taking, and different ways to courageously step into the unknown. You've seen how my story involves new kinds of sex and new places to travel, and everything from athletics and shamanic practices to journaling, art, and career transitions.

Your journey will be yours. And chances are, if you are really reaching for new life experiences, it will involve trying new things, feeling new feelings, and being willing to be seen and to know yourself in new ways.

All of which is to say: Going forward, more and more, this book will involve you!

And since in this section I step more fully into a teaching and sharing role, on a basic level, what that means is that here, my journey has led to you, dear reader.

I want you to know that I consider it an honor. Thank you for meeting me here. I'm excited to see where this leads.

There's a whole new world of experience waiting for us: many new kinds of fulfillment, many new kinds of richness, many new discoveries. Ecstasy is a big energy. Big energy needs clear ground and a resilient vessel to fully express. What follows is intended to help build this foundation for the ecstatic to move through us.

Let's go.

CHAPTER THIRTEEN
Love and Sea Salt

As my body began to wake up, I began to slow down, notice life, trust Spirit and connect with the world around me in new ways. I learned new ways to trust my power with compassion. All these new ways of being set a foundation for what was yet to come. I had been listening for guidance, doing my best to honor that guidance, and doing my own human homework, including some hard lessons. I had even consciously manifested the most conscious, loving, sexually expanding relationship I had ever had.

And it was just the beginning.

Manifesting Dixon

2009 — I peek around the corner in the narrow, dark hallway, smiling. I am on the second floor of the dark, edgy, urban warehouse art space in which I am performing with my fellow troupe members as aerialists. Aerial performance has become a new love of mine. Feeling the strength in my body, in balance with the fluid lines and ability to relax into flow is empowering. We're at an art show held in an industrial space in Detroit, one of many performances where we climb, twist and turn and engage high in the air with aerial fabrics in expressions of emotion, sharing stories with our bodies.

At the moment, I have a break before our next showtime, and I am feeling drawn in by the music cascading from the dark ballroom that I now overlook unnoticed from my perch. The haunting strings, the inspiring music reaches toward me, wrapping around my heart and beckoning me. I see the creator of what I hear: a man, sexy, alluring and powerful on stage, filled with raw emotion as he shares his soul with his audience. I've met him before: We've shared the stage at other events, and I've been bathed by his music during yoga practice. Again I smile, loving the music as it engulfs me, loving him for sharing it. My heart beams.

During my seminal relationship with Paul, we explored sacred sexual healing together, training, polyamory[45] (consciously having many loves with all parties in consent and choice, an alternative expression of relationships) and what it meant for us. Through all this, I got to a place where I acknowledged I was seeking a new masculine energy in my life. A teacher, perhaps? Or lover? Paul and I both knew that loving and connecting with others is often our greatest teacher. I spoke about this desire with Paul and together we held the intention of holding space for such energy to move into my life. Being familiar with manifesting at this point, I journaled about the qualities I was seeking, and opened my awareness to the possibility. Paul and I discussed what our relationship agreements were as we connected with people outside our primary relationship.

However, after a couple of months or so, I really started to feel that although I had stated that I was opening space for this new life experience, something was blocking the possibility of someone entering it. I remembered that Paul and I had held a different intention sometime prior that had been left floating, and it had grown foggy and fuzzy as the months went by. The intention was around the possibility of him moving from his then home in another state to a dual home-base situation of a home near his children and joining me in my home in Michigan. The energetic remnants of this earlier intention felt like a fuzzy ball in my energy field. I realized I needed to get some clarity around it. When I noticed this block, I opened a tough conversation with him. What did we each want?

After some heartfelt, deeply powerful communication, we both concluded it was time to release the intention, and so we did. We decided to continue with our polyamorous relationship as we had been, without moving his home base. Almost instantly, I felt the energy lift and the space really open up. The fuzzy ball had dissipated, I felt clarity in my field. I was now ready.

Within a week, I got the email that changed my life once again.

---

[45] While a full exploration of Polyamory is outside the scope of this book, some writings by others that I have found helpful are *PolySecure* by Jessica Fern, *Sex at Dawn* by Cacilda Jethá and Christopher Ryan, and *Opening Up* by Tristan Taormino.

And my relationship with Dixon emerged.

Dixon and I had met backstage during shows where we were each performing... he sharing Transformational Journeys via Digital Violin, and I exploring and sharing energy through aerial arts, fire performance and intuitive movement. Our art and passion were planting the seeds between us even then. I remember my heart being carried by his music at a live music, raw food and yoga event. This combination of some of my favorite things filled me with joy! We had chatted about the huge life shift he had in conjunction with Burning Man many years prior. It had become an annual pilgrimage for him ever since. His experience was intriguing to me, since I had been feeling the call to participate in the experimental festival for a while prior to our meeting, and I wanted to learn more. I began to feel there was a reason for the connection.

So when I received an email from him reaching out with interest in my life's work and in meeting to learn more about each other, I felt the resonance from a very deep place. We planned a time to meet, and as we acknowledged that we both had incredibly busy schedules, Spirit opened the door for us with some last-minute changes that created a wide possibility.

I come home from the yoga conference, tired and sweaty — energy well spent, and now eager and excited for this meeting with Dixon. I quickly freshen up, brush my hair and change clothes, donning a fresh top and flowy, casual skirt to replace the sports bra and yoga pants I had been wearing. As I zoom around the house getting ready, I move past the glass front door. Glancing through it, I see him bounding up my front steps in a sexy shirt, dark jeans and black cowboy boots. His signature joyful bounce, full of smiles and energy announces his arrival! A huge smile beams across my face and fills my body and heart as I turn to greet him at the door.

Our first meeting was magical. I invited him down into my Temple space, an intentional space where I held my spiritual practice and rituals, saw clients and created conscious connections. Descending the stairs into the lower level, we came to the entry way, then opened the door made of dark, rough-cut wood. Inside, the Temple walls were painted shades of deep reds and mustards, with deep purple cushions and mats that we used to support our bodies on the floor. There we created a conscious space, lighting a candle at the altar, and sat facing each other to align to what may wish to come into our space.

Together, we shared stories, learned more about each other and our dreams, desires and relationships. We discussed what we each might like in a connection, and honored the others in our lives. We had a common history with corporate careers, life shifts and sexual exploration phases, and clarified our current relationship agreements and desires. We felt the alignment happen, a merging together, in parallel at high speed. We had each done our individual human homework to arrive here together, each making conscious choices to call in the next piece of our lives and create the space. What proceeded to unfold was a deeply connected, magical experience of emotional, physical, sexual, mental and spiritual bonding — all in this first day together. We were both struck with awe and wonder at how fast and deep our relationship began and continues to grow even now as we share and co-create this life together more than 14 years later.

We have proceeded to honor the amazing beautiful gifts we each individually are here to share with the world, as well as nurture and cultivate this beautiful gift of a relationship, in which we co-create, grow and share deep vast love with ourselves and others. As my friend and colleague, Sasha, who loves to cook says…

"The right amount of salt makes anything taste more like itself."[46]

I heard this as "sea salt" when they first shared it with me, and it stuck. In the clean, supportive way that he lets me be more authentically me, I can connect more with who I am, center and ground and find sweet ease in connection with him: Dixon is my sea salt.

ॐ ✿ ॐ

As Dixon and I began our journey together, my time with Paul shifted rather quickly, perhaps even in ways I didn't expect. This was early in my journey of polyamory and I was still navigating the inherited social constructs around monogamous partnering that I had been conditioned to. So maybe I felt I had to let go of Paul to a greater extent than perhaps was true? My love for Paul continues to this day, and his for me, as he now has a new primary beloved

---

[46] Sasha Lasdon, Somatic Sex Educator and Intimacy Coach, Certified Sexological Bodyworker, integratederos.com

partner. As our relationship evolved, we consciously reshaped it to open space for each of us to be who we are.

Two months into our newly deepening love and partnership, Dixon invites me to a party his friends are hosting. It's a special type of party, what circles in the BDSM, kink, sex-positive and leather family worlds may know of as a "play party."

I am used to co-creating in conscious sexual spaces and am excited to go with him, even though I was also a little nervous, with us being so newly partnered. We arrive and I begin to meet some of his friends. As we're standing in the kitchen, the door opens and in walks this stunning woman. She has a long, lithe body with creamy skin, ginger hair pulled gracefully atop her head with curls escaping the wrap and cascading around her face. She has dozens of piercings, most are along her ears and nose with a delicate chain, a nath, connecting them. Rainbow bracelets join the many others that line her arms and I feel a sense of relaxation into her open queerness as I am simultaneously struck by her presence and clear blue eyes.

As she enters, she sees Dixon and they embrace and share an intimate kiss. Instantly I'm intrigued by her. I feel she has this similar quality of the energy that I had met and felt in Girijah years before (we meet her in the next chapter). She felt familiar, and I felt an affinity and closeness with her right away.

They complete their embrace and she turns as Dixon introduces me to her and totally welcomes and accepts me into this friend group with her eyes and her gaze and her hug. That night the three of us explored and played together.

In this realm of our newly forming leather, kink and BDSM family, we came to be known as "the hippie love children." Xaina and I fall in love this day, and the three of us fall in love, adding to the love already shared between her and Dixon. We make love and explore together and embark upon a journey of really embracing the polyamory with a widening of partnership of love and care for each other.

To this day, over 14 years later, Xaina and Dixon and I journey together still. We have moved through so many changes and so many dynamics together. Xaina's and my relationship has changed, flowed and flexed through the course of time in many ways.

As this loving relationship emerged, a friendship blossomed also. Lovership blossomed open. Triads of connection blossomed open. And later Xaina became primary partners with another member of our leather family. The four of us opened up together as well. Mike and I started a journey of partnership that supported the awakening of my cock energy, as we played in a realm of me in a dominant role with him. It was a loving, caring role that developed over years together. What we shared was beautiful, and we were just beginning to explore new layers of this dynamic when Mike was diagnosed with lung cancer. And over the course of a very short time, the four of us reshaped our love and care to include us bringing meals and sharing hospital visits.

Mike died only three months later. I mourned the loss of a dear lover and friend, and later I mourned for the pause I felt in the claiming of my own cock energy. I mourned for Xaina losing a fiancé, a love, an artistic co-conspirator, a co-creator of home and care for her daughter. I mourned for our community losing an artist and friend and incredible human.

As Xaina prepared the Celebration of Life, an event in remembrance of Mike that was our version of a funeral with our community, she asked me to lead the spiritual ceremony which I accepted with great honor. One hundred people within our wider family and community participated in the ceremony.

The love we share with partners teaches us so much about ourselves. We learn and grow through this relational space when we cultivate and care for ourselves and each other in these partnerships.

Importantly, however, finding a partner is not the purpose of sacred sexuality, nor is it in any way required to embark upon this path. Partners can and do show up as a reflection of our ongoing alignment with our authentic selves. They support us with relational healing. That relational healing also happens in the relationship we have with ourselves and our bodies. This path of self-realization is the real journey.

Now let's explore the foundation that supports that journey.

CHAPTER FOURTEEN

Container and Foundation

In 2009, the year prior to the events described in the previous chapter, I was still partnered with Paul and very much engaged in the process of coming into a deeper alignment with a more authentic physical and emotional self.

I am in training with a room full of 30 or more people. My partner Paul is paired with another person in the room, as he and I have chosen the delight of learning and connecting with many beautiful beings as we explore this path together. I am paired with a stunning woman named Girijah. She intrigues me — I really like her style and energy and I am curious to learn more about her. The exercise we are exploring at the moment has us standing across the room from each other, with instructions to invite the other to move (using hand gestures) either closer to us, further away, or to stop. Two rules: We are not to talk, nor to touch, during the exercise.

It's my turn with the controls. I gesture for her to move toward me, in one action, all the way toward me without pause, to a point just an inch or so away. Our eyes are connected, nearly touching noses, and there I have her stop. We wait. At first, this feels great — yay! I like her and having her this close seems like a good idea to my rational brain.

Then as a moment passes, I start to feel a shift in my body. With a sharp intake, my breath gets high and shallow. At the same time, my heart races, belly contracts, tail bone and buttocks tuck under, my shoulders creep up near my ears.

Meanwhile my head says: "What? You're fine! She's not going to hurt you. Just suck it up and deal with it." Secondly, my head says: "Besides, if you have her back up she may think you don't like her, and you don't want that." So I leave her there — we don't budge. For the rest of the several minutes, other pairs are exploring space, back and forth, noticing. Yet I am holding her in this close-up spot.

The exercise comes to a close and we sit down to reflect on the experience.

I exhale. Whoa. Now it hits me. I notice. Wow, I just did "that." Not only did I just do "that" right now, a portal of awareness opens up into my past and I begin to see all the times that I had done "that" before.

What is "that" to which I refer? **All the times where my body was screaming a message, and my head overrode and shut it down.**

These are the sensations I experienced:

- Breathing high and shallow
- Heart rate increase
- Lower belly contraction
- Buttocks clenched and tailbone tucked under
- Neck tension, shoulders up near my ears

These body signals I now know to mean: "I don't feel safe and I don't feel good. I need a change." And yet, I was overriding it. My rational brain was saying, effectively: "Body, you are not important. I am not listening to you."

Wow, I began to notice how prevalent this had been in my life and in my sexuality. The times with a partner where I would feel like I had to push to overcome the stereotype that said women don't like sex as much as men. The times I would say to myself, "I want sex too, so let's get started and get him inside me now." If that meant I need to grab the lube to force my body to be ready, then that is what I did, not recognizing then that **my body could present herself to be ready all on her own, if I would slow down, listen and allow her to.**

Through this experience with Girijah, I began to see how much I had patterned this into my body. In my recognition, I began to rewrite those old stories, slow down, and deepen in my path of Listening to My Body. I also began honoring my Yoni — my vagina, my womb, the holy Temple of my body — in new ways.

This was the day that the sense of Container began to open: a safe space to support freedom and transformation. In the concept and reality of Container, I have seen the most profound means of supporting human growth and freedom I had ever known. This opens the possibility for love. In lovingly building my Temple I have created Container. With my agreements I create Container. In my relationships I create and co-create Container. So profound and widely applicable is this principle that I believe it is key to unlocking who we are and supporting us as we move into our most authentic brilliance, and ultimately to our very existence as a whole human consciousness on this planet.

Take a moment now. Notice your breath. Notice your body. What does your breathing feel like? Can you notice the parts of your body in contact with the surfaces you are seated or lying upon? What sensations are there? Invite a deeper breath. Where is your awareness now?

To explore the concept of Container more deeply, let's first pull together three of the energetic concepts that have been dipping into our journey thus far: Infinite Being, Gift of a Body, and Feminine and Masculine Dynamics. These three will set the stage for the understanding of Container and much of the rest of our work together in this book.

Infinite Being in Finite Form

"We are infinite Beings in finite form." This is a statement my teacher, Jean Houston, used to often make in her Mystery School, and one that resonated deeply then and continues to hold true for me. Some may say we are "energetic Beings in a physical body" or "spiritual Beings having a human experience." When I use the term "Energetic Being," "Energy Being" or "Soul Being," I am referring to the deep infinite aspect of ourselves. One might call it a soul, or the part of us that persists beyond the 3D world and this human experience.

Reflecting on my experience with Girijah at the beginning of this chapter, how does being an infinite being in finite form show up?

It started with feeling her presence. She was definitely there, showing up with me. I remember her eyes, these bright, vibrant sparkly eyes and smile, and her willingness to just be right there only inches from my face — to simply be there and not waver. I felt her infinite self, right there present with me in her physical body.

Additionally, our pairing for this shared experience felt like it had been led from the infinite realm. We connected strongly through the course of this workshop, and it was a spiritually led connection. I don't even remember how we picked each other or how we were paired up.

Regardless of how it happened, the partnership forged in this seemingly simple exercise really kicked off a huge thing for me personally, and in this instance both of us felt the depths that were opening up between us. It was at the infinite level that we were guided together and that we connected in a way that went way beyond our finite forms. In these moments we can sense ourselves as spiritual beings having a human experience, spiritual beings guided to have a human experience for our own individual growth journeys.

A lot of healing can happen in 10 minutes. This is another sign that the infinite is expressing through form.

The relational space that opens up goes way beyond the two physical-organism bodies to also include two *energetic beings*. It's like: "Here we are! *Ding! We're meeting through physical form!*"

That's our gift. We can learn through our physicality, but that's not the only thing that defines us.

No matter how we wrap words around it, one important feature of being infinite beings in finite form is that we have the capacity to tap into the realms of the infinite, which is incredibly empowering and full of possibility. Imagine our capacity as humans when we connect with these realms and wake up areas of our body and brain that have been dormant. In doing so, suddenly we realize that we do have the ability to create our reality. Contrary to the view of the world that likens our existence to lab rats in a cage, tolerating and working around an environment we have no choice over, I invite that through our ongoing connection with the infinite, our thoughts and intentions do shape and form the world around us. That's not merely my idea — many influential writers, visionaries, scientists and spiritual leaders have expanded on this in depth.[47]

As George Leonard, who wrote extensively about education and human potential,[48] offers in his book, *The Silent Pulse: A Search for the Perfect Rhythm that Exists in Each of Us*:

> Our key choice is whether to become aware of and take responsibility for the power of our intentionality.[49]

---

[47] See Additional Resources to Explore for many such teachings on intention, including the movie *What the Bleep Do We Know?!* and books including but not limited to Lynn McTaggert's *The Intention Experiment* and Masaru Emoto's *The Hidden Messages in Water*.

[48] https://en.wikipedia.org/wiki/George_Leonard

[49] *The Silent Pulse: A Search for the Perfect Rhythm That Exists in Each of Us* by George Leonard, Kindle location 1506 of 2214.

This power of our intentionality draws upon this infinite reservoir. Once again, there are as many spiritual paths as there are beings on this planet, and I honor that each of us has free will and choice on how we meet the infinite for ourselves.

Energy Being, Gift of Physical Body

My experience with Girijah also beautifully illustrated the gift of being in a physical body, in that through the body we get to *relate* in this world as infinite beings. The body may be finite, but people and the relational spaces generated between us are not. If we aren't incarnate, we don't get this readily available gift of relating with others in the physical plane,[50] to lean against the tree or feel a deer across space in the forest, or share a hug with another human.

With Girijah, the gift of the physical body meant that I could have a conversation to set the space, then feel her energetics and her physicality through my field, even without touch, and have an experience that led to an awakening through all the messages and realizations that came through me. My longstanding "brain in charge" pattern came into view, and with this new awareness, I could begin to change that pattern. And by no means was this the end of the gift. Standing in this new place of awareness, I also had a new friend, compounding the possibilities for both of us to grow into.

As infinite energetic beings, every single human on this planet has access to the incredible potency of the infinite realm, AND has such a sweet gift of being, here on this planet now, in a Physical Body. Through our Physical Body form we can access and transform energy into energy usable by our bodies… we eat food, feel sunlight on our skin, and take in 'prana' (life force energy) with each breath. Likewise, imagine the power of our Sexual Energy! Our sexual energy can be doubled, tripled, even exponentially grow, and in ways we don't often associate with sexuality.

One of my teachers whose work resonated with me is Kenneth Ray Stubbs, PhD.[51] I met Ray in person for the first time at the 10th Annual Conference of

---

[50] Sure, for those paying attention with awareness in the infinite realm we can still build a relationship with disincarnate beings, but for the sake of most 3D reality conversation creating relational space in physical form is much easier.

[51] Kenneth Ray Stubbs, who has now passed into the realm of the ancestors, www.sexualshaman.com

Sacred Sexuality & Consciousness Educators in April 2011. A sweet man with a spunky, geeky side, Ray had a narrow-framed body and long, neatly braided silver hair. His hands rested gently in his lap as he sat gracefully in his wheelchair at the front of the room. Witnessing him, I had a powerful transmission experience that day that launched me into working with Ray over the next few years.

One of the things Ray said during the course of our work together is, "We can only grow as Beings when we are incarnate." In other words, our soul-being Self only has the possibility of expanding our abilities and functioning when we are in a physical body, or we wouldn't have chosen to show up this way. It is through our body we experience the world, relate to others, relate to nature and the Earth, and it's through these experiences and our energy systems that we are informed in new ways of being and open up to expanding our amazing possibilities as humans.

This is big.

This is about the value of "Be"-ing. We grow and change through relating. We can set down the pressure of having to "Do" something to be of value. What is it like to sink into the awareness that we are worthy merely by our existence? How does it feel to let go of the to-do list? What is it like to rest in the moment of the now and trust that is enough?

Additionally, this sense of relating reopens our discussion on the relational field from Chapter 12. Part of the magic of healing work, whether in a formal session or simply in our relationships with others, ourselves, plants, animals, Earth and other beings, is the love and care and establishing of a settled relational field. This is an important piece of the Container. **Healing can happen when the relational field settles.**

As we settle, what can be seen has a chance to arise. Having a witness is crucial… yes, we can track what's going on in our own bodies, and developing this witness consciousness is an important piece of this work. That said, another human can witness through a different lens. We're human, and we need other humans to thrive, learn and grow. We don't exist in a vacuum.

As we work with the framework of understanding ourselves as energetic beings and recognizing our power of choice and intention, whole new vistas of possibility emerge. Let's build on this to continue to explore energy.

Feminine and Masculine Energies: Energy as Balance and Flow

When I viewed my own masculine and feminine as they showed up in the exercise with Girijah, I could see the way my masculine — the analyzer, the doer — was running the show, saying, "Hey, this is what we're gonna do."

But then my feminine — the listener, the part of me about feeling and slowing down and opening — had no space. Those energies were getting squashed. The masculine-analyzer was taking over, but not paying attention, so there was no space for the feminine-receptor to be heard around what she needed. In fact, I kind of trampled over her. Thankfully, due to the container of the exercise, we had the space afterwards to integrate. I noticed all the sensations in that space and sat down and talked about it. That was when I could notice my "doer-thinker" had taken over and my "being-feeler" was ignored... I'd lost my balance. I wasn't creating a safe space for my own feminine energy to be there.

Self-awareness and growth are all about balance. They depend on complementary energies through which, as they come together, we can find healing and then weave and integrate them through and as our bodies into: One. Union. The very word "Yoga" means "to yoke" or bring union, and that is the nature of that path: finding and connecting with what I will call the feminine and masculine energies that are in us all, allowing them to integrate and find balance within. The word "Tantra" can be translated from Sanskrit in many ways, and one is "to weave." This weaving and integrating of this fabric of Self is the very essence of the practice of Tantra.

Notice that throughout this text I have used the words "Feminine" and "Masculine" in the context of applying to us all. These words as I use them are not about gender. We all, regardless of how we identify in our gender expression, have qualities of both within us.

This is important, so let me reiterate:

Feminine and masculine are qualities of energy within us all, regardless of our sex and how we identify in gender. When I use the words feminine and masculine, I do not mean female and male. There is a whole spectrum of how we may identify in gender. Gender is not binary.[52]

The path of Sacred Sexuality and Tantra is about meeting and exploring the integration of these complementary energies within us.

So let's explore the words in more detail. Despite the potential confusion with gender, over the years I have found that, given the limitations of the English language, these are still the best words I can find to describe the complementary energies they name. For the purposes of this book, I will use them in this way:

Our **Masculine energies** are those facets within us of drive, purpose, getting things done, thinking and planning. Our Masculine is solar, fiery and active, and is about things outside of us. These energies are about *doing*.

Our **Feminine energies** are cool, lunar, receptive, feeling. They are about slowing down, feeling emotions and opening, allowing, being vulnerable and surrendering to the flow. Our Feminine is about *feeling* to balance the *thinking*; *being* to balance the *doing*.

Deep inquiry into both of these energies and the balance between them has been a part of my journey for some time. I explored them in my yoga teacher training, and wrote about them in my paper, "Sri Yantra: The Sacred Geometry of Yoga."[53] Below, I include a summary of my research and study via one of the tables from that paper here (See Table 1).

Table 1: Feminine and Masculine Principles[54]

Feminine		Masculine
HA		THA
lunar		solar
Left nostril & body		Right nostril & body
Right brain hemisphere		Left brain hemisphere
PRANA shakti		MANAS shakti
Vital force		Mental energy

---

[52] An excellent and accessible read on this topic is *Beyond the Gender Binary*, a book by Alok Vaid-Menon.

[53] *Sri Yantra: The Sacred Geometry of Yoga* by Leslie Blackburn.

[54] Ibid.

Life force		Mental force
"All Matter is Alive"		"All Matter is Conscious"
Life = prakriti	in Yoga	Consciousness = purusha
Shakti	in Tantra	Shiva
Ida (tamas)	in Hatha Yoga	Pingala (rajas)
Yin	in Taoism	Yang
Matter	in Physics	Energy
space		time
passive	in Buddhist Tantras	dynamic
dynamic, creative, manifest	in Hindu Tantras	static, unmanifest
female principle		male principle
introverted		extroverted
orientation in space, artistic, creative, musical		logical, sequential, mathematical, analytical
subconscious		conscious
positive	neutral	negative
	sushumna (sattva)	
flow of vital energy	flow of spiritual energy	flow of consciousness

And I giggle as I look at the table that I created! As I reflect on my journey with this, I see that the "masculine approach" to the Feminine and Masculine dynamic is to make a list, in this case my table!

My analytical self began this journey by trying to distinguish and label each quality, create two lists or buckets, sort things out, get them organized in my head. Yes, this was helpful for me and the way I process information, and I include it because you may find it supportive as well. Yet what keeps showing up is that this concept is more slippery than what can be held in a table alone. There are arguments that can put each quality on either side: "Looking at the table I see 'positive' under 'feminine' and 'negative' under 'masculine.' But wait:

I thought the feminine is negative because of being the open vessel to receive the shaft of the masculine penetration?" So one might argue. Yes: That's another way to look at it.

I now see that a feminine approach — a more fluid, creative approach — widens my perception and gets me out of the tension of analysis. While there was a point in my journey where I felt the value of creating the schema in Table 1, I can also now feel the value of *releasing* it. Both are important. As a friend of mine who is a bodyworker shared in a workshop she taught recently about how her work has deepened as she as brought her authentic self to it: "I spent the first 10 years learning the techniques and details of the practices I was taught, and the next 10 years unlearning them."

Over time I came to recognize that it is less about which one is which, and more about honoring the complementary dynamic between these energies and the wholeness they generate, and about recognizing what happens when they get out of balance.

Over the last millennia, Western culture and society on this planet, and most recently the culture in the US, have derogated, subordinated and devalued the Feminine energy ways: the ability to feel and be guided by body wisdom and our connection with nature, the shamanic way. These encompass fluid ways of learning: breath, sound, movement and touch practices that have mostly been dropped from mainstream educational, political, economic and corporate systems and structures.

What gets valued in the corporate-normative world is: analysis, planning and goal-setting within rigid structures and narrow points of view. I speak this having lived it. As we explored in Part 1, for the first decades of my adult life I did my best to fit into that structure. I excelled in school and in my career, doing my best to "man-up" to the job and "walk the company line." I was rising up through the promotional ranks, getting big bonuses, glowing performance reviews and awards, and all the while, the top criticism of my performance was: "You're too emotional." My perfectionist self had a hard time with this. I shoved my feelings away and got even more analytical.

Recall my story of sitting in a boardroom meeting one day, presenting on a topic to senior management, where I began a sentence with "I feel that…" I was immediately verbally squashed and told:

"I don't care how you feel. Show me the data!"

And it worked: I trained myself well in those analytical ways. I even found myself on the other side of that boardroom table, where I was the manager raging in anger when someone didn't "perform" or "do" something "right." As if anger and meanness were an expected part of getting the job done.

Notice even how, years later, in the exercise with Girijah, my analytical self took over and ran the show, despite what I was feeling in my body.

What is it like to let the Feminine be heard? I have spent over 20 years in that inquiry. Deeply feeling the value of slowing down, of listening to my body, I have come to know in my body and mind that these ways aren't inferior to the masculine analysis… they are a crucial complement! Both are needed. As acclaimed author, mystic, and Founder Director of the Institute of Sacred Activism, Andrew Harvey[55] says:

> Unless we really return to the feminine wisdom and marry the profound feminine knowledge and wisdom and passion and concern for all forms of life with what you might call the masculine gifts of precision and order and clarity and brilliant intellect and real focused action in the world, we're simply not going to survive.

As I started seeking to find a better balance than this masculine, hyper-analytic path, I started to recognize, trust and feel my body again. I began to notice changes and openings in my sexual energy and vibrancy. And as I had Body Awakenings (times when old armor or shields in my body would let go and I could feel new vibrancy move in) and started to experience bliss, pleasure and ecstatic states I felt like, "Whoa! I need to stand on top of the mountain and shout: EVERYONE DESERVES TO KNOW ABOUT THIS!"

I began seeking teachers and guides and then weaving what I learned from them to create my own unique path. I hope this book can be a similar support for your path. This ongoing process of gestating and giving birth to my work in the world and how I teach and share is unique; it's not part of a single lineage or teaching certification. It is a weaving from many teachers, teachings and traditions, as well as my own direct experience and downloads from Source. It is about honoring that we each have access to the wisdom within our own bodies, and it's about empowering each of us to claim that knowing and trust our capacity to find and connect with our own Truth. It is life and love brought forth from my own inner connection with the divine. I share my work from a place

---

[55] http://www.andrewharvey.net

that acknowledges that Art and Science, East and West, blend and overlap in many ways.

What were the practices and foundations that I was meeting in my life that supported me to have these experiences that sent me to shout from the mountaintops?

Let's explore them in the deep foundation of Container.

Container

Container: This concept is perhaps the biggest, most profound foundational concept to support change and healing for each of us as Energetic Beings, or Soul Beings, as well as for the healing of the collective consciousness on this planet. The rise of the Divine Feminine on planet Earth at this time relies on the physical embodiment of "Container" in our bodies and in the world around us. I shared about this with every private client I saw and every group class I taught. It shows up as part of my life on a daily basis, in many forms. I feel it support me. I embody it. I live it. This is the concept of "Container" — a safe space to support freedom and transformation.

We not only create Containers with others, we also create them within ourselves. Recall my journey with the exercise at the opening of this chapter: I didn't notice how I wasn't holding a safe container for myself until after we sat down to integrate and discuss. This self-inquiry is an important component to how we also co-create container with a partner. Here's another example:

I am exploring touch with a client, we have called in our Sacred Circle and spoken our boundaries, fears and desires — effectively co-creating our Container for the session. As we come into contact, our bodies and energy begin to harmonize and as the session proceeds, the cultivation of energy begins. We raise the energy and spread and share it, continuing to build the energy we are cultivating. He starts to creep his hand slowly in a way on my body that ends up violating one of our Boundary agreements.

Immediately, the energy pours out, draining away. We both feel it. I sense he is disappointed as he is no longer feeling the energy. Yet he can't articulate it. He tries to ignore what happened and try something else. I feel frustrated that he violated a boundary, almost ready to yell — I feel my defenses prickle — yet I also recognize that there is a teaching point to be offered. Spirit is clear that me yelling in anger (an old thing for me) is not what is being called for, yet I also cannot let this just slide away and be ignored (also an old thing for me). This is also clear: It is not about punishment or hatred. I stop, take a breath, allow my body to soften.

This pause took a minute, and the reason it only took a minute was that I had done a lot of personal human homework to be able to transmute the heavy energies and shift so quickly.

After allowing myself that space to shift, I open a discussion, witnessing with compassion.

"Hello beautiful, what are you noticing?"

Closed, stoic, dark face, gazing down. "Um, I don't know."

"Can I share what I am noticing?"

Shrugs. "Mm."

I share from my heart, smiling, "I am noticing that we were building and cultivating some energy and it was feeling really wonderful, yes?"

Face brightens, lifts a little, feeling acknowledged: "Yes."

"And then something happened and that energy dropped away and felt 'meh.' Make sense?"

Definitely resonates for him, his face softens a bit. Yet he's also hesitant, looking confused as if he's surprised he's not being yelled at. He slowly replies, "Yes."

"I notice that you moved your hand and crossed a boundary, and what happened at that point was you cracked the Container we had co-created to be our safe space for this relating. When the Container cracks, it can't hold the energy anymore and the energy pours out and drains away. Then it feels icky — for both of us. Mmmm, all the yumminess dropped away. Do you feel that?"

In his confusion I offer gentle invitations to see from a different lens. He moves from expecting to be yelled at and either trying to ignore it or defend it — old defensive mechanisms from a lifetime of patterning — to opening and widening in awareness to how his choices and actions are part of what creates the world around him, and how they impact not only himself but others. He's surprised.

"Oh my god! I have never looked at it that way before!" He gets it, and a new layer of healing emerges. Yes, we've discussed this before, many times. The difference is that now it is not just something offered at a mental level, not just about "thinking" — now, he FEELS it — his body has caught up to the knowing. This is when true healing can begin.

We smile together and share a loving embrace.

Let's explore Container from three directions.

Transformation

First, let's look at the importance of Container in the nature of Alchemy. Alchemy is about creating change, transforming. Often this is the very nature of what we are seeking in our lives. We notice something about our life and we want to change it. This concept of Container is crucial for that possibility of change.

Let's illustrate with one of the simpler alchemical transformations: changing liquid water into steam. For this example, imagine you have the desire to transform liquid water into steam. You have the water, and you realize you need an energy to apply to the water to evoke the change... you acquire fire. If you only have those two things, and you dump the water on the fire, what happens? The fire goes out, and it leaves a messy, wet puddle! This is because a third crucial component is missing: the Container!

Alchemy is transformation, change. To support change, we need three things:

- The **substance** we wish to transform (for example: liquid water)
- An **energy** to apply to it to support the change (for example: fire)
- A **Container** (for example: a pot)

Now, we have a pot, put the water in the pot and put the pot on the fire. Ah! We can easily see how in a short amount of time, the water will boil and transform into steam.

This is a simple example of the necessity of the container. We must have the container to support change, or transformation.

Now let's look at the nature of Container a second way.

Divine Feminine & Healthy Masculine

Reflecting back on what we've explored about Feminine and Masculine energies, let's expand on this. Our Healthy Masculine does three things for us:[56]

- Creates safety
- Holds space
- Witnesses without judging

---

[56] A teaching from ISTA, https://ista.life/

When we hold space for someone, we allow them to be who they are without trying to fix, change, take from, or demand anything of them. When we witness in this way, we call it non-judgmental. However, as humans, we also acknowledge our own vulnerability and notice that even with our best intentions in holding safe space and witnessing, we may have judgments of others arise. So to support people in their ability to "witness without judging," I expand upon that: "Notice our judgments when they arise and acknowledge them as our own without projecting them onto the other person."

I like to express this with a body gesture like a relaxed safe comfort-figure with arms open in a welcoming way, saying in effect: "Ah, I have your back. You are safe to let go here." This energy is that of, "I'm not going to touch you inappropriately, I am not going to laugh at you if you are crying, I am not going to yell at you, I am simply here now, loving you and holding you with no expectations." In the presence of the Healthy Masculine you feel safe. You can be true to yourself. You could fall asleep in their arms.

The thing is, for so many of us on the planet, we have no role model for this: We didn't feel it in Mom, we didn't feel it in Dad. Consider this: We can find it *within* our own Being. How empowering to recognize that we can find this within ourselves, once again noticing that a partner is not required. As we can connect with this energy, we can hold space for amazing possibilities — in our own individual path of self-awareness as well as with others.

In fact, as we connect with our Healthy Masculine, our Divine Feminine will finally feel safe to emerge. She will peek out and burst forth with a "WHEEE!! Yay! I can come out and play!" She is our za-za energy, juice, our vibrancy, our joy and light! She will not come out to play if she does not feel safe.

Author in ecstasy, the flow of vital energy moving through their body.

So imagine the infinite possibilities when we create the safe space, the Container, for the very nature of our passion, creativity and juice and zest for life to emerge and shine its light in the world!

For example, when I was held in the safe space of my experiences of shibari with Paul, he was embodying the healthy masculine. My teacher Rose embodied this quality when she met me and held space for my new layer of self-awareness to integrate as she affirmed my spirit name. I have embodied this when I held a boundary with Jay's tearing out the sacred space that had been created when a child planted a flower.

As we awaken to healthy masculine ways of being, we find we are creating containers all the time and we can make a choice about how to shape them. It's a constant checking in with self and others.

To expand even more deeply, let's look at the nature of Container a third way.

How Boundaries Support Freedom

There was a research study done with children on a playground.[57] Imagine a large open space with playground equipment in the center. At first the kids come

---

[57] Ibid.

out to play and they cluster in close to the playground equipment. Now the kids leave, and a fence is erected around the perimeter of the open space. Next, they come out to play again, only this time they play fully, ranging wide. Out to the edges of the fence. It's as if at first they say, "That spot of grass over there... hmmm, I don't know if I can go there. Is it safe?" And when that question of safety is not clear, there's a contraction and they behave as if the space is not available.

However, when the edges become clear, the fence is in place, they think: "Ah, yes! I can play there!" And they do. In other words, when the Container is known and the boundaries of the space are clear, the children are supported in the freedom to expand into the space. This is what I call "How Boundaries Support Freedom."

Important — note that this is counter to our typical patriarchal cultural assumption of the nature of Boundaries. I know, even in myself, I found that the word 'Boundaries' used to evoke in me a sense of: "Oh I don't want those... those are just a list of restrictions. Those things hold me back, I want to feel free, not bound!" We even see this in literature, mainstream advertising and pop culture with phrases such as "pushing boundaries" and "no-boundaries experience" as being an encouragement to step out of your comfort zone and meet new goals.

I invite that Boundaries are just the *opposite* of restrictions. By being able to connect with our authentic body wisdom around what feels safe and good, we can discern our Container needs for the moment, hold those for ourselves or with our partners and open the space to let go into Freedom. **Boundaries are what support us to let go into Freedom.**

That said, while the concept may be cognitively straightforward, to embody this is not easy. There are a few complications.

Barriers Are Different than Boundaries

Sometimes Boundaries get confused with Barriers. In this book, as I refer to 'Barriers,' I mean armor, shielding, numbness, protective mechanisms that we have erected over time. While these barriers can be perceived as holding us back from being fully aligned with our Truth, or from opening our heart in connection with others, they are also really important "skills," or coping strategies. We learned and sometimes fall back on these skills to get through really hard things in life. I invite us to be gentle on ourselves when we begin to notice them. As we build our resources and learn new things, we may find that barriers have a chance to crumble and fall away. In particular, cleanly connecting with our boundaries, communicating them and holding space for our authentic selves to come forth in our fullest are some of the new skills that support releasing the barriers and opening to new ways of being. It's a journey of exploring new possibilities, listening to your body for what it has to say, adjusting based on the messages, and noticing the changes. The structure that a Container provides gives space for the freedom for this exploration.

Recall my story in Part 1, I noticed myself erecting many barriers in the form of "Don't let anyone in" and "Don't feel" for many decades of my life. To be clear, it was through connecting with my authentic body wisdom and discerning my boundaries (aka the things that I needed in order to feel safe to let go) that I was able to allow those barriers to crumble away, expand into new expressions of my deep being and begin deeply reconnecting with my divine feminine juiciness. It didn't happen overnight. It is more like a widening spiral: learning new things about what my body needed, offering new ways to create safe space, listening and honoring the next step in the journey. Supporting liberation one step at a time.

A key piece of our self-inquiry then becomes discernment. How do I know the difference between an authentic boundary and a barrier? How do I tell the difference in a body message between authentic body wisdom and a message from a wounded place or place of resistance, or fear, or from a place of ego-mind? Indeed, these are the very nature of exploring embodied awareness. It's a practice in which we learn and listen and our bodies guide us. It's an ongoing exploration.

Now that we've done the Container deep dive, recall the three energetic concepts of: Infinite Being, Gift of a Body, and Feminine and Masculine Dynamics. What do those concepts have to do with it? As we are infinite beings in a finite form, we can begin to acknowledge that our bodies are a vessel that uniquely houses our energetic being or soul. This opens the door for the awareness that our bodies are indeed a tremendous gift. Without the Container of our organism, which is literally formed by the union of masculine and feminine energies to become a vessel for our expression, we cannot access energy and come into relationship with other beings to learn and grow. Many spiritual traditions miss this important piece and instead degrade the body as something to escape from or teach that our bodies should not be trusted. We are indeed swimming against mainstream US cultural currents as we rebuild that trust.

However, essentially the body is one level of Container, and it is a crucial piece of the creation of safe space for our soul to be incarnated here on this planet. Our journey of Sacred Sexuality then becomes more clearly one of listening to the body and building resilience and capacity in our physical and energetic bodies to be with the bigness of who we are as energetic beings, remembering and trusting who we are and our power.

It also means doing all this in right relationship with the other beings we share this world with, because we are all connected.

CHAPTER FIFTEEN
More Container to Support Soft Power

Dancing with Polarities & Balance

Think of the last time you held a container in your hand: a coffee cup, a glass of water. The container's function marks a boundary between what's going on inside the container — the water, say — and what's going on outside of it — the person drinking it. With a glass of water this boundary is pretty rigid and brittle. In humans, our boundaries are by necessity flexible, alive, and responsive — as individual as our own skin. Our boundaries are best thought of as movable balance points. And, because we are all different, consciously creating container for our growth will mean different things to each person and involve different approaches in different times and situations.

So for example, as a recovering over-achiever who long thought working harder was the only way to get things done, my ways of finding the needed balance point for my container may be completely different than someone else's.

I share the following to empower you with the self-awareness tools to assess what pieces of the practices are right for you, based on your personal nature and choice.

For example...

Recall our journey of energy balance: Rarely can we categorize something as rigidly right or wrong, or good or bad. It is all about the nature of balance. Noticing where we are on the spectrum of possibility helps us make choices that invite balance for our particular body and in a particular situation or moment. In the same way a dowsing pendulum, or any object hanging from a string, may jump and bounce, spiral and circle and dance between various points on a spiral — we find balance by approaching, touching and feeling our edges, adjusting with our choices, finding a new center. We reach, stretch and open; we condense, curl, pull inward. This is a moment-to-moment dance without a singular right answer.

All too often we may think of our choices in binary terms. Then it can feel like we are in the daunting momentum of a large grandfather clock, bonging on predetermined cycles with little room for curiosity or creative new possibilities. Instead, let's be in the dance.

I believe the description of the *Gunas* helps shed some light on our patterns. "Gunas" is the Sanskrit term for the "nature of mind" described by Patanjali in the Yoga Sutras,[58] the philosophy of life in the yoga tradition. There are three gunas — Rajas, Tamas and Sattva — and they are all three present in a spectrum as we dance among them.[59]

One portion of the spectrum is Rajas. Rajas nature is fiery, active, bound up, tense. "Militant attention" is how I think of Rajas. When I feel Rajas, I feel tense and stuck. Energy isn't freely flowing due to binding. Rubbing out a quick orgasm, or pushing my body into finishing races despite injury and illness are just two examples of many of my own Rajasic tendencies.

Another quality in the spectrum is Tamas. Tamas is lethargy — a dull, couch-potato quality. Meh. Energy isn't freely flowing due to flaccidity, lack of tone. It is very different than Rajas, yet neither feel so good. Tamas shows up for me with screen time. Back in my passive television watching days, I would sit for hours in a dull energy of disconnection. I wasn't present to sensations in my body, and instead stayed "checked out," sometimes without even noticing the TV was on. This is the nature of the low, lethargic, addictive passivity of television left unchecked.

The sweet spot of the gunas is Sattva... ah! The absence of both Rajas and Tamas — or perhaps more accurately the presence of all three in balance. Clarity, feeling deeply rooted like seaweed at the bottom of the ocean, yet vibrant and alive in our movement with the currents. When I feel a quality of Sattva, I feel grounded and connected to the earth, with a relaxed ease allowing currents of

---

[58] *The Yoga Sutras of Patañjali* by Satchidananda and Patañjali.

[59] I am taking a bit of artistic liberty here with working with the gunas in a spectrum. To meet the full inquiry of the gunas requires a deeper exploration of the sutras and yogic philosophy, which is beyond the scope of this book.

energy to move through my toned and alive body — without force, without collapse. Balance, vibrancy, aliveness, awareness, ease. These are the qualities of Sattva. These qualities align well with the journey of transcendence and enlightenment.

The Sattvic difference is the presence and clarity — vital energy becomes more accessible through and by our bodies. None of this is to say that being driven to finish endurance races or chilling out and watching an occasional show are inherently bad things. We each need our own balance, ways to support our bodies in rest and recovery as well as in active participation with life. The ways you find balance and nourish your bodies may be completely different than the practices someone else may need.

With this in mind, as you explore the invitations and practices in this book, I encourage you to check in with yourself. What qualities of mind do you notice in you right now? How do these inform how you meet this work?

Soft Power and Balance

And next, as we draw upon the ways we dance in the balance of feminine and masculine energies, and the spectrum of the nature of mind (the gunas), let's meet the way this spectrum shows up in our personal power.

There are three dynamics in this dance:

Codependence ~ Interdependence ~ Hyper-Independence

Hyper-Independence

In my own journey I started down a path of fierce independence. I built walls and armor and shields in an attempt to protect myself from feeling. So I got really good at creating barriers. Barriers are when we are in an energy of (with a stiff arm): "NO! I don't want to let you in. I am guarding my heart and it feels scary to let down the shield." Here, I am in "Hyper-Independence."

With hyper-independence, the masculine can dominate in "power-over" aggression. There is often an underlying fear of scarcity, as if someone else having their power somehow takes away from my own. This quality shows up not just in my own journey, it is at the forefront of colonization culture mindset, setting out "every man for himself," to conquer, take over and claim dominance. This mindset not only harms the people and land that get oppressed in the process, it harms the people and culture perpetuating the mindset by disconnecting us from nature, connection and belonging.

Recall my journey with my aerial teacher as I wanted to share newfound skills. In my genuine desire to stretch my wings and step into new roles as a teacher, I unconsciously pushed past a limit and in the fallout learned a lot about how to hold space for my own needs without trampling on someone else's. I learned more about this balance later and came to know it as Soft Power. I experienced this as a journey with my solar plexus, the seat of our power dynamics with others and our self will. This balance is key to releasing the competitive scripts and healing our relationships with others.

Codependence

Another piece of the power spectrum is Codependence. One way this expresses is that we grasp at people to fill a hole in ourselves, believing that somehow we cannot be whole without another to fill us in. When I am in this place I feel lacking, incomplete and not good enough. I grasp at others, perhaps at first seeing it as love. Then I notice it can easily swing toward hate, toward resentment. Perhaps I notice myself trying to be like someone or something else to make others happy, and I lose that connection of happiness within my own being. I felt this voluntary shrinking early on, in attempts to date and "make people like me" during adolescence.

My relationship with my first boyfriend had many codependent themes: I was needy and grasping, I clung to him to fill in emotional connection that I wasn't getting from my parents. I was overly involved and obsessed by the relationship. I had passive-aggressive ways of interacting that were met with similar patterns, something I brought in from my mother's lineage.

As I experienced the end of that relationship and made the decision to numb out and not feel, my codependency shifted, ironically fueled by the hyper-independence, to becoming a "fixer."

From a Codependency in Relationships website:

> Some people are "fixers." This means that one of the partners wants to fix the other and solve their problems to make them a better person and a better person to be dating. This is commonly known as falling for someone's potential. Ironically, the person being the "fixer" is generally the codependent partner. They can see themselves as having their own responsibilities in order and strong enough where they can handle helping their partner. This is

dangerous because this person is constantly bearing the load of the relationship in order to help the other improve or change, which, unfortunately, does not usually happen.[60]

I can see the ways I tried to control and change my husband, coming from what I thought were good intentions at the time. This type of codependency wasn't as obvious as my needy graspiness, but was certainly just as painful to unwind from, if not more so.

It showed up later in other ways, too. One of which was my relationship with Jay.

As I reflected on our time together, I noticed another pattern in my relationship with Jay, one that had begun with my husband. I noticed that while with my husband I had grown to the place of not enjoying "doing things" together, with Jay we really did enjoy "doing things" together. I thought this shared interest in activities was what I was looking for. Yet part of the glue that held the relationship together was that Jay was really into me, and that attracted me to him. I found myself in the same "loving him for loving me" place that I had begun to notice I had done in my ex-partnership. There's something that happens when we meet this type of energy — a sense of one partner filling holes in the other, and an unhealthy grasping at or pushing away often emerges. This place is called "codependence."

I am guiding the boundary exercise described at the beginning of Chapter 14 with a new client. She is healing from a traumatic marriage that had begun shortly after her grown children left the nest and ended recently in an abusive spiral. In the embodied practice we are exploring, she has an "aha moment" related to her falling in love with and marrying the partner who later had abusive behaviors: "Ohhhh! I see now how I let it happen!" she says. "When my children grew up and moved out, they left a hole in my heart. I tried to fill it with this other person. I see now that I can meet the loving needs of my heart, and my WHOLE-ness within me. I don't have to rely on another to fill the hole!"

And even later, I could clearly see the codependent thinking involved in my experience with the boundary exercise with Girijah. I found myself worried about what she would think if I asked her to move back: "Maybe she'll think I

---

[60] https://codependencyinrelationships.weebly.com/better-understanding-of-codependency-and-why-it-happens.html

don't like her." I didn't want that type of rejection, and was violating my own body wisdom thinking it would safeguard the possibility of connection with her. Which was not actually true, and doesn't work anyway.

Interdependence

As we dance in the spectrum of balance in our power, we find a sweet spot, the place that's filled with lightness and ease, or what I call "Interdependence." The dictionary definition of interdependence is "the dependence of two or more people or things on each other." In this balance, we allow each other in, but do not suck each other in. When I dance in my life here, I feel good and clear and connected with who I am. I trust my capability and value. I let people in. I relate, I learn and grow. I know that when I am in my power it doesn't take away from anyone else's, and that when someone else is in their power it doesn't take away from me.

Together, in this shared Soft Power, I can co-create with others. I can rely on and trust in our connection and in my own presence, and not grasp at it nor push it away. When I feel clear and bright in who I am and open to learning new ways, I feel myself in a balance of interdependence.

This balance becomes important as we meet the various energies in our lives. Often we're in a place of judgment, and we decide that something or someone is good or bad and we make choices on what to "do" accordingly: follow the "good" thing, reject the "bad" thing. Have you ever noticed in your attempts to fight off or hide the "bad" thing, it just keeps showing up? Maybe you start to notice that you keep dating new versions of the same person, or that your relationships have a pattern that keeps showing up. If we think we're going to shove away, cut off, kill or destroy some facet of that energy, we're fooling ourselves.

Energy cannot be created or destroyed, yet energy can be transmuted, meaning, changed in its form or nature. We can meet it, learn from it, change it, release it. Shame, low self-esteem, jealousy, judgment and hatred are some of the many parts of ourselves that we tend to want to reject, yet we can transmute these, actually make a change at our core. Perhaps we can find the ally in it and merge with that supportive facet of ourselves. Perhaps we can release into the support of the Earth. When we dance, move, sing, breathe, we are in relationship with the energies in our bodies and can make choices to transmute and change.

The Earth can safely transmute and clear a lot, if we ask her to, if we allow her to. We can shift the vibration, change the state and find the balance and integration that is right for us in each moment of our growth and transformation. This alchemy and embodied practices for exploring it are the focus of this book.

In fact, not only do we have that power of choice, being of service and change and growth are the very reason we, as soul beings, are here on this planet... *it's what we're here to do*. Each of us arrives with different assignments, a unique calling into the path of lessons and experiences that shape our growth and transformation together.

As an experienced colleague and friend of mine, clinical sexologist, author and lecturer Francesca Gentille shared with me: "Our lives are shaped by the questions we ask."[61] This stuck with me because I had been trained throughout my childhood to be small, stay out of the way, and not ask questions. The message I received was that it would be wrong to ask questions because they were intrusive. It took years to unwind that conditioning. Now I invite, yes, let's meet the world with inquiry: asking questions with playful curiosity. We allow ourselves to learn by asking questions and relating with the world — with animals, plants, fellow humans, nature.

And, how we ask our questions really matters.

An example of a career path question is: "How can I make money?" Eventually someone will give me effective information. But what if instead I asked, "How can I make money while expressing my soul's purpose?" Now the information I receive will guide me in a very different direction.

Likewise, in relationship if I ask, "Why are you being such a jerk?" I may get a defensive reaction. On the other hand, I may receive a much more connective response if I ask, "I am curious about why you speak or make choices in this way. Is it something you saw modeled growing up? Or something else?"

Further, the intention with which we form the question and the depth with which we design the question will shape the responses, as well as the journey in life that unfolds.

So as we ask questions and relate with each other, nature and the world around us, let's feel into how those inquiries can reshape our lives.

---

[61] Francesca Gentille, http://www.francescagentille.com/

More Learning About Power: Responsibility & Accountability

As I related with new beings and with the world in new ways and deepened in the realm of Sacred Sexuality, my journey of learning about power continued. I found that it is not only about claiming my own balance and power, but also about learning where not to take on someone else's, even if it is being handed to me on a silver platter.

My hands are in contact with his body, one set of fingers woven through the toes of his left foot, stretching to provide a sensation that pleases him. The fingers of my other hand cradle under his heel, delicately dancing between light touch and firm pressure. At his request, I begin to stretch and tug his foot and toes... he responds, "Yes please, more!" I breathe, we breathe together, he beckons me to pull harder, "Yes please," feeling the intensity of our breaths and the tugging at his root. The energy builds; it's palpable.

Shortly before, we had set the container. As an exercise in our training, we are exploring a practice of relating with bodies with consent. We had each made a choice to come together for this learning, which has energetic as well as physical aspects. Whether or not we chose to make actual contact with the body depended completely on the choices and consent of each person involved. As the person offering, I had asked questions to guide the creation of our container together. In the course of our sharing, he as the one receiving spoke a fear: "Please don't hurt me."

I, in my eager desire to support him fully and to learn this path, agreed completely, "Of course I won't hurt you." I committed to holding him safely. We finalized other details and open our sacred space. The session then began.

As we continue the tugging, the pressure builds. He asks for more and I give it, until the moment happens.

"Ouch!" he exclaims.

Oh no! I've hurt him! I feel awful, instantly shifting my touch, apologizing for doing the one thing he had asked me not to do. I feel as if a gate has opened, all my energy begins pouring out. He says he's fine, it's okay, no harm done.

I continue the best I can, trying to move past the mistake, beating myself up inside, and doing my best to stay strong to complete the session.

As we deepen in the session, he takes my face in his hands, gazes at my eyes, sharing gratitude for my touch and support of him. I feel an emptying... as if he is drawing my energy out of my body. Sucking out my life. Feeding on me.

I make it through. We close the session. I move to a break and find myself in a heap of tears. I'm exhausted, drained. I feel awful. I can't think straight. What just happened?

Girijah is there, the soul sister I had only just met in the training, yet connected with immediately and deeply, as well as sweet Paul. Holding me and loving me, they check in: What has happened? I share the story. As I get to the point of his request, "Please don't hurt me," and my response, Girijah brings me to a halt: "Right there, Sister! That's it!"

"What's it?" I ask.

"Right there: He tried to hand you his power... and you took it! And the result was he was able to drain you of yours. No one can drain you like that unless you let them. By setting up the contract you chose in the beginning, you set the stage for the possibility of what happened next."

The thing is, my partner in this exercise likely isn't even consciously aware of what he did. He probably didn't mean for it to happen that way. Most people don't drain others on purpose.

Girijah compassionately and lovingly helped me see a new way.

In that moment, another way to meet my exercise partner began to grow in me: "I hear you asking to not be hurt and I indeed I will do my part to hold you in the safe space we are co-creating. That said, you are responsible as well. I ask that YOU share with me if you feel near that edge of pain. You have the power to choose to ask for us to stop or shift at any time."

In this way I am not taking on his responsibility for self-care, I carry only my own responsibility in the relationship. I meet it in compassionate, loving ways... holding us each as Divine beings.

Through this experience, I learned one of the most important lessons of my journey in Sacred Sexuality and stepping into my own power: **Do not let others give me their power — simply stay present and clear in my own.**

And this applies in both directions, not just about the edgy or hard bits, but the wonderful or magical ones as well. As I relate with beings in life, if they have an amazing experience, that is just as much a shared responsibility, co-created as the not-so-wonderful experiences. Ego has a hard time with this lesson; it's a layer of shedding. It's counter to a common mentality when seeking spiritual guidance that someone is "better than" and therefore should be followed unconditionally. As Rachel Naomi Remen, MD,[62] a pioneer of Wholistic and Integrative Medicine who has helped thousands of patients to remember their power to heal, shares:

> There is distance between ourselves and whatever or whomever we are fixing. Fixing is a form of judgment. All judgment creates distance, a disconnection, an experience of difference. In fixing there is an inequality of expertise that can easily become a moral distance. We cannot serve at a distance. We can only serve that to which we are profoundly connected, that which we are willing to touch. This is Mother Teresa's basic message. We serve life not because it is broken but because it is holy.[63]

Being of service, I am an equal. It's not about fixing or changing another person. Nor is it about making them happy. It's about meeting each other in divine relationship, and learning, healing and growing together. I invite we each are our own teacher; our Truth is within. Our bodies know the way… let's slow down and listen.

Summary

So far in Part 3, we've introduced **the foundational pieces for our journey with Sacred Sexuality and recreating our relationship with our bodies**:
- We are **energetic beings** with the gift of being in a **physical body**.
- We're on the Earth at this time to be of **service** to ourselves and others and to **change and grow** as energetic beings.

---

[62] Rachel Naomi Remen is an internationally recognized medical educator whose innovative discovery model course in professionalism, resiliency and relationship-centered care for medical students, *The Healer's Art* is taught at more than 90 American medical schools and schools in seven countries abroad. http://www.rachelremen.com

[63] Rachel Naomi Remen, In the Service of Life, handout from BCST training, also found here: https://www.infj.com/ServingVsHelping.htm. Accessed 2024-11.

- Shaping the **container** creates the safe space for transformation and freedom for new possibilities. Clear, honest communication is important in creating a container.
- **Witnessing without judgment** is a powerful and often under-appreciated spiritual practice. We can hold this for ourselves and others. And we can notice when judgment comes up that it is our own stuff, not to be projected on the other person.
- **Boundaries** are part of a powerful container supporting freedom, not the restrictions that mainstream culture often makes them out to be.
- **Dancing with balance** — because we are unique and changing, the ways we meet this work and its practices will be different for each of us and will continue to evolve. Becoming aware of the various spectrums we inhabit (feminine/masculine, tamas/rajas/sattva, codependent/hyper-independent/interdependent) can help us make choices that are right for each of us.
- We can learn to meet our bodies with **curiosity instead of fear**. And this also applies to how we relate to others, nature, animals and the world around us. This will take the form of being curious and in inquiry, rather than expecting a right or wrong answer to a test or quiz.
- Each of us has the power of choice and **free will**.
- Growth in this path often requires **slowing way down** and **noticing with love and respect.**

Let's go into the deep territory of listening to body wisdom. How can we hold the space we need to feel safe and let go, and to meet the world in the ways that support us on our journey? And what great possibilities lie ahead as we listen deeply to our bodies and unlock the wisdom from within? As George Leonard suggests, we can see:

> All the cosmic patterns, the "secrets of the universe," are embedded in our muscles and bones and cells, in whatever makes up the context of the self, and that these patterns must in some way influence the way we think feel and act.[64]

Let's slow way down. With love and respect we can invite this deep wisdom to reveal itself. This means having respect for ourselves as much as we hold that for

---

[64] *The Silent Pulse* by George Leonard, Kindle location 1572 of 2214.

others. Body messages are subtle and emerge at a slower pace than the 99 mph we're used to in the way many of our rational brains think and plan and analyze. Let's give ourselves the love and respect of slowing down to listen and allow these powerful body messages to be heard, and then do our best to honor them.

As we do, often the first pieces that show up are the ones that have been screaming the loudest. Often these pieces are related to what we could name as trauma, and it's really important that they be heard.

$$\wp \, \text{❀} \, \wr$$

Welcome to a new section of the book that will continue throughout Part 3. In Questions for Self-Reflection (QSR), you will find an invitation into revealing more information from your body through inquiry. Our first QSR includes suggestions for how to work with this section to make this real in your life.

Questions for Self-Reflection

Notice the ways you create "container" for yourself and others: Do you set aside time for your self practice? Have you quietly witnessed and admired your children at play or sat by the bedside of a sick relative? Have you ever held space for a friend who needs to emotionally unload after a difficult week?

Notice the ways others have created container or held space for you: Did a teacher, elder or friend ever see your potential and encourage you to grow into it?

Suggestions for how to work with QSR in this section:
- Journal your answers to these questions.
- Write a letter of gratitude to someone who held space for you. Send it.
- Reach out and thank the space holder in person.
- Next time someone calls you with an emotional need, be a space holder instead of a fixer. Notice the difference.
- Next time you are in a gathering, explore expanding your awareness to encompass the whole. Can you remain in awareness of your body at the same time?

CHAPTER SIXTEEN

Trauma as Information in the Body

As we begin this next section, notice if you see the title and find yourself wanting to skip ahead: "Oh, this section doesn't apply to me. I don't have any trauma or abuse in my history, so let's move on to the ecstatic stuff!"

Whoa… Hold on there!

I invite you, keep reading. This section is important for all of us, no matter what we've labeled our experiences. We're humans who have been living in the recent millennia on planet Earth, so chances are, ALL of us (especially those in Western cultures) have some layers of information that our body is carrying that don't feel good. That's trauma.

Trauma can manifest in the body in many different ways: tightness, discomfort, pain, and dis-ease, to name a few. The word "trauma" may evoke immediate thoughts of abuse and molestation. Yes, these events can indeed create trauma. However, in addition, it may have been a time in sixth grade when a bully knocked your books out of your arms and laughed. It may have been a parent who yelled at you to stop singing because they had a headache, or a time when you were told you were ugly or not good enough. Any of these types of experiences, and many more, can cause your body to hold on to stuck energy, which is what I will refer to throughout this book as a "trauma."

Trauma is the way the body is carrying information. It's not the event. As Resmaa Menakem, author and therapist with decades of experience specializing in trauma, body-centered psychotherapy, and violence prevention, says: "Trauma is the body's protective response to an event — or series of events — that it perceives as potentially dangerous."[65] When we heal from trauma, we release the patterns we are holding related to the past event and love our bodies back into wholeness.

Trauma can be initiated by any number of a huge range of events and can land with varying impacts on our bodies and systems. Sustained or intense events that can often create complex post-traumatic stress include:

- experiences in war
- gun violence
- mass shootings
- chronic child abuse/neglect
- violent rape
- torture
- abduction and captivity

Trauma in the body can also be initiated by:

- physical abuse
- sexual abuse
- emotional and/or verbal abuse
- bystander trauma from witnessing abuse or other intense events

...as well as by other, less obviously violent, situations:

- birth
- accidents (car collisions, sports injuries, falls)
- illness
- surgery
- loss of loved ones
- being bullied
- being shamed, yelled at, teased, told you are not good enough
- having emotional or physical support withheld, parents not physically present or parents present but not emotionally available

---

[65] *My Grandmother's Hands: Racialized Trauma and the Pathway to Mending Our Hearts and Bodies* by Resmaa Menakem, pg 7.

And other types of stressors:

- global pandemics
- economic downturns
- being fired from a job
- divorce
- being evicted
- natural disasters
- robberies
- fires/floods in home
- homelessness

Sometimes the worst traumas are the ones we don't even know we've experienced, particularly if they become "normalized" because many others around us have experienced them, too. For example, there's often invisible academic trauma that results from being shamed or compared, the pressure of being measured and graded, or having a different way of learning that was ridiculed or suppressed.

I've noticed in my own body and with most clients I work with the shutdown that can come with fear of being judged and graded. I gently remind myself and my clients that when we are inquiring and noticing with our bodies, it's not about a "test or a quiz" or "doing it right or wrong," it's simply about curiosity and the joy of inquiry and the "aha moments" of noticing. This "allowing to be" is lost in most of our school systems, so much so that we don't even see the problem. You'll recall examples of my own story in this book, and each of us brought up in the US school systems of the last century have our own unique stories, each being impacted in different ways. Even more traumatic is the impact on individuals, families and humanity as indigenous children were forced into boarding schools to strip them of their native ways and force assimilation into mainstream cultures.

Similarly, there is religious trauma: systemic teachings that tell us not to trust our bodies or our own innate knowing, or being told we are "sinners" and that we must prove our way to goodness, instead of acknowledging the innate intelligence and goodness in all. Such beliefs can get deeply ingrained into our psyches and deeply impact our relationships with our bodies and our sexuality. This systemic trauma is hard to unwind, because it is connected to our value system, begins at an early age and may appear to be universal from the young child's perspective. Perhaps not coincidentally, there is often more overt abuse (sexual, emotional, physical) that has unfortunately been perpetrated in many churches.

We can say some of the same things about workplace trauma and cultural trauma. The white American, dominant cultural worldview perpetuates hierarchy, power-over-another, commercialization of happiness-as-needing-to-buy-stuff, and the subordination of self. That worldview is blasted at us from all directions and hard to unplug from. TV screens in airports, bars and many restaurants, bus banners and billboards, bench backs and shopping carts, web page popups and video insets… are positioned so dominantly it's hard to orient our bodies to rest and avoid the view. And woven through all that is systemic racism, sexism, classism, ableism, and more, all contributing to cultural trauma.

The more we allow our awareness to be ripped away from our source of belonging — the land, our bodies, authentic human connection, Spirit — the easier it is for oppressors to oppress. It makes their job easy.

Traumas can also have extensive reach over time, culture and lineage, and can be classified as Historical, Intergenerational, Personal or Persistent institutional. Resmaa calls this "HIPP theory." In his book *My Grandmother's Hands: Racialized Trauma and the Pathway to Mending Our Hearts and Bodies* he describes how our bodies hold racialized trauma passed down through generations, with a focus on unwinding from white body supremacy.

Trauma lives in the body, and our bodies hold the keys to unlocking how it is held. This book in your hands is about listening to the body, *your* body, and offers a somatic approach to trauma release as a path of connecting with your power and sexual sovereignty. Again: our bodies hold the keys to unlocking the way we carry old pain. You have the power to listen and heal. And you don't have to do it alone: We're in this together.

Notice also the **relational** theme. The events that can create trauma in the body listed above describe things happening between you and someone or something else. Most of our trauma happens in this relational space, and our healing happens in this relational space also. This is another reason why, as humans, we are not meant to heal this alone.

Experiencing any given event does not automatically mean your body will hang on to it as trauma. It's also about how it was met in the moment and how the body and brain responded. An event that has no long-term effect on one person can create lasting trauma in another, or an event that results in one type of response in one person can cause a completely different response in another.[66] The events that happen in our lives intensely shape our bodies and our minds, and then drive our actions into adulthood. Sometimes the ones that are particularly mysterious or terrorizing are the ones that occur in the early stages of life as our brains and bodies are newly developing, often before we have a way to verbalize what's happening or before we've developed the resources to process them. Yet any of the events listed earlier, at any time, can cause trauma.

Bessel van der Kolk, MD, is a specialist in trauma who serves as the Medical Director of The Trauma Center in Boston, Professor of Psychiatry at Boston University Medical School and Co-Director of the National Center for Child Traumatic Stress Complex Trauma Network.[67] In his book, *The Body Keeps the Score: Brain, Mind, and Body in the Healing of Trauma*, Dr. van der Kolk describes trauma as creating a feeling of a wretched state that seems like it will be forever.

> In other words trauma makes people feel like either *some body else*, or like *no body*. In order to overcome trauma, you need help to get back in touch with *your body*, with *your Self*.[68]

Notice how the theme here is the *body* consequence. Trauma is not just in our heads, it is carried in the body. For most of the population, trauma is bigger than we know, more multifaceted than we know, and is affecting more parts of us than we know.

On the pervasiveness of trauma in our society, van der Kolk emphasizes:

> Child abuse and neglect is the single most preventable cause of mental illness, the single most common cause of drug and alcohol abuse, and a significant contributor to leading causes of death such as diabetes, heart disease, cancer, stroke and suicide.[69]

For some of those coming from a background in traditional psychotherapy, seeing the link between the body and trauma can be difficult. In psychotherapy and related disciplines, trauma is often conceptualized as a mental illness.

---

[66] An excellent example of this is in the car accident story with Ute and Stan in Chapter 14 of *The Body Keeps the Score: Brain, Mind, and Body in the Healing of Trauma* by Bessel van der Kolk.

[67] http://besselvanderkolk.net

[68] van der Kolk, pg 247 (emphasis added).

[69] van der Kolk, pg 351.

Babette Rothschild, MSW, a body-psychotherapist and specialist educator in the treatment of trauma and PTSD,[70] provides a courageous bridge from the realm of traditional psychotherapy to the importance of body awareness in her book *The Body Remembers*,[71] where she explores the body as a resource and ways to resolve the effects of trauma. Also, as she sets the stage, she describes the different names, categories and diagnoses that relate to the nature of trauma. Stress, traumatic stress, post-traumatic stress (PTS), post-traumatic stress disorder (PTSD), anxiety and different types of anxiety all have their own definitions and categorization. Rothschild shares reference to the Diagnostic and Statistical Manual of Mental Disorders 4th edition (DSM-IV). She also brings in the concept of complex PTSD (CPTSD), stating that "these clients have suffered such massive and/or multiple trauma that they lack the resources and resilience necessary for any direct confrontation of traumatic memories to be constructive."[72] For all beings suffering from trauma, remembering the resourcing within, connecting with and trusting resources outside ourselves to support it, and building that resilience are key to healing.

The diagnostic codes describing and naming these conditions can be helpful as they relate to insurance coverage and accessing traditional medical support. They can help our brain get a grip on things that feel very uncomfortable. However, sometimes naming can create limitations, too.[73] We don't have to build an identity around a diagnosis. We often grasp at a diagnosis to make sense of things, and yet it isn't always helpful. If a diagnosis leads to a solution, great. If it's getting in our way or showing up as a limitation, we may need to find other ways of conceptualizing our condition.

Peter A. Levine, PhD, pioneer in the field of trauma and developer of the Somatic Experiencing[74] method, describes how we can heal trauma through awareness of body sensations:

---

[70] Babette Rothschild, http://www.somatictraumatherapy.com/

[71] Babette Rothschild, *The Body Remembers: The Psychophysiology of Trauma and Trauma Treatment*.

[72] Rothschild, pg 83.

[73] See *The Body Keeps the Score* by Bessel van der Kolk for his view on the limitations of naming and his quest for adding Developmental Trauma Disorder to the DSM.

[74] Peter Levine, http://traumahealing.org/about-us/#founder

> I learned that it was unnecessary to dredge up old memories and relive their emotional pain to heal trauma. In fact, severe emotional pain can be re-traumatizing. What we need to do to be freed from our symptoms and fears is to arouse our deep physiological resources and consciously utilize them. If we remain ignorant of our power to change the course of our instinctual responses in a proactive rather than reactive way, we will continue being imprisoned and in pain.[75]

And on the importance of FEELING, something our analytic, rational brain often shuts down and something most of us have been socialized to fear and avoid at all costs, van der Kolk says it well:

> As long as you keep secrets and suppress information [from yourself], you are fundamentally at war with yourself. Hiding your core feelings takes an enormous amount of energy, it saps your motivation to pursue worthwhile goals, and it leaves you feeling bored and shut down. Meanwhile, stress hormones keep flooding your body, leading to headaches, muscle aches, problems with your bowels or sexual functions — and irrational behaviors that may embarrass you and hurt the people around you.[76]

In other words, healing requires us to be willing to see and acknowledge that the sensations we are noticing in the present, likely catalyzed from something happening now, are actually tied to something that happened in the past. This noticing allows the healing to begin. And it's crucial: when we are reliving old scripts, it's not that the person or situation we are interacting with now is traumatizing us — they are triggering a trauma response in us from the past. They are providing a "gift" of inviting something old to come up in a new way, with a new possibility for a greater understanding or deepening in the healing. The person catalyzing our awareness in this way is often an intimate partner, and it can be hard to see this as a "gift" because it can seem like a frustration or even a threat.

Sometimes we know what the sources were, sometimes we may not know what started it, but we can still find relief as we witness our body and tap into our resourcing to allow the old patterns to unwind.

What are the signals that old trauma response patterns have been triggered? Recall for example what happened during my boundary exercise with Girijah: shallow breathing, increased heart rate, clenching in the buttocks and tucking of

---

[75] *Waking the Tiger: Healing Trauma: The Innate Capacity to Transform Overwhelming Experiences* by Peter A. Levine and Ann Frederick, pg 31.

[76] van der Kolk, pg 233.

tailbone to name only a few possibilities. Likewise, we can notice when we reach for numbing behaviors that we use to avoid feeling: mindless eating, TV shows, drinking alcohol. These cues can help us notice when something is rising up within us, trying to get our attention.

In working with my own body and in thousands of hours with clients, I have developed a new way of looking at trauma. While for me this began as an intuitive process in the deep territory of the shamanic nature of my path, what I've also learned in my research is that it aligns with the teachings of these pioneers in the field of healing trauma somatically. I've seen over and over that it all really comes down to:

- **Being in your body:** Can you settle more deeply into your body?
- **Being present:** Are you in the present moment? Is your body online? Brain research has shown that certain areas of the brain shut down in trauma (when they were knocked offline, that's how the trauma got rooted to begin with) and again later in the moments of trauma response symptoms. These areas must remain online to be able to heal from trauma. Therapy won't work if we keep being pulled back into the past. We MUST be grounded in the present. This opens the possibility of deeply knowing at a body level that the horrible events belong in the past.[77]
- **Listening to your body:** Noticing your body and breath. When we're in highly activated, hyper-aroused states, can we slow down and listen? When we're in lethargic, hypo-aroused states, can we spark an action to go a different way?
- **Honoring free will:** Would you like to make a change?
- **Balancing the polarities:** Are you willing to feel? To balance the thinking that usually takes control?

When all those answers are a "Yes," then when held in a Container of safe space, with some guidance and awareness, we can release the patterns and rewrite the old scripts that we have been reliving. We can let ourselves go into the wisdom of our body. All the wisdom is in there. We don't need to name it or

---

[77] *The Body Keeps the Score* by Bessel van der Kolk.

cognitively plan it out. We also don't need to feel like we're stuck in the box of a diagnosis forever. Our body's capacity to heal itself, to align with its original template of well-being, is immense. Sometimes we just need to get out of our own way to allow it to happen.

It's really about listening to the guidance and wisdom of the body, and the willingness to be in it. So no matter what name we give it, I invite you, slow down and take note. When your body gives you a message, listen to it.

An Empowering New Way to View Trauma

In 2014, I had an epiphany in my understanding of trauma. At the time I was well into a three-year training program on Biodynamic Craniosacral Therapy (BCST), a powerful and gentle modality of supporting the body and engaging our healing potential. My teacher was Jan Pemberton, a peaceful powerhouse of a woman with long, dark, wavy hair and kind, deep eyes. In many of our classes we worked with the BCST concept of Inertial Fulcrum.

After Jan defined and described the concept, we did practices to explore it kinesthetically with props, then we discussed as a group. Finally, in one such class, I felt the knowing click into my body.

The Inertial Fulcrum is a way of looking at how we respond to the force of experience, and helps us understand why similar experiences can impact different people in very different ways. For example, if a person gets hit in the shoulder with a soccer ball, the body must meet that experience in some way. If the particular circumstances (the speed, angle, timing of the ball, etc.) combine in that moment with our resources and body integrity in such a way that the force vectors can be resolved, then we may shake it off and move on with our day, hardly remembering that it happened and with no lasting effect on the body.

On the other hand, if the body is unable to resolve the impact within a short timeframe, the body's life force helps to center, contain and minimize disruption from that impact. Body systems reorient, meeting the force and holding it there in a way that limits the consequences on the total body system in the most efficient way it can in the moment. This profoundly life-supporting response to incoming energy creates a centering/ordering spot called an Inertial Fulcrum. It becomes a center for organizing the movement, activity and energy flows in the body. Over time, body tissues will start to organize differently in this new holding pattern.

For example, do you ever notice the way your body holds tightness differently on one side or the other? Or how twisting can feel for you on one side versus the other? We may have one shoulder that grips a little tighter than the other, or notice difficulty having someone approach us from one side of our body or another.

We can also acknowledge how the emotional and the physical dance together. Attitudes of defeat may come across in posture. Perhaps a chronic feeling of "Oh, poor me; I suck" goes along with a hunched over, rounded back. Perhaps feeling that the world is loud and dangerous comes along with contraction in the face and body. Some of the deepest patterns we can hold may even arise from the process of being born, how we were lying in the womb, and what path we took and how birth attendants and mom related to us in the process of moving through the birth canal or being born via C-section.

Originating in the body's good-faith attempt to limit the impact of an emotional or physical trauma, such patterns can be held for days, weeks, or years. Maybe sometime later, even decades later, the body feels a new sense of resource and there can be a little loosening, a shift, or even a full-on release of the original forces that had been held for so long in our energy field and body tissues. At that point, the pain associated can resolve, and the energy that had been holding for so long becomes free and available.

There are several important takeaways from this view of trauma, and each of them has profound implications for our work in sexual healing and the recovery of a more embodied spiritual presence in our lives:

1. The body is implicitly understood to be working as best it can at all times and in any given circumstances. Knowing this, we can stop blaming or disdaining the body for holding trauma.

2. This shift in our perspective on the pains and trauma patterns we carry entails an emotional shift that can open the door to healing. Instead of the disdain or hate for our body parts and responses, we can relate to them from a place of curiosity, listening, care and love. Just as we as individuals tend to relax and open to change in the presence of love and the absence of judgment, so too do our bodies sense and respond to our new orientation toward our physical experience with a greater openness to shift and change.

3. As we move out of judgment and other defensive postures related to the trauma patterns we're carrying in our bodies, we can stop the labeling and start listening and noticing. Again, just as we as individuals tend to open up when others stop labeling us and begin to notice and listen, so too does our most intimate partner: our own body.

4. As these patterns are released, the life energy that had been trapped in the holding-pattern dynamic is liberated, becoming available to the total body/energy system. **This gives us access to more energy for our lives!**

On a basic level, the release of old information in trauma patterns allows us to "repattern." Things that once felt really hard to hear or situations that made us feel uncomfortable no longer carry the same charge. Something that may have burned like lemon juice in an open wound in the past, rolls off painlessly once the pattern is released. Instead of living in a victim mentality that says, "I am stuck in my pain," we stand in the liberating knowledge that our bodies and Spirit have the wisdom to both limit the impact on our systems as incoming energies affect us — could be a soccer ball, could be a rejection — AND the ability to release those patterns when it's time! This is an empowering new way to witness the body and any stuck or numb spots we carry, giving us more space for finding loving forgiveness, both for ourselves and for the people and experiences we encounter going forward.

Tips for Noticing a Trauma Response

The keys to supporting ourselves in this process are awareness and presence. First we need to Notice that something is happening in a way that is not congruent with the situation in the current moment. We will explore examples of this in the next chapter. Second it's about staying Present for the sensations. If we get drawn into the past, we cannot heal. Healing happens in the present.[78]

I call this type of awareness being in my "Witness" consciousness or "Witness" awareness. We'll explore this more in Chapter 19. Developing this Witness awareness of self is a life path on its own. Mindfulness practices of many traditions emphasize noticing and observing our own thoughts and sensations,

---

[78] Jan Pemberton shares this in her trainings, it is a core tenet of BCST work.

without attaching to them. I invite there is a balance: Noticing, with enough Presence to also take action and make a Shift.

For example, take a breath right now as you are reading this book. What do you notice about your breathing? What do you notice in your body? Is there a shift that is being asked for to support your comfort? Does your bladder need emptying? Is there a pressure against a leg, foot or other body part that needs adjusting to find more ease? Take a moment to tend, and come on back to reading.

Here are some tips for noticing a trauma response in the body so you can observe it from a witness place. This creates space to support you to acknowledge how the present experience is relating to the past, instead of being pulled into the spiral as though trauma is happening now:

1. Notice if your body slows to a stop or your focus narrows to a really small spot.
2. Notice if there is tightness in your body, or a sensory experience of contraction. For example, do you find yourself gripped into stillness and staring at a spot on the carpet?
3. Notice if there is tightness in the belly, or nausea.
4. Notice if there is stuck movement... meaning, a repetitive, obsessive, mechanical kind of movement, like fidgeting or pacing, one you can't get out of. This is different than the cathartic type of movement that supports expression and release.
5. Notice any accelerated heart rate, sweating and/or rapid or constricted breathing.

These can be signs that your body is preparing to respond to a danger. If the current circumstances are such that there is imminent danger, then of course these body responses are here to help you to fight or flee or freeze; honor that.

Yet what we are focused on here is the very common situation that these body responses are happening AND there is no imminent danger — even though it feels like it. The key here with witnessing is that you also notice that the danger is not in the present moment. You notice there's no need to respond to it — you're reliving an old experience. You may not be able to name what it is or have any cognitive awareness of it. That's totally okay. You don't need to. All that is needed is to stay Present and Notice the sensations, and be able to pull out of a spiral and make choices/changes.

When your capacity to stay Present and Notice these sensations is there, you notice that there is no imminent danger, and you can pull yourself out of the trauma spiral (loop), then you have the resources to work with it.[79] In the next chapter, we explore specific ways to support yourself to unwind traumas from the body.

If you are unable to Notice and pull yourself out of the loop, healing is still available. Allow yourself to rest. Then seek support, guidance, and additional body resources to meet this layer of your human journey.

> Neuroscience research shows that the only way we can change the way we feel is by becoming aware of our inner experience and learning to befriend what is going on inside ourselves.[80]

Our bodies are so wise, and we are powerful beings that can support our own healing in ways many of us don't even realize. That said, depending upon how the trauma is lodged in the body, you may also need support from outside resources. However, whether we are getting help from therapists or friends, trees or mountains, the process moves forward because we support it from within. Regardless of what path you choose, you will be relying on the astonishing inherent power of the body to heal itself.

---

[79] From Jan Pemberton's lectures teaching BCST.

[80] van der Kolk, pg 206.

CHAPTER SEVENTEEN

Resources to Support Unwinding Trauma

What Are Resources?

We are not alone. As noted in the previous chapter, the way we hold information in our body often comes from the relational space, and it is in the relational space that we can heal. This does not mean we have to re-engage with a past abuser. The journey of sacred sexuality is about shifting how we relate with our own bodies, each other, nature, Spirit and the planet. When we can cultivate a relationship that feels safe and connected, it becomes a Resource. This can be any relationship, not just a relationship with an intimate or romantic partner. We can cultivate a relationship with, for example: areas in our body, a place in nature, a trusted friend, a therapist, or a pet, and these can become Resources.

In my practice I have found that healing from trauma is greatly facilitated by an awareness of the importance of resources. Resources are those places we go to, whether inside or outside the body, to know we're okay. Where is that safe space that you can always rely on? Knowing what your resources are and how to access them adds a layer of support for the entire body-centered process of healing.

2011 – Dixon and I are driving to Canada for a conference, and at the border we're stopped, pulled over and searched. It's a common occurrence when driving in Betsy, my partner's touring van. As a small RV, Betsy attracts a lot of attention when entering another country. My partner is used to this as he travels regularly. For me it feels tremendously disrespectful, rude and violating. I have sacred objects in my mesa (a cloth wrapping that contains my altar items, special objects that are part of my spiritual practice). The border agents pull it out and rather brutishly open it up, the objects cascade out of the wrap and some hit the pavement outside the back of the van. I am cringing from afar, not permitted to be near the space as they trample through my belongings. The man behind the desk is grilling me about the conference: What's it about? Why am I going? They poke around on the Internet, and they see me listed as a presenter. Yes, I am presenting. No, I am not getting paid. I've done nothing wrong. They keep poking, as if trying to find something to make a problem.

I feel it landing as if they are poking at my work with Sacred Sexuality, as if they are poking at my very soul. They are triggering an old trauma, the sensations from the dorm room phone call with my father so many years ago arise, as well as sensations perhaps from past lifetimes and from the field of sexual healers being oppressed and burned at the stake so many generations before me. I feel my body tightening, I feel overwhelmed, shaky, ready to cry but desperately trying to stuff it away, desperately trying to appear rational, logical. As if trying to be something they want to see, so they'll leave me alone.

Finally they release us to pass into the country. Dixon drives us in. I am gripping, hitching, trembling, holding on the best I can, yet as we pass into relative privacy and safety I have a huge panic/anxiety release. I feel sobs, tears flow and tremors run through my body like I hadn't felt since that day in college on the phone with my father. I feel judged, like I am a bad person. At my request, Dixon gets us through town and pulls over to a spot of grass — I need out of the van, I NEED the Earth, to feel her, to let go into her. I barely let the van come to a stop as I tear open the door and pour myself out onto the Earth. I run to a spot, jump, scream, fall to the Earth, pound on the ground, roaring into the support of her, letting the tremendous vibrations of fear, anger, shame pour off of my body and into the Earth. I feel the roars shift to sobs, I feel myself settling, I'm feeling more present, I invite myself back in my body, feeling held, safe.

Ahhhh, Gratitude! Gratitude for the resource within me of knowing I can plug back into my body, my capacity to acknowledge when I need to feel this support to do so, Gratitude for the Earth for always being there, and Gratitude for my partner who supports me by holding space for the release.

Resources can be External or Internal. And as we explored before, Dancing with Balance becomes important with Resources as well. As we build our external resources, we may strengthen our capacity to connect with the ones within, and as we feel a clearer sense of self and internal resourcing, we trust connection with external resources. Building our resource pool diversely supports stabilizing our transformation and growth.

My border crossing experience lit up old trauma in me. To work through it I was able to access internal resourcing that I had developed over time through practices of connecting with nature and the land. The Earth and Dixon are external resources that really support me to remember the internal resource of my body, and that connection with my body is available. I was then able to move the energy and let go of another layer of the oppression that I had been carrying so long.

And once again, this is a dance in an array of possibilities rather than a firm binary. As we meet resources, some are inward, and some are more external. There is a reason the child's teddy bear is not my resource — I don't have the connection to it the child does. The child feels a soothing sense of nervous system settling when she snuggles with the bear; it's powerful. Even when the resource is more external, it's the inner landscape we are working with at the core.

In the border crossing example, I saw the Earth as a friend and craved a tangible connection with her as a resource. Thus the desire to pull over and dive my body into her arms. This is a resource for me that may be less available to someone else. Others might only see it as landscape flying by.

Whether we name them as internal or external, ultimately our resources support us within, they support our body and our nervous system to settle. In a sense we also have the opportunity for initiations: These are points when we realize the resource is actually within us. At the same time, we can also claim the power of making a choice to seek external support to access that inner ease. Reclaiming our sense of connection — with the Earth, our bodies, with each other and Spirit — reinforces our sense of belonging and settles our nervous system, opening space for layers to let go. In this relational space, we heal.

"We are not alone." The statement may sound reassuring to some, creepy and spooky to others. But it's really a simple fact. We inhabit, shape, and are shaped by relational space at all times. The essence of Resource is developing the awareness that we can access, lean into and even cultivate authentic support for our growth.

External Resources

External Resources are the people, places, and other beings that help us find our joy and wholeness, just by connecting with them. We have a sense well up inside us of: "Wow, I am capable, and good enough. Everything is going to be okay. I don't have to do anything to be loved, I deserve love just as I am." When you feel connected with a resource, a smile spontaneously moves across your face, your body relaxes, and you settle into simply being in the moment. The value of these external resources is in the internal shifts they provide.

Some examples of External Resources are:

- Favorite spot in nature you like to go to
- Pets
- Loved ones: family members, friends, chosen family
- Safe space: perhaps your home or a specific spot in your home (remember the spot in my closet in my childhood that I shared about in Part 1, this was a Resource for me then)
- Altar space: a place centered around connection with Spirit
- Cozy object: blanket or plushie for example
- Power object: crystals, stones or other meaningful symbols that bring you support
- Group of people: your allies, a support network, conscious queer community, women's or men's or fellowship circle
- Spiritual/religious guides: both in person, such as ministers, rabbis and priestesses, as well as in the spiritual realm
- Spiritual/self care practices: animal wisdom, see the Recipes
- Ancestors
- Herb and plant allies

Even though External Resources can and do support this sense of well-being, I also advise a bit of caution with my clients. Sometimes, external resources end up not quite being the resource we expect them to be. Relying solely on something outside ourselves to validate our "Okay-ness" can backfire. Maybe that beloved pet runs away, or we break up with the loved one. If our main connection with resource, our sense of "I'm going to be okay," is external, then its disappearance can really pull the rug out from under us, or even cause more trauma.

Also, if escalating engagement with external resources doesn't produce greater benefits, it's time to start looking within. In other words, if higher and higher amounts, numbers or intensity levels are needed, that's an indicator that we're trying to change the outside when we need to actually internalize the wisdom. For example, in almost all cases, meditation is an excellent resource. However, it can happen that it morphs into an abandonment of relationships with the body and others instead of leading to enlightenment. We need a variety of resources to better stabilize us in our growth.

Internal Resources

Internal Resources are the places within the body and our inner awareness where we can notice a sense of wellness, a sense that everything is going to be okay, regardless of the things swirling about in our lives. In the journey of life and this path of Sacred Sexuality, I invite connecting deeply with our internal resources. As we connect with internal resourcing, we build a sense of wellness that we can always come back to, even when things feel tough and regardless of what's available externally in that moment.

That said, going within as a resource can be incredibly hard for many people. Slowing down and paying attention to our internal landscape and body are hard when life experiences have told us it's not safe to be here. And so many of us, myself included, had experiences early in life that taught us that "checking out" was safer than being in our bodies. The complex journey of sacred sexuality and listening to the body is the core topic of this book. Be gentle on yourself in this process of rebuilding your relationship with your body.

Sometimes, we need the external resources to support us in finding the internal ones. Once we connect with our internal resources, our capacity to discern and hold space for the external ones that truly resource us deepens.

Both internal and external are welcome. When Resources come together, there is even more power in our sense of capability and knowing who we are, strengthening our trust in the flow and our zest for life.

So let's take a moment with Internal Resources.

Pause here and engage with two of the experiential practices introduced earlier to explore our inner awareness: R6 Center Ground Orient and R7 Exhale with Sound.

In my experience, the single most powerful Internal Resource is our capacity to center and ground. Slowing down, taking a breath, dropping awareness back and noticing our center, our midline, and allowing our body and energy to ground down to the Earth can support us to trust that everything is going to be okay. Sometimes this practice takes time to open what may feel like a new relationship with our bodies and the Earth. That's okay too. Take all the time you need to deepen with this sweet resource that is always available. The more I plug into my own body and connect with the Earth, the more I trust everything is going to be okay. Being embodied, deeply present and aware of our physical body is a Resource that we can carry with us anywhere and rely on, any time, day or night.

Building Our Resources

Every day, often many times a day, I bring conscious awareness to my center and my ground, honoring my connection with the Earth and with Spirit. I ask for support in creating and feeling that connection. I pray. I share gratitude for that connection, and in that loving gratitude, the connection deepens.

Every time I met with a client or taught a class, hosted a radio show or shared a video, I invited some level of the centering and grounding for my own body and for those engaging with me.

And as I shared in Part 2, I've also done some human homework to open my heart and allow someone in to meet me, to be a Resource, rather than to hold them at arm's length as I had learned to do so many years ago when I built the walls.

March 13, 2014 — I'm on the land, and it's cold, and there's another blanket of snow on the ground, and it has already been such a long and cold winter... I am DONE.

Connecting with the Earth and the land is one of my resources. At least once daily I get my body in connection with her (a practice I call "Barefeet Earth," see Recipe 8 introduced later in this chapter), and at least one day a week I spend in solitude and deep connection with her, year-round, regardless of weather. I call this my "Day on the Land" (see upcoming Recipe 9 for an invitation to create this for yourself). Yet today, I am having a really rough morning and I am having some trouble connecting and feeling grounded. I come back to the van and I call my sweetie and I vent and cry and he receives me: He does not try to fix it, judge it, change it, he does not yell at me, he simply holds me. We share a virtual hug at distance, he wraps his arms around me and I sink into him. We've learned to share this energetically across distance. Today it helps me so much.

It is exactly what I need and I am feeling a little better. I feel the heaviness lift away.

Over the years I've really come to clarity in finding Earth and Spirit and grounding as my Resources. I've really found that Internal Resource, the one within, my connection to my Body and to the Earth and with Spirit.

So there I was thinking that while things are feeling tough all I needed that day was time on the land, but what I was missing was another piece that's also very real, and in the past I resisted it. I had well learned the lesson not to let anyone in, especially not any men, and to not feel. I had become good at not expecting to find Resource in a person.

However, later after I got home on that March snowy day, it hit me:

Here is this sweet man in my life! Yes, I am allowed to rely on him, to ask to be held. He is a Resource for me. He's my sea salt. He lets me be more authentically me, and I can connect more with who I am and more in my center and ground and find sweet ease in connection with him.

In the past I would have thought, "No, I can't do that. I can't rely on anyone else. I will do it myself. I shouldn't call him, I don't want to be a bother or a nuisance. It won't help anyway."

And now I see he really is supporting me to be me. I'm not relying on him to fill a gap in me. I've done that before. But no, this is different. There's this clearness and cleanness in it, and I can reach out without energetic dramas. This isn't about what I can't do, it's about how together we can be even brighter. I'm allowed to feel that support. I feel it, and I feel everything is going to be okay.

Once again, the dance of balance — allowing an external resource in supports my internal resources which in turn allows me to trust receiving external resources even more deeply.

RECIPE 8: Barefeet Earth, pg 316

RECIPE 9: Day on the Land, pg 318

Questions for Self-Reflection

What are your External Resources? How do you connect with your Internal Resources? How have they changed over time?

Reflect on the times you experienced exquisite joy. If this feels hard to access, consider a time where you felt at ease, where life's troubles were set aside even if for only a moment. Where were you? Who were you with? Describe it: What colors, textures, temperatures, sounds, smells and sensations did you notice?

As you sit with the memory, what do you notice in your body *now*? Notice your face, your body posture, the sensations in your heart and your belly. Allow yourself to feel these sensations in this moment.

What message can you offer yourself about your Resources from your place of enlightened awareness?

What mantra can you create from this message that will support you to remember the wisdom?[81]

For support in connecting with your Resources see the prior Recipes: R6 Center Ground Orient, R7 Exhale with Sound and R8 Barefeet Earth.

Plus this practice:

RECIPE 10: Resource Meditation, pg 320

It's okay to have and connect with things outside of us that feel safe, as well as internal ones. The balance of the two can feel really lovely.

Now that we've set the stage with some conceptual framework for understanding trauma, and how resources can help us approach it, let's meet some of the ways we can release trauma from our bodies and continue on the path of remembering who we are.

---

[81] The inspiration to create a mantra came to me from my teacher Leyolah Antara and her book *Kundalini Dance: Sacred Alchemical Evolutionary Keys.*

CHAPTER EIGHTEEN

Fruit Flies and Releasing Trauma from the Body

To explore ways to release trauma from the body, let's continue with my personal story we began in Chapter 7, the G-spot healing.

When my lover came in contact with my G-spot, "Fruit Flies" began to swirl about my head: memories of my experience with the babysitter, the images, the feelings. They came in, but I didn't notice them at first. Then when I did, I denied they were there.

So what are "Fruit Flies" and how does noticing them help us identify and begin to release trauma?

Fruit Flies

Here's why I call these trauma-associated thoughts, images, and momentary flashes of feeling Fruit Flies:

- They seem to appear out of nowhere.
- They seem random.
- They are persistent.
- We tend to swat at them and brush them away, not wanting to deal with them right now.

These memories, thoughts, images, feelings or sensations arise when a part of our physical body or energetic bodies is activated in a way that invites that old information stored there to resurface. Even the sense of a smell from the past can be reactivated in the present.

It's like our bodies are computers, living libraries of information. On a computer, we may have a software program, for example a word processor. If we open the computer and look, we may not even know that word processor is there. Yet once we activate the program, the word processor opens up and there it is. We can even work with it to create a new document.

Similarly, Fruit Flies can lie dormant under the surface, sometimes for years, not showing up on the internal "screen" of our awareness. Or they may be flying around in the background noise of our heads in such a way that we are not able to pay attention to them and they go unnoticed. But one day, *when the body is ready*, something can activate it, whether it be a touch, a sound, a movement, a breath. It may be a body position, or a certain threshold we reach as our sexual energy blooms open in pleasure. It may be a certain smell that sets it off, or a constellation of bodies in space around us — a certain position, for example face-to-face, shoulder-to-shoulder, standing or sitting, that someone takes in relationship to our bodies. Any of these things can trigger a response, activate the old energy that has been held, and initiate the Fruit Flies to come up. Or it may be that the day comes when that Fruit Fly has visited thousands of times, and it is finally time to really *see* it.

I've found that noticing and really allowing Fruit Flies to come into our conscious awareness and not just be lost amidst the stream of awareness or background noise in our heads **can be some of the most difficult work of our lifetimes.**

Yet Fruit Flies are actually a gift, not an annoyance as they may seem. By noticing them, we can begin the process of transforming them into "Fireflies," illuminating our path through the stuck place, moving us through the trauma and into the clarity of who we are.

Noticing our Fruit Flies is crucial to inviting awareness of new possibilities in the body.

Yet for a long time, I kept shoving them away, at first not even conscious of them. As time progressed and my body became ready, I started to notice them. Then, I was finally able to seek support to ask about them and, with guidance, unlock the underlying trauma from my body.

This has been empowering and freeing! I no longer have the thoughts or shameful feelings associated with the experience with the babysitter, even when my G-spot, the part of my body that was carrying them, is touched in various ways. The energy has released and my body has integrated (see the following Recipe) into a new vibrational space: The wound has healed. I can now share about the story, recount it, talk about it, and it no longer triggers me into the sensations of the past. There's an ease, clarity.

RECIPE 11: Integration, pg 324

Since that pivotal change, what I call my first major conscious Body Awakening, my capacity to meet the Fruit Flies and work with new layers has expanded. More pieces have emerged, and I have experienced more freedom as I have been able to let them go. In addition, I have learned new ways and supported countless clients to release layers from their bodies as well.

Learning to pay attention to the Fruit Flies that come up can lead to profound healings. Let's explore another example.

"Hurry Up and Clean Up Before Mom Finds Out!"

When I came to this work, and even as I started to dive into it, I noticed some things about my sexual patterns that challenged me. One of them was the way I felt and acted around self-pleasure.

I knew I wanted to be open and relaxed and happy and lovely about it, but as I started to pay attention to my habits I knew there were things I needed to explore, because I wasn't as open and relaxed and happy as I wanted to be.

I had the right attitude; I had the right ideas.

But when I went to make love to myself, when I touched myself, when I pleasured myself, I would keep my body tight, or my eyes closed; my whole body was run through with an old, rushed, secretive energy. There wasn't much lovely and sweet and open about it. It felt good, but I knew there was so much more, and that's when I started to experiment.

I'm in my early 30s, in my home in Michigan. My Spiritual Awakening has opened my eyes, and my Body Awakenings have begun. I've been reconnecting with my juiciness and my sexual nature and feel delighted to be in a self-pleasure practice, masturbating in my bedroom, alone at home.

I touch all over my body, my breasts, neck, arms, legs, backs of thighs, I brush my fingers across my face, scratch them through my hair to my scalp. I grab my feet and press into the soles with my thumbs. It feels nice. I stretch. I feel my skin open up, cultivating my arousal and desire from within my body. The time feels right: I check in with my yoni and she says, "Yes, please" to being touched. I bring my hand to my mound, press my fingers along my labia, and simply hold here. I breathe, bearing my awareness and energy down into my pelvis, meeting my hand. "Ahhhhh...." I exhale with sound and pleasure.

As my touch and desire build, I decide to get a toy... the beautiful G-spot stimulator that has become a favorite. Providing firm, gentle pressure, without vibration, this wand helps me access the territory of the deepest section of my G-spot that's hard to reach on my own with my fingers. I insert the toy, as my yoni says, "Yes, more please" and invites me into her juicy, warm, succulent space. I meet her lovingly, I build in pleasure.

As I continue to touch and play and breathe and move... I feel tension across my face as the pleasure builds. It builds and builds, my breath faster, heart rate increasing, and I feel my body building toward an orgasm. However, in a moment just nearing that place of orgasm... SMACK! It's as if I hit a glass wall. The energy drains away. I feel stopped, stuck. A Fruit Fly comes swirling in. This thought flashes into my head:

"Oh no! What if Mom walks in?!"

Now mind you, I haven't lived with my mother since I was 17 years old. She has lived across the country, over 2,000 miles away, for nearly two decades by this point. We don't visit, and at the time, only communicated a few times a year by phone. So this underscores, from a rational brain perspective, the seeming ridiculousness of this fear to come in at this particular moment: "What if Mom walks in?!" What? She's nowhere near here! Which makes it all the more clear how strongly the body remembers: The body carries these old energies and experiences.

To be clear, it's not ridiculous to feel these feelings... as much as our rational brain might think that. **They are very real to the body and deserve to be heard.** I had patterned in at a young age that it was bad to touch my body, that I shouldn't do that: It was "wrong." I carried fear of my mom walking in during those times as an adolescent when I was masturbating, as if it would mean I am a bad person to be seen in it. Now here I was, a grown adult, making a wonderful healthy choice of exploring my sexual energy in my own home, and BAM — the old Fruit Fly came in.

In this case it was easy to see. So I continued to explore:

...I feel my body tighten up and shut down the energy. Yet at the same time, very quickly I laugh — literally, out loud — as I notice that being in the old energy of "hurry up and clean up before Mom finds out!" is ridiculous. I am SO allowed to touch my body, and to feel pleasure. I am allowed to feel good about who I am and enjoy my sexuality, my desire, my pleasure and orgasm.

I giggle a bit more, shake it off, relax. I let myself rest for a moment, or "Trust the Valley"[82] *as I call it: giving space, slowing down and allowing the energy to widen, soften and be shared with my whole body rather than be only genitally focused. Sure enough, as I do, the energy starts to build again, and to reveal a new readiness. I follow it, I touch myself and build and let go into an exquisite orgasmic release.*

I speak out loud my intention to repattern this. I ask Spirit for support, and I speak the affirmations: "I am allowed to touch my body. It is okay to feel pleasure. I am a good girl and a powerful woman. May this sexual energy bring healing to my body and the field of consciousness of sexuality on this planet!

"It's okay to feel good.

It's okay to feel good.

It's okay to feel good!"

I allow myself to breathe the affirmations into my body, fueled by the energy and power of my sexuality that brings healing to my body and the world.

As this example demonstrates, sometimes the Fruit Flies are obvious and they can be noticed quickly and worked with on the spot with lasting results. My cognitive brain had known that it is okay to feel good and touch my own body for some time. The gift in this experience was that this new layer of body awareness was now ready to open up to match it.

Yet not all traumas are released quickly. For example, in the case of my G-spot memory (the babysitter memory), it took years for a piece to fully unlock. Both are perfect. The timing of what our body is ready to reveal is Divine and known within. There's no need to force anything.

2014 – Dixon and I are traveling cross-country for an event in Betsy, his touring van. He is driving, I am in the passenger seat, and I delight in this relaxed feeling of expansion

---

[82] Trust the Valley – a term I use to describe an invitation, as sexual energy is building strongly, to relax, give space, slow down and allow the energy to widen, spread and be shared with my whole body rather than be narrowly genitally focused. See also the work of Mantak Chia (regarding Valley Orgasms).

in my body. I feel my sexual energy peeking through and I choose to start touching my body. As I am in self-pleasure, exploring my body and building in energy, I realize I want to invite being wider in that awareness. Not in an exhibitionist sort of way; it isn't that anyone else is seeing me, and I don't want that anyway in this moment. Instead, as we are driving down the road there are trees and nature that we are in and passing and I feel delight in letting my energy interact with and be wide into the space around me, to merge with the trees. It feels wonderful to let my awareness expand out wider than inside my physical body, and not close myself down. As I start to gently widen in that and invite that space of relaxing and expanding, I notice there are places that I bump up against.

One is a fear that someone is going to see. I remind myself, "I'm safe and okay." I remind myself that I am just fine, I don't need to push past it, which is something I may have done in the past. I relax into it and unwind the layers.

Second, a couple of Fruit Flies come up.

I am feeling that Dixon is starting to delight in this too — and run energy, and get aroused. I immediately feel worried. I am writing the story in my head of, "If he does that he's not going to be paying attention to the road and that doesn't feel safe while he's driving," and I feel my energy curl up and contract and close down.

I don't want it to close down so I have a check-in conversation with him. I speak it: "Sweetie, I am feeling a little shut down. I need to hear, you got me? You're driving and responsible for that in this moment. Are you holding us safe?" And I hear him speak it and hold it, yes, he's got us, this is not about him running energy right now. He shifts to be really present with that, as a space holder. We hold the intention that this isn't about him and me engaging in sexual energy right now. It is about our holding space for the energy running through my body.

When that shift happens, I relax back wide again. Yes. I can feel it! Ah! Acknowledging that Fruit Fly, the worry that I am bumping up against in the moment, helps me release it and re-expand and shift and rebuild the container that I feel safe to relax into.

Then a second Fruit Fly emerges. I worry that "I shouldn't be doing this" or "someone else will see — I shouldn't be touching my body inside a moving car"... and in my Witness consciousness I look at that and wonder, "Why not?!" I affirm for myself: I am allowed, it's my choice, I am a consenting adult touching my own body. Why is that a bad thing? It's not a bad thing. I acknowledge the imprinting I had with that old story and I let myself relax past it. As I touch my body and build, I affirm the beauty of simply being who I am and allowing energy to move. I ejaculate, and I build to an exquisite orgasmic release. Ah!

Later, I recognize the first Fruit Fly: This fear of my partner getting distracted from the road is connected with a car accident I had been in years prior as a teenager when the driver was distracted in sexual energy, ran a red light, and we were hit by a car in the cross traffic. This time, my body remembered this old experience, and I was able to state what I needed to relax into the present.

I notice that when the thoughts in my head include "should" or "shouldn't," those are often reliable signs that they are limiting or from my place of self censor, instead of my place of authenticity. These cues help me notice.

Also, as I've worked with countless others in supporting witnessing and repatterning and healing, I have had times when the Fruit Flies are hard to acknowledge, and then other times when they are super clear. What follows is a lovely example of when the message from the body is profound and clear. While it doesn't always happen this cleanly and clearly, it is a great illustration of the power of Listening to the Body.

I am with a client in session. He is lying on the dark purple Thai bodywork mat and I am literally stepping on his arm: My foot is on his left arm. In Thai bodywork, one of the influences in my touch work, it is common as the practitioner to use other parts of the body in addition to the hands to apply pressure, make contact and support the client in movements and body release.

Suddenly he proclaims: "Oh, I have this Fruit Fly!" He goes on to share a memory that is coming in and the "aha moment" he is having about it:

"I used to Give to try to get my wife to Receive and be aroused so that then I could become aroused. I realize that I was relying on her or other things outside me to arouse me and now I can see that I need to trust my arousal from within."

This is a powerful body "aha moment" for him, to really get it from his body (not just talk about it, as we had done already). It really clicks for him, and he is surprised. He says, "I don't understand. Where did that come from? How did that come out of my arm?!"

I sit down with him and have an intuitive hit. I ask, "By the way, are you left-handed?"

He replies, "Yes."

"Well," I offer, "your dominant hand, in your case your left hand, is your giving hand, your giving arm. Our arms and hands are connected with our heart." We had noted already that this is a strong heart issue for him, he feels a lot of tension and absence in his heart center. "Perhaps it's connected with that?" I invite as a self-inquiry. Yes! Our work that day deeply resonates for him and opens up a new layer in his self-awareness.

I share this story as an example of how wisdom can come directly from the body, through breath, sound, movement, touch or visualization. In this case it was firm pressure touch at his left arm that woke up awareness that he could reclaim his power of opening to energy from within.

Body wisdom is not always this clear or direct. Sometimes it can be really hard to hear or discern, but my experience is that **once we work with the key principles, the process of noticing becomes easier and easier.**

We are at a particularly profound time on our planet right now. In this era, the time is ripe for shifting consciousness. Things can happen fast, and linear clock time becomes less relevant as we are opening to the realms of the infinite where lifetimes of changes can happen in seconds. I say this not to force it or expect it, but to allow — to invite and open the possibility that yes, we really can make changes in our bodies, including tangible, physical changes, in ways that we've been taught by traditional science and Western medicine to believe aren't possible.

Changing and healing our body is possible. My shamanic self, my spiritual self knows this deeply. And my skeptical rational brain self has come to the point of figuring this much: It can't hurt to stay open to the possibilities, and our thoughts and intention really do shape our world. So instead of locking our thoughts into what we think is not possible, let's remain open to what could be. We really can heal our bodies, change our lives and create our reality.

Releasing Trauma from the Body

Here are the principles of the practice I have found most effective in releasing trauma from the body:

- **Slow down** with love and respect.
- **Create the Container** for holding safe space for change. See the next two Recipes for practice to create Sacred Circle and speak our needs for the Container.
- **Connect with Resource** — the sensations and feelings of joy in your body — to come back to as needed.
- **Listen to the Body** — the Body has the wisdom of the universe. We just hold space for it to remember its original template of health.
- **Presence** — Healing happens in the present. Some ways to remind ourselves to come back to the present if we find ourselves drifting into the past or wondering about the future is to notice our orientation in space, our body position and contact with the surface we are on, notice colors and smells in the room, notice our position relative to another being or an object in the room.
- **Mindfulness** — see the upcoming Recipe 13 for practices to support this.
- **Reclaim the Power of Choice** — work with conscious movements, breaths, sounds, touch.

RECIPE 12: Sacred Circle – Invoking the Directions, pg 326

RECIPE 13: Mindfulness Practices, pg 330

Accessing trauma can feel scary, like falling into a pit of fire. We don't need to dive head first into a bonfire of old trauma. Instead, when feeling resourced and ready to explore, I encourage gently standing close enough to the fire to feel the warmth. This allows the body content to light up, to awaken, to come into our awareness. Then we can work with it, gently dipping a toe back and forth, to feel the sensations in the body, and to notice and to stay in present time to invite the unwinding. Peter Levine describes this as moving between the Healing Vortex and the Trauma Vortex.[83]

---

[83] Levine and Frederick, *Waking the Tiger*.

As van der Kolk describes, also referencing Peter Levine's work:

> We start by establishing inner "islands of safety" within the body. This means helping patients identify parts of the body, postures or movements where they can ground themselves whenever they feel stuck, terrified or enraged. These parts usually lie outside the reach of the vagus nerve, which carries the messages of panic to the chest, abdomen and throat, and they can serve as allies in integrating the trauma.[84]

Van der Kolk elaborates with examples of these islands of safety, maybe hand or arm movements, feeling the weight of your body in the chair, etc. Tapping acupressure points can be a good anchor for some. Turning the head from side to side, opening eyes and noticing other areas in the room is also helpful, as it makes a brain-body connection that is supportive for being in the present.[85]

To me this is about empowering people in their body awareness so they can tap into this as a way to resolve what's emerging. As van der Kolk goes on to say, also acknowledging Peter Levine's work:

> This sets the stage for trauma resolution: pendulating between states of exploration and safety, between language and body, between remembering the past and feeling alive in the present.[86]

And while the principles can be named, it's not about a to-do list of actions that will release or integrate the trauma, nor is it about a certain protocol with a magic solution. Each person and each situation is unique. Often the very tool that works in one situation would create a re-traumatization in another.

The key once again is Listening. Being able to access a Witness space, either for your own body/Self or as the practitioner holding space for someone else. In the work of BCST, this is known as acknowledging the body's own "Inherent Treatment Plan." As we listen deeply, the system, the body, will reveal what's next. It will reveal the next piece, and each step, when it's ready.

Our job then, whether for ourselves or in holding space with others, is to deeply Listen to the Body. This requires us to do our best to ground and center and be of service as a Witness. It also requires us to spend less time analyzing and trying to plan what to do, and more time in deep reverence of the guidance that is inherent as wisdom within our own bodies and that of our clients.

---

[84] van der Kolk, pg 245.

[85] Training with Jan Pemberton.

[86] van der Kolk, pg 245.

As we listen to and honor this deep wisdom, it is also important to be gentle and go slowly. Often in the excitement of noticing that yes, we really can make changes and heal in our own bodies, there rises up a sense of urgency around "doing it all right now." I know I've felt that. Nonetheless, I encourage us to go slow, listen, and feel for the inherent pace being asked of us. There's no need to rush. Sometimes, trying to rush can create more harm if we try to force things that are not ready. Here the concept of titration may be useful.

I remember in a chemistry lab in middle school, we learned the concept of titration through an experiment involving slowly adding one clear solution drop by drop into another clear solution. At first, as each drop was added, nothing seemed to be happening. Then, with the addition of a single extra drop, the clear solution in the beaker suddenly turned a bright purple color! In this experiment, despite the temptation to hurry things along, it was crucially important to go one drop and one step at a time to get the correct measurement. Similarly, as we work with making changes in our bodies and learning new information, we will most benefit from the cumulative changes we are introducing to our bodies and awareness if we take each step as it comes and truly integrate those changes. This builds our resilience and helps us be ready for the next steps as they reveal themselves.

To open to this inherent body wisdom and guidance, let's deepen our exploration of what it means to Witness, and to hold space.

CHAPTER NINETEEN

Witness

Witnessing is an essential capacity to develop as we learn to release trauma from the body this way. The Witness self is simple awareness without judgment or analytical thinking attached. In the examples given in the previous chapter, each realization and trauma release required a moment of quiet awareness to notice the messages that were coming through. **The challenge is that in our society, the power of witnessing to reveal things and precipitate transformation is often as invisible as that which witnessing is capable of revealing and transforming.** Becoming aware, witnessing the witness, is an essential step for us both individually and collectively to repattern old programs and step into a new way of being.

Recall Fruit Flies. Emerging from all kinds of buried traumas, they can be buzzing around our heads for years until we start to notice them, but when we do, things change.

Being a Witness is about seeing, listening, being fully present, holding space for what is.

Being a Witness is not about judging, analyzing, trying to fix, categorizing or labeling what we are witnessing. It's not about trying to figure out what we are seeing or molding it into meaning.

Although I had been exploring the power of this Witnessing self for some time, my experience with a practice called "Authentic Movement" with facilitator Stefanie Cohen[87] helped me to embody and articulate Witness in important new ways. In the practice, we are held as a group in various constellations of moving and witnessing. The common thread in all Authentic

---

[87] Stefanie Cohen, https://www.somastories.net/

Movement practice is that while a person or group of people are moving, there is always at least one person holding space as Witness.

What is it like to move in ways that the body wants instead of ways that we have scripted? Over my years in this practice, I have watched the layers of past scripting inform my movements. I noticed how a lot of my movements matched familiar ways — a yoga pose, walking, stretching, a qigong movement pattern. Yes, they are important, and also I began to feel so much more as my body kept inviting inquiry beneath these habit patterns.

Today as we meet for our Authentic Movement class, something is different.

2017 – I come to the practice feeling tired and raw, like the tender skin exposed from being torn on jagged ground. I have met a sense of deep tenderness and tightness in my solar plexus, xiphoid at the tip of my sternum, and the base of my head… sensations that arose when I felt a deep sense of violation at my core. Two days before, my physical sacred Temple space had been literally, LITERALLY trampled upon and not protected. My body temple mirrored the violation I felt. Through the day and night afterward, I met and worked through these sensations in my body through my ecstatic embodied practice. Arriving to class this morning, I am exhausted. I speak my needs to the group, as each of us in our circle do, and we hold space for each other, open our circle and move into the practice. I curl up in the corner and rest.

My little girl voice begins to emanate from deep within. She's sad. Tears move. Soft songs whisper from my body like dew droplets in the morning fog. I rock softly, I sing. I feel the presence of my fellow classmates, like mountains, strong and present, around the valley of my foggy morning.

I feel my censor talking to me: "Shouldn't I be moving more overtly? After all, I am just lying here."

And yet my body knows this is exactly what is needed in the now. There is movement even in the stillness. As I witness for myself, I affirm it. I suck my thumb, something that has brought me huge fear and shame in the past, now meeting my need for self soothing, and really allowing myself to be seen in it. I rest, deeply, and the time of the class passes. My head writes the story that I should get up and move to witness, and yet it's already been clear that I can choose what is needed for me today. I rest. I am held in safe space by my peers, who are co-creating this class with me.

As we close the circle and reflect, I find myself feeling refreshed. There's a softness to my edges, a gentle space that has opened in my body. I notice this with gratitude. I am gentle on myself, as are my fellow classmates. I have been seen, simply in the moment, without judgment. When I notice my own self judgment, I watch it as such, and shift to noticing myself with loving kindness. So many layers.

This is the power of Witness.

My years holding and being held in witness space have offered so much to my awareness, but in particular the Authentic Movement practice highlights the power of Witnessing in relating to both myself and others.

Most importantly, to witness, all one needs to do is be present with the experience. Sharing about the witnessing is not required. However, if I am moved to share and speak about my witness time, I do so holding this premise: I do not know *others'* experience, my reflection is of *my* experience. We can only speak from a place of our own filters and perceptions. We can never really truly know someone else's experiences. Only they can speak to those.

So, in relating my experience as Witness, I speak from "I." For example, I may describe the specifics of their movements. For example, "When I saw your hand in the air, the…"

- story that came to me...
- image I had was...
- feeling I had was...
- sensation it evoked in my body was...

Owning my experience and not projecting onto others promotes a deep honoring of each Being, honoring their experience as theirs and humbly not presuming to know what that may be. Again, to Witness is powerful whether anything is spoken or not. Yet there can be a gift in sharing our experiences as witnesses: "I am the one who saw… I am the one who felt…"[88] Often, we miss the value in simply be-ing with another and allowing them to authentically **be**.

This also really helped me to embody the Healthy Masculine energy, to feel into those three things: creating safety, holding space, and witnessing without judging. Through these, the practice of Witness enables us to bring awareness to our Self and Others.

This may not be easy at first. As Stefanie reminds us in practice: We are human. Do judgments come up? Yes! Do we try to make meaning? Yes! We're human, so these things tend to happen as our rational brains engage. Making meaning and judging can be of service in many contexts of our life. We learn how

---

[88] Cohen, in-person teachings.

to move through the 3D world by judging situations and creating meaning of our experiences. It's how we learn to survive. The key is to not attach to them or promote them as someone else's truth. To witness is to simply acknowledge them as our own, through our own filters and perception. **Neither our experiences as witness nor any judgments that arise in us are about the people we are witnessing.**

In my experience, I have found that these principles are fundamental in my journey of mindfulness, self-realization and remembering who I am.

The power of witnessing shows up twofold:
1. Witnessing others and providing the gift of holding space and simply being.
2. Going WITHIN to witness ourselves, seeing and recognizing what's going on in our own bodies and allowing it to emerge in its own time.

In practical terms, as we embody our sexual and spiritual lives, this means that we can witness ourselves and recognize a body sensation without going into the old story or script that was patterned into it. We can hold the space lovingly without trying to analyze, fix or critique it. Likewise, we can encounter our personal "Fruit Flies" with an open and questioning curiosity about the messages they offer us. This can be challenging. However, as we learn how to step into this place we can create profound shifts and changes in ourselves.

While the context of witnessing we've explored so far has been in non-sexual spaces, this also all applies right in the depths of our sexual energy. When we can meet our sexual energy with guidance and in a witness space, it can open profound changes in the body.

Now as we practice Witness and open to exploring pendulation between the Trauma spiral and the Healing spiral, we come to a case where I worked with both of these really directly in my own body:

Trauma Release Example

Dixon and I have a sweet set of agreements with each other about the ways we feel good about connecting with other people. We call these our Relationship Agreements. We have chosen to have ways that we can consciously connect sexually and romantically with other people. It's been important to us since the beginning that we honor the part of ourselves that feels sharing love and relating in wider ways only adds to the overall love for ourselves, humanity, nature and the planet. Even the phrase "making love" can be interpreted to be about *creating* more love. Love that can be shared with consciousness of humanity. This deep relational space is powerful for self-growth and being of service here in this lifetime. Dixon and I really appreciate this way of journeying together even when it's tough — other lovers have been part of our relationship from the very beginning.

Yes, there are challenges in this kind of relating, just like there are challenges in every kind of relating. At the time of the events I'm about to share with you, Dixon and I had been together for three years, with other involvements of various kinds happening throughout. As of this writing, we have now been happy in our consensual non-monogamy together for over 14 years.

Pause. Breathe.

Yes, this may be a very different kind of relating than the kind you are used to. In many people's expectations, any sexual relating or even romantic interest outside a relationship with a partner can be seen as cause for grave concern. Sometimes even emotional connecting is felt as a threat. Fights ensue, tears are shed, relationships end.

The reality is, whatever kind of relating we are engaging in, from our romantic involvements to our family and professional lives, old traumas stored as physical and emotional patterns can and do get triggered.

As mentioned earlier, polyamory and/or ethical and consensual non-monogamy are topics that are outside the scope of this book. See Additional Resources to Explore for the gifts others have written on these topics.

For now, the most important thing to know is that the story you're about to read was not an unusual or wrong thing to be happening. I offer this example because it brings together many of the elements of trauma healing explored in this and previous chapters.

May 2013 – Dixon and I are on the phone. He's been touring and performing his concerts and is now driving home from across the country, a journey of several days. We set this time together to check in and catch up, sharing about each others' days and lives as we've been apart. This is a time we both look forward to, and we have found is really necessary as a prelude to reconnecting physically upon his return. It is a deeply intimate time for both of us.

He left a voicemail earlier, then he called back to say that he has something he is so excited to share. I had felt sexy intention in his voicemail and now I am acknowledging I was wishing it away. As he shares all about his night and day, I feel relief as his excitement seems to be around sharing energy in other ways (dancing, playing his gig, receiving hugs from fans). My mind has calculated, based on the timing of his stories, that he couldn't have connected physically/sexually with someone, so I register that I can let go now… I no longer need to "brace for impact" for a story of sexual connection. Yes, sometimes his connection with others is still tender for me.

Once again my head was saying one thing and my body was saying another, and a new layer of listening was emerging.

However, now he shares with me an important discussion he had with a woman on the phone. He shares that he is interested in her, that together on the phone they shared about their mutual interest in each other and that they had the Relationship Agreements conversation, which is an important and regular part of how we share with other people. All of this was a simple conversation on the phone on the road; they weren't even physically present in the same room together.

Since I had already let go of the "bracing for impact" sensation, my heart and body are open. Therefore, his story of the discussion hits especially hard: My guard isn't up. It hits way harder than I would have expected…

Whammo! I feel a clenching in my deep belly and solar plexus.

I start walking and moving, then crawling — I feel myself come back in my body but resist again.

I feel the urge to cough, to vomit and it scares me and I hold it back.

Tears, snot, crying. Dixon holding space over the phone.

I feel the fear of being seen as dirty and not liked if I throw up. I speak it to him. He holds me even more.

I get scared, hit a block in my body. I will not really let go into this for fear of vomiting.

Then I realize I need to be witnessed in that space (of feeling the urge to vomit), right in it, with a pail or something to feel safe and just let go into it, and feel where it takes me.

But it is too much for right now. I back off.

All of these really strong body responses — sensations I've equated with fear and jealousy in the past — take over. Witnessing this in myself is really quite interesting, with sensations this strong from a mere conversation. I can tell it really has nothing to do with the fact that he just had a conversation with a person. But the sensations are real in my body, and need to be acknowledged, not swept away as "no big deal" as I have done in my past under the guise of: "He didn't do anything to violate our agreements, so I 'should' be totally okay with this." It evokes deep undercurrents in my body and I witness this right away. I can see the conversation as being a trigger for me. This is important.

I begin speaking it out loud with him, and he holds space. I am noticing the now familiar sensations of the trauma response and I share with Dixon what I am noticing:

I want to throw up and I want to freeze. I am moving in ways that aren't conscious. I am rapidly pacing and feeling stuck in a pattern. My breathing is shallow, my focus is really narrow. I seem to be staring at this little white dot in the carpet pattern. My body is curling up and getting small. I feel overwhelmed with heat and a sense of helplessness.

As all of these sensations come up and flush through my system I am noticing them, I am able to also step aside a bit and Witness: "Wait a minute. This has nothing to do with this moment. It was simply a conversation he had. There's something more in here, more in my body."

As I share this, Dixon is supportive. We've walked though these things together so many times now. We're learning from each other.

He witnesses, holds space, isn't trying to fix or defend — he is just loving me and holding space. In the midst of the body sensations, the heat, the nausea, I am able to step aside and say, "Yes, I need some time to process this, and we can reconnect later." We hang up the phone.

Immediately, I go down to my Temple space, instinctively seeking the Container I have built there as a place to access my Resources. I engage in some pillow-hitting, some journaling, letting myself feel the sensations in my body and giving form to the thoughts that accompany them. I vow to myself and to my body: I am not going to keep shoving these feelings away like I have so many times in the past. I promise to do my best to listen and to feel. In my journal, I write the "stories" that are bringing up fear and dread in me:

...He's on the phone with her, I try to call and he laughs at me. They both laugh at me.

...I am jealous — she's young and is dealing with facets of her sexual energy that she doesn't understand (as she reached out to me in the past about).

...Will they connect and he wows her and it becomes more? Or she wows him and he doesn't want me anymore?

And she's been reaching out to him about my work, but not to me — feels frustrating. Does she have ulterior motives?

He says that he feels she has an open and loving energy.

What's his piece in this? Not just for me to deal with.

And I feel like a hypocrite — talking and teaching about polyamory — am I not really living it?

How come he can be so okay with me being with someone else, but I can't be for him?

Anger, frustration, fear, jealousy, sadness. Wow.

Part of me feels sad that I can't be open to supporting him in this.

Part of me says I must honor my body — she is clearly telling me she doesn't feel good. I listen to her.

Through the night that night, I awoke many times, still grinding and roiling in the body undercurrents.

The next few days were filled with ways that I met this inquiry in my body. These are regular pieces of my life and practice now. Doing my human homework, listening to my body, and opening to Spirit guidance have become integral to my way of living life. The synchronicities of how it was all aligning affirmed both the need for and the power of meeting these tough emotional obstacles as gifts of healing, recreating my relationship to my body, reclaiming my power.

I did a specific practice that has been part of my Spiritual journey called "Chöd – Feeding Your Demons"[89] to face this shadow. Chöd is an embodied part of my shamanic practice, and can help bring awareness to these parts of ourselves that we have held subconsciously out of our awareness because they make us uncomfortable.

---

[89] This is a powerful spiritual practice with roots in the Bön Sect of Tibetan shamanism. The original teacher is Machig Labdrön, it was brought to the west by Lama Tsultrim Allione and taught to me by my shamanic teacher Rose Khalsa. A description of the practice is here, I recommend seeking live guidance from a practitioner if you wish to learn and embody it: http://taramandala.org/about-kapala-training/the-process/

In my Temple space I set up the meditative, visualization practice; I call in my guides and allow the demon to take shape...

I face this shadow, experiencing it as a cold steel ball and thick plate at my solar plexus — cold, hard, impenetrable — and meet the demon. As a Chödma, I transmute the terrorizing energy of the demon and meet my ally in it: On a serene lake, there is a single creature resting lightly on the surface in a ring of circlets of water ripples... I look closer, is it a Turtle? A Crab? No, it's Spider. Spider, are you my ally? Yes, she is. She promises to help me by weaving a gentle web bed for me to rest in, lightly, gently, safely protected. She promises everything will be okay and that I can call on her anytime by noticing the web around me. Rest. Yes, Aho![90] Deep gratitude to my teachers, the process, Spirit and to Spider.

I also reached out to Deb:

I call Deb and she answers! Yay! It feels good to feel supported. I share with her how I had been feeling so great for weeks and had been meaning to call her to set up an appointment while I was in this great space, and yet now the shit has hit the fan and I feel triggered and contracted. She immediately affirms — yes! That happens a lot: When we reach a new stage of growth, new vistas for continued growth become available. Then Whammo! The Universe often brings in another one... the next layer to be seen. Yes, of course. This resonates and I start to feel better already. I book a session with her. "In the meantime," she reminds me, "be sure to record your dreams."

Sure enough, that night I dream:

End of trip for Dixon, I'm about to head to airport to pick him up. He's exhausted, but he wants to address it. Give him time.

On trip myself, how did it go by so fast?

My best friend from high school asks me to buy her and a friend gold bras for the "Super Bowl." Fine. Sure.

---

[90] Aho: an expression that I first learned from one of my shamanic teachers, Rose Khalsa, and her teacher Grandmother Lillian. It came through her to me from the Lakota tradition, meaning "amen" or "yes, I agree" or "thank you" with a sense of "we're all connected." During the times of my life described in parts of this book, I often used it when acknowledging the spiritual and the physical coming together, so I keep it intact in the stories here. Since then, however, I have reoriented to connect with traditions from within my own bio-lineage and have released using this word in respect of the native culture from which it comes.

I feel numb. A man from my corporate past comes by and I hop on him and he carries me.

Afterwards, I am cutting wood underwater, standing in a river. Others were doing it too, on film.

Woman speaking — her iPad audio is producing feedback — switches to another device. I turn mine off in case it helps reduce the feedback.

We see a swallow overhead, pink head feathers on sides and back. It feels good.

As I processed this the next day, I used tools that have been a part of my practice for some time now. I originally learned them from the book *The Dream Game* by Ann Faraday, PhD.[91] By capturing the dream as I first wake up, later I am able to explore its messages by noticing its core theme, characters and symbols in conjunction with what's been happening in my waking life. Then by rewriting the story using what the characters and symbols mean to me, I am able to glean some messages to myself:

Let myself be nourished and suckle.

Let my little girl (that inner piece of me that is my younger self) be cared for.

Don't fall into the old passive-aggressive behaviors to avoid walking this yourself.

Also — don't just drown out (with talk and emotions) the need for cutting through the anger and transforming it.

Heal Through Love. The gender-bendy newness.

Pause the book process to allow clarity to emerge in my voice.

Give my healthy masculine time to be present for me.

Thank you, dream power, for this guidance. I will do my best to hear and honor your messages.

In the course of my day, I spend some time on the land, another key Resource I have developed through relationship over years.

I've walked back through the woods to my special spot near the river, and as I stand there barefoot, Grackle flies in, squawks and presents itself. I hear its message as: "Look at

---

[91] *The Dream Game* by Ann Faraday.

life differently; it is not always what it seems. Take a new view past the emotional turmoil and find joy. Take action. Don't just rehash and talk and not do anything."

Then I feel called to feel the support of a tree at my sacrum. I rest against it and meet my own sexual energy rising up. First I shut down a little bit, like: "I am not allowed to do this," or "Dixon needs to be here." No! I AM allowed and it's important to be ME, fully alive and here! I lean back then began to touch my body — at first through my pants — then decide to touch my breasts and yoni directly (under my sarong). So I do. I feel worry and guilt — what if someone sees me? Then I let that go and allow the energy to rise up. Birds come in to honor the energy: a Kingfisher and a Robin. As I build, they land, singing to me. I let go in an orgasm, holding the intention of healing… healing for me, my solar plexus, for the land and for sexuality and consciousness on the planet. Aho! I sit with the land with a much wider perception, and notice it is much easier to sink in now.

In my meditation, Sea Turtle makes itself known, slow rhythmic undulating swim… new dimensions opening for me. The worst is over. I will encounter much less resistance. As keeper of the doors between dimensions, Sea Turtle invites me to see that new ones are opening. She offers her medicine: heightened senses, subtle vibrations, and hearing.

Meanwhile, through all of this, (wow, the synchronicity!), I happened at the time to be reading *Waking the Tiger: Healing Trauma, the Innate Capacity to Transform Overwhelming Experiences* by Peter Levine and Ann Frederick.[92] As I live these experiences, this book becomes an embodied resource, much different than the times I've read books only with my head. It feels as if the Universe is bringing this series of events in as catalyst to really learn this deep medicine in my body. I make some notes in my journal, little bits from the book that are resonating for me:

> *"Trauma has the power to rob our lives of vitality and destroy it. However, we can also use it for powerful self renewal and transformation."*[93]

> *"'Memory' is not what we think… It's not a fixed linear record (limiting). It's a mixed bag of information, images, and responses (freeing!). Transformation — change your relationship with your memories."*[94]

---

[92] Levine and Frederick, *Waking the Tiger.*

[93] Levine and Frederick, pg 196.

[94] This is a quote from my journal notes, inspired by but not necessarily directly quoted from the *Waking the Tiger* book.

Two days after the phone call with Dixon that precipitated all of this unwinding and personal growth, I did a Yoga asana practice and felt my body. I noticed my solar plexus felt disconnected in *savasana*, almost like I needed to be more rounded in my back to connect down my front.

Also that day, another call with Dixon:

I share a bit of the new trauma awareness I've learned and get stuck at a point. I feel safe to just ask for his patience, which he is giving freely. I am truly in love with him. I know this process is meant to unfurl together in love.

My old ways of pushing away or controlling or passive-aggressive behavior are no longer of service.

"One step at a time, my sweet love," I remind myself.

Journal Self-Reflections:

I realize all the "what-if" scenarios my inner censor is creating — how I think he could've done it differently or why didn't he tell me first or etc. — none of this actually addresses the root. It's actually perfect the way it happened. This really was the gentlest way to activate this place in me. I experienced strong body response, yes. Yet I am able to see and feel some safety. Resourced in a new way... I am willing to learn and grow here.

At this point in the process, all the awareness, presencing and human homework I had been doing — the spiritual and mental pieces clicking and coming together — created a huge Resource for what happened next. Still unwinding in various ways two days after the phone call that triggered this old traumatic response, it was time for my Body (the Physical and Emotional pieces) to meet this once again, and something amazing happens.

Early in the afternoon, I get into the shower.

Shower time, Ah!

Cleansing.

I let myself tap back into the sensation of tightness in my body: in my solar plexus, where I noticed it when I was on the phone. I don't go very deep into it. Some coughing, tense body. I let it unfurl, I go into it, just tap into it a little bit, not overwhelming myself, not stressing myself to the point of throwing up. I simply let myself feel it a little bit, let it light up in my system.

And I can feel that it is tied into something big. It is bringing up Fruit Flies, chunks of my old stuff:

...remembering being seven and vomiting in bed and Mom's reaction.

...feeling ashamed, feeling dirty and disgusting, feeling needy, needing to stuff it away so I'm not a bother.

As it's coming up and I dip my toe into the physical and emotional content, I feel this hit: I stretch up, I do this really strong movement with my arms like the butterfly stroke in swimming ...

I notice it comes out of nowhere! I hadn't planned this! It's not like I said to myself: "I'm going to go into the shower and use my Resource Movement." Yet with the influence of the wisdom in the book I am reading, I realize: It's there, my body knows.

As a longtime competitive swimmer, ever since I was little I had associated this movement with real strength, power and success, with stepping into who I am. I now put it all together for the first time: The powerful energy of that stroke is a Resource for me.

So this comes out of an intuitive hit... I feel the need to shift my body so that it will let go, and it just goes into that butterfly movement. Like it knows exactly what to do. I sense, "Oh, YES! I remember this feeling. This feels really good, I feel the strength and power of stretching and reaching, feeling so expansive, alive, beautiful and powerful and I am proud and strong and in my Light and feeling really good about who I am!" Yes.

Then... I curl up into a ball, fetal "child's pose" on the floor of the tub, with the water of the shower pouring over me.

I feel relief — I feel permission to just rest and be held.

I don't have to move or rush away to clean up.

I'm not bad or dirty.

Next I gently let myself go a little back into the feeling again, I move my arms overhead to feel my forearms crossed against the wall above the tub as if hovering over a toilet bowl to vomit. I feel the saliva brew in my mouth and the spit starting to drain from my mouth, and I let myself meet the sensations and... ugh... I begin feeling the raw intensity of the overwhelm again... I spit, and more Fruit Flies emerge:

Memory of the morning after prom... I drank too much the night before, and now, while everyone is eating breakfast and enjoying themselves, I am vomiting in my friend's parents' green bathroom, spitting the disgusting red remnants out of my mouth after each retch.

Then I stand and move, butterfly strokes in the air, strong and powerful… and I feel the discharge. The sense of wellness, my Light, floods through my body.

I feel reassured and relaxed. I have all the time I need. I don't have to rush.

Relax.

Energetically I feel Dixon holding me like he has done when I was up in fear all night. Feeling held, patient, loving, no action needed — just rest, relax, let it out.

And I do this for a few cycles, "pendulating" between the intense trauma feelings and the resourced, grounded, "I am strong" space.

And it UNWINDS!!

It's okay to let it out and let it go.

Unwinding slowly.

Standing now at the end of my shower, I feel myself ground to the Earth, ground lines from my sacrum and inion, at the base of my skull.[95]

I move my body… I shiver, shake, let the energy pour down and out.

A little bit lets go, discharges.

Time now to rest a bit.

The sensory experience of the deep helplessness LETS GO… and the aha moments come… I write about my experiences.

Having a cognitive connection to what it's all about sometimes happens and sometimes does not. Sometimes I can intellectually come into a place that says. "Oh yeah, I know what that was about," and sometimes I don't, and it doesn't really matter. That's what I like, what's so simple and elegant about this. We're just letting the body be heard and letting it release things that no longer serve. We don't have to "figure it all out." Simply allowing the body to remember its truest place of health and aliveness. It is always there: Health is never absent, it's just a matter of remembering it.

And that place felt really beautiful to let some of this unwinding go, so that as I go back into the memories or the thoughts of this experience they just flow off my body, instead of grasping at or poking me right in that place of trauma re-

---

[95] The inion is a protuberance at the back of the skull. Through my training in BCST practice, I learned to ground from straight sinus through this point and it has felt beneficial in my grounding practice.

engagement. **These stored emotions, images, memories and body patterns no longer have the power over me as a trauma trigger. I have reclaimed that power.**

It feels wonderful.

$$\wp \, \circledast \, \wp$$

So how does this all tie together in support of the release of trauma? **By creating a Container, staying in the Present, and Listening to the Body, we can Witness our sensations, and through making choices with intention, breath, sound, movement and touch, we can release the charge that has been held as trauma.** As needed, we can access our Resources. In this example, some of those were: Deb, shamanic and tantric practices, body awareness, Witness awareness, Temple space, sacred land. Through this process we can transform the body without diving into the old stories and scripts that stored them to begin with.

As these practices emerged and developed in my self-awareness and shamanic work with clients, I was inspired to see the way van der Kolk articulated a similar strategy in his Top Down/Bottom Up options for regulation:[96]

Top Down: Strengthen capacity of the part of the brain[97] that hovers calmly and objectively over our thoughts, feelings and emotions ("mindfulness") to be able to monitor your body sensations. Practices such as mindfulness meditation, yoga, qigong and more support this (see the next Recipe for a simple way to begin with a Five Breath Meditation practice, or explore more in the R13 Mindfulness Practices shared earlier).

Bottom Up: Recalibrate the Autonomic Nervous System (ANS) by accessing the deep territory of the brain stem (the instinctual, non-rational emotional/reptilian brain). In other words, make a shift in the body to release the charge.

---

[96] van der Kolk, pg 63.

[97] This is the Medial Prefrontal Cortex (MPFC), an area of the frontal cortex van der Kolk calls the "Watch Tower," which has connections to the Emotional Brain (reptilian brain) and has the possibility of changing it. The rational analyzing part of our brain, the Dorsolateral Prefrontal Cortex (DLPFC), the place where we "think about it" has no connections to the emotional brain and cannot effect changes there. This is perhaps why so many people reach a point of feeling stuck in traditional talk therapy modalities.

Van der Kolk notes that we can access this through breath, movement or touch. Incidentally, I will add, these are some of the very modalities of working with energy that are the tenets of Sacred Sexuality and Tantra. Breathing is one of the few body functions under both conscious and autonomic control.

With practice, our capacity to notice and regulate ourselves will deepen, enabling us to connect with Healthy Masculine to support Divine Feminine to feel safe to come out and play, and to help us to embody Witness consciousness. Creating safe space, holding a Container... these are some of our Super Powers. As a facilitator of this work, I am really blown away by the changes I have experienced in myself and have seen in others through doing this work together.

RECIPE 14: Five Breath Meditation, pg 332

Questions for Self-Reflection

What have you noticed in your body? Have you noticed Fruit Flies — times when seemingly random thoughts or memories swirl about and you feel like shoving them away? Do you find they often feature the same thought or memory repeatedly? What do you notice about your energy or the situation you are in when this happens? What do you notice about your body when this is happening? Do you notice a pattern? Write in your journal about this.

Reflect on your Resources. Choose one. Allow yourself to feel the sensations associated with your Resource, feel your body change and respond. Notice the changes.

The key is: **Listening to Our Bodies**. Practice how to listen when you are feeling relative calm and ease, developing your capacity to witness within. Building this practice during relatively easy times helps us to bring our Witness consciousness into the times when it feels harder to notice. I find it feels much harder to listen when my nervous system is activated in a trigger (lighting up an old trauma), or when a Fruit Fly is coming to the surface that I don't want to see. I suggest practicing in a "cooler" emotional and biophysical state to integrate this witness consciousness capacity into your life so that you can consciously choose to access it in the more activated states as well. Practice using mindfulness practices (yoga, meditation, qigong, etc.) and practice the following Body Wisdom Toolkit.

What message can you offer yourself about your body messages from your place of enlightened awareness?

What mantra can you create from this message that will support you to remember your newly acquired wisdom?

RECIPE 15: Body Wisdom Toolkit, pg 334

Extra Support

We've covered big territory here. Meeting our body this deeply and holding space for old information to unwind is not a small task. A huge range of experiences may arise, and in various levels of intensity, as we saw while looking into the nature of trauma in the last chapter.

If you are finding that your body is holding trauma in a way that feels overwhelming to explore on your own with the resources offered here, or is not resolving with your self-guided practice with the tools and methods I've outlined in this book, be sure to consult a trauma-informed healer, practitioner or therapist, ideally one who works with somatic practices. This type of investment in your own self care can be invaluable.

With these tools of self-awareness and listening to the body, let's now explore the nature of touch, both for our own bodies and as we relate with our fellow humans.

CHAPTER TWENTY
The Nature of Touch

Naked, I touch my lover's skin with my hands. We breathe.

I listen through my hands, notice the texture, the warmth. I feel my partner breathe, I acknowledge their[98] body. I nuzzle my face against their neck, my muffled breath near their ear. I feel them press into me. I lean into the pressure, I sense them receiving me. Aha, I sense myself dropping into my own body awareness. I offer more of the weight of my body, I feel it pouring through their body into the support of the Earth. We roll in contact together, shifting our weight. We settle, finding a place that says, "Yes, please." We rest, my body touching their body, the sustained pressure invites a release. We feel an exhale into the moment. Skin-to-skin contact, gentle pressure, the joy of touch. We give ourselves permission to simply notice and be.

Slow down. Notice. Make choices. Listen.

Sound familiar? These elements are central to many of the practices we've been exploring. They are also the basis for our next exploration: the power of Touch.

Throughout this book we've been working with energy in the body and our energy bodies by noticing, slowing down and feeling. There is a wide spectrum of ways to meet and work with energy in the body. At the most subtle end of that spectrum, we can impact our bodies and our environment through intention and

---

[98] While she/her and he/him are two sets of individual pronouns, there are also more, including they/them and others. If this is new to you, check out more about pronouns and gender identity and why it's important: https://youtu.be/gXLFdYNEl_I
Also see the Miriam Webster dictionary definition of "they": https://www.merriam-webster.com/dictionary/they

visualization. And as we move to the more physical, tangible aspects, the spectrum includes breath, sound, movement and the subject of this chapter: touch.

The Shit That Went Down

Touch has gotten a bad rap in Western society, often lumped together in people's minds with "inappropriate" behaviors. And as we meet collective trauma-inducing events such as wars, conflicts and pandemics, our human family feels the effects of creating distance from each other, sometimes in support of community health, sometimes for protection.

Whatever their origin or source, over time the distances between us can impact our bodies and psyches. Many of us, when isolated, experience an intense impact to our nervous systems from the lack of touch and human contact. Noticing this, each person has the power to slowly, consciously choose new pathways to relate to touch and contact with other beings.

This can take many forms, with countless gradations of subtlety. What's it like to slow down and create deep connection at a distance that actually supports our nervous system? Then, when it's time, what's it like to come back into physical contact? How do we hold the intention around our contacts? What do we need to allow our bodies to feel safe to be truly receptive to touch once again?

USA & Western Culture Patterning

We are in an early 1970s hospital room: clinical, sterile and gray. The woman giving birth is attended to by multiple doctors and nurses, shuffling about in thick, white shoes, face masks and gloves. Her husband is not allowed in the "operating" room that is her designated birth space, even though she is progressing through a healthy, vaginal birth. The baby is born, the cord is quickly cut and baby is whisked away to be "cleaned up," wrapped in layers of blankets and returned to mom in a "neat little bundle."

Mom, wearing her own layers of hospital gowns and bedding, receives her little one with delight, following all the instructions that "they" give her. Doing her best to be the best mom, she takes the bottle of formula they bring her, offers the artificial nipple to her child and begins to feed her through the layers of clothing separating them. When she is finished, the nurse takes the baby away to sleep in the isolated bassinet in the nursery across the hall. Mom is happy that at least her room is right across the hall from the nursery, so she doesn't have to walk very far to come gaze at her new baby through the window.

This was the scene of my own birth as reconstructed through my mother's sharing about it. It was a common pattern for those of us born into mid-1900's dominant culture in the USA. I've noticed the effects of this patterning in my own life and as I've worked with others in thousands of hours of client sessions. This was the first life experience of many born during that era, and many still today: separation from mother, isolation from skin contact, isolation within a clinical setting. And this pattern continued, taking on other forms as we grew up. Here's a common experience for those of us born into mainstream USA cultural patterning:

Maybe we are touched and held, which is great, but then we typically find ourselves in a crib in a separate room (with an electronic monitor on for "safety"). Parents and children sleep in separate beds. Going forward, there is a rushed drive toward weaning us away from parental contact and getting us off to another room, and soon enough, under other people's care. We start to toddle, then to walk and are rushed through the learning experience under the guise of encouraging independence: "Oh, yay: Let's hurry to get them to walk on their own!" Then comes a time when we're heading off to kindergarten and we hear: "Keep your hands to yourself." Quickly we learn: "Don't touch anyone else." We are socially trained early on not to make contact with other bodies. All through school, that's what many of us experience. Traditional public and private schools as well as many other facets of our social programming ingrain this as a message.

Part of me sees why that happens: It's a necessity because in a typical classroom the ratio of caregivers to children is way off. This basic imbalance requires stricter rules than would otherwise be needed to provide for the physical security of the children, which in turn result in further imbalances and distortions *within* the children as they grow up.

So, in school we're taught "don't touch," and oftentimes we aren't given a way to meet our innate human touch needs even in the family setting. Then we progress into puberty, and our hormones lead us to a place where we start to become aware of our sexual human selves in a new way. We *need* to make contact. This instinctual, hormonal drive fuels our need to make contact. That's big. We can't ignore it. We may think (at an intellectual level) that we're not going to touch, but our bodies have an innate drive to make contact. Thus the need for touch gets reawakened, patterned in with the charge of sexual energy, because that's when it gets strong enough to drive us to overcome earlier conditioning and make changes.

In this setup, we don't learn about touch so much as we sort of stumble into it. When we're socialized not to touch others, puberty becomes a collision between our socialization and our biology. It can later manifest as anxiety when relating with others, in not wanting to be touched, or in feeling shame, suppressed desires, and awkwardness in intimate situations. The results of this collision can also be a factor in those who end up perpetrating violence.

Exploring touch is often secretive, hidden, not talked about, or rushed because "we shouldn't be doing this right now," but the drive inside us says we must connect. Therefore we feel conflicted, and then all sorts of patterns can get created. For example: "I need to touch, but if I touch I'm bad. So I'm touching and I feel good because it feels good, but now I'm a bad person because I feel good."

Often in this scenario, since touch was patterned with sex, what shows up is either: "Touch means sex. Good, I need and want that." Or: "Touch means sex. I don't feel ready for that or I don't feel safe, so I'm going to push even my basic touch needs away." Neither of these stories support a flexible and conscious approach to touch, and many other stories are also created at that time.

All of this adds to a convoluted spiral, a set of patterns that can go all sorts of different directions, ranging from: "I can't stand to be touched! Don't touch me, ever!" to "I need to touch so I'm a bad person, but I'm going to do it anyway. 'Being bad' turns me on." These and other patterns can get repeated in various ways, leading to confusion and less-than-satisfying relationships.

In the end, every person has different touch needs. Some don't want much touch or any, and that should be respected. Some really desire snuggles and cuddles. Touch needs are different for every person, but recognizing our patterns can help us to shift them if desired. While most of my clients have been raised in US culture, I also work with people from other cultures and societies, and I definitely see differences among both individuals and cultures.

Let's explore an example, a composite scenario drawn from many cisgender, heterosexual, white, US-based couples I have worked with in my practice.

As you read this next example, notice that touch is energetically directional. Who is this about? Who's this for? What's it about? All of these can really influence the nature of the way touch feels.

A couple comes to me to deepen their intimacy and improve their sex life. They're middle class, parents of teen children and in their forties and fifties. We'll call them Joann and Michael. Joann runs her own home business, Michael works long days in his corporate office. They share with me that they miss the connection they used to have before the children were born. Joann misses her own desire for sex. Michael's desire for sex is higher and they feel mismatched. They both have frustrations about the relationship, and yet love each other at the core and want to make it work. They both desire to make a change and want to feel the joy of connection again.

We've set the foundation by creating the container: setting intention, opening sacred circle, speaking agreements and opening into touch coaching and guidance. We explore the dynamics of touch through interactive practices that I guide them with. During one of the exercises as Michael is touching Joann, I notice that Joann's body appears closed and contracted, her arms are loosely crossed at her wrists on her solar plexus. Her energy has turned inward. Michael's hands are moving quickly and his body is in an awkward position that doesn't look comfortable for him. His breathing is shallow and braced, and he seems off balance. Joann isn't talking. Michael moves his hands faster and also remains silent. Joann's body contracts even more. The exercise comes to a close. I have to remind Michael to remove his hands from Joann's body as had been agreed in the container for the exercise that we set up at the beginning. As he does, I see Joann exhale and her body soften, arms relax from across her body to down by her sides.

This is an incredibly common scenario that I've seen in my life and practice. Most of the time, while it's happening, folx in the scenario are noticing only a portion of what is going on. That's totally normal: We each perceive from our own filters. The advantage of having a coach or guide is that you get an additional witness and one who can perceive through a different lens, with experience and training in a realm you desire support with. The beauty in this case is Joann's and Michael's willingness to acknowledge things that are hard to see about themselves, and their desire to make a change. With such willingness, there is a way through. If one or more of the partners is not willing to open to these possibilities, it's a much tougher ride.

As we complete the exercise, I open space and ask them to share what they noticed. Joann shares that at first it felt okay to have her husband's touch. Michael shares how much he enjoys feeling Joann's skin.

I ask Michael, "What did you notice in your own body?" He struggles, not really able to answer.

I asked if I might offer a response about what I had seen and sensed, allowing space for them to take or leave any of it. They consented to hearing the offering, so I shared what I noticed.

My sense was, fairly quickly into the exercise, Joann energetically left the room. Michael, who depends on his wife's arousal to create his own and may not even realize this, then subconsciously tried harder to get her to respond, to "make" her feel good. His touch shifted into a energy of "grasping." All the while, he thinks he's "giving" touch — he believes he is doing this for his wife's benefit.

However, Joann is no longer present, let alone communicating what she wants or needs. This may be because she doesn't really know. Or she doesn't want to make her partner feel bad for "not getting it." She may sense more in the energetic realm than Michael does, and expect or at least wish him to have that same awareness, when in reality he simply may not have those skills.

For Michael to be giving and for Joann to truly receive, the touch needs to be about her... for her. The only way to know what she really wants and consents to is to ask her.

If Michael is "giving" something he thinks is for her, yet hasn't heard from her or had her consent, then he is actually "taking." And if that "taking" is also without consent... he's stealing.[99] He is exploring a touch to try to make himself feel good in a nonconsensual way. This doesn't feel good for the person being touched, which feels unsatisfying for all involved.

Remember here the important point that Joann and Michael are in this together. They desire to make a change, they know that they each inherently want to support each other and their relationship. They're not here to behave without integrity, or to intentionally create harm.

---

[99] These dynamics of touch come from the Wheel of Consent® work of Dr. Betty Martin and the School of Consent: http://bettymartin.org/ www.schoolofconsent.org

Given that, can we learn a way to shift the energy of what is happening here? Let's support Joann and Michael to create the intimacy they both seek.

To begin this process, we'll need to explore the biology of touch, its healing power, and how we can consciously repattern old stories held in the body.

Biology of Touch

Skin: it's the largest organ of the body, and it's central to the sensation of touch, one of our most primal ways of relating to the world. Physically, this flexible, porous boundary between our insides and our outsides serves many vital functions. Beyond these, there are also psychological and even spiritual dimensions to the skin and how it works. Touch as a shared experience combines all of these dimensions of relating, which is why it is so powerful as a vehicle for both trauma and healing. By tuning in to the qualities of touch, we can receive and transmit enormous quantities of information and bring about shifts in consciousness and our physical being.

Because of all this, touch is one of the most profound ways to work with the energy of the body. It is critical in human survival. Let's explore the nature of touch more deeply.

Standing in a barn, my daughter and I are gazing at a momma pig and all her babies. The little ones are nuzzling in, pressing their tiny faces against her body, swimming with their legs in the sea of fellow babies to meet the destination of mom's nipple. Occasionally a little hoofed foot presses against a head or an ear, a butt pushes against another back, tails wiggle, snouts snorfle and suckle to make contact and receive nourishment from mom, for support, for life. I feel them all delighting in a pile of piggy love. This is what they know. No one taught them this. Their little bodies know exactly what to do.

This is not accidental. There's a reason piglets are born into that type of contact — it has to do with *connection*. Likewise with humans, as we are consciousness coming into form, we meet and grow through *experience*, through *relating* with our bodies. Contact and touch are crucial to life. Like our fellow mammals, human contact with the earth, mammals and other humans is critical for our survival on this planet.

It is such a gift to be in a physical body. Yet many of us feel times in our lives where we don't like something about our body or we feel compelled to cut, poison, starve, torture, neglect, get rid of or push it away. When we experience self-loathing, we sometimes think our bodies aren't good enough. We can reset our awareness about this. It is really important to start to shift the way we relate to our OWN bodies, as well as to other people's bodies.

Contact and pressure with another body, feeling the physiological exchange, feeling heart rate and warmth and pressure and breath — all of this supports us into "Ahhhh"… a sense of relaxing into ourselves. Studies have shown many benefits of skin-to-skin contact. Twenty to 30 minutes of sustained contact can shift the brain and body to release the feel-good chemicals/hormones (oxytocin, etc.), that are about relaxing and opening into the nature of who we are. It helps us bring our parasympathetic nervous system (PNS) back online. The PNS is the part of our automatic body processing that helps us rest, integrate and heal. Often we are rushing around in high sympathetic nervous system (SNS) states of vigilance, rushing to get things done, or feeling like we have to defend who we are just to exist. Bringing the PNS online supports us to drop that vigilance and feel ease.

The Healing Power of Touch

As I was researching touch many years ago, I watched an online report featuring an interview with a couple in Australia.[100] The mother had given birth to twins at the hospital. One of the babies was pronounced dead at birth, and was brought to the parents to pay their last respects.

Momma and Daddy stripped off their shirts, resting the baby in skin-to-skin contact with their bodies. They held him, stroked him, told him how much they loved him and told him what his sister's name was.

Within minutes, he started to move. Then he opened his eyes, and in a few minutes more, suckled breast milk from his mother's finger! They called for the doctor to come back in, but the doctor brushed them off, stating that it could not be possible. The baby's movements were only reflexes, and they should not get their hopes up.

Finally, two hours later, they fibbed a little to get the doctors to come back into the room. The father said to one of the physicians, "We've come to terms with his

---

[100] See the story and interview here: https://www.youtube.com/watch?v=FJ39-KJr_vA

death and we have some questions." The doctors finally returned only to find the child had totally stepped back into life!

As I first watched this interview I found tears streaming down my face. The two parents, holding their healthy five-month-old twins, shared their story. What moved me was their capacity to really hold open the space and effectively say "We love you. You are wanted. You are welcome here." The sense I got was that their loving acceptance and touch helped this child step back into life.

Also clear to me was what it wasn't. I noticed pretty distinctly that it wasn't about grasping at their newborn baby, even though the interviewer's questioning seemed to presume this was the case. It wasn't the energy of, "Oh, the torture! We can't have you leave us!" It was simply: "We love you and welcome you."

There is a real difference in the quality of acceptance and love and respect and holding space through touch when compared to grasping or trying to pull at. I believe that the parents' loving, accepting touch invited the space for the beautiful little being to say, "Yes, yes! Actually, I AM coming in."

It was profound to see these parents share their story. It emphasized the importance and power of touch, especially when held with a grounded presence. I notice the role that the quality of touch played in this story. I've also experienced it myself when I'm being touched or when coaching others to navigate their relationship with touch.

Conscious Repatterning

Whatever our personal history with touch, there is a way to process, listen, unwind and repattern. We can let these things move through our bodies and really honor that we are emotional, spiritual, mental and physical beings.

If we are only paying attention to our mental bodies, which is often the case in our society, we're thinking-thinking-thinking, or talking-talking-talking. And if we live from that place exclusively, which, again, is pretty common in our culture, we're missing three really important facets of our being: the spiritual, emotional and physical. Letting ourselves actually widen to meet all of the aspects of our energetic being helps us heal and reclaim our wholeness. This includes clearing our emotional field, clearing our physical body, letting ourselves be authentic and aligning with who we are.[101]

---

[101] Recall our journey and the prior practice on Clearing Clutter in Chapter 6 and Recipe 4.

Touch can draw upon and help us connect to all of these aspects of our being. Touch is about relating and connecting, and it is part of how we learn and grow. In fact, this is why touch is often so highly charged. Touch can often feel really good, regulating, or supportive or feel really horrible, triggering, or traumatic. Whatever touch is to you or however it is working in your life right now, it can not only *shift* in a direction that is deeper and more profoundly satisfying, but that shift can involve all the many layers of our being. Part of that shift could be learning not to hold ourselves away from it in a pattern of isolation. Instead, can we gently meet it? The shift can also be about how deeply we allow ourselves to explore the experience of touch. When held in a safe space that we co-create together, the body can unwind the messages it has carried — maybe old patterns adopted to help us feel safe when we were little and something happened but we didn't have the ability to process it.

When we're little beings, we need parents and other people to support and love us and show us the way. When this support is not there, we're awfully darn good at doing whatever it takes to carry on. We survive. That's how we're here now.

We're here because we built skills, created patterns in our bodies, to meet the challenges and do our best to feel safe. Maybe we check out of our bodies, maybe we numb out, maybe we dissociate, maybe we push others away. There are all sorts of ways that we try to protect our little hearts, and our little selves. And guess what? Those patterns aren't bad — they are skills that protected us, they held us safely.

Now, as we become more deeply resourced, we can be in the adult place of meeting old patterns in a new way. We can unwind them without swimming around in the past. We can meet them in the now, the present, and let them be heard. We can grow, learn and move forward. We can allow anything that prevents our joy, love and growth to release from the body. We can allow our body wisdom to reveal itself, and then move on. This is powerful. Touch is one of the most profound ways to connect with and see our old patterns as well as build the biospiritual wherewithal to rewrite them, discovering the deep wisdom of the body as we do. Recall our Body Wisdom Toolkit from the last chapter: slow down to Notice, make a Choice, Notice the shift and Celebrate that you are supporting your body to change.

Create What We Seek

I slow down. Breathe. Notice my body.

As I surrender to rearward and downward flow, I begin to remember my back body. I notice my seat and make adjustments to feel more comfortable, more supported. I allow my back to be supported by the chair. I notice how far forward my awareness often is. I breathe, and drop my awareness rearward in my body.

Ahhhh…

I check in with my body. How would I like to receive self touch in this moment? I feel a call to bring my fingertips to my scalp, scratch my nails through my hair, down the back of my head and neck, then drag the pads of my fingers to squeeze along my traps and to the front of my chest. I feel another layer of settling happen.

Now I spend some time with my hands. My right hand asks for touch, yes please. I feel a "yes" to that and my left hand, in my case my nondominant hand, answers the call. I start by simply holding my right hand, allowing it to settle into the support of my left. I breathe.

I remember all those years ago how my partner was inviting me to allow my hand to rest in his, and how hard that was. Like I had to hold up my own weight, I couldn't possibly allow someone else to support me. The intentional practice it took to really allow my weight to be held by him. I feel a warmth in my body that I let this in. A gratitude swelling in my heart.

Returning my awareness to the present moment, I begin to move my left hand, bringing slow intentional touch to my right. Taking all the time I desire, pressing the center of my right palm. Then moving with rhythmic, gentle squeezes outward from the center along each thumb and finger. One squeeze per bone, between each knuckle, then drawing away from the center to wring out each fingertip, and gently coming back to center to start again with the next finger. I add a squeeze at the webbing between my thumb and fingers, and at the webbing between each finger as well.

Now I rest my hands, no longer in contact with each other, palms up in my lap. I feel the buzz and hum as aliveness in my body. I notice the differences in that sensation between my hands. I crave feeling the aliveness in more of my body. I breathe, allow it to spread out and inform my arm and shoulder. I feel the buzz spread.

Then my left hand asks for touch, and my right hand delights in a yes. I repeat the practice for my left hand's pleasure. My arm asks for more, my right hand obliges and squeezes up through my forearm, then upper arm and shoulder. I feel my breath and I allow a bearing down of my awareness through my body and pelvis, into my sex. This naturally emerges, I don't think about it or force it to happen. I simply notice it begin and follow it.

I pause. Breathe.

Bring my hands back to resting palms up in my lap, no longer in contact with each other. I ask my body, What is your delight? What will you have me do next? How would you like me to touch you for your pleasure?

As we've explored, often we carry so much baggage around touch that we lose sight of something really special: We can actually center pleasure and desire, and hold clear boundaries, instead of focusing on what we don't want to happen. Where and how we place our attention has incredible power in our energy fields. Take some time to experience this for yourself with the following exercise.

RECIPE 18: Touch Exercise, pg 343

What do you notice in your body? What showed up? What surprised you?

Let's place our attention on pleasure and desire, and explore the beauty of creating what we seek.

Desire

Do you find it easy to know what you want, and ask for it? Be honest with yourself. If you are like so many others, myself included, the answer to that question is either "no," or it has been "no" at some point in your life. You may also find the answer changes depending on how clear you feel in yourself and your power, which may change moment to moment, depending on who you are with or what environment you are in, or over the arc of time.

Let's explore the layers of the permission field for creating what you seek.

Number 1 – NOTICE what you desire

As we take a breath and go into our own body, slow down and go inside, can we **notice** what it is: What do you desire? What does your body want right now? What do you not want right now? What feels unclear? It can take time and honest exploring to notice what that is sometimes. For example, maybe I know I want to feel contact yet I am unsure how much or where. Take a moment to imagine touch in one area, maybe sitting back-to-back with someone, and feel what your body has to say about that. Allow the need to decide about the rest of your body another time, leave it out. Receiving the body's messages indicating what would feel good, comfortable and safe can be quite a journey on its own. One step at a time. Take a breath and release the pressure — allow the space to notice.

Number 2 – ADMIT to yourself that you want it

After you notice what you want, which can take time, can you **admit to yourself** that you want this? Many people, especially those assigned female at birth (AFAB), those socialized as girls and women, trans women and cis women, feel overwhelmed with so many grasps and attempts at nonconsensual taking from them over their lifetimes that did not feel good. One way we've defended from that is to simply shut down and say: Forget it. It becomes: "None! I want none!" and we might be really good at just holding people at arm's length and saying "Stay away," keeping people out. Yes, holding our boundaries is an important skill to hone. Also, we all need human contact and there's benefit in it. So instead of only holding to our arm's length "no," can we feel into and find our "yes"?

Continuing with the back contact example: Can I admit to myself that I would like this shared contact at my back, and only my back, for the moment? And, I always reserve the right to change my mind.

Even admitting our desires to ourselves can take time, courage and intent. This layer of the process may also have old stories patterned in. Admitting we might like a certain type of contact can carry its own old baggage, times when we were told, "Don't touch yourself like that" or "Don't be touched like that," or "You're a bad person if you want that." As we grow up we might also think, "I shouldn't need or want cuddling. I'm a modern, independent, fully grown adult." These are only a very few examples of the vast numbers of old stories that pattern into our bodies.

Number 3 – ASK for what you want

Now that we've noticed and admitted to ourselves what we want, can we **actually ask** for that? Can we clearly speak and communicate to someone else what is starting to peek open inside ourselves that we might like? Chances are, we're nervous, and communicating can be another opportunity for growth. So acknowledge that, give yourself permission to ask: "Could we sit and rest our backs against each other and breathe together?"

Finally, Number 4 – ALLOW yourself to receive what you want

Let's say you've gotten the courage and you've figured out all these pieces: You've Noticed what your body might like, you've Admitted to yourself what it is, and you've created the situation for it or gotten the courage to Ask. And your partner has shared an enthusiastic yes, indicating their clear consent. Can we go into the fourth step and actually **allow** ourselves to receive what we just asked for? We've asked for touch; can we really relax into receiving it? Do we feel worthy of it? Because, yes, we're worthy and yes, we deserve to feel contact.

Notice what shows up for you as you read these words.

All of these layers, all four of them, have so much in them. They often bring up old stories and brain connections patterned into our bodies and psyches, stories that can make it really hard to give ourselves permission to meet our own desires and seek their fulfillment. Practice. Allow yourself to explore small steps in experiencing what you desire, in small doses, then let yourself integrate these experiences. Remember our titration example from Chapter 18? Taking slow sips and allowing your body to adjust to the new sensations can help you widen your capacity for creating what you seek.

Let's pause together, here, now.
And breathe.

Practice in Action – The Capacity to Transform

Now, let's return to Joann and Michael. Recall the directionality of touch and how consent and acknowledging who the touch is for can bring to light shadowy areas that are hard to see and support all involved to feel good in the exchange. As we practice the skills, we build our capacity for really creating what we seek. The possibilities are endless. You can transform your relationship with touch and connection, and feel good about feeling good.

After Joann and Michael have been exploring the work for some time, they've gotten more comfortable in the practice of creating the container together and navigating an exploration of pleasure within it.

We meet them again here. The structure for this play is that Joann is invited to receive the gift of touch from Michael within the context of a 5-minute timed container.

Joann first asks for what she wants:

"Michael, I have been enjoying our new play involving more contact and pressure. At first I thought I only liked soft touch. I am curious about the intensity of firmer touch, and even scratching and squeezes. I am curious and a little nervous. I want to start slow."

Michael is sitting comfortably near Joann. He found a new way to sit near Joann as they explore on the floor that is more comfortable in his body, and he took the time to get the cushions he needed to feel that support. He's able to be present in his body and listen to Joann.

Then she shares her hard limits for this 5-minute touch container:

"I ask that you not brush roughly across my nipples, intentional slow contact there is okay. Please stay on the outside surfaces of my body — don't touch my eyes, inside my nose or mouth or penetrate my vagina or anus. Don't grab tiny amounts of skin in pinches or bites that could break the skin, larger amounts are okay, go slow and check in."

Note that it may seem like some of the things Joann lists are obvious that they wouldn't be part of a 5-minute touch exploration, yet by her naming them it becomes clear where her edges are and this supports Michael to trust in her capacity to speak her truth and therefore it expands his capacity to meet her more deeply in a way she desires.

Michael repeats what he heard and checks in that Joann feels heard by him. She answers that she does.

Michael asks, "Are you ready to begin?"

Joann answers, "Yes."

Michael sets the timer and proceeds with the touch practice.

He starts with his hands on her belly and heart, still, breathing, listening... noticing her breath, noticing his own. After a few breaths, he begins to slowly move to her hips, then lean more pressure into her body from a grounded place in his own. He remains present to his own body comfort and ground, and he notices her body response. They exhale together with a bit of sound. As he feels into what's next he slowly offers more intensity of pressure, then begins to scratch his fingers along her thigh. He notices her breath and follows it. At the right moment he squeezes by grabbing a handful of her leg and holds… she startles, then squeals a bit and a smile opens across her face. He gently releases the squeeze and stays present with her, and present with his own body. He holds. He shifts position to adjust for his own comfort and rolls her body into contact with his own. He checks in, "How's this?"

She smiles and moans a "Yes."

He now has access to her back and he slowly begins to rake his fingernails from the nape of her neck down her back. She responds with a moan of delight and an undulation of her body into his touch. He's able to take a few moments to amp up the scratching as her body and her voice indicate their yes, then he slows it down and pauses with his hand flat in contact with her back to ground again as the timer goes off. He takes a few more breaths to notice her body as he holds her in stillness. Then they close the session.

Afterwards they check in together.

Michael asks, "What did you notice?"

Joann shares, "I so appreciate your presence with me. I really feel you with me in new ways. I love going slow, and listening for the moments to build in intensity of sensation. I was surprised by the squeeze, yet as you held it with me, I noticed how delightful it was to let go in it. I loved feeling you pull my body into yours, and the scratches on my back were divine! I appreciated you taking the time to hold still, breathe with me and listen to let the energy settle at the end. Going slow and checking in help me feel safe to let go into the faster moments. I am loving how much more pleasure I am starting to feel in our touch together."

Michael expresses gratitude for Joann's share and offers his own: "I am appreciating you sharing your words around what you like and what your edges are. It helps me know where to place my attention. I love getting your body movement and sound feedback as we engage together because it helps me know where you are with what we're creating together and supports me to shift gears if needed. And I delight in your pleasure, it feels good to me to share it with you."

They share their love for each other and rest in an embrace with smiles.

Consent

Notice how consent and boundaries were central to Joann and Michael's transformation. Self-knowledge is the foundation of our capacity for consent. As we grow in our self-knowledge, we better understand who we are and what we want in a given moment. The practices in this book help us build the self-awareness needed to be clearer in our "yes" and our "no." And, as we really get to know ourselves, we can trust ourselves and our partners even more to lean more deeply into what we desire.

In much of the book we have focused primarily on our intrapersonal journey, the way we listen to our own body as a guide for taking actions in the world. We've explored how listening for our body's permission, i.e., consent, makes a difference in how we're able to receive self touch and care that we desire. Remember from the Body Wisdom Toolkit exercise, the story of the man who was holding the energy of picking a fight with his body because that was the only way he knew how to relate with it? When he shifted from fighting his body to listening to it with loving kindness he was able to experience changes that felt good.

Notice as you read the self touch story earlier in this chapter, did you pause and give yourself time to explore the associated practice for you?

If you haven't already explored the Touch Exercise recipe, take some time now to do so.

Now that you've experienced this embodied practice, what do you notice in your body?

Let's open the door to bringing this embodied awareness into our interpersonal connections. Here we open new pieces of the Consent discussion.

A lot has been written about consent and navigating connections with partners, from a place of speaking boundaries and navigating what not to touch or do. This is important. Notice that Joann and Michael really started to experience more pleasure together when boundaries got clarified. Recall what we saw in Chapter 14: By finding the edges and communicating our limits, we create the playground for freedom. We have explored the basics of boundary setting, holding and container creating. It is also important to center the joy and pleasure of desire so that we begin creating the experiences we seek, not only avoiding the ones we don't.

To really support each other in collective liberation and wellness, it is important to explore pleasure and desire with the trauma-informed awareness we've been establishing in this book, as well as with the lens of social justice. Noticing where we rest in the power dynamics of a space helps us navigate the co-creation of consensual space. This includes the lens of race, gender, economic status, teacher/student dynamic, individuality and uniqueness in cognitive functioning and body ability.

Also important is to ask ourselves questions like: Did I get enough sleep last night? Am I in an altered state? How well am I feeling in general right now to make choices? Learning where we and our partner(s) are with these questions becomes a basis for co-creating together. Being able to see with these lenses, acknowledge differences and make choices to support all beings involved can deepen our capacity to create the experiences we seek without harming ourselves or others. It also supports us to build resilience and capacity for moving together through consent accidents, times when integrity is present yet harm happens, without creating more trauma.

Finally, working with the tools we have learned in this book, let's explore creating a container, navigating consent and boundaries, and letting go into something wonderful.

We're outside in nature, we three, in a safe, private space. A warm summer night, the grass is moist with dew, the bats have come and gone with the sunset. Now in the darkness, the fireflies continue to sparkle ecstatic brilliance around us as the rest of the animal world falls into silence — even the chorus of frogs has grown quiet — for now. I feel the support of my ancestors, and the ancestors of place, in addition to the nature beings all around us.

We stand and sway in a hug, breathing and feeling each others' bodies and the calm stillness of the night. After some time, my body feels tired and I desire a shift from standing to lying down. I speak the desire, the other two welcome the shift and we move to a space on the picnic blanket. We have chosen to open a container together to explore touch and contact.

What do we each desire? What are our needs and limits for contact? How do we each feel in this moment? What power dynamics are at play? What relationship agreements and dynamics do we each bring into the space? We co-create the intersection of our delights and share an incredible night of sexuality and play under the stars. After we close our container, we head to our separate sleeping spaces for the night.

The next day we check in. How do we each feel? What are we noticing? What after-care is needed? All voices are heard and we delight in knowing the truths of each being involved.

I felt such gratitude. Our willingness to speak up, have the conversations, and care for each of us made it possible for us to dive deeply together. We built trust because we heard each other acknowledged our edges and limits, and we trusted that we each had the capacity to offer our consent and to stay in the relational field if a consent accident showed up.

One of the biggest things that can limit how much trust I have with someone is hearing them say: "I have no boundaries" or "Anything is okay." We all have limits. If the person I am exploring with cannot speak where their edges are, I find it difficult to trust that they will be able to communicate with me in real time about what's true, and I am less likely to go into deep spaces with them.

I invite you to practice this. Create small timed containers to let go into freeing experiences. Over time, you can shape these in new ways to create new levels of pleasure possibility. Here's a simple practice that can be used as a scaffolding for creating experiences you love.

RECIPE 19: Container for Pleasure, pg 345

Notice how the practices in this book have offered a deepening in self-awareness that supports relational healing, and how the relational healing supports our self-awareness. I am grateful and honored to be connected with amazing humans who have been a part of my own relational healing and the evolution of my explorations about this, and you may benefit from building your own network of co-explorers and teachers as well.

As you look to build your connections and support, consider the work of Dr. Betty Martin and her Wheel of Consent mentioned earlier. Betty's work created a touch foundation for my own personal learning and for my work with clients for 14 years. Also see Embody More Love,[102] the work of Zahava (Z) Griss, a friend, peer, teacher and co-visionary for a pleasure- and love-based world. My connection with Z and our shared community, which began only six years ago, is very special to me. Through a powerful transmission and deep work together, they helped me see myself and my relational sphere more clearly and how to hold myself in deep care and be held in community as I noticed and transformed

---

[102] Z's website: www.embodymorelove.com
And in particular their Eight Steps to Creating the Intimate Explorations You Love: https://www.embodymorelove.com/blog/8-steps-to-creating-the-intimate-explorations-you-love/

things that were uncomfortable to reveal. And finally, check out the work of friends and colleagues Emma Daley and Fuzzy Konner, Consent Beyond Yes,[103] for more recent explorations in this territory. I have appreciated their centering of pleasure rather than fear, and how to navigate the gray areas with a trauma-informed presence as well as through a social and transformative justice lens.

Ultimately, touch is about connection: connection with self, connection with others. Connection with the most primal levels of human experience, and connection with the most sublime. Connection that brings healing, pleasure, learning, and new kinds of awareness. Connection that brings spiritual insight and personal growth.

And the amazing thing is, however we've been conditioned to experience touch by past experiences, through communication, focus, study and facilitation, we can shift our relationship with touch in helpful ways. By connecting our inner experience with our outer experience, touch can serve as a vehicle for relationships that go much deeper than physical contact. Through these relationships we can find joy, discover ourselves and move toward our current best place and best ways of being in the world.

Because of this, touch plays a key part not only in sacred sexuality but also in how we show up in life generally. Situated at the intersection of two of the main areas where people's experience tends to get disrupted — body and community — touch can help reweave those connections. In the next chapter we will complete the foundation that we've been building and show how it all fits together.

---

[103] https://consentbeyondyes.com/

CHAPTER TWENTY-ONE

Ancestors and the Four Foundations

This book thus far has placed our attention on rebuilding our relationship with body, nature and spirit as a way to connect more deeply with ourselves and others for a more meaningful and enjoyable life. Along the way, growth in these areas was facilitated by seeking, finding, and building communities that support these explorations. As we saw in my own journey shared in these pages, there's no way to know ahead of time how such a path will unfold for any particular individual. So, there was no way for me to know when I started writing it 14 years ago that, as I continued my learning, I would awaken to the need for developing a relationship with my ancestors, which I now consider critically important to share with you.

'Awaken' being the key term. I really didn't see it before about four years ago. This, despite Deb all those years ago sensing into my field and asking about my mother. "Something's there," she'd say, an invitation to get curious about something that needed healing or tending. The topic came up often. I would brush it away, saying to myself: "Nah, everything's fine," not seeing the rupture, secrecy and shame that my mother line held so tightly — maybe even because it *was* held so tightly, invisible to those within it. Here's a relevant line from Chapter 1: "Childhood is when our ideas of what is normal are established. We're building the lens through which we view the world, and then we don't see it anymore because it's a lens. Because of that we can easily normalize things that are not okay, including things that were profoundly traumatizing."

While not at the forefront of my own awareness during the events described in Part 1, the patterns in my own family and the need for mother line healing were there, ever present below the surface. I caught a glimpse in 2008, during my Vision Quest journey described in Chapter 11. As I returned from that journey, it wasn't only synchronous that I left to enter my quest as I left the corporate world, it was also divinely timed that when I returned to integrate the journey afterwards, my grandmother — my mom's mom, Violet — was in hospice. I returned from my quest in an exquisite, heart-open space to witness how my mother and the other women in her line were present — or not present — to the experience of my grandmother dying. I saw the shame in my grandmother's body, and I saw her fear. While intellectually I didn't know to do anything different than the responses I saw in my family members — I am one of this line just as the rest of her children and grandchildren — I was fresh from my quest and my heart knew a different way.

Accordingly, I trusted my intuition. I came to her bedside, I sat with her, I felt her afraid, not knowing what to do. I whispered to her that it was safe, it was okay to let go. I witnessed her children around her with pursed lips and silence, assuming their physical presence translated as support, when none were actually sitting with her or seeing her face or holding her hand. None were there to softly speak to her. They sat in the room staring off in another direction. There was even an unspoken ownership of who sat in which chair, defended as if that was the only way they could show their care. I watched as some of my cousins tried to encourage more interaction between their mothers and our grandmother, to no avail. Violet's children were physically present, but not emotionally present. I finally began to see a pattern that had been so pervasive throughout my life that I thought it was "normal."

Years later, as my ancestral healing awakening continued, I was able to more clearly see the rupture and trauma in my mother's ancestral lineage. And as I placed my attention there and built my resources and resilience, even more was revealed. As my capacity to receive it grew, the universe, and the ancestors, began to show me even more.

I realized that if I were to continue moving in the direction of healing, it would never be enough to heal my relationships with body, nature and spirit on my own. I saw and clearly felt that I was the product of lineages that stretched back deep into time. Much of the trauma work and healing I was doing in my own life was traceable to these sources. And not only that, I had resources in my ancestral lines to help with this. Our ancestors want this healing to happen, too.

In my ancestral healing work,[104] I had met a guide in my mother line (the ancestral line of my mother, her mother and all the mothers before them) and I sensed her walking with me. When I asked her name, she shared that for now, for the current ways I know how to relate with words, I could call her Sarah. My sense is she may have been known by another name or even a song in her time. She has long, straight gray hair with high cheekbones and sparkling mischievous eyes that light up when she smiles. When I encounter her, she is wrapped in a hooded, dark-colored cloak. She lived in a time of cooking over open fires and living in simple structures on the land. She exists as one with the herbs and plants from the land on the rocky, grassy ledges and cliffs near the ocean. She is an ancient Druid.

I had called for someone in my lineage who was well, deeply and truly well — someone who was well, capable and also willing. When Sarah showed up, I sensed her wellness and I asked her if she would be willing and able to help heal the line. I sensed a vibrant yes. As I connected with her, and we began to build a relationship, she helped bring the healing forward in the line so that the gates could open from the collective wellness of her time to assist with the challenges of mine. With her consent, she became my guide.

Sarah is from a time of intact wellness around 1,500 years ago and has been helping me bring that wellness forward through the generations. After a year of working with my mother's lines, the time opened up in April 2021 for something more. The work we had explored included 3D reality types of genealogy work at the computer, visits to the past homes and burial sites of my people, as well as deep work in the ritual space of spiritual and ancestral realms.

I open my sacred space and plan for another ancestral healing ritual. I'm seated at my ancestor altar in a space in my home with windows overlooking our outdoor space in nature filled with trees and birds. Two mourning doves are resting on the backs of the chairs outside. I call in my guides, asking for their support: Will you help bring the healing forward to the more recently dead?

They answer: Yes.

---

[104] Based on the book and work of Daniel Foor: *Ancestral Medicine.* Also Simon Wolff, somatic practitioner who offers ancestral and cultural healing in service to collective liberation, has been an incredible resource for me personally as I have worked with ancestral healing. You can find them at: https://www.simon-wolff.com/ancestralhealing

As I hold open the space and start the ritual, it begins… I feel Violet's mother, Opal, finally now join the well ones, then, oh wow, Violet steps in easily. Then the floodgates open, the flow ignites to become bright and spacious on my right side, which happens to be aligned to the west during this ritual, the place I connect with my mother-mother line.

Songs move through me, first ecstatic, then grief… deep grieving waves actively come up and through. I wail, "I am soooo sorry for your pain… Violet, Opal, Della (Opal's birth mother)," and my mother, daughter and other living family members, lovers and friends.

I cry and grieve and wail their names and express how sorry I am, which, as the alchemy happens, moves into how thankful I am, and the ecstatic waves shift to joy.

The mourning doves are present during all this — I love you! Grandma Violet, I love you! The doves have been with me always, reminding me of your land since I was a little human. They are here, making love during this ritual.

This knowing comes in loud and clear and puts a fine point on the bigness of what had just transpired:

"I've gained freedom from a mess that has had me bound for years!"

I rest.

The next few days move with ease as I integrate the new liberation.

After that, more revealed itself through my research. What I now know to be true is that the ancestors make things happen when they are ready, and when we are in a position to help clear unfinished business. The ancestors had my back in a way that the shift in my heart with my mom and my mother line was possible. I moved into a new place of care and forgiveness, a place of: "Family, I love you. Ancestors, I love you." And wow, yeah, my people made some decisions and did some things that really sucked. I can find new space around that and I can hold you with the new care and not bring blame or more shame or more heaviness to it.

Moving into this space, I feel a freedom, a freeing, as if the ancestors are saying: "Oh, thank god… finally, we can bring this information into the light of day." They feel the space we've created together.

There's relief. I'm on their side. We can let some of these stories and secrets be heard, not as a way of creating more blame, anger, judgment or finger-pointing, but as a way of expressing, "Oh! All of our people have had to carry the weight of this guilt and this shame too long in our blood, our cells, our bodies, our lines. Let's not have our descendants carry this anymore."

We can free that up. Just as energy becomes available to us when we heal personal trauma, so too does more energy become available when we heal the collective trauma that is still reverberating up and down our bloodlines.

One of the miracles was with my 71-year-old mother. I had shared nothing with her about my own experiences with my ancestral guides, and in fact we didn't often speak at all. I now see how affected I have been, starting back in childhood, by the presence of so much held back in her: big things she wasn't saying, things she maybe didn't even know herself. Six months after the wellness flood gates opened during the ceremony just described, I was on a phone call with my mom when she said, "No more secrets, Les. It's time." I felt a huge shift in her, a relief, a new curiosity and hope. My uncle, her brother, called me and said he noticed a peace in her he had not seen in her in a very long time… perhaps ever before. And I feel that through this healing work my grandmother and my grandfather as ancestors have been welcomed back into the collective wellness, have come to a new place and been welcomed in a way that they finally feel safe to reveal this information: "Yes, please. Let this stuff be heard."

And in the wake of all this, the miracles continued happening. I believe it's with the help of my ancestors that I keep finding pieces of information in the 3D world that weren't available before.

Once the ecstatic healing happened, the repair and connection to the collective wellness opened, and that's when all the other pieces were able to emerge. For example, new information revealed that my mom's biological father is not who she thought it was her whole life, and we learned about children and partners on both her parents' sides whose existence had been actively hidden from us.

While the full story is beyond the scope of this book, the essence is critical to it. We are all descended from a long line of survivors. Go back far enough in time and you will be able to connect with those whose life ways were relatively intact and who enjoyed a strong connection with the wellsprings of their own vitality. The wellness of these ancient ancestors can be extended through the line to benefit the living. All of us.

The Four Foundations

This is how my work on the path of sacred sexuality, self-awareness and remembering expanded to encompass a greater appreciation for the role of ancestors — the support they offer, and the healing needed there. All the work that I've done over the last two decades I now see clarified into four resources of support — key relationships that are often ruptured in our experience. These include our relationships with:

1. our own bodies
2. community
3. nature
4. ancestors

I have seen a deepening relationship with Spirit emerge as a common thread as we connect with each of the four.

Breaks in these four key relationships represent the biggest obstacles to overcome as well as the biggest opportunities to find support and create healing for many of us. Once again, since our traumas happened in a relational space, the opportunity for healing happens in a relational space as well. I've found this to be true in my personal journey, and with thousands of folx I've worked with in our Western, US culture.

The thing is, we don't know what we don't know. Most of us live in a culture that normalizes broken or severely compromised relationships with the body, the earth, ancestors and community. Because of this, we often don't know how these breaks and ruptures may be contributing to our problems. While all four of these areas require dedication and practice to restore conscious connection, ancestral healing often occupies a particularly large cultural "blind spot." True, some people are aware of this missing connection. Others never lost that felt connection to begin with, and may not even realize what rupture from it feels like. However, the majority of people in Western cultures do not know that the experience of a felt, living connection with their ancestors is possible, or haven't even given it consideration.

My experience is that restoring connection with any of these areas — body, community, nature or ancestors — makes restoring connection with other areas easier. For example, as we start to connect with our bodies, it often becomes easier to connect with nature, and vice versa. As we do, everything clarifies. Life becomes more easeful, more rich, vibrant and colorful, and access to pleasure and even ecstasy is more available.

Let's elaborate on these four foundational relationships, the first three of which — plus Spirit — make up the largest part of the book. Connecting with my ancestors came most recently for me. I will touch on the three others first then elaborate on the ancestral healing that is very alive in me right now, and I believe also for many folx seeking their next level of personal growth.

Body

Repairing, listening, trusting, and rebuilding our relationship with our bodies is central to this path. We meet the physicality of spirituality through the living body. For me, my body became an access point into Spirit, and vice versa — bringing Spirit into matter. Often we are taught not to trust our bodies and that we should leave our bodies to meet Spirit. This teaching is perpetuated by many religious structures that break the connection between body and Spirit. What if we reframe awareness and instead see that the lived experience of spirituality is all about embodiment — of spirit coming into matter? That coming home into our own bodies *is* connection with the divine?

As we looked at in depth in Chapter 16, the body is an enormous bank of stored information. What's it like to slow down, remember, and unwind the information that's been held there? Much of this information and the opportunity for healing can be identified and connected to events within our own lived experience.

However, bringing our ancestors into our awareness makes clear that a great deal of this stored information does not originate from our own personal experience and lifetime. Our body holds intergenerational wisdom, communal wisdom, societal structural wisdom and the traumas associated with all these levels as well. When we touch our bodies, move, make sound and breathe, we open some of the many access points to increasing our body awareness.

Community

As we repair our relationship with our body, we may feel more clear to be able to navigate, for example, our relationship with community. This is especially true if we consciously choose a community as a vehicle of healing our relationships with our bodies. The healing then works on both levels: Because our relationships with our bodies are to a large extent formed through person-to-person interactions, some people may choose to begin to build relationship with community first. We can remember that people love and support us, and this helps us to feel better about our bodies. By 'community,' I mean friendships, loverships, groups of people and chosen family that may or may not include biological family. People that we feel supported by and care for. Webs of relationships that give us a sense of belonging, a sense of being held in community together. There's an "in-ness" of belonging, a sense of connection. This helps us connect with our own body. While it is true that some communities can be formed around shared beliefs and values that inhibit body awareness and empowerment, the invitation here is to choose relationships where the people involved support body sovereignty and care together.

Typically, our relationship with community, with each other as a wider human family, has been ruptured or compromised. While there was a rupture even before the global pandemic, it was brought to a peak with COVID-19, which necessitated isolation and quarantine and intentionally distancing our bodies from other human bodies to slow the spread of the deadly disease. During this time, many people lost the kind of social contact and connection that our mammalian bodies need for nervous system resourcing and co-regulation.

Whether in relationship to self or with others, touch is where physicality stops being a concept and starts getting real. Touch can be a literal point of connection between the healing of our bodies and the healing of our communities. While hugging, snuggling and other forms of directed, physical contact with chosen family, friends, lovers are certainly a part of that, touch as a kinesthetic connector shows up in other ways as well. Maybe we carry a couch together to move it across a room. Maybe I hand you an onion to chop as we share time in the kitchen, preparing a meal for our friends. Maybe two people sit shoulder to shoulder to watch a performance, sharing space together. How do you experience touch in community?

Nature

The third foundational relationship is nature or earth, landscapes, animals, plants, mycelium, soil — the very planet we're on that we're interconnected with. Most of us have inherited or been socially conditioned into a broken connection with earth. This adds another layer to the ruptured relationships with body and community. Connecting with the earth can also be a point of healing that benefits the other two.

Reclaiming our connection with the Earth and soil is more important to our well-being than many recognize. And by reclaiming, I mean remembering. It's always there — in some ways it can't be lost — yet we have gotten really good at ignoring our connection with the planet, even putting in place barriers to the most optimal flow. We wear rubber- or hard-soled shoes and we spend a lot of time inside structures or on cement, isolating ourselves from the energetic and physiological connection with the vital force of the planet. In losing this awareness and connection, we lose access to the vitality available to us through it.

As described earlier in R8 Barefeet Earth, the practice of getting my bare feet on the Earth daily while I was still living in corporate suburbs made a huge difference in my awareness and growth. I did this practice for several years, then opened into spending one day a week in nature. This happened during a time when I also explored earth-connected indigenous practices and ceremonies such as vision questing. And along the way, a curious thing happened in my physical body practices: I shifted from intensely linear, goal-directed athletic pursuits like triathlon competitions into the more 360-degree, omnidirectional and relational awareness that aerial arts and acro yoga can offer. This shift illustrates how connecting with body, community and nature can work synergistically.

Building my spiritual awareness in all these areas set the stage for my current work as well, the new piece of awareness that opened up through connecting with my ancestors.

Ancestors

The fourth foundational relationship is that with our ancestors. Like the other areas, rebuilding our relationship with our ancestors is a path of connecting to Spirit. However, because most of our ancestors are no longer as accessible as body, community, and nature, it may be more difficult to undertake this path until one first feels resourced with their connection with Spirit, which is an especially important vehicle for ancestral healing. Yet, many of us come from lineages fragmented from intact culture or relationship with spirit as well as our bloodline ancestors. Myself included.

Some people in my family had their way of connecting with Spirit. To me it looked like religious dogma, and simply never resonated. I resisted it, pushed it away and rejected it. I rejected the idea of going to church, and I rejected my extended family. I didn't like them and I didn't feel like I fit in; why would I want to hang out with them?

What I'm coming to see now is that some of my immediate ancestors were more spiritually connected than I previously thought. I saw the religious dogma, but I couldn't see past it.

It wasn't until recent years that my journey with the ancestors helped me see more clearly and find forgiveness, acknowledging that yes, there was true spirituality there. Interpreting their spiritual experience within inherited religious frameworks was how many in my lineage were able to maintain a spiritual perspective in their lifetimes. And it's okay. We can clear and repair and complete unfinished business by working with our ancestors to free ourselves, and them, and support our collective liberation as a human family.

What do I mean by rebuilding intact relationship with "ancestors"?

For me and many of us who have felt disconnected from cultural or spiritual practices in our family, it may actually start with borrowed tradition and spiritual practices we connect with through teachers in this lifetime or through lineages that we may feel at home with because of our past lives. This can create a lovely sense of connection with the ancient ones as guides. While this "borrowing" also needs additional action to honor the original peoples of the traditions,[105] in my experience the resourcing and wisdom gained from this

---

[105] For me, this includes guides in the many traditions I have been blessed to learn from and resonate with but weren't part of my family's cultural teachings: Native American shamanism, Peruvian shamanism, tantric yoga, kundalini yoga, hatha yoga, Bon sect Tibetan Buddhism, Taoist sacred sexuality, and Egyptian sexual alchemy. I have deep gratitude for these teachings and the teachers I have learned them from. However, the work continues from there. If we rest only in a borrowed tradition, while ignoring our own need for repair, we risk cultural appropriation and continuing the harm that has been carried through our past generations. I now see this as an ongoing conversation, with no single answer. I am taking action to pay reparations, speak up to educate others, and bring equitable relating such that I honor the original people of these traditional practices and healing modalities, as well as the work itself. And I also see that more is needed.

helped open my eyes to the next crucial piece of the ancestral healing needed: repair of my actual bloodlines.

As we who have inherited a broken culture seek healing in traditions that remain relatively intact, the reason this chapter needed to be added for the book to be complete is that I have come to understand — clearly, distinctly — that it's also really important to include rebuilding our relationship with our *actual bloodline ancestors*. How did our people relate to Source, to Spirit? How did they successfully negotiate maintaining the connection with Life? We all have access to that. Even if we feel like we don't.

I acknowledge this may be hard to grasp — it was for me. I feel this needs some emphasis: **We all have access to the collective vitality and wellness of our actual bloodlines, even if we feel like we don't.**

Thus, while many and varied traditions from around the world can help us build our spiritual connection, we can then bring the capacities we have built to explore, heal, and access the vitality and wellness in our own ancestral bloodlines. And the good news is — just as in any community — in making this connection, we are not alone when faced with the heavy lifting this may require. We can rely on and rest in the support of our healing-oriented, well-intentioned ancestors. We only need to do our part.

Building these relationships through inner connection requires clear and strong boundaries, just like with the living. I am not suggesting torturing ourselves with relationships with bloodline ancestors that are harmful. Instead, it's about meeting and tending to relationships with the really vibrant and well ones and those in our bloodlines who best align with our healing intent. Depending on the culture we are from, these guides may have lived 2,000 or more years ago. Our most well-resourced, most intact ancestors see where we are today. They know what happened, and they want to help. We are, after all, their children.

As we repair our relationships with our bloodline ancestors, it feels like: "Ahhh… my people have my back!" There's an accessibility, a power, a potency for everything else in our lives.

Spiritual practice is essential in this healing process. In addition, just as with our relationship with community, body and nature, touch and physicality can also be a pathway to connect with the ancestors. The ancestors are the land, their bones returned to the Earth. What do we notice when we walk the lanes of our ancestral village?

In 2015, I was encouraged by a very conscious health practitioner to return to the place of my grandparents and find forgiveness as a part of the journey of healing my gut. I was struck by the suggestion, and resisted it or at least didn't really pay it much attention at first. Several years later I actually did it, and it was crucial in my healing process. Visiting the houses, the cemeteries, the land, the space that my ancestors lived, breathed, drank of the water, ate of the food, returned their bodies into the land... all these are acts of touch and contact. Some people will notice powerful sensations and even receive messages by holding an object that belonged to an ancestor. In the cultures that maintain physical touch, physical community and physical communion with nature, people tend to have more durable connections with their ancestors.

Ancestor healing is the leading growing edge for me right now, a new green shoot. It feels really important to recognize that this is happening now because of my 20-year journey of connecting with my own indigenous wisdom, my own body sense.

The word 'indigenous' gets confusing for some folx, especially those of us in white bodies whose ancestors came here from other lands. By 'indigenous wisdom,' I mean the inner wisdom we all have access to through our intact relationship with wellness in our bloodlines. Every human on this planet has a lineage that, if we go back far enough — and sometimes that may mean thousands of years — had intact relationship with the land and with collective wellness. And the more we connect with our own indigenous wisdom, the better the practices of any tradition (working with breath, sound, movement, touch, energetic practices, etc.) will work for us. Ultimately the truths and understandings we are accessing are our own.

Regardless of where we start: Developing our awareness of the body, healing community, connecting with nature or even with ancestors, healing happens as we meet and rebuild each of these foundations. While becoming aware of the multiplicity of breaks can feel daunting, the opportunity is to see that every break in the system can be a point of effective focus in healing it. Just as fragmentation and loss can lead to further fragmentation, so too can the reintegration process build on itself. It's a journey, a dance and flow. We can start anywhere.

Through this work we build capacity in our organism for meeting big energy. The big energies we encounter can include the power of our sacred sexuality, feeling the depth of grief, and meeting the discomfort of anti-racism work, which includes unwinding racism from our bodies. It can include supporting collective liberation, or simply remembering who we are and stepping into the world in a new and bigger way. In all these ways and more we are meeting big energy and building our resilience and capacity to be present for it and each other.

The conversation between us and our worlds is now open. As you have read this book, you may feel yourself getting curious about your relationships with your body, nature, community and ancestors. Feel into each one. Which of the four do you feel drawn to place your attention on next? What do you notice about your energy as you do?

CHAPTER TWENTY-TWO
More Energy Available

So here we are in the final chapter.

You may have come to this book wanting better sex or relationships. You may have wanted a better orgasm or to learn how to connect more deeply with partners or be a better lover. You may also have wanted a more spiritual experience of life, one that includes your sexuality and goes beyond.

And as we grow together, we find out that to heal our sexual life is to heal our whole life, our whole self, our relationship with ourselves and each other and the world around us. This shift changes everything. It changes our work, our relationships, maybe it clarifies our sexual orientation or how we experience gender, sometimes even how and where we live.

We have seen how a part of that is to heal our connection with nature, body, community and spirit. And now even the ancestors. We may wonder, what the heck do the ancestors have to do with it? Think about it. For you to be here in this body, your ancestors had sex, a lot of sex, all the way up the ancestral line. We grew inside our birth mother's womb, steeped in her energy field and the field of her relational interactions during that time, including how she related to your birth father and how he related to her and the unborn you. Before that, your mother grew inside her mother. As she did, the eggs she would release for her entire lifetime grew, at least one of which would become fertilized and begin the body vessel that you inhabit today. This means that a part of you was also physically present, *even in your grandmother's womb*, and was exposed to her field. And, she was similarly influenced by her mother and grandmother, and they theirs. Does it start to make a little more sense how deeply impactful our ancestors are, even if we may not know them or have any strongly felt connection with them at this time?

All of this highlights how powerful sex and sexuality really are. This fundamental connection is why sex is more than just "biological" procreation — as we've seen in this book, it can be explored as a path of liberation. When we look at the intergenerational dimension of how we hold information in our bodies, the vast potential for learning, unwinding and liberation on this path can reveal itself in a deeper way.

Throughout this book, I've shared some of my own story and a collection of foundational practices — exploring the body as a primary modality for reclaiming our authentic inner wisdom and power, and our own sacred sexuality. My intent from the outset was to offer a resource for you to create the life you choose, rejuvenate your body, and reclaim your sexual sovereignty. My hope is that this can connect you with the deeper resources you carry as you witness and learn from the places in your own body, releasing old patterns and limiting beliefs. And in the previous chapter, I open the door to gather the resources needed to shift even intergenerational patterns, reclaiming our power and our choice to really let ourselves feel good about feeling good by listening to our body and building our relationships with nature, community and our ancestors.

In this way we spiral back once again to: "It's Just the Beginning." As we explored in the first parts of this book, ecstatic states of bodies merging, energetic orgasms, opening to and embodying love are indeed possible. This journey of listening to our bodies is what makes it possible. Yet the processes outlined in this book create the foundation for so much more. All too often in books on sacred sexuality, this foundation gets glossed over in the drive towards ecstatic states. And yet without that foundation, this drive can mislead us and even burn us out. This book fills a gap in literature between higher levels of ecstasy described in the sacred texts of old and the realities of achieving them in our own, oppressive, materialistically oriented time and culture. How can each of us get there, given the ruptures and confusions involved, as well as the systemic, structural and intergenerational trauma that exists?

Ultimately, all of this is about following our own unique inner guidance and connections, trusting in these relational spaces, trusting in our own power. Access to our unique inner guidance can really bloom open to be trusted in deeper ways as a result of this work. What follows is a share from a recent inner body experience after exploring this journey for over 20 years.

While I often prefer to be outside in nature, this time we set the space inside our home because it's wintry cold outside in Michigan. We have a space heater, blanket and pillows and a soft space to snuggle. My beloved Dixon and I create a ceremony together with the intention of opening our hearts together, listening to our bodies, and exploring deep connection. We slow down and begin our practice.

After exploring and connecting together, we shift to him holding space for me as I explore a deep dive with my womb, allowing my own descent into my pelvis and listening to the wisdom there.

I find myself noticing my daughter, who is now 20 years old, and I am internally guided through a practice of gently inviting a deeper release of her from my womb, offering her more space into her own freedom in her adulthood, what I come to call offering her more "birth freedom." I feel a warmth and ease in my womb as I let her go. I smile, gentle tears flow.

After some sweet moments to complete that portion, I place my attention back in my womb and I listen. I notice my mom comes in... oh wait... it's actually me inside my mother's womb as a fetus! From this perspective, suddenly I feel a new compassion for my mother. Ohhhh, I feel it! My frustrations with her dissolve for now. She is so young! *She loves me so much, yet is so unsure of herself. She really wants to do her best, yet she is naive to the ways of motherhood. Rifts with her own mother and her mother's mother have disconnected her from the teachings of the ways. She does her best, yet she doesn't know how to be in her own power in her pregnancy and body choices. She gives them up to the white male doctors who say that cutting the cord quickly is the way. But it is too soon! There's a vitality from the pulsing of the cord that I as the newborn can receive, an ignition into life. I now allow myself to reset and receive it.*

"You can't cut the cord yet. Wait!" This declaration comes from my present adult self and my newborn infant self as one.

I breathe, I receive. I receive the potency, the vitality. No, it's still not time: Don't cut the cord.

I receive, I take all the time I need.

I receive, ahhhh.

The space is finally available.

I rest, so good.

The cord is cut in the right moment, it just happens, it's easy and smooth, not rushed.

I feel a new empowerment and vitality, able to let go a bit more from my own mother. Not only have I offered more birth freedom to my daughter, I have received deeply a new layer of birth freedom from my mother.

This is an *embodied* experience, not a cognitive "idea." After energy body shifts of this kind, relationships often transform. Growth trajectories can accelerate. Creative energies may be liberated. **More energy becomes available.**

Tuning in to my body as resource for information — this is what this very book is about. I find it sweetly affirming and synchronous to share this revelation from my womb as I write this final chapter and prepare to release this book into the world. I didn't plan the ceremony for the purpose of the book, yet it showed up. It allows seeing something really important.

As I came to completion with these womb aha moments in ceremony, wisdom about the overarching experience came through and I captured the following in an audio note:

This is a really big deal: The awareness that women of ancient cultures, meaning in this case all those who identify[106] as womb-bearing beings, who were often the spiritual leaders and the seers and the witches — our capacity strengthens and deepens and opens with womb clarity.

I mean, I think it's womb linked up with third eye, linked up with heart. It's more than just womb, but if the womb is cluttered with information or overwhelmed with trauma, our access to womb wisdom is cloudier and it's confusing.

And unfortunately, most beings with wombs walking on the planet at this time in history have a lot of trauma and clutter — which has its own burden of grief that needs tending as a part of the path of unwinding it.

I can now see that all these years of unpacking trauma, stories and clutter and unwinding all these signals that have been confused and convoluted in my womb have **opened a tremendous access to my own seeing.** *Holy shit, of course we can't see clearly when all of that is present. But most people don't realize that because they don't see that the womb is a place where we see! Wow, it's just really huge to have this aha moment.*

---

[106] Including multi-spirited beings, known as Two Spirit beings in some traditions. Also includes third gender or other non-binary expressions of our human family.

Like: "Oh, what… my womb is clear?!" I say that out loud and my womb stays clear and soft and wide and warm, right? If I say that and it's not true — if there's something that needs to be seen — I will know, especially right now because I'm cramping and I'm getting ready to bleed. When I speak that and it's untrue, my womb will contract and tighten and tell me that I need to listen to something else. As we bleed, it is a particularly potent time because I think our wombs are on higher alert for conversation.

This is a huge revelation. Wow, duh! And it's so simple, I'm thinking, "You're not saying anything surprising, and you're not saying anything new," which seems to happen when a new layer of body awakening of a remembered truth happens. Yes I may have known this cognitively before, but now my body has opened to a deeper knowing, and this is what is so potent. Womb wisdom is a powerful thing… and I don't think it's a thing that most people think about. Oh, Wow.

I noticed bigtime in this ceremony how my confidence with intuition and seeing have opened in a deeper way after all these years of unwinding trauma, messages, stories and frankly, the clutter of information that my body and my womb were holding. I didn't even know I was holding these things because the traffic was so busy that I just figured these random thoughts were "normal."

But now, as I meet my body and listen, I can slow down into the clarity that has emerged from the unwinding. I have so much more space available and it frees up energy, releasing the way my body held these bits of information and did its own energetic work to find the right balance to get me through, which has been awesome. There's no resentment or blame for that.

When we find enough silence amidst the static and overlapping signals, new channels of information become open to us. The analogy I see is that it is like radio traffic, scanning the dial and hearing all of the different ways we could be tuning in to information and the universe. There are a lot of channels of information all trying to come through. As we unwind, we can receive this information in more intelligible ways. We can trust what's coming up now, trust that there's an intelligence at work in the seemingly random events and thoughts and feelings and so on. Listen to them.

We can listen. We can pay attention to our feelings, to the memories that crop up, to the annoying "Fruit Flies" buzzing around our heads. We can pay attention to synchronicities, chance meetings, words, encounters. We can notice body sensations. We can feel into and distinguish our authentic yes and no. We can discern when something needs attention, or when we can simply let it go. We can become aware of habits and habitual responses and unravel their origins.

We can ask ourselves questions. What is the story there? What needs to be said? What can go a different way? What's now complete? As we listen and unwind, the static clears. Those many, many voices clear. And we have access to a clear channel of our body vessel for the messages, for the guidance.

In this quest, I wish to acknowledge there is not only one right path. We can let go of the assumption that there is one way and we have to find it, and that if we don't, we somehow aren't doing it right. Or that we missed getting the message and aren't working hard enough. These add the violence of perfectionism to our journeys and it simply isn't helpful. Also honoring that it's ongoing. As I write this today, while I feel so much more clarity compared to where I was 20 years ago, I love that I'm still learning. It opens the door to further development, bigger experiences of life, deeper knowing. It doesn't mean that there isn't more. There is so much more.

Along the way, I've found having a daily practice to really drop underneath that static and keep the pathways clear has become really important. I've shaped my life to create the space for it. Creating the space for these somatic practices can help us stay centered, grounded and present to our own experiences.

Then whenever we spiral out into other awareness or feeling overwhelmed, we can re-engage with the tools of practice we've explored together here in this book to come back, center, and listen to our bodies.

Also notice: Not all of these changes were comfortable. It's important to let ourselves be in the messiness. We've seen it in my stories and I know I am not alone in the messiness — the broken trust, the broken fingers, the vomit, waking up hungover and grimacing as the light shone on all the things I didn't want to see that I was stuffing away. For a long time I was running my body, overriding my body's sacred wisdom, telling my body what to do, rather than listening. In fact, it still happens — and I feel more able to notice and shift than ever before, and to treat myself with care when I do notice.

Our sacred sexuality encompasses all of this: being in the hot and sweaty pile of bodies and sex juices with your lover, being in the grief and tears, the wails of rage. Being less afraid of the goo and the mess on all levels! Discovering our sacred sexuality dredges up our stuff — that's why it works, that's why it's an authentic spiritual path. Listening to our bodies means less time running and driving and forcing our bodies to do things, and more time listening and making space for what the messages are.

I didn't know before, or even as it happened, that some of my spiritual growth would happen with a salesperson at a clothing store. Or hearing song lyrics on the radio. Who knew a dragonfly landing on me and cleaning its eyeballs in such an unassuming way would launch my experience into a deeper awareness of my self and the world around me?!

Yet I learned as I went, more ways to be compassionate with myself as I saw things that were hard to see, more ways to be compassionate with others in my work and with all of you as readers here in this space together. Reflecting back helps the story clarify and get organized in these pages, and it also helps bring a softness to whatever may be coming next. Because the messiness will still come. And in our changes, we build resilience and strength and deeper resourcing that allows our experience of that messiness to change.

This is why this story is worth telling. It's an offering, a demonstration from a place of authenticity, of what can be as we meet the shit and the mud and the pain and transform through it. My goal as I write is to offer relationship, a place where we learn together and grow together. A story that meets you where you are, and me where I am. We can do nothing else, really.

And we end up in a place I couldn't have predicted when we started. But isn't that how love works?

Likewise, you will find your own teachers, practices, and explorations. Yet the outcomes will never be entirely predictable before you go into it.

The field of possibility is WIDE!

Working with a client couple,[107] *I offer excerpts of this book manuscript as homework readings to support them between our sessions. They immediately feel a real resonance with Michael and Joann's story from Chapter 20. After beginning the work and doing the practices, they notice that "life starts to take over," leaving their commitment to this work*

---

[107] Like many, but not all, of the client couples I worked with in the first decade of my practice, this couple was heterosexual, white passing, able-bodied, cisgender man and woman.

on the sidelines. They feel guilt and shame and embarrassment that they're not doing it right or they're not doing it enough.

I share with them that what I see is their deepening care for each other and their willingness to slow down and pay attention to even the subtle things that arise in the practices that allow them to see each other more clearly.

They're bringing more care to what they see, both within themselves and each other, and they're recognizing the power of the change in their lives that the practices offer. They share with me, "We came to you wanting to deepen our sexuality and improve our intimacy, and what we're finding is that it's big, it's a lifelong path, and so interconnected."

Like many couples, they originally thought in terms of "sex in the bedroom," as if that aspect of their relationship were literally in a separate box, and they expected to simply address it that way. Then they began seeing how much deeper and richer the transformation is.

They were curious as they completed this series of sessions together with me: Is there a way to continue? Yes, there was more work we could do together. I also invited them to see that the work really is being done through them, even in the times they feel most uncomfortable. When life feels like it's taking them away from what they want to do — it may be directing them right towards it. Working through and unpacking the embarrassment and shame they are feeling may turn out to be the first step toward the bigger, deeper kind of relating that they are looking for. And yes, it will translate into "the bedroom."

This awareness is part of the journey: where they place their attention, how they care for themselves when they realize something about themselves they don't like and they want to shift. At some point they will likely have to look at how they care for themselves in those moments when they realize they've created harm, even if unintentional. And how they care for each other as they each learn and grow.

The growth catalyst for this couple may be that as they see how things are taking them away from their practice, this noticing can actually help bring them closer. Their worries and fears may be past-stuff patterns that are arising. Oppressive constructs woven into our systems may be showing up in their bodies: the drive for perfectionism, fear of "doing it wrong," urgency, avoidance of discomfort, and other ways we sabotage ourselves. Bringing awareness to these patterns is crucial in creating new ways to relate to these often unspoken, subversive energies, so that we can open and the unwinding can begin.

Here's a gift in the final moments we have together before the book ends…

That thing that you think is taking you away from what you think is the thing? THAT'S the thing!

In other words, whatever is showing up, show up for that. This may be exactly where to place your attention right now. I call this subtle level of attention: following the bioluminescent threads, a feeling or knowing of awareness that expands into more color and vitality that can be followed. Arthur Mindell calls it "second attention,"[108] a level of dropping below the "first attention" of everyday reality and noticing that there's something else asking for attention on another level. It requires being with what arises, with what is here now. It requires recognizing that this is what's being asked for and seeing its innate perfection, even in all its messiness. This presencing is also the essence of tantra. When we listen and follow, this is where the vitality is. Colors get brighter, the world opens up, time slows down, and joy and ecstasy emerge.

Notice this takes the element of practice — perseverance, which comes from an inner wellspring. We can practice shifting where we place our attention.

It's a lot like the whole story I've shared in this book. We start from someplace and think we're going somewhere, we follow the path and we listen and we explore. We shift in so many ways, sometimes becoming whole new versions of ourselves, closer to our authentic being.

Each step is a new place to emerge from. It's the first day, once again, of the rest of our lives, and we really don't know what's next.

Then the way becomes clear.

And yet we still don't know what tomorrow or the next decade will hold.

ৡ ❀ 03

---

[108] From the book *The Shaman's Body* by Arnold Mindell.

Aspen, eh-yah aspen.

Tremble. Fears. Facing the shadow. Moving through the fear. Dancing messenger of the wind. Beacon. Resist — bend but not break.

My body is submerged in water. The winds are speaking — we are having a conversation about this book via another descent into my womb. I listen. Here the final piece comes in.

Aha moment as the wind rises up and says, "Yes."

Yes to collective liberation.

Name the Gifts

This book ends with a reflection on our journey to this point, and an expansive invitation into what's next. This is the "Yes, AND..." of more energy being available as we liberate old stories and trauma from our bodies and experience more vitality, joy and pleasure in our lives. With more energy and vitality available, and through practice with awareness, the gifts of the second attention emerge.

This book and the practices shared here can continue to be a resource for you to create the life you choose, rejuvenate your body, and reclaim your sexual sovereignty. Yet the true gift in all of this is your own connection with yourself and with the deeper resources you carry — access to your wholeness.

Call to Action

With this vitality and increased awareness comes also the gift of service, the accountability and responsibility to our fellow humans and the planet.

In addition to listening and tending to your body, how are you tending to community? Tending to nature? How are you tending to and listening with your ancestors? How does your lineage influence the types of intergenerational stories you are meeting? In what ways does all this influence your service on the planet? In what ways are you resting and tending to the oppressed places in you? In what ways are you recognizing the places you have privilege?

As we journey with this book and our life, we explore our own personal growth, transformation and authenticity. This is so important. And it's not just about our own liberation and freedom and access to vitality but about everyone's right to it.

In what ways are you tending to our human family as you create more space, joy and freedom in your life?

So this path, one of powerful liberation, claiming our sexual sovereignty and creating space in our bodies, is also one of reciprocating care with community with activism and service. Here I am reminded of, and encourage you to explore, adrienne maree brown's work with *Emergent Strategy* and *Pleasure Activism*.[109]

Now, we can open with even more curiosity as to what's next and how we can make a difference, not only for ourselves but for and with each other and the planet. Finding and following our unique paths of service is an important part of tapping into the deeper wellsprings of **more energy available**.

Celebrate

I celebrate you. I encourage you to take time to celebrate. Celebrate you, your path, your joy, and how far you've come. Celebrate and give thanks for all the teachers and gifts. Celebrate the hope that more and more of us recognize that we're all in this together, and that together it's going to be okay.

So let's celebrate together. Celebrate what we know about ourselves, what we've learned through our journeys thus far.

Take some moments now to reflect and breathe.

Where do you feel your power in your body? Explore the sensation there. Maybe even write about it in your journal, or paint it or dance it.

Take some time to create pleasure, to follow joy and truly let yourself receive it. As you do the human homework on this journey, be sure to allow yourself to play, too.

---

[109] *Pleasure Activism: The Politics of Feeling Good* and *Emergent Strategy: Shaping Change, Changing Worlds* by adrienne maree brown.

Prayer

My prayer for all humans: May we remember who we are. May we remember wisdom and compassion and accountability and care.

May we all feel good about feeling good, so that we can support each other to rise up and be authentically who we are, in right relationship with our bodies, with each other, with nature and the planet.

May we remember our interconnectedness and acknowledge our differences as valuable in how we co-create together. May we see and honor the unique experiences that we each have on the planet, and allow them to inform how we equitably relate with each other.

May this book offer healing, awakening, and empowerment for the purposes of our collective liberation and pleasure.

I love you. Let's do this together.

PART FOUR

THE RECIPES

As promised in Chapter 6, here are the Recipes. Each Recipe includes:

- Title of Exercise
- Time to Allow: minimum needed to fullest extended
- Description & Benefits: short, easily accessible description and outline of main benefits, short-term and long-term
- Ingredients: space, settings, materials
- How-to: the steps to take
- Stories and other resources

Feel these out for your own body. Allow the structure of the practices to become art and flow. "Give Your Brain a Chance" by allowing the time and space of at least 21 days to introduce a new pattern. Explore new practices for at least that length of time before making a decision about them.

The intention is to support you to get these practices off the page and into your life. That's where your transformation potential really is.

May these Recipes guide you into listening to and trusting your body and the energy moving through you. May we remember who we are and claim our power so that we can all rise together.

R1 SELF-LOVE & ACCEPTANCE PRACTICE

Time to Allow: 3 - 10 minutes for the Short Sweet version,
30 - 60 minutes for the Luscious Bath version
Description & Benefits: Transmuting self-loathing to self-love; shifting your relationship with your body to allow more love and ease into your life.
Essential Ingredients: Short Sweet version: You.
Luscious Bath version: You, colorful eye or body makeup pencil or paint, warm bath.
Optional: Candle, oils or herbs.

Reflection and Intention-Setting (both versions)

Introspect. Have you ever hated your body or wanted part of it to look or be different than it is? In what ways do you wish you could change your body? Do you criticize or hold a sense of loathing for any aspect of your physical being? Have you tried to control or force your body to be something different? Do you hurt yourself?

You are not alone. I lived my version of this for years. Many people experience their own versions of self-loathing: "I hate my thighs." "I wish I were more muscular." ...and so on. Be honest.

Notice how you feel in your body when you bring that critical awareness to it. Do you feel your body? What sensations do you feel? How does your body respond to your criticism?

Make a new choice. Are you ready to feel better about yourself? Are you ready to feel better about being in your body? Would you like to feel good about feeling good? Your intention and thoughts impact your reality, including the very body you inhabit.

Let's explore Transmuting Self-Loathing to Self-Love. It begins with your choice.

Short Sweet Version:

1. Pause. Breathe. Rest on a chair or lying down. Turn your awareness to your body.
2. Place your hands gently on places on your body that you have a hard time relating with: belly, thighs, face, genitals, a scar. You'll know what this is for you.

3. Set an intention to shift the way you are relating to your body from one of fear, mistrust and disdain to one of curiosity, playfulness, and love.

4. Say it out loud: "I am choosing to shift how I see my body and how my body sees me. I send love to my body now."

5. Next, say out loud whatever has been true for you until now, and your willingness to shift it. Here's an example: "I've been hating you in many ways, or trying to force you to be something you're not. I invite you to be who you are, and to really let yourself be you."

6. Now give yourself space and permission in this ritual to love your body, just as it is — all the stresses and imperfections still right here, and you in the middle, part of it all. Sit with this. Rest in the love. Feel your body as love flows into all your parts.

What do you notice? Do you feel your body? What sensations do you feel? How does your body respond to your love? Let yourself feel a shift to allowing your body to be what it is.

Luscious Bath Version:

Make sure there's time and space for this. Remove yourself from your phone or other sources of distraction. Prepare your bath, gather towels, eye liner or makeup pencil. If desired, have ready the oils, candles, herbs, etc.

If you haven't already, I encourage you to see the movie that Deb invited my friends and me to see all those years ago.[110]

Set an intention to shift the way you are relating to your body from one of fear, mistrust and disdain to one of curiosity, play and love.

Say it out loud:

"I want to shift how I see my body and how my body sees me. I want my body to know that I love it."

- Draw a bath. Optional: light a candle, add oils or herbs to the water.
- Take your eye pencil and release yourself into the healing bathwater.
- Draw hearts and spirals and soft, lush waves all over your body.

---

[110] *What the Bleep Do We Know!?*, the 2004 film that posits a spiritual connection between quantum physics and consciousness.

- Write "I love you" and other loving messages all over yourself.
- Shift how you interact with your body in this moment.

Say out loud whatever has been true for you and your willingness to shift it. Here's an example:

> "I've been hating you in many ways, or trying to force you to be something you're not. I want to feel what it is like to invite you to be who you are, and to really let yourself be you."

Now give yourself space and permission in this ritual to love your body, just as it is — all the stresses and imperfections still right here, and you in the middle, part of it all. Sit with this. Rest in the love.

Feel your body as you offer it love.

What do you notice? Do you feel your body? What sensations do you feel? How does it respond to your love?

Let yourself feel a shift to allowing your body to be what it is.

Closing (both versions)

It's okay if it seems like you don't feel anything. I have felt so numb and disconnected that I didn't have any idea of what it meant to "notice sensations in my body." That is okay. It's also okay if this feels frustrating. Feel it. Be gentle. Release any pressure for this to be anything other than what it is.

Take all the time and space you need. When it feels complete, tell your body thank you and draw your time to a close.

R2 BODY BRUSHING

Time to Allow: 2 - 3 minutes

Description & Benefits: Dry brushing the skin can help stimulate the lymphatic system to clear toxins, smooth skin, invite energetic and physical body connection, integrate and regulate, and increase sense of physical safety.

Essential Ingredients: Body dry brush with firm bristles (purchase at health food stores or online); comfortable, safe space to be naked.

How-to:

Body brushing is an important part of my daily body care ritual. When I began the practice I was surprised to notice the energetic clearing and connection that I could feel in the circuits of my body. Through Body Brushing I experience coming into myself and remembering all my body parts. I acknowledge to myself: "Yep, here I am. I am a whole being."

I offer my own version of this practice as an invitation for you to explore. I do Body Brushing first thing in the morning while I am still naked, before getting dressed, before bath or shower.

First, separate the brush head from the handle.

Begin brushing from the limbs and extremities toward the body's center at the heart. I have seen it taught to stop at the heart center. However, I encourage much more overlap. Brush so that the downstrokes from the raised arms and upper body fully overlap with the upstrokes from the legs and lower body. Also, be sure to cross the midline. For example, move your brushstrokes from your right hand and arm to your shoulder and across your body to left belly, hip and thigh. This crossover invites physiological balance and healthy right–left brain connection.

I start at the tips of my fingers and hands, using short brushstrokes to bring the yumminess down the arm and into armpits, along breasts, give a jiggle (super helpful for breast tissue and moving fluids). Be gentle at nipples. Bring it all the way down into the center of your torso and deep belly area, then from the neck and along the shoulder and down. Then repeat on the other side.

Feels AHHH! I notice my arms are expressions and extensions of my core. My arms, which had sort of felt "attached" to my torso like a marionette, became a PART of me, a wonderful energetic feeling.

After I complete my upper body the best I can reach, I move to my feet. Stroking along the feet — toes, soles, tops — brushing up the legs, draw the brush up the butt and into the core and repeat on the other side. Be gentle with the groin area, where skin is thinner. Check in on what your body likes.

Next, reattach the handle and explore the back body to reach places that were hard to reach without the handle. Brush up from the sacrum and down from the back of the neck.

I then set the brush aside and use my hands to brush through my scalp and face and down my neck and into my chest. This completes the practice.

Your brush may feel a little intense when you first use it, but it will soften and feel better over time and as your skin gets used to it. Many folx I've shared this with have found this revitalizing, with little zings waking up our skin.

A term used in some shamanic practices is that we "re-member" our body. In addition to the traditional definition of "remember," this also implies the opposite of "dismember." We are putting our parts back together. In the course of our day we sometimes scatter our energies as we put ourselves out in the world, and we may not even realize it. This is a chance to experience: "Oh! I remember I am here. I remember these edges."

You can also do this without a body brush, using your hands only, getting comfortable to touch and be in connection with your skin and strengthen that feeling of connection. Touch yourself inclusive of your butt, genitals, and breasts. Notice if you find yourself trying "not" to touch certain areas. It's really common. Let yourself have that contact. Remember that this beautiful physical form that you are in is a gift. Delight in being in your body.

R3 JOURNALING & FREE WRITING

Time to Allow: Ranges from a few seconds to hours.

Description & Benefits: Capturing thoughts, to-do lists, "aha moments," and self-reflections to support you to widen awareness, deepen integration of healing moments, create space for your mind to settle, and allow a safe space for you to express and remember who you are.

Essential Ingredients: Basic journal; pen or pencil.

Optional: Colored pencils, sparkly stickers, photos, art, clippings, found items in nature, paint.

Story & How-to:

Although I'd already been journaling for years, in 2002 the book *The Artist's Way* by Julia Cameron[111] took my process to the next level and ultimately guided me into the next phase of my life. The reason journaling works is that it helps us connect with the deeper layers of who we are while producing a tangible, durable record of that interaction that we can access. The self-discovery and self-awareness that result support the growth process, so I encouraged my clients to begin journaling if they had not already.

Here are some of the ways I've seen journaling be helpful to myself and others:

- **Clear the Mind** – You may notice when you try to settle in for meditation or to slow down, a flush of information coming at you. Let those seemingly random but important bits of information find a home in your journal. This allows space in the mind. This can be a wonderful foundation for R4 Clearing Clutter.

- **Jot Down To-Do Lists** – I find writing down the things I need to do gives space for the mind to let go of them, knowing they are held safely in the journal and can be returned to when needed.

- **Capture "Aha Moments"** – Insights can be slippery to hold on to. They often come from a place in ourselves that sometimes only peeks briefly into our everyday awareness. Writing them down helps capture those strokes of brilliance of clarity and gives them a place to take root.

---

[111] *The Artist's Way* by Julia Cameron.

- **Stream-of-Consciousness** – This is the mainstay of Julia Cameron's Morning Pages.[112] Set aside a time in the morning to simply fill two to three pages with the words that flow through your pen to the page. For me this was hard at first. I found myself literally writing "blah blah blah I don't want to write right now but I am doing it anyway..." But then, Wow! A big thing would show up that needed to come through. Often it was the same big thing, every day, and it was the thing I didn't really want to look at. This practice created space for it to be heard. Gently I was able to meet it and start to listen.

- **Questions for Self-Reflection** – Use your journal as a repository for your answers to the questions and self-inquiry invited in this book, and in any other portions of your self practice. As you explore workshops, books, training courses, videos, audio, and guided practices — do the practices, answer the questions, reflect on your experiences in your journal. This is your life! It's worth writing about. Make your journal yours.

- **Art** – Sketching ideas, drawing what's alive in me in the moment helps me to remember something easier than words alone. My journal becomes a safe space to create without judgment.

- **Your Unique Flair** – What other ways do you use your journal?

Everyone has a different approach to journaling. Some love exquisitely bound journals, while others just grab a spiral notepad and start the process. Even a basic legal pad serves well. Do what works for you, and make room for your preferences to change over time. I started out journaling on lined pages and then shifted to unlined pages. Blank pages allowed me to open to a fuller range of expressive possibilities through drawing, color, insets, quotes, pasted-in inspirations. The most important thing is to start, then keep going.

Once you get your journal, I invite you to initiate it. Hold a simple ritual to begin your writing. As I begin a new journal, I often read back through the old one, or sit and meditate and hold space for what I am noticing in my life as I begin the new one.

---

[112] Ibid.

Here's a "Free Writing" practice that can be helpful to get you started. Free Writing is simply about connecting to your inner guidance and opening to what flows through you:

- Settle in with your journal and pen or pencil. Release distractions (turn off phones, etc.).
- Take five deep belly breaths, and call to Spirit for guidance in your way. See R12 Sacred Circle for some ways to do this.
- Ask: "What do I need to know right now?" You can supplement this if there is a specific inquiry in your life you are seeking clarity on. For example: What do I need to know right now to support my project? To manifest my partner into my life? To transition my business? To support my authentic path? To open in my sexual empowerment? Yet this question can stand alone really well. Simply: "What do I need to know right now?"
- Put pen or pencil to paper and start writing without judging, censoring or stopping yourself.
- Write continuously for 3 - 5 minutes. These few minutes of clock time are all you need to open to your answer.
- When the time is up, ask if there is more. Continue if you feel inspired.

Once you feel complete, take a breath of gratitude for Spirit, and for yourself for taking time for you. Rest in silence for a few breaths and allow the response to integrate in your body.

R4 CLEARING CLUTTER

Time to Allow: Varies. Devote manageable chunks of time to this based on the size of your project.

Description & Benefits: Clearing clutter in your life leads to better sex, more vibrancy, more clarity. It opens space to move energy through your body, receive it, share in it, and to relax open to vital life force. It also makes room for relationships or opportunities you seek.

Essential Ingredients: Stuff you are ready to clear.

Optional: Emotional Support Crew, ritual items and fire, device to take photos, staging area, bins, boxes or bags and a marker to label them to help with sorting and moving stuff out.

Story & How-to:

One step at a time.

It doesn't need to happen all at once. For me, decluttering involved quite a spiral of unwinding layers: layers of emotional content, things held back and stored in my body and my sexual energy. Things felt heavy. They weighed on me.

Not doing it all at once and taking baby steps helped me. This is not true for everyone — some people do it all in one big chunk. Listen to your body for your pace. Dixon taught me a lot in the clearing clutter phase and has definitely moved through many cycles himself — he's made DEEP cuts. For him, his body was alright with, "Okay, it ALL goes!" So he did!

Take baby steps if you need to, and listen to your body. Here's a way to do that:

Decide on one chunk.

Example: Kitchen clearing. I noticed a bunch of stuff stored in the backs of my kitchen cabinets. Items seemed to get hidden back there and then multiply when I wasn't looking. Suddenly I had 15 small, trinkety glasses I didn't need anymore. Does this sound familiar?

Instead of going through and pulling out only the things you don't want, decide on one chunk — in this example, the dishes-and-glasses cabinet — and then…

Pull EVERYTHING out.

Empty out everything from this chunk of the kitchen and move it to a staging spot — in our case, the dining room table. Not just one or two things: everything! There is something that happens when you pull everything out all at once. The energy breaks up a bit and this gives you a chance to free the items from your space.

Make a choice.

Next, decide what stays and what goes. Select ONLY those things to keep that are intentionally going to stay.

Listen to your body.

As you engage with this energy, watch your body position. Dixon was also helping me see this. He would notice that all of the sudden I had curled down into a ball and I was reading something I filed away back in 1983. I was touching it, reading through the details and it was sucking me back into the inertia of a past time.

When you notice this, stand up and move and release from that draw. There is a kinesthetic memory that happens when we touch things from the past that can feel overwhelming and suck us back in. The way out is to notice and move your body.

Call in an Emotional Support Crew.

Having someone watching, supporting and doing a lot of the touching and moving of things through this process with you can be very helpful. Dixon had been in my life only a few years as I was unpacking and unwinding stuff from decades prior. Dixon's support helped me see things from an impartial point of view.

I call this your "Emotional Support Crew" — people you trust who are not tied up in the emotional content you are going through. Call them in advance to be there with you. They can help you see things in a new way, one that is not embroiled in some past memory.

There are also people who help clear clutter as a profession. Explore asking for the support you want.

Take a picture.

Consider taking a digital photo as an alternative to storing the physical item if it is something that you want for a memory, yet it's no longer serving in your life. This can honor its memory and give you space to let the item go.

Stage it.

It was tender for me to remove some stuff, especially some big stuff, and I wasn't so sure I was ready to let it go. For some of the bigger items, or emotionally charged ones, it felt overwhelming — like flighty terror in my body, traumatic responses. In those cases, rather than telling myself, "Just toss it anyway! Rip it off like a band-aid!" I found I needed to stage it.

Staging means putting an item aside for a bit before deciding for sure whether it leaves. I designated a spot in the garage for this purpose. If after a little while I didn't notice it missing, I could come back to it and see, "Oh yeah, I really don't need this." Then, it was easier to finally let it go.

The key here is to move the item from its original spot. It starts the energy shift that needs to happen, breaking up the inertia that holds things in place.

Create ritual to let it go.

Remember: Honor this as energy. Continue to do your own human homework in your life and with past relationships, make peace, and invite forgiveness for yourself and others. This is all part of what creates the possibility that you can let some of this stuff go now. And this process can work both ways: Sometimes letting go of stuff is where forgiveness and peace start to open up.

Treat the clearing as an intentional ritual.

Make piles!

I have found having four intentional piles helps me:
1. **Recycling** – Stuff that can go into the recycling bin.
2. **Donations** – Lots of different donation paths, including gifting.
3. **Re-file** – Sometimes in this process I find something in one room that actually is useful but needs to be in a different room or space to fulfill that purpose. "Oh wow! That was here? You are going somewhere else."
   I encourage you to make sure this is a particularly tiny pile. If you haven't noticed it in years, maybe it doesn't need to stay.

4. **Waste** – What is literally going into landfill? I try to keep this pile small, if possible, repurposing or recycling if it's an option. That said, I have also made peace with throwing things out if needed. If the energy required to repurpose or donate becomes overwhelming, then maybe this is the case where I am going to use the landfill.

All of these are wonderful tools to help your process. Here are two more:

Take breaks.

Once I decide to start with a chunk of decluttering, I tend to get overwhelmed, trying to do it all at once. Sprinkling in short breaks as needed to move, breathe, drink water, dance or sing helps my body process and feel revitalized for the next step. As I acknowledge and celebrate my forward momentum, it becomes a much more enjoyable process.

Which brings us to the final and most important tip:

Happy Dance!

Phase 1 is complete. Now you can do a Happy Dance and celebrate that you have cleared some things:

RECIPE 16: Happy Dance, pg 338

Yay! Joy! You can feel new space opening in your home, in your body and energy field — the space you need to feel more vibrant and alive.

R5 WIDENING AWARENESS OF SELF

Time to Allow: 5 minutes
Description & Benefits: Supports us to expand our capacity to notice and be with parts of ourselves, which allows our energetic and subtle bodies to come online. By moving our awareness into the spaces surrounding our bodies, we expand. As we develop our capacities in the physical and energetic realms, more becomes available in our journey of wholeness. This exercise is a synthesis of practices from my work with shamanic awareness, contact improv, qigong and other nervous system/vagus nerve, somatic and body/mind integration tools.
Essential Ingredients: You, a safe space to pause and take time for the practice.

How-to:

Take a seat and get comfortable. Settle in, land, allow yourself to notice your body and breath. Take a few moments to get centered and oriented, perhaps using the Center Ground Orient practice in the next Recipe. As with all the recipes, please adjust the instructions as needed for your body ability.

Close your eyes. Feel into the space around your physical body. Place your attention on the following spaces and notice what you sense:

- The area in front of your body
- The area at your right side
- The area behind your body
- The area at your left side
- The area above your body
- The area below your body

What do you notice about these spaces beyond your physical self? Is it possible to sense what's in them without looking? How available is your awareness to move into these spaces? Can you notice one inch around your body? One foot? One arm's length? Twenty feet? How does the availability change in the different regions?

Now open your eyes. If vision is less available to you, use your other senses in the directions with the same or similar body motions if possible. Once again, modify the body movements as needed to support your ability. Turn your head at the neck to your right, allowing your torso to remain relatively still. This supports a settling into present moment through relationship with the vagus nerve, a major part of the parasympathetic nervous system.

See what is actually in the space there, even if you think you know, come into the present moment of actually noticing what is here now. Describe it: What colors, shapes, textures do you witness? What feelings and sensations do you notice in your body?

Then turn your torso, gently twisting further to the right to look behind your body. What do you notice? Describe it.

Return to center. Feel the spaces at your right and left sides and behind you. What differences do you notice?

Now repeat to the left, and then farther to the left to look behind. Notice and describe again.

Come back to center. Breathe. Close your eyes. Be with what you are noticing and the sensations that are emerging in your body. Take some time to journal about your experience. Repeat this practice as often as you desire. Notice any changes.

R6 CENTER GROUND ORIENT

Time to Allow: 2 - 5 minutes

Description & Benefits: Drops awareness into the body and acknowledges yourself as an energetic being. Brings attention and care to the physical body, expands subtle body awareness and remembering who you are, increases sense of ease and safety through connection with the earth.

Essential Ingredients: You, a safe space to sit.

Optional: Being in nature.

How-to:

Find a comfortable seat. Allow your body to rest with a balance of ease and comfort, along with steady alertness.

Notice the way your body is in contact with support wherever you are — a chair, the floor, a bed, the earth. Feel the surface you are in contact with, what part of your body is touching it? Make any adjustments you need to increase your sense of support and comfort. Invite your eyes to close by either reading ahead then taking a pause for the exercise or recording this as an audio note you can play back for yourself.

Inhale through the nose and exhale through the mouth with some sound (see also next Recipe). Give yourself permission to make sound, to vibrate, perhaps tone an "Ahhhhh."

Drop your awareness back into the center of your head. Notice the central axis of your body, your midline. Exhale. Continue breathing at your own rhythm. Allow your awareness to slowly and gently scan down your midline and offer the qualities of light and length as you notice your body from your crown down through the roof of the mouth, throat, space behind the heart, diaphragm, belly, lower belly and pelvic bowl, pelvic floor, sitz bones, leg bones in the hip sockets, lower legs, heel bones and feet.

Invite your root system from your pelvis and your feet to spiral down through the structures you are resting on, any spaces below them, through foundation of any building you are in and down directly into the soil of the Earth. Feel your roots down through the soil, past the water table and into the deep central core of the Earth, wrapping around the core.[113] Take a few breaths here. What do you notice?

Then gently widen your awareness out to the edges of your skin allowing your perceptual field to expand. Staying present with your midline, notice also your orientation in space and in relationship with the planet. Which way is east? Notice from there the south, west, north, above and below, and then rest within your own heart.

Breathe. Notice: "I am here now."

Rest in this awareness until you feel complete with the practice. Invite a breath of gratitude, and remaining wide in your awareness, gently open your eyes. What do you notice as you rest here in your heart? How does your body feel?

Resources:

Reference my video: https://www.leslieblackburn.com/resources/grounding-centering-meditation

There are so many practices in different traditions that effectively invite this core teaching of noticing center, ground and orientation in space. Ones that have been part of my practice that you may wish to research further include: Kabbalistic Cross, Yoga Sun Salutations, Magnified Healing, Qigong, Merkaba and Druidry practices.

What additional practices are familiar to you that offer presencing and remembering of your physical and energy bodies?

---

[113] Gratitude to my colleague, friend and coach Zahava Griss, aka Z, for inspiring this version of grounding that has become a regular part of my practice. You can find their work at embodymorelove.com

R7 EXHALE WITH SOUND

Time to Allow: 5 seconds – 1 minute (or longer)

Description & Benefits: Make sound. Vibrations move energy, open space in the body, and invite things to go a new way, both in your body and in your daily life.

Essential Ingredients: You, a place where you feel comfortable making sound.

How-to:

Exhale with sound. Sound simple? Great, give it a try. If it's easy for you, there are worlds for you to explore here. If it's not easy for you, you are not alone, there are worlds for you to explore here.

Exhale with Sound is an intentional practice where we explore, allow, and experiment with sound vibrating through our bodies. Maybe it is starting with the airy sigh of the exhale. Then in addition to that, invite sound from a deeper place in your body. Get into the vowels. Experience how different tones from high to low feel in different places in the body. Notice the physical and emotional effects of the full range of vocalizations. This is a chance to explore what it feels like to vibrate and tone: "Ahhhh," "Yeahhhh," "Ayeeee-ahhh hoooo," "Whoooo," "Eeeeeee," "Oooooo," "AHHHH." Let the sound vibrate and shake free the crusty bits and let those crusty bits drop away.

Often in working with clients, whether privately or in group settings, I've noticed that allowing ourselves to make sounds can be a big challenge. This was certainly true for me at first, and if it describes you, this exercise is likely to be particularly helpful in opening pathways in your body and freeing your spirit.

It is common for us to carry loads of vocal inhibition. These patterns are often traceable to childhood settings where making sound was discouraged or punished, while being quiet or silent were praised and rewarded. Some of my clients have fears they can name around it. Some don't like doing it themselves and some don't like hearing the sounds of others.

Some people have just never considered this before. Wherever you are on this continuum, enormous shifts can occur as we connect with what wants to move within us as sound and learn to vibrate our bodies in new ways.

Your sounds will be different than anyone else's. What sound does your body authentically feel called to make in this moment? What edges do you bump up against around this? Do voices in your head say things like: "I can't make a sound." "It feels silly." "It feels childish." Let yourself notice those limiting thoughts and acknowledge them.

Create the safe space, maybe find some privacy, allow yourself to reconnect with your inner child and make some sound!

After making some sounds...

Simply breathe. What does your body feel like now? What differences do you notice? What has changed?

Also, notice if thoughts come in. Some of these thoughts may come from skepticism. Notice any mental resistance. Allow your inner skeptic to be heard, yet also invite it to step aside for a moment and give yourself permission to try something new, even if it's pushing the edges of your comfort zone.

Then, feel it. What do you notice? What happens when you make sound?

Time to Allow: 1 minute – all day. Suggested frequency: twice daily for at least 2 - 3 minutes each.

Description & Benefits: Allowing bare feet or body to be in direct connection with Earth. This allows for energetic reconnection, nervous system discharge and settling, receiving juicy life energy and a sense of "Ahhh."

Many of the benefits are physiological — we are literally "grounded" electrically when we have our bare skin on the Earth. Since our bodies and nervous systems rely on tiny electric charges, the transferring of electrons by touching the Earth can act like the world's best antioxidant to support and settle our nervous system and reduce inflammation.[114]

Fundamentally, we're energetic beings. Plugging into the Earth is our way of being connected with her and our whole consciousness. We cannot survive without the Earth. This physical connection with her can help replenish our vitality.

Yet as a culture we have largely disconnected from the Earth. Pulled up our roots. One way to invite those roots to reconnect and for us to feel safer, more grounded and more present in our bodies is getting our bare feet on the Earth. As we rebuild this necessary connection for human life, it supports the ground from which we feel our confidence and presence, and supports trusting our power and even reclaiming our sexual sovereignty. Yes, it's that big.

Essential Ingredients: You, bare earth: soil, sand or grass.

Optional: Natural fiber socks, natural skin mukluks or moccasins for extreme cold temperatures.

How-to:

Barefeet Earth is also known as "Earthing." For this practice, I invite you to get your bare feet on the Earth, connected on the land, nothing between your skin and the Earth. This means feet direct to Earth… grass, soil or sand. This does not include driveways, pavement, buildings, decks, etc. This practice is about direct, body-to-Earth contact. In particular, we remove the commonly worn rubber-

---

[114] One of many resources about this in scientific research: https://www.ncbi.nlm.nih.gov/pmc/articles/PMC4378297

soled boots and shoes, which block energy flows and disconnect us from the planet.

As you get your feet on the Earth, pause.

Take a few breaths, noticing how you feel and relaxing into your body as you do.

Gaze at the sky. Settle in. Notice the world around you. Notice your body. Notice your breath.

When you feel complete, invite a breath of gratitude to Spirit and Earth and move on to the next piece of your day.

Note that even here in Michigan in the depths of February in two feet of snow and −10°F, it is possible to get out at least once a day, year-round. Yes, it is possible without damaging your body. In colder weather or in snow and ice, try having a natural skin or fiber (cotton socks, wool socks or simple thin leather moccasin or mukluk) to protect your skin and still allow an energetic connection with the Earth.

R9 DAY ON THE LAND

Time to Allow: 4 - 12 hours

Description & Benefits: Being outside in nature for one day a week. This creates space in our bodies and our lives that allows for moments of clarity to emerge, aligning us with Source and our soul purpose. This practice also magnifies the benefits of Barefeet Earth exponentially: energetic reconnection, nervous system discharge and settling, receiving juicy life energy through breath and body, invites a sense of "ahhh," reduces inflammation and associated dis-eases. Like Barefeet Earth, this practice improves our confidence and presence in the world, and supports trusting our power and reclaiming our sexual sovereignty. We are also helping the planet and our community as we engage in supportive environmental practices.

Essential Ingredients: You, nature.

Optional: Journal, water (in your own reusable glass or metal container), spiritual offering, birdseed in a small pouch, drum/medicine bag. Other items, depending on season and location: small backpack, hori hori knife, bandana, natural bug spray, sunblock, hat, sarongs, big fluffy coat, rain gear, boots, two pairs of socks, possibly also spare reused plastic bags and gloves to pick up litter if you feel moved to do so.

How-to:

Spend a day outdoors in nature. I suggest doing this weekly as the benefits will be cumulative. However you start out, you'll get the most from the practice if you find a rhythm that works for you and stick with it. Bring what you need (see list above).

Consider nearby parks and nature centers. Look on a map for spaces that are green and go check them out. Consider asking friends who have private land or finding hiking trails or bike paths. Take a walk and explore near the space where you live — you might be surprised by what is nearly right under your nose.

For example, after I had been doing this practice for several years living in the same home, my partner Dixon saw a green space on Google Maps that was not marked and found we could disappear into a wooded area by the river only a 12-minute walk from our home!

Some "parks" are overly groomed and rigid, and even though on a map they "look" green, they are actually mostly ball fields, cement, and groomed lawns. While this is better than nothing, I find the sense of land and spirit connection I crave is harder to access in spaces like these. Walk a bit, explore, get off the beaten path and see what gems await you.

Personal Experiences:

Years ago, my teacher Rose encouraged me to spend more time in nature. I began with small nuggets, reclaiming a space in my backyard and acknowledging that it didn't have to take a ton of time or a lengthy drive from my suburban home to let my body plug back into the Earth (see R8 Barefeet Earth practice). In time, I began to crave more. I noticed how good I felt when I would travel and spend time camping or away in nature.

Reinforced by the spiritual calling that demanded it, I eventually re-created my workweek to dedicate an entire day each week to spending in nature. Today I still spend at least one day a week in solitude and deep connection with the Earth, year-round, regardless of weather.

The day shapes differently each time. Sometimes it is sitting in meditation, practicing qigong, moving, singing, dancing, offering prayers. Sometimes I walk and pick up moop (matter-out-of-place, aka litter) to dispose of properly. Sometimes I take hikes, meet with animals, and get called to offer healing practices. Sometimes I open my body and meet new ecstatic awakenings, sometimes I cry, roar and scream. Sometimes I run sexual energy. Sometimes I harvest wild edibles. Sometimes I allow my naked body to be submerged in water. Sometimes I lie down on the earth and just be.

As a side note, as with any practice with the potential to produce real life changes, the Universe may test you. How committed are you to your practice and holding space for what you need?

What you choose to do is up to you. My practice has evolved as I have. See how your practice evolves for you.

R10 RESOURCE MEDITATION

Time to Allow: 30 minutes for two people together, 20 minutes for solo.
Description & Benefits: A guided meditation to offer the possibility of feeling what our Internal Resources offer in the body. Feeling the way our bodies change as a result of attuning with these resources builds confidence in Self and in the capacity to feel safe and know we are okay. It also helps us access this safe space in a way we can rely on, and supports building resilience for deeper work.
Essential Ingredients: You, a timepiece, a way to record your voice to self-guide, or a copy of this to read aloud to yourself. It's helpful, but not required, to have already read more details about holding space as a Witness in Chapter 18.
Optional: A second person to practice with.

How-to:

You can explore this exercise[115] in one of two ways. Do it solo and be your own Witness, or engage with a trusted friend to support each other as Witnesses.

If you are doing this practice solo: Read through the practice below and record audio notes of each of the Partner M sections. Then play those back to do the practice. Set a timer for yourself to complete each section with the time as noted in the Partner W sections.

If you are doing this with another person: Find a comfortable place to sit together. Choose who will first be Meditating (**Partner M**) and who will be Witness (**Partner W**). Partner W will also be timekeeper and read the meditation prompts.

Take a breath and R7 Exhale with Sound. Settle in, R6 Center and Ground.

Begin.

Partner M (*Record or have your partner say to you*): Take 1 - 2 minutes and be with Joy. Think of a time when you felt exquisite joy: Who were you with? What were your surroundings? Let your body go back into the sensations of that

---

[115] I created this exercise inspired by an exercise Jan Pemberton offers in BCST training, along with my journey with Authentic Movement.

moment. What sensations do you notice in your body? What colors, smells, sounds and textures do you notice? If recalling a time of joy is difficult for you, be gentle. If recalling a time of joy is easy, allow that and go into it. Notice the sensations you are feeling right now that let yourself know everything is okay.

Bring this awareness into this current moment. Let it develop and expand within your body right now. What sensations in your body do you feel right now?

Notice all this. Harvest in silence, without judging yourself. Harvesting is a gathering of the fruits of our inner awareness — this supports integration of the work.

Partner W: You are timekeeper and holding space, witnessing without judging. This means noticing any judgments that may arise and acknowledging they are your own and not about this person, then setting them aside.

After about 2 minutes of the Joy meditation, invite Partner M to shift their awareness.

Partner M (*Record or have your partner say to you*): Notice now an Irritant. This does not need to be a big source of frustration or anger in your life, simply a minor irritant, or something that rubs you the wrong way. Be gentle, and allow this irritant to rise in your awareness and feel it in your body. Be with it for about 1 minute.

Notice your body. How is your position changing? What sensations do you feel? What changes in temperature or vibration do you sense? What areas of your body make themselves known that you weren't aware of before?

Partner W: After about 1 - 2 minutes of Irritant, prompt Partner M to shift back again to the sensations they felt during Joy.

Partner M (*Record or have your partner say to you*): Releasing the Irritant, shift your awareness back to a time of Joy and the sensations you noticed in your body during Joy. Allow yourself to breathe and smile! These are Internal Resources, felt-sense experiences of knowing that everything is okay. Tap back into your Resources.

Spend 2 minutes coming back to Resources. Notice your body sensations, position, temperature, movements. Harvest what you are noticing in silence.

Partner W: After 2 minutes of coming back to Resource, prompt Partner M to come to completion.

<u>Now take 5 minutes to discuss, using this format:</u>
Partner M: Share from your experience transitioning from Joy to Irritant, then back to Joy/Resource. What did you notice? What changes emerged? How long did it take to shift gears from Joy to Irritant? From Irritant back to Joy/Resource?

Partner W: Listen, hold space. When Partner M's sharing is complete, if you wish to offer a Witness response, ask Partner M if they would like to hear a Witness response. If the answer is No, hold your share. If the answer is Yes, offer what you noticed, keeping in mind these guidelines for being Witness:

Name the specifics of their movements (for example, "When I saw your forehead wrinkle," OR "When I saw your body round forward," OR "When I saw your body extend and lengthen" the…)

- …story that came to me was…
- …image I had was…
- …feeling I had was…
- …sensation it evoked in my body was…

Avoid statements claiming to know what Partner M was feeling. For example, instead of "When I saw your sadness…" describe what you observed that suggested sadness to you. For example: "When I saw the tear roll down your cheek…"

After 5 minutes, close sharing with gratitude for each other.

Switch roles and repeat.

<u>When everyone has experienced the practice, come back to these notes:</u>

What did you notice in the exercise? Let yourself claim your awareness of body-level Resource that you were able to meet in this meditation. This is available to you at any time. Call upon it when you need.

If you noticed that it can be easier/quicker to tap into Resource when you are not already in an Irritant, this is not uncommon. It can take a bit longer to allow the Irritant to drop away and move back into Resource once the recollection of the Irritant has risen to the surface. This isn't bad. You're not "doing it wrong." Simply notice it as information. This can provide insight on the amount of time you may need to make the shift in different circumstances.

Sometimes what rises up is way bigger than a minor irritant. Move that energy safely. Give it space to go. Moving Bulk Energy helps clear the way for positive change and healing. See more about this in the upcoming Recipe:

RECIPE 17: Emotional Processing Toolkit, pg 340

Then bring in these presencing and Resource Meditation practices to return to feeling the support and joy of being you.

Remember when working through and healing trauma:

- If you have the Resources to pull back out of the loop, you have the Resources to deal with it in this moment.
- If you don't have the ability to pull yourself back out of the spiral, healing is still available. Also, do not force yourself to stay in the spiral. Take time and self care to rebuild your Resources before proceeding. This may include reaching out for support from a trauma-informed practitioner.

R11 INTEGRATION

Time to Allow: varies

Description & Benefits: Integration is "the space in between" that allows us to deeply receive the benefits of a practice and have it connect to our being in a deeper way. This supports lasting and cumulative positive changes to our bodies. It is a valuable practice in itself and it can be added to other practices for heightened benefit.

Essential Ingredients: You, time and space you give yourself.

Optional: Body of water to immerse in, water to drink, nourishing food, journal, safe space to sleep.

How-to:

Integration is about the space in between. Examples of integration include savasana at the end of yoga practice, resting with your lover after lovemaking, taking space after listening to music, an after dinner tea or rest with friends. Notice where we are placing our attention. Are we rushing to the next thing? Or are we giving space for listening to what is now?

Naming this space in between can help us to remember its importance and make room for it in our practices and daily lives. At the conclusion of an exercise or practice, many of us rush past this space assuming it has no value and that we must race to the next thing to do. In fact, taking time to observe and use the space in between allows us to deeply receive the benefits of the practice and have them become a part of our being.

An example of how integration works from my endurance athlete days: When we work out at the gym, if we do "bicep curls" today, we aren't actually strengthening our biceps. In fact, the workout tears them down a bit. It is the space in between, drinking water, eating nourishing food and rest, that allows the muscles to rebuild and strengthen in a new way.

Similarly, with our spiritual and sexual practices, our physical and energetic bodies need time and care to help new patterns and possibilities "click into place." This gives these changes a chance to become an ongoing, fully *integrated* part of our being.

The most important piece of any integration practice is to give yourself space. Integration happens, you don't have to "do" it. Yet there are ways to support it.

Integration is often a time for rest, nourishment, drinking plenty of water, slowing down, soaking your body in a warm tub of water. Through this you are creating the fertile ground in your body for the new seedlings of possibility to grow. It is also time for the initiations and doors you open in your "body wisdom library" to continue their processes.

Your body knows. Trust yourself. Integration space allows for your vibration to shift and change at a cellular level, and it's not about "Doing," it's about allowing the change to integrate into your "Being." This can seem so simple and yet be so hard. Often, we just need to get out of our own way! Be gentle with yourself, trust and notice what emerges.

In terms of timing, integration can take from a few moments to many days or even weeks or more, depending on the intensity and duration of the experience being integrated.

During integration, also notice the whisperings from the Universe. Things that seem like coincidences are messages. Pay attention. Notice dreams. Journal about what you notice.

R12 SACRED CIRCLE – INVOKING DIRECTIONS

Time to Allow: 1 - 5 minutes or much more, depending on how elaborate you wish to make your ritual.

Description & Benefits: Acknowledging and inviting support, guidance and protection, and giving thanks for it. This creates a container for opening new possibilities and helps build a sense of our ancestors and spiritual support having our back, which strengthens our confidence and presence in our work in the world.

Essential Ingredients: You and your presence, intention and desire.

Optional: Candles, a simple cloth to help delineate your intentional space/altar, local herbs/plants for offering (be mindful of harvest methods and sustainability), natural objects you have a connection with that relate with the qualities in each direction, inspirational art or sculpture, other ritual tools related to your practice and tradition.

How-to:

Here's one way to work with this practice.

1. **Begin by settling into your body**. Feel into your body, plug in and connect with ground and root. Notice your breath, your midline and allow yourself to settle into this moment. (Remember the R6 Center Ground Orient and R5 Widening Awareness practices, and do these here if you wish). Welcome in vital energy and deepen your presence.

2. **Call in the benevolent ancestors**. "Calling in the well, kind and resourced ancestors, the ones who know this work. Please encircle us in a pillar of light. Guide and protect us for this time together. Please hold the less well ones outside the circle, tend to them to support healing and welcome them into the collective wellness."

3. **Bring your awareness to the East**. You can stand and face the East, or sit and simply bring your awareness there. Speak from your heart to acknowledge the qualities of this direction and to share gratitude and ask for their support, guidance and protection. Invite them in for the purposes of your ceremony or practice. Breathe your prayer into the offering, ask them to join you, and complete it with Amen, Awen, or

another proclamation that resonates for you and your culture and traditions. Then make the offering, leaving it with the Earth (or if you are indoors, into a shell or container to collect for returning to the Earth later).

4. **Repeat** for the remaining six directions, turning your awareness each way to move with the sun (East, South, West, North, then above, below and within).

5. Once complete, **offer a breath of gratitude**, and it is so.

Proceed with whatever ceremony or practice or gathering you wish to be held in this Sacred Circle.

When the practice is complete, share gratitude and release the Circle. An example: "Thank you thank you thank you (Ancestors, Great Spirit, Elements, Guides and/or however else you refer to them) for holding us safely in this Circle, we release you from the Circle but not from our hearts."

Below is my own Table of Correspondences for the directions: the qualities I have met and resonated with there, drawn from the teachings I have been honored to receive in my life. These are an example, and not the only way. **Create your own correspondences** by feeling into what's true for you based on your traditions, community, culture and ancestors, your relationship with your own body and spirit, your relationship and orientation with the land around you.

1. **East** – yellow, air element, mental/masculine, rebirth, new day, archangel Rafael/Rafaela, winged ones, eagle/condor, hawk soaring in the wind, community foundation,[116] father-father ancestral line.[117]

2. **South** – red, fire element, physical body, sacred fire, passion, desire, playful child, reclaiming innocence/awe/wonder, archangel Michael/

---

[116] Explore more about these four foundations: community, body, nature and ancestors in Chapter 21.

[117] See the Ancestral Medicine teachings of Daniel Foor. Your father-father line is your father, his father and all the fathers before him.

Michaela, serpent, stag in the heat of the chase, body foundation, father-mother ancestral line.[118]

3. **West** – black/dark blue, water element, emotional/fluidity/feminine, deaths/shedding old skins in preparation for rebirth, archangel Gabriel/Gabriela, jaguar... sometimes I feel owl here, salmon of the waters of wisdom, nature foundation, mother-mother ancestral line.

4. **North** – white, earth element, bone, stone, Spirit/wisdom, ancestors, archangel Uriel/Uriela, hummingbird or buffalo are often named... sometimes I feel owl or wolf here; bear and the starry night sky, ancestor foundation, mother-father ancestral line.

5. **Above** – blue, Father Sky, Great Creator, Star Beings, Ascended Masters, Jesus, Buddha, Sacred Masculine, Shiva, up into the gold, central sun.

6. **Below** – green, Pachamama, Gaia, deep dark Mother Earth and all her support, allowing us to release to her, providing abundance to nourish us (in conjunction with Sun), Sacred Feminine, Shakti, realms of the sidhe of the Tír na nÓg, mineral realms of the Earth, mycelium networks, tree roots.

7. **Within our hearts, all around** – All My Relations, purple, the seventh divine direction in the center of the sphere, the Light that shines in each of us and how we are all connected, people we love and support and teach, and those who love and support and teach us, etc. "We're all in this together, and everything is going to be okay."

Explore a regular practice and begin to feel what is resonant with your truth. Meet your ancestors and listen for what the people of your lineage knew, even if that was from hundreds or thousands of years ago and wasn't a part of your upbringing in this lifetime. Borrow and learn from human teachers and guides who offer their teachings, yet also be mindful to be in right relationship with those teachings rather than misappropriate them.

Personal Experiences:

In my experience, Invoking Directions began as a practice taught to me by my teacher Rose, and over time became an amalgamation of practices from various

---

[118] See the Ancestral Medicine teachings of Daniel Foor. Your father-mother line is your father, his mother and all the mothers before her.

paths and teachers. This elaborate ritual, including naming the qualities traditionally associated with each of the directions, was so helpful to support me into new layers of embodied wisdom that those elements and qualities offer. As I related with these qualities, I've also experienced that over time we can learn to hold them in new ways, so that sometimes a simple breath and widening of awareness can invoke the same guidance and protection. In fact, it's always there, so the ritual is really about placing our attention on it with gratitude. Sometimes now I love using an elaborate ritual with many items, and sometimes I simply take a breath and feel my subtle bodies expand to remember.

Gratitude and praise for the traditions that have influenced me here that helped me remember who I am after the rift from my own ancestral culture: Native American – Lakota, Tibetan Buddhism and Bön Sect Tibetan Shamanism, Peruvian Shamanism – Q'Ero, Tantra Yoga, Egyptian Sexual Alchemy, Taoist Sacred Sexuality, Western ceremonial Magick, Paganism and Ancestral Medicine teachings. Most recently I have been remembering and deepening in the nature-based path of my ancestral people: Druidry. Note that my lens is through current living in the Midwestern United States, in the northern hemisphere. Differences exist around the world based on relationship to the equator, poles and ecological regions. For example, in Peruvian shamanism, the heat/fire is in the north toward the equator instead of the south.

R13 MINDFULNESS PRACTICES

This segment is a mini recipe booklet in your Recipes. See the individual recipes for more about their Ingredients, Time and How-tos.

Mindfulness[119] is about becoming aware of something in the present moment. This presencing, or calm acceptance of what is, is a skill that can be developed through practices. Some examples of such practices are described in this book. There are many others. Here are some practices to consider to develop your mindfulness:

- Breathe
- Slow way down
- Notice sensations
- Listen to your body (for example: R15 Body Wisdom Toolkit)
- Spend time in nature (for example: R8 Barefeet Earth and R9 Day on the Land)
- Meditation (for example: R14 Five Breath Meditation)
- Journaling (for example: R3 Journaling & Free Writing)
- Art, music, crafts, cooking, anything creative
- Conscious body movement practices (for example: Continuum Movement, Body Mind Centering)
- Yoga (explore asana practice at a studio near you, or follow a video)
- Qigong
- R4 Clearing Clutter
- Walking meditation
- Gratitude practices
- Mindful eating
- Biodynamic Craniosacral Therapy (both as a receiver and as a practitioner)

---

[119] Google Dictionary defines mindfulness as: 1. the quality or state of being conscious or aware of something; or 2. a mental state achieved by focusing one's awareness on the present moment, while calmly acknowledging and accepting one's feelings, thoughts, and bodily sensations, used as a therapeutic technique.

In my own journey of self-awareness and building mindfulness, I found that I needed to begin with practices that had more gross, tangible actions and movements before the practices that involved more subtle awareness could emerge. For example, yoga asana practice helped me slow down to even begin to notice there could be value in a seated meditation. Meditation opened the awareness of my subtle bodies beyond the layers of physical. For me, qigong felt like it "wasn't doing anything" at first, then opened to be a profound practice of energy awareness and cultivation. Later, when Biodynamic Craniosacral Therapy came into my awareness, I trusted the call into the three-year training and was once again amazed to find another layer of awareness of the infinite power accessible to us all.

Explore the practices in the way you feel called. What resonates as important for you now? Great! Be with that for a bit. To give your brain a chance, I suggest exploring any practice for at least 21 days before making a decision about it. As you do, also stay open to the possibility that something you assumed doesn't work for you might actually be supportive at a different time in your life. Notice how practices involving touch, movement, sound and breath can move from gross to subtle, and invite layers of slowing down that may be new to you. Allow yourself to let go and explore new possibilities as you feel the call.

R14 FIVE BREATH MEDITATION

Time to Allow: 1 minute

Description & Benefits: A breath practice to create more space and time in your day and increase your self-awareness. Helps to reset body, mind, emotions, focus and attention. Loosens reactive patterns and brings us into the present, connecting us with that power.

Essential Ingredients: You.

How-to:

This practice is simple and requires less than 1 minute of clock time. Are you ready? Here it is:

Slow down, and notice five breaths.

Yep, that's it: five breaths.

This practice requires no special preparation, planning or location. It can be done seated, or standing or lying down. You may be in the car, in the bathroom, or taking a pause on a short walk on a break from the office. It can be done as you hold your sleeping child. It can also be done in nature, in your own backyard or in a special place you designate as your Sacred Space, with an altar and a candle.

Simply pause, take a breath and notice the next five breaths. Inhale, exhale, inhale, exhale... five sets of these. After those five breaths, if you feel complete, then close with a breath of gratitude and move on with your day. If after those five breaths you notice it might feel nice to continue... do. Breathe, notice, bring awareness to your Self.

Discussion:

Give yourself permission to explore this Five Breath Meditation daily for at least 21 days. What do you notice in your body? What changes begin to appear in your life? Allow this to become a seed planted for your Self Practice, giving a fertile ground for additional practices to take root. Invite it as a gift to your authentic Being.

Personal Experiences:

I often see clients who feel they have no spare moments in a day. This resonates with a time in my life when I felt that, too. My life was full to the brim with being an endurance athlete with hours of daily training, a corporate engineering manager on the fast track, and a single mom. The thought of carving away time for a meditation practice seemed impossible. And when it seems that way, we tend to avoid even trying. Or, we try to change very fast from the beginning, like someone who has never practiced yoga or meditation tries to take on an hour of silent seated meditation in the lotus position daily. Often we cannot sustain it: Our bodies complain, we assume we just aren't trying hard enough or we must not be good enough. Whew... Let's release that!

As my awareness shifted and I began to slow down and re-create my life, I learned that some basic practices actually *create* more time in the day.

Five Breath Meditation can be such a starting point, as it is simple yet profound. The practice is powerful on its own, and can become a foundation for others.

R15 BODY WISDOM TOOLKIT

Time to Allow: 5 minutes
Description & Benefits: Connect with your body by feeling, responding, and listening. This can help open infinite possibilities by accessing the wisdom of your body.
Essential Ingredients: You.

How-to:

1. **Notice.** Slow down. Turn your awareness inward. Take a few moments as needed to do this. Then, notice a sensation in your body. Describe the sensory experience. What is the texture? The color? Is it smooth or rough? Soft or hard? What is the shape of the sensation? How is it moving? Get underneath the emotion of it, and get into details. Is it tightly wound like a steel trap? Fluffy and soft like downy feathers? Witness the sensation without judging or labeling as good or bad. If you find yourself labeling it as "I feel nervous" or "I feel sad," ask yourself: What sensations in my body do I associate with the labels "nervous" or "sad"? How do "nervous" or "sad" feel in my body? Describe.

2. **Choose.** Take a moment to make a shift or change. This is about choice and free will. It can be by giving some space and doing nothing, inviting a breath to simply inform the place in your body that you are noticing. Options here also include a more overt action such as shifting body position, etc. Can you visualize a boundary around the area, encompassing it like a bubble? Invite your breath to fill and inform the area, to simply meet it. Notice if you are trying to push or pull at it, to fix it, or to make it go away. Notice these things and let them drop away. Come back to simply informing and meeting the area with your breath.

3. **Notice.** Once again witness your body and listen. Describe the sensation in this new awareness. What has changed? How has it changed? What is the color, texture and shape now, in this moment? Notice that you made a change in your body, perhaps one that felt good, by simply choosing to.

4. **Celebrate!** Do a HAPPY DANCE (see R16 Happy Dance)! Look up, smile, do a happy wiggle! This may include: wriggle your fingers, lift your arms wide, dance around the living room, wiggle your butt! Move

your body in the way that feels accessible and best for you. Your dance is your way, including stationary from a chair, movement with walkers, canes or wheelchairs. What other ways do you express your celebration with your body?

Yes, celebrate, even if you feel like it didn't change that much. Or even if you feel that one thing changed but there are 20 others. Or even if you feel like it's not over yet, and there's still more there. If you start judging yourself, this is your censor sitting on your shoulder saying, "This is childish. You shouldn't dance. You can't just wiggle your butt like this. You should be more mature."

Yes, you can wiggle if you want to. It *is* childish, in all the delicious, vibrant, being-authentically-who-you-are senses of being a child. Give yourself permission. Happy Dance that you made a change in your body that felt good, simply by *choosing to*.

Extension:

Once you get some practice with listening, a great extension of the Body Wisdom Toolkit is to ask your body for guidance or a message, and listen to the answer.

Notice, Choose, Notice, Celebrate

- In the first step, as you notice, now ask your body:
    - How can I love you? How can I help you feel safe? OR:
    - What do I need to know right now?
- Listen for the answer and apply that in the Choose phase or beyond. Maybe a part just wants to be held and loved as it is. Offer that. Put your hands there, send some loving kindness to your body.
- Listen, notice again.
- Celebrate and share gratitude with your body.

Discussion and Examples

I am guiding a client in the Body Wisdom Toolkit who had been in chronic pain for years, and he asks with some playful seriousness:

"What is the intention I should hold for the Noticing part? Is it 'Okay, you motherfucker'?" he asks as he directs the energy of picking a fight to the painful place in his body.

I reply, "Well, nope, not that! It's Loving Kindness. Hold your body with Loving Kindness."

We both giggle!

Yet when this client asked his question, on one level he was quite serious. He really did not know how to relate to his body any differently than with a disdain and hostility that had grown over time. He had been dealing with pain for so long he had lost all kindness for himself.

This is really common. We judge ourselves so harshly or are so angry with our pain or so angry with the places in our bodies that are lighting up that it's common to relate to them with anger.

Instead, take a breath. Pause. Acknowledge one thing your body has done for you that you are grateful for and bathe that part in love. Then allow that feeling to inform the place you are frustrated with.

Examples:

1. Maybe you have chronic knee pain. You get mad at your knees often. Pause. Notice how your feet have served you for years, supporting you to walk and move across the planet. Can you bathe your feet in loving gratitude, smile and feel it? What do you notice? A softness? A warmth? Now allow that soft warmth to expand and inform the place in your knee that has been so painful. Simply be with that, allow your judgment of your knee to shift. Notice what happens. And be sure to Celebrate. Smile!

2. Perhaps you often have a tightness and pain in your neck. Pause. Notice your lungs and your breath. Feel the gratitude of how your breath has served you so deeply, even when you are not noticing. It's always there for you, always present for you. Fill your lungs and your body deeply with your breath, allow loving care to fill and buoy your chest and allow that support to spread and inform your neck. Simply be with that, allowing your judgment of your neck to shift. Notice what happens. And as always, be sure to Celebrate. Smile!

There are many ways people feel their bodies are betraying them. Some people feel they are too big or too small. There may be times when we do not like our shape, our looks, our skin, our hair. We may be experiencing disability or disease. All of these can be met through the Body Wisdom Toolkit. Here the invitation is radical acceptance of our bodies, just as they are.[120] Be gentle with yourself, and listen.

---

[120] A resource for more exploration is the book *The Body is Not an Apology* by Sonya Renee Taylor.

R16 HAPPY DANCE

Time to Allow: A few seconds to a minute or more.

Description & Benefits: Find a way to move your body that expresses joyful connection with yourself in this moment. This lights up our bodies and shifts our mood, and signals feel-good chemicals to be released in our system to support the integration of new experiences, allowing joy to be present.

Essential Ingredients: You.

How-to:

It's so simple. Here's how it goes:

Smile, and give your body a little wiggle!

If it feels available for your body, maybe even look up, stand up, lift your arms up in the air and bounce. Dance around the room, give yourself a happy wiggle. Move your body in the way that feels accessible and best for you. You may be sitting a chair when you dance. It could include standing movement, maybe with the support of walkers or canes. What other ways do you express celebration with your body?

I encourage this practice every time you acknowledge you've made a change for yourself that feels good. My family and I practice this regularly. Often several times a day you will find us Happy Dancing in the studio. Perhaps one of us just finished a project, or had a conversation that felt really hard and we knew we needed to do it. Once we complete it, we HAPPY DANCE!

Also, as described in Recipe 15, the last and most important step of the R15 Body Wisdom Toolkit is to Celebrate with a Happy Dance!

I invite you to learn and practice the Happy Dance often. It can be applied in many ways in our lives.

Notice if you find yourself resisting this. Does that censor inside you say: "I can't possibly do that" or "It's too childish (or silly, or stupid)"? I invite you to notice the chatter, and let it move on. Give yourself permission to smile and celebrate that you did something that supported you.

Notice also if you find yourself saying, "Well, yes, I finished that project but I still have 10 more to do today," or: "I made that change in my body and it feels a little better, but it is still there." Or: "Yes, that ache is gone but I still have these other pains and problems." This kind of self-talk might convince you to skip over the Happy Dance celebration, thinking it's not time, or even that it's a waste of time.

I call bullshit. It is time, and you are important. Notice that censor and give it permission to go offline. Celebrate each moment. Not only does this feel good but it also starts to repattern the brain and body to be receptive to the "Yes!" of life. Receptors in the cells of your brain[121] will literally start to shift to acknowledge the joy in your life and let go of any old self-deprecating habit patterns. Among these patterns, maybe the most important shift this practice offers is to allow yourself to feel good about feeling good.

And yes, it can start right now.

Happy Dance!

---

[121] See the work of Candace Pert: https://en.wikipedia.org/wiki/Candace_Pert

R17 EMOTIONAL PROCESSING TOOLKIT

Time to Allow: 1 minute to an hour or more

Description & Benefits: Building capacity to notice, feel, name, own and express emotion. This helps create spaciousness and ease in our bodies and our relationships, allowing vitality to enter to support us in feeling more connected, present and alive.

Essential Ingredients: You, safe space to move energy.

Optional: Pillows, journal, practice partner – for example a trusted friend or trauma-informed practitioner.

How-to:

When we are triggered into anger, frustration, jealousy, fear, etc., it is important to acknowledge and feel it, and to create space to let it move safely. Sometimes this can be in the moment, sometimes we need to delay that expression until we can find a safer space to move the energy. Over time, emotions that aren't honored but are instead denied or otherwise stuffed away, tend to get stuck in the body and eventually manifest as tightness, pain, or even disease.

Emotions are portals to our power and are important to feel. I find it helpful to process them as they arise and not allow them to fester.

Personally, I have noticed that as emotions arise, very often the triggering event has little to do with the current situation, and a lot more to do with what I had previously stored away. This is very common.

Also, oftentimes the triggering event is something that an intimate partner says or does. This is one of the gifts of our closest connections: Our intimate partners help us reveal these old stuck stories so we have an opportunity for things to go a new way. That said, whether it is an intimate partner, a dismissive or abusive boss at work, a careless driver on the road, disrespectful sibling, child or parent, or someone else, these people become catalysts for the alchemical process of change in our bodies. Many of our original traumas happened in the relational space. The healing of these traumas happens in the relational space as well.

For the sake of clarity in this Recipe, we will use the term "catalyzing partner" for the partner who may have helped old, stuffed-away emotions to come to the surface for healing.

When emotions come up for healing, you may choose to seek partnership with another person to support you in your emotional processing. This person will most likely not be the catalyzing partner, but instead a friend or coworker who helps by holding space and witnessing. This we will call your "practice partner."

As you begin your Emotional Processing practice, you may find a lot more to process than you expect. Allow yourself to follow it, and you will find the old stuff will release and defuse. The triggered emotional backlog will surface less and less, and in smaller ways. Here are some steps to processing in the moment:

1. **Recognize**[122] the emotion in the moment. You may suddenly feel disconnected, paralyzed, or out-of-body. You may notice sensations in your physical and energetic bodies. Often these are in the areas of the gut, heart or throat.

2. **Own it** as your own. Say it out loud. This takes your catalyzing partner, if present, out of the picture and allows that partner to become witness. This acknowledgment can be really hard for our ego, but it's okay. Breathe. Each step in this process gets easier with practice.

3. **Communicate.** If they are present, tell your catalyzing partner, "I need some time for myself to move some energy and I will return soon." Don't play games. Release any old "subconscious contracts" that drain energy. You know the ones. Like: "You get angry, I get frustrated, you get sad, I feel guilty." Notice if you have a particular pattern when responding to these kinds of situations. This helps you step outside of it to break the pattern.

4. **Create a Container** to move the energy (see the Recipes R12 Sacred Circle and R19 Creating Container). Within that safer space, be active. Move the energy. Get out of your head and move your body: walk, run, hit some pillows, wail, scream or silently bring a groan from deep in the belly to avoid hurting your vocal cords.[123] Three basic rules: Don't hurt yourself. Don't hurt anyone else. Don't damage anything. For example, do not direct anger at your partner or punch a wall.

5. **Follow the energy**. As it moves, get curious about what's underneath the feeling. Follow that. After some time, allow your body to find

---

[122] Portions of this toolkit are inspired by the book *Tantric Orgasm for Women* by Diana Richardson, pg 148.

[123] Inspired by similar practices shared by ISTA.

completion. Rest, breathe, be. Journal about what you noticed. Share gratitude for yourself, your body, the land and your supportive guides. Drink plenty of water.

6.   **Get curious.** Based on what you noticed, would you like additional support from a practice partner? If so, who? Make a note in your journal to call that trusted friend or practitioner and set a time to meet.

Importantly, do not make your catalyzing partner responsible for creating unhappiness in you. If you must stay in proximity to a catalyzing partner, remain in the "I feel" discussion, not the "blame" or "you did" discussion.

Once you release and move some energy and feel some spaciousness, if appropriate, return and acknowledge your catalyzing partner and yourself. This assumes this person is part of your ongoing life, not an unknown driver on the freeway. If it's possible to share in the moment, do so. Alternately, create an intentional time and space for this sharing to take place in the near future. Journal about what you've noticed for yourself. Give yourself a breath of gratitude for taking time for your own healing and growth. Be gentle with yourself.

Note: Like other dynamic processes in this book, it's a dance. Sometimes we need to move the energy to feel the empowerment of being here in our bodies, and sometimes we can get addicted to big cathartic movements that actually take us further away from our center. Remember that healing happens in the present — our grounded, present-moment awareness makes a difference in how big energy can move. Pendulate between the release movements and presence and stillness. Come back to your resources often. This builds resilience in our bodies' capacity to contain and be with our vitality and power as well as move and be with the flow.

If you feel called to additional support, seek out a trauma-informed practitioner who understands how to facilitate emotional release and body and somatic processing. This is different than talk therapy, though they can complement each other. Advocate for yourself in seeking support on your journey of self-healing and awareness.

R18 TOUCH EXERCISE

Time to Allow: 5 - 30 minutes
Description & Benefits: Learning to follow and respond to the desire messages of your body and honoring your boundaries so that you create what you seek.
Essential Ingredients: You, safe space.

How-to:

Create a safe space. Settle in. Perhaps you are seated for this exercise. Alternately, you could be lying down or in another position you find delightful.

Close your eyes. Slow down. Breathe.

Notice your body.

Drop your awareness rearward. Notice the rearward and downward flow of energy that can feel different than the forward and upward energy we often get swept into during our day-to-day activities. Notice the way the chair, blanket or other support beneath you holds you at the point of contact. Remember your back body.

Notice your seat and make any adjustments to feel more comfortable, more supported. If seated, allow your back to be supported by the chair.

Check in with your body:

1. In what way would you like to receive self touch in this moment? **Notice**: Listen for the answer. **Admit**: Give yourself permission to do what your body is asking for. **Ask**: What does the area you wish to touch have to say about it? What about the part of your body that is being asked to do the touching? If both are an enthusiastic Yes: Do it now. **Allow** yourself to receive the benefits of the touch.

2. Pause, listen. How do you feel? What sensations do you notice? What old stories or patterns arise? Can you witness the stories and let them pass on?

3. What else does your body desire?

4. If you feel stuck, here's a sequence to get you started. Have your dominant hand (DH) ask for receiving touch from your nondominant hand (NDH). If you don't have access to your hands, choose two other

body parts to explore an intentional touch practice with. Listen for the answer. If both hands say Yes:

- Start by simply holding your DH, allowing it to settle into the support of your NDH. Breathe.

- Begin to squeeze your NDH, bringing slow intentional touch to your DH. Taking all the time you desire, press the center of your DH palm. Then move with rhythmic, gentle squeezes outward from the center along each thumb and finger. One squeeze per bone, between each knuckle, then drawing away from the center to wring out each fingertip, and gently coming back to center to start again with the next finger. Add a squeeze at the webbing between the thumb and fingers, and between each finger as well.

5. Now rest your hands, no longer in contact with each other, palms up in your lap. Feel the sensations. Notice the differences in sensations between hands.

6. What's next for you? Ask your body: What is your delight? What will you have me do next? How would you like me to touch you for your pleasure? Notice and follow these messages for at least three more minutes.

Pause. Breathe.

Share a breath of gratitude for your body and draw your practice to a close.

R19 CREATING CONTAINER FOR PLEASURE

Time to Allow: 15 min or more

Description & Benefits: Working with the tools we have learned in this book, we explore creating a Container. This process supports us in navigating consent and boundaries to create freedom and let go into something wonderful. For a full discussion on Container see Chapters 14 and 15.

Essential Ingredients: You and a partner for creating pleasure. That partner can be a platonic friend or family member, a lover or romantic partner, an emotional intimacy partner or anyone else you feel safe navigating with. You'll also need a timing device such as a timer on a phone or watch.

Optional: Space in nature, music, items for sensory play and delight. Examples: berries, flowers, various textured objects, water, ice, kinky play items such as impact toys, rope, fabrics, oils.

Before we begin: Please note that Creating a Container for Pleasure does not have to mean you're about to "have sex." This container-setting is just as powerful for platonic cuddle time or having a delightful back scratch from a friend. In fact, if you desire to create more intimacy and connection, start with timed containers where clothing remains on with no genital contact and watch what happens in your body.

Remember the power of the Container for creating freedom, which we explored in Chapters 14 and 15: Err on the side of more structure than you think may be needed, and notice what your body has to say as the experience unfolds within these boundaries. Do not broaden your container structure midway through a given timed experience. In other words, things that you define as "no" at the start remain a "no" for the duration. However you are always at choice to change something that was a "yes" to a "no" at any time.

On the other hand, if you feel a desire to expand your "yes" during a timed container, pause instead and delight in what is now. Then note what you get curious about so you can possibly bring that into a future container. Follow your pleasure and create more containers to lean into changes slowly and watch what happens.

During the last 15 years of learning and professional offerings in this path: I became a timer geek! When I mention timers in these practices, it's not only for facilitating groups or working with clients. I often use timers (effectively a container in itself) to create freedom in my exploration in my personal life as well. The timer gives built-in checkpoints for communication, which can help really open conscious connection, especially with experiences with new people. Set a timer for 2 minutes, then harvest and check in. Then maybe create a new container for another 2 minutes. Or 5 minutes. This practice really opens a deeper flow of vitality and pleasure, and it is so yummy to share that with others.

How-to:

Create your safe space, call in R12 Sacred Circle.

Give each person a chance to speak and name their **intention** and what they **desire** to create during your time together.

Next, name your **limits, boundaries, fears** and other things arising on top. The questions below were created by Zahava (Z) Griss, a friend, peer, teacher and co-visionary for a pleasure- and love-based world. I've included them here, with their permission, as a great structure to start from:

1.   Are you clear and present to make aligned choices in this moment?
2.   What's your intention for connecting?
3.   What power dynamics are present?
4.   What are your desires and limits with this person?
5.   What is your health status? Check in about COVID or other respiratory health status for needs/desires around sharing air space or kissing.[124] If you want to explore genitals, check in about sexual health status and testing.
6.   How do you experience gender?
7.   What relationship agreements do you have?
8.   What would you like for integration (aftercare)?

---

[124] Expansion of the scope of this question added by Leslie Blackburn.

The full article and descriptions of the questions can be found at Z's website.[125]

As you now have created your container, decide on your time structure and set your timer, then co-create within it! Allow the space for breath, sound, movement, touch and play within the structure that is supporting you into freedom in this moment.

Explore, open, feel.

Delight in the sensory experience of the now.

Be you.

Let go.

Co-create.

Delight in this shared, co-created experience.

When this timed container is complete, invite a breath of gratitude for each other, and for Spirit. Decide if you want to create another timed container, and if so, create one. Repeat.

When the time with containers is complete for now, close the Sacred Circle. One way to do this is: "Thank you, Spirit, for holding us safely in this Circle. We release you from the Circle but not from our hearts."

Honor your body with what it needs in this moment, perhaps: snuggles, rest, mammal-pile pressure. Drink water, integrate, breathe.

Take some time here for honoring the relating you are creating with yourself and with any partners with whom you choose to share.

You can use this practice with any kind of relating and play — sexuality, kink, BDSM, intimacy, dance, sensory play. When embarking on particularly edgy play, such as some forms of kink and BDSM, there are additional considerations and tools involving safe words and other harm-reduction strategies, the full scope of which aren't included in this book. It's also important for holding space for healing and trauma release, which can be a crucial component that may arise during play. When you create the container and hold the space for what you choose to co-create, the possibilities are infinite.

---

[125] *8 Steps to Creating the Intimate Explorations You Love* by Zahava Griss: https://www.embodymorelove.com/blog/8-steps-to-creating-the-intimate-explorations-you-love

To find more ideas and inspirations for "ingredients" to be included in your creation of Container, see the next Recipe:

RECIPE 20: Touch Laboratory, pg 349

This book is about building the foundation to relate together pleasurably and responsibly in a way that feels good for all involved. By listening to our bodies we can learn to relate consciously with beings in all areas of our lives, including our sexuality.

Having completed the book, you now have a foundation for deeper play and creating the empowering relationships you wish to explore within.

This segment is a menu of ideas — options to play with in the context of that foundation. Please be sure to complete the book before working with these ingredients in your Container creations. Recall the directionality of touch and how consent, boundaries and acknowledging who the touch is for can bring to light shadowy areas that are hard to see, supporting all involved to feel good in the exchange.

Listed below are some ideas you may want to sprinkle into your Container explorations from Recipe 19. Think of these as ingredients you can test out in your own personal Touch Laboratory. Experiment with them. I also give two suggestions for the structure of the container.

1. Choose Your Own Delight

"I kinda already know what I want. Let's explore!"
  a) **Receiver's choice**: Pick one or two from the ingredients below of the types of touch you would like to receive.
  b) **Giver**: As you negotiate, honor your boundaries about what you feel available to offer. Once you've decided together, set the timer for 2 minutes.
  c) Explore the touch with your partner(s).
  d) Harvest a bit about what you noticed. Begin with the Receiver sharing first. Then, if the Giver has a witness response to offer, ask the Receiver if they'd like to hear it. The Receiver answers what is true for them. Proceed accordingly. Not always will a witness response be desired even if there is one to offer, and that's okay.

Ingredients/ideas for touch/sensory play:

- Different types and strokes of touch
- Light gentle fingertips
- Fingernail scratching
- Slaps with the fingers together, fingers only
- Slaps with full hand
- Slaps with cupped palm
- Pinches
- Bites
- Tongue
- Textured fabrics/objects (pine cones, forks, fluffy things; look around your home)
- Fur or faux fur
- Rope sliding over skin
- Allow your hair to brush across your partner's body
- Ice
- Warm or cold water
- Massage oil
- Firm pressure and hold
- Varying speeds
- Invite pauses and holds
- Varying pressures
- Lying on top of the whole body or an area of the body.
- Hair pull (full hand at base of hair right against the scalp with fingers woven through a large volume of it, start with simply squeezing; go slow and listen; avoid tiny amounts or pulling hair from a distance away from the head)
- Explore very light touch at sensitive areas: inside forearms, inner thighs, backs of knees, neck, throat, soles of feet, hands and see what you each notice
- Explore those areas with your breath
- Bring mouth to body and make sound/tone in/on various body parts like shoulder blades, sternum, sacrum, pubic bone

2. Learn New Things About Delight

"I'm not sure what I want. Here are my edges and let's get curious together about what's new and build capacity for pleasure."

a) **Receiver**: Name your limits (at least two things you are a "no" to for this particular timed experience, see following list for ideas if you aren't sure).

b) **Giver**: Reflect back what you heard and ask, "Do you feel I've heard you? Did I miss anything?"

c) **Receiver**: Answer and clarify any pieces.

d) Once you are ready, set a 5-minute timer and Giver explore creatively within that.

Use the safe words: Red, Yellow, Green (see below for definitions).

Receiver: You always reserve the right to change your mind, even if you initially thought you were a "yes" to something. At any time you may call "Yellow" and pause if desired (see below), or call "Red" to stop the play.

Ingredients / Ideas around Limits:

- No penetration of body orifices: vagina, anus, mouth, nostril, ear, eye.
- No pinching or biting small skin amounts, only okay if working with larger skin amounts or what I call "big meat."
- Ask your partner to wash hands before you begin.
- Face touch okay?
- Hair touch okay?
- Feet touch, toes?
- Only intentional slow touch at nipples, don't brush across them quickly nor pinch/bite/twist them.
- Or simply no touch at nipples and/or breasts.
- No touch at genitals.

When working with impact play, unless you already have some training with this, stick to well padded/protected areas: butt, thighs, upper back on either side of spine (not on spine).

In general, avoid intense pressure at joints, spine, kidney area and any other areas you sense or ask to be avoided.

Safe Word Definitions:

- **Green** – All is well, I am staying present for and enjoying this experience.
- **(Grey** – This is sometimes used for "All is well, I am staying present for this experience even though it may not be particularly enjoyable.")
- **Yellow** – I am nearing the edge of my capacity to stay present for this experience and am asking for a pause so I can feel into it. Yellow doesn't mean stop and leave. Giving partner: If you hear "yellow," pause, hold where you are, stay present and listen for what's next.
- **Red** – I am no longer able to stay present for this experience, please stop. This is not bad — this means you have both leaned into an edge, and that can be really useful information.

Giving partner: Do your best to stay present and listen for and go at a pace that your partner stays present with you. If you find yourself losing focus or having a hard time being present, bring the play to a close at any time.

APPENDICES

GLOSSARY

Included below are terms that readers may find helpful in understanding this book.

3D Reality: the world we experience with our conventional sight and senses; including, for example, the book in your hands, the chair you are sitting on, the floor beneath you, and your physical body. Often called 'consensus reality' or 'default reality.' Note that there are other fields of awareness in which we also exist, and we can make choices about from where we operate. The possibility of expanding our awareness into these other modes is an important focus of this book.

Aha Moment: a time of seeing something we haven't seen before, or getting it in a deeper way. Capturing such nuggets of wisdom in a journal or audio note can help support their integration.

Aho: an expression that I first learned from one of my shamanic teachers, Rose Khalsa, and her teacher, Grandmother Lillian. It came through her to me from the Lakota tradition, meaning "amen" or "yes, I agree" or "thank you" with a sense of "we're all connected." During the times of my life described in parts of this book, I often used it when acknowledging the spiritual and the physical coming together, so I keep it intact in the stories there. Since then, however, I have reoriented to connect with traditions from within my own bio-lineage and have released using this word in respect of the native culture from which it comes.

Barriers: protective mechanisms that we have erected over time. These are important skills that protected us in tough times. Yet once resourced in new ways, we can learn new skills and perhaps let go of anything holding us back from being fully aligned with our truth or from opening our hearts in connection with others.

Body Awakenings: times when old armor or shields in the body let go and new vibrancy can move in, often resulting in experiences of understanding, bliss, pleasure and ecstatic states.

Body Block: armor, shielding, restrictive tension, or energetic stuck spot; a place in which the body is holding old information in the best way it knows how. These spots may feel numb or painful.

Boundaries: edges, limits, the fence at the edge of the playground. By being able to connect with our authentic body wisdom around what feels safe and good, we can discern our container needs for the moment and hold these boundaries for ourselves or with our partners. Boundaries support us to let go into freedom. They are the opposite of restrictions.

Container: a safe space to support freedom and transformation.

Energetic Being or **Energy Being** or **Soul Being**: the deep infinite aspect of ourselves, one might call it a soul, or the part of us that both exists in the present and persists beyond the 3D world and this human experience.

Energetic Orgasm: a physical body orgasm inspired by exploration of energy in and through the body. This can result from practices with breath, sound, movement, visualization and intentional energy exchange with other beings (tree, Spirit, Earth, or humans for example).

Fruit Flies: memories, thoughts, images, feelings or sensations that arise when a part of our physical body or energetic bodies is activated in a way that invites old information stored there to resurface. These trauma-associated thoughts, images and momentary flashes of feeling seem to appear out of nowhere. They seem random, they are persistent, and we tend to swat at them and brush them away, not wanting to deal with them right now.

Gunas: the Sanskrit term for the "nature of mind" described by Patanjali in the Yoga Sutras,[126] the philosophy of life in the yoga tradition. There are three:

- **Rajas**: is fiery, active, bound up, tense. Energy isn't freely flowing due to binding.

- **Tamas**: is lethargic — a dull, couch-potato quality. Energy isn't freely flowing due to flaccidity, lack of tone.

- **Sattva**: is the absence of both Rajas and Tamas, or perhaps more accurately the presence of all three in balance. Clarity, feeling deeply rooted like seaweed at the bottom of the ocean, yet vibrant and alive, moving with the currents. Balance, vibrancy, aliveness — these qualities align well with possibilities of transcendence and enlightenment.

Harvest: I use 'harvest' in the context of gathering what we notice — the fruits of our inner awareness. This helps integration. When we explore inner work, taking a moment to gather the noticings. This can be done silently and in inner space, written down in a journal, painted, danced, moved, or spoken out loud in sharing with a partner.

Hit: a spiritual knowing, an intuitive knowing, getting spiritual guidance in the moment that helps make a decision or gain better understanding. Often used in the phrase "having a hit."

Holding Space: being present to listen and witness without judgment, creating space for what may emerge through another being with compassion and care. This also means not trying to fix or change anything or drive towards an outcome, acknowledging any judgments that do come up as our own. When we hold space for another person we are also becoming a Resource for them. There is a humility and beauty to being someone else's resource. We can hold space or be present for ourselves as well as for our partners or others. See also chapters on Container and Resources in this book.

Human Homework: the processes we engage in as we grow into new ways of navigating our experience and redefining our relationship to life. As infinite beings in finite form, this is the work of how we meet this human body and learn

---

[126] Satchidananda, and Patañjali. *The Yoga Sutras of Patañjali*. Yogaville, VA: Integral Yoga Publ., 1990.

from it and our experiences, owning our stuff, walking our talk. It's about supporting our own transformation as soul beings, through walking in life as human. It includes paying attention, noticing what is emerging in our life as information to guide us, taking action based on the guidance, unwinding old stories from our bodies, being willing to have the hard conversations or do the right thing even if it feels uncomfortable so that we live in alignment with who we are, therefore having even more access to vital energy and the joy of being alive. Like other types of homework, it isn't always easy but it is important for our learning and growth.

Infinite Realm: the world we cannot touch or see with our traditional senses; the realm of the Other, the Spirit world, the energetic realms, including energetic beings.

Intention: the dictionary definition is "noun: an aim or plan," yet this is just the beginning on an energetic level. Energy follows intention. Intention can be the precursor to things happening, it has a causative quality. And while that quality can be powerful, we also need to meet intention with the complementary sense of allowing spirit to move through us. We don't always get to pick what happens, and we might not want to, even if we think we do.

Lightworkers: beings with a desire and drive to be on a path of self-realization (remember who they are) and who are here to support others to remember and align with their soul paths as well, supporting all of humanity to wake up and shift toward higher modes of consciousness.

Lingam: meaning "wand of light" in Sanskrit, a term I use to honor the penis or cock of the penetrator body.

Mammal-Pile: a term for lying with a group of other humans in platonic snuggles.

Manifesting: a spiritual practice of magnetizing someone or something into your life with intention.

Polyamory: multiple loves; consciously and ethically having many loving relationships with all parties in consent and choice; an expression of relationships that is an alternative to modern societal norms.

Relationship Agreements: conscious set of choices, boundaries, and ways of sharing time and energy with our intimate friends and partners.

Repatterning: noticing the themes in our past experience and how our body carries them, and then inviting a new way of experiencing that opens new possibilities. Repatterning quite literally invites "neurons that fire together and have wired together" to fire in a new path and create new neural networks in the brain.

Sacred Spot: deep in the holy temple of the body, this refers to the area of the G-Spot or prostate. These and other places in the body energetically store our sexual history and therefore serve as keys to unlocking and unwinding old stories and patterns to make space for reclaiming our power and sexual sovereignty. The G-spot is actually a misnomer that has gathered enough traction in popular culture that I use it in this book for simplicity. Counter to the idea that it is a "spot on the wall" of the vagina, it is actually a whole three-dimensional body of tissue that includes the glands that support ejaculation. A full exploration of pelvic anatomy is out of scope for this book. An excellent and empowering resource for female body anatomy that is a must see is *A New View of a Woman's Body: A Fully Illustrated Guide by the Federation of Feminist Women's Health Centers* by Suzann Gage and Sylvia Morales.

Self-Realization: a path of awakening to remember who you are.

Soft Power: a reclaiming of power in a soft, gentle way of holding space for oneself without trampling on others. We all can be in our power; soft power doesn't take away from someone else. This type of power is not about having "power over" another person, or aggression, or creating the harm that toxic power creates.

Synchronicities: events and occurrences that seem to connect in meaningful ways with precise timing, but which have no apparent causal relationship. An example would be writing in your journal that you feel it's time to find a new job and then minutes later unexpectedly hearing from a friend who knows someone looking for your skills. Synchronicities were first noted and described by Swiss psychiatrist Carl Jung. For many people, synchronicities often seem to coincide with periods of intense personal growth and change, and/or strong alignment with Spirit.

Tantra/Tantric: as used in this book, tantra, a term borrowed from ancient yogic traditions, broadly encompasses a spiritual path of personal transformation and growth that incorporates sexuality and celebrates and strengthens our connections with all of life. The essence of tantra and the tantric path have deep roots in the yogic tradition. I've had teachers in these paths, and I deeply respect these traditions and value the transmissions I have been able to embody. The term *neotantra* has also arisen, which separates newer, Western views that have sometimes misappropriated from the history of these spiritual traditions. In light of this, while the word *tantra* applies to portions of this book I don't use the word extensively.

Transmute: to change in form, nature, or substance.[127]

Trust the Valley: a term I use to describe an invitation, when sexual energy is building strongly, to relax, give space, slow down and allow the energy to widen, spread and be shared with my whole body rather than be narrowly genitally focused. See also the work of Mantak Chia regarding Valley Orgasms.[128]

Yes AND: a way of approaching life that affirms what is and then engages with life on that basis to navigate forward. *Yes, AND* is also a mainstay mindset principle in improvisational theater because of the way it encourages responsive adaptation to emerging developments. Works offstage, too.

Yoni: meaning *sacred space* in Sanskrit, a term I use to honor the womb, vagina, vulva; the holy temple of the receptive body.

---

[127] Google definition.

[128] *Taoist Secrets of Love: Cultivating Male Sexual Energy* by Mantak Chia and Michael Winn.

ADDITIONAL RESOURCES TO EXPLORE

Sacred Sexuality & Tantra

Anne, and Claire Heartsong. *Anna, Grandmother of Jesus: A Message of Wisdom and Love*. Santa Clara, CA: S.E.E. Pub., 2002.

Camphausen, Rufus C. *The Yoni: Sacred Symbol of Female Creative Power*. Rochester, VT.: Inner Traditions International, 1996.

Charles, Amara. *The Sexual Practices of Quodoushka: Teachings from the Nagual Tradition*. Rochester, VT: Destiny, 2011.

Chia, Mantak, and Douglas Abrams Arava. *The Multi-Orgasmic Man*. San Francisco: Harper One, 1996.

Chia, Mantak, and Maneewan Chia. *Healing Love through the Tao: Cultivating Female Sexual Energy*. Huntington, NY: Healing Tao, 1986.

Chia, Mantak, and Michael Winn. *Taoist Secrets of Love: Cultivating Male Sexual Energy*. New York, NY: Aurora, 1984.

Deida, David, and Marianne Williamson. *Dear Lover: A Woman's Guide to Men, Sex, and Love's Deepest Bliss*. Boulder, CO: Sounds True, 2005.

Deida, David. *Blue Truth: A Spiritual Guide to Life & Death and Love & Sex*. Boulder, CO: Sounds True, 2005.

Deida, David. *Finding God through Sex: A Spiritual Guide to Ecstatic Loving and Deep Passion for Men and Women*. Austin, TX: Plexus, 2002.

Deida, David. *Intimate Communion: Awakening Your Sexual Essence*. Deerfield Beach, FL: Health Communications, 1995.

Deida, David. *The Enlightened Sex Manual: Sexual Skills for the Superior Lover*. Boulder, CO: Sounds True, 2004.

Douglas, Nik, and Penny Slinger. *Sexual Secrets: The Alchemy of Ecstasy*. New York: Destiny, 1979.

Feuerstein, Georg. *Tantra: The Path of Ecstasy*. Boston: Shambhala, 1998.

Kirsch, Jonathan. *The Harlot by the Side of the Road: Forbidden Tales of the Bible*. New York: Ballantine, 1997.

Lai, Hsi. *The Sexual Teachings of the White Tigress: Secrets of the Female Taoist Masters*. Rochester, VT: Destiny, 2001.

Mann, A. T., and Jane Lyle. *Sacred Sexuality*. Shaftesbury, Dorset: Element, 1995.

Mary, Magdalene, Tom Kenyon, and Judy Sion. *The Magdalen Manuscript: The Alchemies of Horus & the Sex Magic of Isis.* Boulder, CO: Sounds True, 2006.

Mookerjee, Ajit. *Kundalini: The Arousal of the Inner Energy.* New York: Destiny, 1982.

Muir, Caroline. *Tantra Goddess: A Memoir of Sexual Awakening.* Rhinebeck, NY: Monkfish Book Pub., 2011.

Nichols, Baba Dez, and Kamala Devi, *Sacred Sexual Healing: The SHAMAN Method of Sex Magic.* Zendow Press, 2008.

Radford, Gail. *Tantric Reiki: How to Use Reiki to Enhance Love and Sex.* Hod Hosharon, Israel: Astrolog House, 2005.

Richardson, Diana. *Tantric Orgasm for Women.* Rochester, VT: Destiny, 2004.

Rose, Sharron. *The Path of the Priestess: A Guidebook for Awakening the Divine Feminine.* Rochester, VT: Inner Traditions, 2002.

Schumann-Antelme, Ruth, and S. Rossini. *Sacred Sexuality in Ancient Egypt: The Erotic Secrets of the Forbidden Papyrus: A Look at the Unique Role of Hathor, the Goddess of Love.* Rochester, VT: Inner Traditions, 2001.

Shaw, Miranda. *Passionate Enlightenment: Women in Tantric Buddhism.* Princeton, NJ: Princeton UP, 1994.

Sundahl, Deborah. *Female Ejaculation and the G-spot.* Alameda, CA: Hunter House, 2003.

Svoboda, Robert. *Aghora, at the Left Hand of God.* Brotherhood of Life, Inc., 2013.

Taylor, John Maxwell, and Linda E. Savage. *Eros Ascending: The Life-transforming Power of Sacred Sexuality.* Berkeley, CA: Frog, 2009.

Tigunait, Rajmani. *Tantra Unveiled: Seducing the Forces of Matter & Spirit.* Honesdale, PA: Himalayan Institute, 1999.

Ward, Tim. *Arousing the Goddess: Sex and Love in the Buddhist Ruins of India.* Rhinebeck, NY: Monkfish Book Pub., 1996.

Shamanism, Dream time, Indigenous & Nature Wisdom, Ancestral Healing

Buxton, Simon. *The Shamanic Way of the Bee: Ancient Wisdom and Healing Practices of the Bee Masters.* Rochester, VT: Destiny, 2004.

Faraday, Ann. *The Dream Game.* First Harper Paperbacks, 1990.

Foor, Daniel. *Ancestral Medicine: Rituals for Personal and Family Healing.* Rochester, VT: Bear & Company, 2017.

Isaacson, Rupert. *The Horse Boy: A Father's Quest to Heal His Son.* New York: Little, Brown and Company, 2009.

Jenkinson, Stephen. *Come of Age: The Case for Elderhood in a Time of Trouble.* Berkeley, CA: North Atlantic Books, 2018.

Kimmerer, Robin Wall. *Braiding Sweetgrass: Indigenous Wisdom, Scientific Knowledge and the Teachings of Plants.* Minneapolis, MN: Milkweed Editions, 2013.

Mindell, Arnold. *Sitting in the Fire: Large Group Transformation Using Conflict and Diversity*. Florence, OR: Deep Democracy Exchange, 2014.

Mindell, Arnold. *The Shaman's Body: A New Shamanism for Transforming Health, Relationships, and Community*. New York: HarperCollins, 1993.

Morgan, Marlo. *Mutant Message Down Under*. Perennial, 2004.

Morgan, Marlo. *Mutant Message from Forever*. New York: Harper Perennial, 2004.

Villoldo, Alberto. *Shaman, Healer, Sage: How to Heal Yourself and Others with the Energy Medicine of the Americas*. New York: Harmony, 2000.

Waggoner, Robert. *Lucid Dreaming: Gateway to the Inner Self*. Needham, MA: Moment Point, 2009.

Weed, Susun S. *New Menopausal Years: The Wise Woman Way*. Woodstock, NY: Ash Tree, 2002.

Wohlleben, Peter. *The Hidden Life of Trees: What They Feel, How They Communicate*. HarperCollins UK, 2017.

Yunkaporta, Tyson. *Sand Talk: How Indigenous Thinking Can Save the World*. New York, NY: HarperCollins Publishers, 2019.

Early Books on My Path of Healing & Spiritual Awakening

Aïvanhov, Omraam Mikhaël. *Creation: Artistic and Spiritual*. North Hatley, QC: Prosveta, 2000.

Aïvanhov, Omraam Mikhaël. *Sexual Force or the Winged Dragon*. North Hatley, QC: Prosveta, 2000.

Aïvanhov, Omraam Mikhaël. *The Symbolic Language of Geometrical Figures*. Fréjus: Prosveta, 1988.

Bach, Richard, and Russell Munson. *Jonathan Livingston Seagull*. New York: Macmillan, 1970.

Bach, Richard. *Illusions: The Adventures of a Reluctant Messiah*. New York: Delacorte, 1977.

Bass, Ellen, and Laura Davis. *The Courage to Heal: A Guide for Women Survivors of Child Sexual Abuse*. New York: HarperCollins Publishers, Inc. 1994.

Beck, Martha. *Expecting Adam: A True Story of Birth, Rebirth, and Everyday Magic*. New York: Times, 1999.

Beck, Martha. *Finding Your Own North Star: Claiming the Life You Were Meant to Live*. New York: Crown, 2001.

Beck, Martha. *Leaving the Saints: How I Lost the Mormons and Found My Faith*. New York: Crown, 2005.

Beck, Martha. *The Joy Diet: 10 Daily Practices for a Happier Life*. New York: Crown, 2003.

Biziou, Barbara. *The Joy of Ritual: Spiritual Recipes to Celebrate Milestones, Ease Transitions, and Make Every Day Sacred*. New York: Cosimo, 1999.

Brizendine, Louann. *The Female Brain*. New York: Morgan Road, 2006.

Brown, Brené. *Daring Greatly: How the Courage to Be Vulnerable Transforms the Way We Live, Love, Parent, and Lead.* New York, NY: Avery, 2012.

Buzan, Tony, and Barry Buzan. *The Mind Map Book: How to Use Radiant Thinking to Maximize Your Brain's Untapped Potential.* New York: Plume, 1993.

Cameron, Julia. *The Artist's Way.* New York: Jeremy P. Tarcher/Putnam, 1992.

Carroll, Lee, and Jan Tober. *The Indigo Children: The New Kids Have Arrived.* Carlsbad, CA: Hay House, 1999.

Castaneda, Carlos. *The Teachings of Don Juan: A Yaqui Way of Knowledge.* Berkeley: University of California, 1968.

Clow, Barbara Hand, and Gerry Clow. *Alchemy of Nine Dimensions: Decoding the Vertical Axis, Crop Circles, and the Mayan Calendar.* Charlottesville, VA: Hampton Roads Pub., 2004.

Clow, Barbara Hand. *The Pleiadian Agenda: A New Cosmology for the Age of Light.* Santa Fe, NM: Bear, 1995.

Clow, Barbara Hand. *Nine Initiations on the Nile,* DVD, 2007.
http://handclow2012.com/books-cds-videos/

Coelho, Paulo. *The Alchemist.* San Francisco: HarperSanFrancisco, 1993. Print.

Edwards, Betty. *Color: A Course in Mastering the Art of Mixing Colors.* New York: Jeremy P. Tarcher/Penguin, 2004.

Emoto, Masaru. *The Hidden Messages in Water.* Hillsboro, OR: Beyond Words Pub., 2004.

Fox, Matthew. *Creativity: Where the Divine and the Human Meet.* New York: Jeremy P. Tarcher/Putnam, 2002.

Grey, Alex. *The Mission of Art.* Boston: Shambhala, 1998.

Harvey, Andrew. *The Return of the Mother.* New York: J.P. Tarcher/Putnam, 2001.

Houston, Jean. *A Mythic Life.* New York: HarperCollins, 1996.

Jalāl, Al-Dīn Rūmī, Fereydoun Kia, and Deepak Chopra. *The Love Poems of Rumi.* New York: Harmony, 1998.

Javane, Faith, and Dusty Bunker. *Numerology and the Divine Triangle.* Rockport, MA: Para Research, 1979.

Jenkins, Elizabeth B. *Initiation: A Woman's Spiritual Adventure in the Heart of the Andes.* New York: Putnam, 1997.

Lamott, Anne. *Traveling Mercies: Some Thoughts on Faith.* New York: Pantheon, 1999.

Laozi, and Brian Browne Walker. *The Tao Te Ching of Lao Tzu.* New York: St. Martin's Griffin, 1995.

Laszlo, Ervin. *Science and the Akashic Field: An Integral Theory of Everything.* Rochester, VT: Inner Traditions, 2007.

Marciniak, Barbara, Karen Marciniak, and Tera Thomas. *Earth: Pleiadian Keys to the Living Library.* Santa Fe, NM: Bear & Company, 1995.

McTaggart, Lynne. *The Intention Experiment.* New York: Free, 2007.

Melchizedek, Drunvalo. *Living in the Heart.* Flagstaff, AZ: Light Technology Pub., 2003.

Melchizedek, Drunvalo. *Serpent of Light: The Movement of the Earth's Kundalini and the Rise of the Female Light, 1949-2013.* San Francisco, CA: Weiser, 2008.

Melchizedek, Drunvalo. *The Ancient Secret of the Flower of Life: Volumes 1 & 2.* Flagstaff, AZ: Light Technology, 1998.

Melchizedek, Drunvalo. *The Mayan Ouroboros: The Cosmic Cycles Come Full Circle: The True Positive Mayan Prophecy Is Revealed.* San Francisco, CA: Weiser, 2012.

Myss, Caroline M. *Anatomy of the Spirit: The Seven Stages of Power and Healing.* New York: Three Rivers, 1996.

Northrup, Christiane. *Mother-Daughter Wisdom: Creating a Legacy of Physical and Emotional Health.* New York: Bantam, 2005.

Pink, Daniel H. *A Whole New Mind: Moving from the Information Age to the Conceptual Age.* New York: Riverhead, 2005.

Ra, James Allen McCarty, Don Elkins, and Carla Rueckert. *The Law of One, Books I, II and III.* West Chester, PA: Whitford, 1982.

Redfield, James. *The Celestine Prophecy.* New York: Time Warner, 1993.

Rueckert, Carla L. *Living the Law of One 101.* L/L Research, 2009.

Ruiz, Don Miguel. *The Four Agreements.* Hay House, 2008.

Ruiz, Miguel. *The Mastery of Love: A Practical Guide to the Art of Relationship.* San Rafael, CA: Amber-Allen Pub., 1999.

Sark. *Eat Mangoes Naked: Finding Pleasure Everywhere and Dancing with the Pits!* New York: Fireside Book, 2001.

Sark. *Make Your Creative Dreams Real: A Plan for Procrastinators, Perfectionists, Busy People, Avoiders, and People Who Would Really Rather Sleep All Day.* New York: Simon & Schuster, 2004.

Sher, Barbara. *Refuse to Choose!* Emmaus, PA: Rodale, 2006.

Singer, Michael A. *The Untethered Soul: The Journey Beyond Yourself.* Oakland, CA: New Harbinger Publications, 2007.

Spina, Edwin Harkness. *Mystic Warrior: A Novel beyond Time and Space.* Deerfield Beach, FL: Higher Dimensions Pub., 2004.

Talbot, Michael Coleman. *The Holographic Universe.* New York: Harper Perennial, 1992.

Virtue, Doreen. *Healing with the Angels: Oracle Cards.* Hay House, 1999.

Yin, Amorah Quan. *The Pleiadian Workbook: Awakening Your Divine Ka.* Santa Fe, NM: Bear & Pub., 1996.

Energy, Meditation, Body Wisdom, Yoga

Apfelbaum, Ananda. *Thai Massage: Sacred Bodywork.* New York: Avery, 2004.

Beinfield, Harriet, and Efrem Korngold. *Between Heaven and Earth: A Guide to Chinese Medicine.* New York: Ballantine, 1992.

Desikachar, T. K. V. *The Heart of Yoga: Developing a Personal Practice.* Rochester, VT: Inner Traditions International, 1999.

Eden, Donna, and David Feinstein. *Energy Medicine for Women: Aligning Your Body's Energies to Boost Your Health and Vitality.* New York: Jeremy P. Tarcher/Penguin, 2008.

Feuerstein, Georg. *The Yoga Tradition: Its History, Literature, Philosophy, and Practice.* Prescott, AZ: Hohm, 1998.

Hartley, Linda. *Wisdom of the Body Moving: An Introduction to Body-Mind Centering.* Berkeley, CA: North Atlantic, 1995.

Iyengar, B. K. S. *Light on Yoga.* London: Allen & Unwin, 1976.

Leonard, George. *The Silent Pulse: A Search for the Perfect Rhythm That Exists in Each of Us.* Utah: Gibbs Smith, 2006. Kindle.

Masters, Robert E. L. *The Goddess Sekhmet: Psychospiritual Exercises of the Fifth Way.* Ashland, OR: White Cloud, 2002.

Maurine, Camille, and Lorin Roche. *Meditation Secrets for Women: Discovering Your Passion, Pleasure, and Inner Peace.* San Francisco: HarperSanFrancisco, 2001.

McHose, Caryn, and Kevin Frank. *How Life Moves: Explorations in Meaning and Body Awareness.* Berkeley, CA: North Atlantic Books, 2006.

Muktibodhananda, Saraswati, Saraswati Satyananda, and Svātmārāma. *Hatha Yoga Pradipika = Light on Hatha Yoga: Including the Original Sanskrit Text of the Hatha Yoga Pradipika with Translation in English.* Munger, Bihar, India: Yoga Publications Trust, 1998.

Satchidananda, and Patañjali. *The Yoga Sutras of Patañjali.* Yogaville, VA: Integral Yoga Publ., 1990.

Schiffman, Erich, *Yoga: The Spirit and Practice of Moving into Stillness.* New York: Pocket Books, 1996

Stein, Diane. *Essential Reiki: A Complete Guide to an Ancient Healing Art.* Freedom, CA: Crossing, 1995.

Taylor, Sonya Renee. *The Body Is Not an Apology: The Power of Radical Self-Love.* Oakland, CA: Berrett-Koehler Publishers, 2018.

Yogananda. *Autobiography of a Yogi.* Los Angeles: Self-Realization Fellowship, 1998.

Embodied Trauma Healing

Antara, Leyolah. *Kundalini Dance: Sacred Alchemical Evolutionary Keys.* Australia: Destiny, 2014.

Becker, Rollin E., and Rachel E. Brooks. *The Stillness of Life: The Osteopathic Philosophy of Rollin E. Becker, D.O.* Stillness Press, 2000.

Levine, Peter A., and Ann Frederick. *Waking the Tiger: Healing Trauma: The Innate Capacity to Transform Overwhelming Experiences.* Berkeley, CA: North Atlantic, 1997.

Remen, Rachel Naomi. https://www.rachelremen.com/

Rothschild, Babette. *The Body Remembers: The Psychophysiology of Trauma and Trauma Treatment.* New York: Norton, 2000.

Sills, Franklyn. *Foundations in Craniosacral Biodynamics (Vol 1 & 2)*. Berkeley, CA: North Atlantic, 2013.

van der Kolk, Bessel. *The Body Keeps the Score: Brain, Mind, and Body in the Healing of Trauma*. New York, NY: Viking Penguin, 2014.

Anti-Racism & Doing Good Work in the Movement

brown, adrienne maree. *Emergent Strategy: Shaping Change, Changing Worlds*. Chico, CA: AK Press, 2017.

brown, adrienne maree. *Pleasure Activism: The Politics of Feeling Good*. Chico, CA: AK Press, 2019.

Gonzalez, Juan. *Harvest of Empire: A History of Latinos in America*. Penguin Books, 2022.

Menakem, Resmaa. *My Grandmother's Hands: Racialized Trauma and the Pathway to Mending Our Hearts and Bodies*. Las Vegas, NV: Central Recovery Press, 2017.

Penniman, Leah. *Farming While Black: Soul Fire Farm's Practical Guide to Liberation on the Land*. White River Junction, VT: Chelsea Green Publishing, 2018.

Pleasant, Bernadette – Sacred Grief Rituals, Unlearning racism through the body, storytelling, and deep listening. https://www.theemotionalinstitute.com/about-bernadette

Ross, Loretta J. – Calling In course, upcoming book. https://lorettajross.com/

Saad, Layla F. *Me and White Supremacy: Combat Racism, Change the World, and Become a Good Ancestor*. Naperville, IL: Sourcebooks, 2020.

Wade, Sabia – Birthing Doula Advocacy Trainings, Racism and Privilege in Birthwork, Anti-Racism or Business Essentials Trainings for Groups. https://www.sabiawade.com/educator

Queer & Transgender

Chacaby, Ma-Nee, and Mary Louisa Plummer. *A Two-Spirit Journey: The Autobiography of a Lesbian Ojibwa-Cree Elder*. University of Manitoba Press, 2016.

Feinberg, Leslie. *Transgender Warriors: Making History from Joan of Arc to Dennis Rodman*. Boston, MA: Beacon Press, 1996.

Harrington, Lee, and Tai Fenix Kulystin. *Queer Magic: Power Beyond Boundaries*. Anchorage, AK: Mystic Productions, 2018.

Kaldera, Raven. *Hermaphrodeities: The Transgender Spirituality Workbook*. Second Edition, Second Printing, Hubbardston, MA: Asphodel Press, 2008.

Vaid-Menon, Alok. *Beyond the Gender Binary*. New York: Penguin Workshop, 2020.

Polyamory & Conscious Relating

Beneteau, Marc. *Circling and Authentic Relating Practice Guide (2nd Edition)*. Monee, IL: 2021.

Easton, Dossie, and Catherine A Liszt. *The Ethical Slut*. Emeryville, CA: Greenery Press, 1997.

Fern, Jessica. *Polysecure: Attachment, Trauma and Consensual Nonmonogamy*. Portland, OR: Thorntree Press, 2020.

Ryan, Christopher, and Cacilda Jethá. *Sex at Dawn: How We Mate, Why We Stray, and What It Means for Modern Relationships*. New York: Harper Perennial, 2011.

Taormino, Tristan. *Opening Up: A Guide to Creating and Sustaining Open Relationships*. San Francisco, CA: Cleis, 2008.

Sacred Geometry & Visionary Art

Cornell, Judith. *Mandala: Luminous Symbols for Healing*. Wheaton, IL: Quest Books, 2006.

Grey, Alex, et al. *The Sacred Mirrors: the Visionary Art of Alex Grey*. Inner Traditions International, 1990.

Grey, Alex, et al. *Transfigurations*. Inner Traditions International, 2001.

Hart, Francene. *Sacred Geometry Oracle Deck*. Vermont: Bear & Company, 2001.

Lawlor, Robert. *Sacred Geometry: Philosophy and Practice*. London: Thames & Hudson, 1982.

Schneider, Michael S. *A Beginner's Guide to Constructing the Universe: The Mathematical Archetypes of Nature, Art, and Science*. New York: Harper, 2015.

Walker, Barbara G. *The Woman's Dictionary of Symbols and Sacred Objects*. New York: HarperCollins, 1988.

Body & Anatomy

Gage, Suzann, and Sylvia Morales. *A New View of a Woman's Body: A Fully Illustrated Guide by the Federation of Feminist Women's Health Centers*. Feminist Health Press, 1995.

Netter, Frank H. *Atlas of Human Anatomy*. 5th ed., Elsevier Health Sciences, 2011.

Wolf, Naomi. *Vagina: A New Biography*. New York: HarperCollins, 2013.